The
Neophiliacs

Christopher Booker

The Neophiliacs

In this our time, the minds of men are so diverse, that some think it a great matter of conscience to depart from a piece of their old customs; and again, on the other side, some be so new-fangled, that they would innovate all things, and so despise the old, that nothing can like them but that is new.

THOMAS CRANMER
Book of Common Prayer, 1552

Gambit
INCORPORATED
Boston
1970

FIRST PRINTING

© Copyright 1969, 1970 by Christopher Booker
All rights reserved, including the right to reproduce this book or
    parts thereof in any form

Library of Congress Catalog Card Number: 76–112442
Printed in the United States of America

First published in Great Britain, 1969, by William Collins Sons &
    Co. Ltd.

This book is dedicated to all those who enabled me to arrive at its conclusion; particularly to my parents, who laid the foundations, to Malcolm, to Barry, to Diana, whose support has been beyond the compass of gratitude

and also to the memory of Timothy Birdsall d. 1963

Acknowledgments

The probability that I would one day write this book has been with me, in one way or another, ever since I first read Malcolm Muggeridge's book *The Thirties* in 1953. It therefore gave me particular pleasure that, having met Malcolm and his wife Kitty many years later, I was able to write a part of *The Neophiliacs* while staying under their roof in Sussex; for all their hospitality and encouragement I am especially grateful. To name the hundreds of others who have assisted me over the years, wittingly or unwittingly, to arrive at the book's fruition and the ideas which it represents would be impossible; but of those whose help, whether material or otherwise, has been freely and generously given during the long period of writing itself, I would particularly like to thank Miss Eleanor Bron; Mr. Ed Victor; Mr. David Frost; Miss Kay Coupland; Mr. Edgar Rapkin, the Manager of the Westminster Bank, Chelsea; Mr. Richard Ingrams; Mr. Paul Foot; Mr. John Thompson; and my parents— all of whom can only be partly aware of how much I owe them.

To Miss Jan Elson, I am grateful for her exhaustive and imaginative help with my initial research; to the Coxson Typing Service and particularly to Mrs. Barrie for the irreproachable way in which they took on what amounted to a typing of the manuscript three times; to Mr. Philip Ziegler of Wm. Collins, for his readiness to perceive the possibility of extracting a coherent finished product from the confusions of an earlier draft, and for his masterly job of editing which at least brought that possibility much nearer; and finally to my agent Miss Diana Crawfurd, whose almost daily encouragement and refusal to lose heart over four difficult years has been beyond all praise, and without whom, more than anyone, it would have been impossible for me to complete my task.

ACKNOWLEDGMENTS

Any work of this nature must depend to a very considerable extent on contemporary newspaper reports and magazine articles, and in recording my gratitude for permission to quote from some of the thousands of sources on which *The Neophiliacs* is based I must first particularly thank the Editors and Publishers of *The Observer, The Sunday Times,* the *Spectator,* the *New Statesman, The Economist, Encounter, The Times, The Daily Telegraph,* the *Queen, Tribune,* the *Daily Mirror,* the *Evening Standard,* the *Evening News,* and *Private Eye.*

I am also extremely grateful to a number of authors who have surveyed individual areas of recent history, and whose works have been of constant help at different stages: particularly to the Annual Register (Longmans); John Russell Taylor's account of English drama between 1956 and 1963, *Anger and After* (as revised for Penguin Books); Oliver Marriott's *The Property Boom* (Hamish Hamilton); T. R. Fyvel's *The Insecure Offenders* (Schocken Books, Inc.); and *Scandal '63* by Clive Irving, Ron Hall, and Jeremy Wallington (Heinemann).

The quotation from *Memories, Dreams, Reflections* by C. G. Jung, © 1962, 1963 by Random House, Inc., is reprinted by permission of the publishers; the quotations from *Modern Man in Search of a Soul and Other Essays* by C. G. Jung are reprinted by permission of Harcourt, Brace & World, Inc. I would like to thank Weidenfeld and Nicolson for permission to quote from *Box of Pin-Ups* by Francis Wyndham and David Bailey; McGibbon and Kee (*Absolute Beginners* by Colin MacInnes, *Declaration* by several authors, *Bomb Culture* by Jeff Nuttall); Harcourt, Brace & World, Inc. (*Burnt Norton* by T. S. Eliot); Harper & Row, Inc. ("The New Romanticism," from *Music at Night and Other Essays* by Aldous Huxley, p. 189); Jonathan Cape (*The Making of the Prime Minister* by Anthony Howard and Richard West). The quotations from John Osborne's *Inadmissible Evidence,* copyright © 1965 by John Osborne Productions, Ltd., are reprinted by permission of Grove Press, Inc. The quotations from *Look Back in Anger* by John Osborne are reprinted by permission of S. G. Phillips, Inc.; © 1957 by S. G. Phillips, Inc. I would also like to thank the SCM Press Ltd. (*Honest to God* by John Robinson); Little, Brown and Co. Inc. (*Rats, Lice and History* by Hans Zinsser); Penguin Books (*Must Labour Lose,* by Mark Abrams, *British Economic Policy since the War* by Andrew Shonfield, *Love Me Do: The Beatles' Progress* by Michael Braun). The passages from Juvenal's Satires are taken from the Penguin Classics edition, translated by Peter Green; the quotation from the Upanishads is also taken from the Penguin edition, translated by Juan Mascaró.

My thanks are also due to Essex Music International Ltd. for permission to quote from the song "I Can't Get No Satisfaction" by Jagger and Richards, and to Kassner Associated, Publishers for Myers Music Ltd., for quotation from "Rock around the Clock."

I have done my best to check all the points of detail which make up this book, but some errors may still remain. If so, may I please apologize for them in advance.

He was indeed the most striking example we remember of
the two extremes described by Lord Bacon as the great
impediments to human improvement, the love of Novelty
and the love of Antiquity . . . we wish to speak of the
errors of a man of genius with tenderness. His nature was
kind and his sentiments noble: but in him the rage of free
enquiry and private judgement amounted to a species of
madness. Whatever was new, untried, unheard of,
unauthorised, exerted a kind of fascination over his mind.
The examples of the world, the opinion of others, instead of
acting as a check upon him, served but to impel him forward
with double velocity in his wild and hazardous career.
Spurning the world of realities, he rushed into the world of
nonentities and contingencies, like air into a vacuum. If a
thing was old and established, this was with him a certain
proof of its having no solid foundation to rest upon: if it was
new, it was good and right. Every paradox was to him a
self-evident truth; every prejudice an undoubted absurdity.
The weight of authority, the sanction of ages, the common
consent of mankind were vouchers only for ignorance, error
and imposture. Whatever shocked the feelings of others
conciliated his regard: whatever was light, extravagant and
vain was to him a proportionable relief from the dullness
and stupidity of established opinions. The worst of it
however was, that he thus gave great encouragement to those
who believe in all received absurdities, and are wedded to
all existing abuses: his extravagance seeming to sanction
their grossness and selfishness, as theirs were a full
justification of his folly and eccentricity. The two extremes
in this way often meet, jostle—and confirm one another . . .

WILLIAM HAZLITT ON SHELLEY

Introduction

Oh ye hypocrites, ye can discern the face of the sky: but can ye not discern the signs of the times?

Gospel according to St. Matthew, XVI, 3

That we are passing through a cultural crisis of unprecedented magnitude and of a definitely putrid quality nobody doubts, except of course the 999 in 1000 intellectual ostriches who prefer to remain head in sand rather than to face realities.

BRONISLAW MALINOWSKI
Culture as a Determinant of Behaviour, 1936

We are living in an age of revolution: that we can admit at once. We are living in an age of unprecedented problems; that can be admitted, if only with very serious qualifications. But our situation is not so wholly unprecedented, our dilemma not so wholly novel that we are excused independent thought as to how we came to be in it and how we can get out of it.

PROF. D. W. BROGAN
The Price of Revolution, 1951

What force moves the nations?

LEO TOLSTOY
Epilogue to War and Peace

It is becoming more and more obvious that it is not starvation, not microbes, not cancer, but man himself who is mankind's greatest danger, because he has no adequate protection against psychic epidemics, which are infinitely more devastating in their effect than the greatest natural catastrophes.

C. G. JUNG
Epilogue to Modern Man in Search of a Soul

Many an American must have been puzzled in recent years by a curious change coming over his traditional view of the British. The fogbound island of Churchill, thatched cottages, and medieval pageantry suddenly sprouted new growths—the Profumo scandal, the Beatles, mini-skirts, and "swinging London." On the most superficial level, I hope that this book may dispel the confusion somewhat, setting these matters in perspective and giving a clearer picture of just what social strains and stresses produced this "New England" of the sixties. At a deeper level, however, the subject of this book is not just something that has happened to Britain in the past fifteen or twenty years, but to many countries, and to America in some ways more than any. The real theme of *The Neophiliacs* is the "psychic epidemic" which has affected all Western societies in this period—its symptoms such things as the revolt of the young and the "generation gap," the loss of self-confidence by traditional authorities, the wave of permissiveness in the arts and morals, the new importance of the mass media and "images," the striking increase in violence and crime.

The close of the sixties and the turn toward a new decade provide an opportune moment to take a reflective look at just what has overtaken us all in the past fifteen years. The closing stages of the sixties have been a considerably sobering period in which to live. So many of the bright hopes which began to appear in many fields in the late fifties and early sixties turned during the middle sixties into something of a nightmare. And although there have been signs in recent days of the beginning of a comparative lull, and a desire for quieter, less hysterical times, this has been coupled with a renewed sense of confusion and disillusionment, and urgent inquiry about what it is that has been taking place in our societies.

Again and again while writing this book, I have been struck by the similarities in the British and American experience over the past

xii

twenty years: by the rock 'n roll craze of 1955–1958, for instance, which was in both countries the key event marking the emergence of that distinct "nonconformist" teenage subculture with which we have all since become so familiar; by the fact that controversies and legal proceedings connected with the publication of the same books, *Lolita* and *Lady Chatterley's Lover,* in 1959–1960 marked the emergence on both sides of the Atlantic of the same new "permissive" moral climate; by the parallels between the civil rights movement in America and the nuclear disarmament campaign in Britain, which in the late fifties provided focuses for youthful radicalism and developed the techniques of "protest" that later bore fruit both in student unrest—beginning at Berkeley in 1964, in Britain at the London School of Economics two years later—and in the agitations aroused in both countries by the Vietnam war.

In a broader sense, American readers may be surprised to see how close a parallel there was in the politics of the two countries, between the growing desire in the America of the late fifties for some dramatic act of youthful national renewal after the Eisenhower years (bearing its fruit in the politics of the New Frontier and the mythic stature of that supreme dream hero of the sixties, President Kennedy), and the very similar mood being generated at the same time in Britain, eventually bearing somewhat less thrilling fruit in the "New Britain" advertised by Harold Wilson's Labour Party.

Of course, one powerful factor encouraging such similarities has been the extraordinary sensitivity of the British to American "imagery" in those years. Again and again, in this narrative, we shall see the influence on the British of a certain highly romanticized view of all things American, and, although the process of "Americanization" is familiar all over the world, it can be argued that it has recently gone further in Britain than in almost any other country. Partly this is because we share the same language. The influence of American films, pop songs, books, and television programs can be transmitted directly, without the intervention of translation; and slang, catch phrases, and styles of speech can be borrowed from

America wholesale, whether by politicians captivated by all the jargon of the New Frontier, by advertising men using the language of Madison Avenue, or by the young adopting that vital framework of "hip" phraseology (e.g., "cool," "groovy," "way out," "swinging") to reflect their new values and attitudes.

Even so, this does not in itself explain why during recent years the British should have displayed on so wide a scale the psychological need to escape into a kind of Americanized daydream; nor indeed does it explain why we were eventually presented with the extraordinary spectacle of the tables being turned so that, for a while in the mid-sixties, America was hypnotized by a highly romanticized image of Britain, in the form of the Beatles, Carnaby Street, Twiggy, James Bond, and all the other ingredients of "the most swinging city in the world."

The answers to both these questions, as I hope will become clear from this book, lie in Britain's involvement in a much deeper revolution of her own during these years, a revolution intimately connected with all the insecurities consequent on the loss of her traditional position in the world and the partial disintegration of her traditional class system. With the break-up of this familiar framework—as is true of any nation, group, or individual in similar circumstances—the British lost their bearings to a certain extent; and the peculiar eagerness with which they adopted so many different Americanized styles and images, and transformed them into something of their own, was due as much as anything simply to their immediate desire to escape from their own familiar traditions and conventions into the "style" that seemed most readily available and most glamorous.

Nevertheless even this does not touch on the deeper reasons why the British should have found the American image so particularly glamorous, or why any nation should behave in such a manner. Nor does it explain why, for instance, so many societies in recent years have been affected by the same symptoms of general social disorder, intimately linked with the creation of a glamorous dream world, seen through the mass media and inhabited by particular kinds of heroes, such as pop singers, film actors, television stars, and even politicians, writers, artists, and philosophers.

As I wrote in the introduction to the British edition of this book, I believe that for all the sense of confusion and suspended belief which has attended so many of the developments of recent years, many people also subconsciously sense that somewhere there is a simple key to a great deal of what has happened, a common thread binding together all sorts of events and phenomena which on the surface seem quite disparate.

When I began writing *The Neophiliacs,* I had only a dim sense of what that key might be. I simply had the feeling that somewhere a link existed that was not being properly accounted for in terms of conventional history or psychology. There were obviously profound links somewhere, for instance, between all the different expressions of the cult of youthful vitality, whether in the politics of the Kennedy era, or advertising, or the eagerness with which the middle-aged were prepared to pay homage to all the crazes and vogues of the young in their desperate desire to not seem "square." There were links between this cult of youth and the cult of sexual freedom—the hostility to almost any convention which smacked of tradition or the proprieties of the past. Again there were obvious links between this kind of climate and that of the youthful vogue for "protest" of every kind, against anything that could be regarded as established or respectable, from governments to civility in everyday social behavior.

The more I looked into these matters, the more I became aware that I was not just looking into the causes of the "Swinging London" phenomenon, or the Kennedy cult, or student unrest, or even specifically the history of the past two decades at all. I was in fact being brought up against something much larger, which had relevance not just to the past twenty years, but to all sorts of phenomena in history at all times and in all societies.

It is for this reason that I hope this book will not be looked on in

America simply as an account of what has happened to one little island off the coast of Europe in the past twenty years. Indeed, I may say that during its writing, I have been perhaps a good deal more concerned with what has been happening in America and in Vietnam than with what has been happening in Britain itself.

I hope that American readers will find in this mirror from across the Atlantic a miniature reflection of the disease with which their own country has been so sorely wracked. I also hope that, in Chapters Three and Twelve in particular, some readers may find clues to understanding the real and hidden nature of this strange, exhilarating, and painful age.

London   CHRISTOPHER BOOKER
November 1969

CONTENTS

Part One

Chapter One

Portrait of an Image

A dreadful plague in London was
In the year sixty-five . . .

DANIEL DEFOE
A Journal of the Plague Year

The nightlife is just a symptom, the outer and visible
froth, of an inner, far deeper turbulence that boiled up in
Britain around—if we must date it—1958, although some
say as late as 1960. In that period youth captured this
ancient island and took command in a country where
youth had always before been kept properly in its place.
Suddenly, the young own the town.

From an article "London—The Most Exciting City,"
Weekend Telegraph, 30 April 1965

David Bailey has photographed the people who in
England today seem glamorous to him. Some of them
happen to be famous—John Lennon, Paul McCartney,
Mick Jagger, Jean Shrimpton, Lord Snowdon, Cecil
Beaton, Nureyev. Others operate behind the scenes—film
producers, art directors, advertising directors, photographers, and nightclub owners . . . together, these 36
photographs make a statement not only about the man
who took them, but also about London life in 1965.
Many of the people here have gone all out for the immediate rewards of success: quick fame, quick money, quick
sex—a brave thing to do. Glamour dates fast, and it is its
ephemeral nature which both attracts Bailey and challenges
him. He has tried to capture it on the wing, and his pin
ups have a heroic look: isolated, invulnerable, lost.

Publisher's note to *A Box of Pin Ups*
by DAVID BAILEY and FRANCIS WYNDHAM, 1965

Now does it not all sound like some horrible dream?
Could you credit it? And these are the recognised leaders
of fashion in England—the people that we are all expected
to bow down to and give in to on every occasion! Really
and truly, don't you know, after such an experience, one
looks for the Writing On the Wall, and asks oneself, How
long are such things going to be permitted to go on?

W. B. MAXWELL
The Countess of Maybury: Between You and I, 1901

The summer of 1965 was not a good one in England. The rain poured down almost unceasingly. All summer long Harold Wilson's new Government was wrestling with the country's fourth and gravest financial crisis in ten years. The pound hovered for months on the brink of enforced devaluation. And the news from abroad, of the wars in Vietnam and India, was only made worse in British eyes by the inability of the Prime Minister and his colleagues to influence these events in any way.

Yet it was not on these dismal distractions that the attentions of Londoners were primarily fixed in that summer but on something that was happening in London itself. Something indeed which, far more than the utterings of her politicians or even her chronic state of bankruptcy, was beginning to attract to Britain the attention and curiosity of the Western world.

Stray hints that not everything on this traditionally somewhat staid and self-restrained island was any longer all it was assumed to be had been reaching the outside world for two years—ever since, in the summer of 1963, the world had been amazed to learn in quick succession of the Profumo Affair and of the Great Train Robbery. The following year had seen the even more startling emergence of the Beatles as the most celebrated show business phenomenon of the sixties. There had been other strange emanations—the James Bond films, with their colorful dreamworld of sex, violence, and gadgetry, the young British painters whose brightly colored canvases had begun to attract attention at international art exhibitions, the news that Britain was being swept by the greatest gambling boom outside the state of Nevada.

And then, in the summer of 1965, focused by a series of newspaper and magazine articles, at home and abroad, the whole thing had come out into the open—that in the previous few years, England had been overtaken by nothing less than a social "revolution." And that London itself, as the center of this phenomenon, with its suddenly

5

risen legions of pop singers and pop artists, its fashionable young dress designers and interior decorators and fashion photographers, its discothèques nightly crowded with Beatles and Rolling Stones, its hundreds of casinos, its new National Theatre and its daring young playwrights and daring young film-makers and daring strip-tease clubs, with its skyline dominated by the gaunt outlines of soaring new glass-and-concrete towers—all set against a seemingly timeless background of Rolls-Royces and Changing the Guard at Buckingham Palace and the swans on the lake of St. James's Park—had been transformed almost overnight into "the most swinging city in the world."

The transformation that had come over London by that summer was indeed remarkable. In the streets, the eye was arrested by the strangely garbed young—men with shoulder-length hair, girls in skirts for the first time eye-catchingly shorter than even the shortest skirts worn in the nineteen-twenties, and clad from top to toe in the shiny surfaces and violent colors of plastic PVC or the dazzling blacks and whites of Op Art. The "Op Art Look" was the craze of the summer, having spread in barely a year from avant-garde paintings on the walls of Mayfair art galleries to hats, handbags, furniture, wallpaper, and even make-up. Down Carnaby Street and the King's Road the first of a flood of foreign tourists had already been drawn to gaze in awe at this thing which had happened to Old England— picking their bemused way past the little "boutiques" which were springing up almost day by day, with names like 430 and Avant Garde and Count Down and Donis and Domino Male, with their weird decor of garish paintings, cardboard Gothic arches, huge photographic blow-ups of pin-up girls and space rockets—and everywhere the omnipresent blare of pop music. There were other boutiques, to sell not just clothes but almost anything—from copper lamps, ancient theatre bills, and old gramophones with horns, to old books sold by the yard for their elegant bindings to give what was

6

described as "that Instant Stately Home look." There were new restaurants to go to—such as the Villa Caesari, a "Roman Banqueting
Room" on the banks of the Thames, where the waiters were dressed
as gladiators and the menus shaped like scrolls; or The Charge Of
The Light Brigade in Brook Street, described by its proprietors as
not so much a restaurant as an "Experience," where the walls were
hung with flintlocks and bugles, the floors covered with sawdust,
and the Italian waiters dressed in the uniforms of British Hussars at
the time of the Crimean War.

Above all was the cloud of publicity which surrounded the phenomenon, poured forth from the color supplements, the glossy magazines, the national and foreign press—so that barely a day could go
by without some new article on the "revolution" in the English
theatre or English cooking or interior decorating or morals, without
the profile of some new fashion tycoon or film-director, without its
fresh crop of pictures of the latest model girl, the latest pop group,
or the latest assistant in the latest King's Road boutique.

What *was* this phenomenon that had overtaken the English in that
summer? Certainly it was no good looking for an answer to such
sober questions in the color supplements and glossy magazines,
which were as much part of the euphoria as the pop singers, the
fashions, and the restaurants themselves. The prototype of these
journalistic surveys, perhaps as much as anything marking the
moment when the phenomenon finally emerged as a full-fledged
legend, was an article written for the *Daily Telegraph* color supplement of 30 April 1965 by an American journalist, Mr. John Crosby,
entitled "London—The Most Exciting City."

Mr. Crosby's article was not so much an objective appraisal as the
portrayal of a vision, written in the same ecstatic vein as his statement that London was:

> where the action is, the gayest, most uninhibited—and in a wholly
> new, very modern sense—the most coolly elegant city in the world.

He presented a glittering kaleidoscope of "young English girls" who were "appreciative, sharp-tongued and glowingly alive," who "walk like huntresses, like Dianas" and "who take to sex as if it's candy and it's delicious," a stream of disjointed verbal images, dancing breathlessly from "the vitality of the nightlife" and "the muscular virility of England's writers and dramatists and actors and artists" to "the explosion of creativeness and dash in the men's clothing game" and "the revolt of the upper-class young" such as "Hercules Bellville" who "toiled in advertising a while, a socially acceptable occupation, then threw the whole thing up to get into movie-making." On ran Mr. Crosby's prose, in a similar vein, through references to the Beatles and "hotshot" photographers and "a frenzy of the prettiest legs in the whole world," past a colored photograph of "some of the people who make London swing," showing various dress designers, pop artists, photographers, and hairdressers grouped solemnly around a piece of cardboard sculpture entitled "Box 1965," until the impression left was almost as nebulous as a dream, like the dreamworld of advertisements or the world of H. G. Wells's pretty little Eloi, in which everyone without exception was "young" and "talented," "creative," "original," and "glowingly alive."

Yet perhaps the very fact that Mr. Crosby could only write so nebulously, that all the Swinging London articles which followed provided only the same *mélange* of titillating fragments and suggestive images, was a clue to the nature of the phenomenon itself?

Some time in the summer of 1965, references began to appear in the press to the "New Aristocracy" or the "New Class"—describing in particular a group of twenty or so young people who seemed in some mysterious way to be at the very heart of Swinging London. All the New Aristocrats were, in different ways, concerned with the creation of "images"—pop singers, photographers, pop artists, interior decorators, writers, designers, or magazine editors.

Some of them were already famous far beyond the shores of Britain: the pop singers, the Beatles and Mick Jagger of the Rolling

Stones, the model Jean Shrimpton, and the photographer (married to Princess Margaret) Lord Snowdon. Others were already famous at least in Britain itself: the actors Michael Caine and Terence Stamp, the fashion designer Mary Quant, who was described during the year as having become "the major fashion force in the world outside Paris," and Len Deighton, a compiler of strip cartoon cookery hints and author of several best-selling spy thrillers. The rest were becoming well known: the photographers David Bailey and Terence Donovan, the pop artist David Hockney, the interior decorator David Hicks, and Mark Boxer, original editor of the *Sunday Times* color magazine.

By the early autumn of 1965, the popular press had become obsessed by these New Aristocrats—their friendships with each other, the restaurants where they ate, the way in which they decorated their houses, and their views on almost anything. And indeed many of the more public activities during that time were noteworthy—such as the fact that the Beatles had been awarded the M.B.E. by the Queen in June and had given the financially most successful concert in history at Shea Stadium, New York, in August.

But the general interest in the New Aristocracy ran deeper than a conventional concern with the doings of film stars, singers, and minor royalty. Indeed, so powerful was their fascination that they could only be described as the focus of a form of mass hysteria. And, as references to these twenty or so people proliferated, a curious fact emerged: none of them was being described actually as a living individual in himself, but only as representative of a kind of collective "image," the different ingredients of which could be applied to any one of them interchangeably.

Above all, of course, it was an image of "youth," "vitality," "creativity," "originality," "life," and "excitement."

Second, it was an image of "classlessness." The word "classless" could be guaranteed to appear in any article about the New Aristocrats, and it was true that they originated from a complete gamut of Britain's social scale. But it was revealing that the emphasis in describing their social origins was laid on those whose backgrounds were lower-middle or working class. It was only too frequently underlined, for instance, that the photographers Bailey and Donovan came from the East End (the sons of a tailor and a lorry driver respectively), that Terence Stamp was the son of an East End tugboat captain, and that Michael Caine, from South London, was the son of a Billingsgate fish porter. No particular secret was made of the Beatles' origins in Liverpool, or that Len Deighton's father had been a chauffeur. But little attention was paid to the origins of those New Aristocrats who were upper or upper-middle class. The fact that Lord Snowdon (Eton), Mark Boxer (Berkhamsted), David Hicks (Charterhouse), not to say Mary Quant's husband, Alexander Plunket-Greene, had all gone to upper-class, fee-paying, "public" schools was somehow not in accord with the "classless" image.

For the third ingredient in the collective image was that it was one of "revolt" against "stuffy," "old-fashioned," "bourgeois convention." The press was delighted, for instance, with the photographer Bailey's wedding on 18 August to a French actress Catherine Deneuve, when, as the *Evening Standard* put it, "The bridegroom wore a light-blue sweater . . . and light-green corduroy trousers," the "bride arrived smoking," the best man, Mick Jagger, "arrived with a blue denim suit and blue shirt with no tie," and one of the guests had to be asked by the Registrar to put out a cigarette. It was even more delighted with the Beatles' press conference after their investiture at Buckingham Palace on 26 October, when reporters could hear from Paul McCartney that he considered it to be a "keen pad," that George Harrison had found the Queen "sort of motherly," and that when she had asked how long they had been together, Ringo had replied "forty years"—at which Her Majesty had apparently "laughed."

It was in short an image of people who had no time for "fuss" and "ceremony": as *Newsweek* observed of Lord Snowdon, "Tony is impatient with pomp." Like Mary Quant and her husband, in words quoted from their interior decorator, all the New Aristocrats were basically "clean, crisp, and straightforward." And there was no subject about which they were more clean, crisp, and straightforward than sex, ranging from Miss Quant's constantly quoted reiteration that she wanted the clothes she designed above all to be "sexy" to the *Sunday Times Magazine*'s delighted quoting of the little rhyme "David Bailey makes love daily."

But despite all the time taken up with sex, newspaper interviews, and visits to the Palace, a final quality shared by the New Aristocrats was their "superbly professional" attitude toward their work. Without exception they ran their lives on what *Nova* magazine, in an article on Lord Snowdon, called "pure, high-octane nervous energy, rattling leisure into work and work into leisure." Or, as the *Weekend Telegraph* put it in a profile of Terence Stamp:

> His mode is cool, with a fierce respect and admiration for the professional, which at times manifests itself as something almost bordering on contempt for those he finds falling short in this area.

And of course their "tough professionalism" was rewarded with the most up-to-date trappings of success, such as having their houses decorated by David Hicks or being photographed by each other for the glossy magazines.

The same ingredients of this "classless," "unstuffy," "straightforward," "toughly professional," "down to earth" image could be found almost everywhere in the British press in 1965; as, for instance, in the caption to a photograph of the pop singer Marianne Faithfull looking for a maternity dress and saying that she wanted something "simple, uncluttered, really 1965." They were even made the basis of advertisements for a brand of vodka, the theme of which was "the social revolution" that had made Britain "such an exciting place to live." Each advertisement in the series, which appeared in the glossy magazines and color supplements, purported to be a short profile of

some figure typical of the "revolution." Their subjects ranged from
the inevitable "dress designer":

> Maggi Shepherd's been in and around the fashion business most of her
> life . . . some of her old Harrow pupils are today's young designers.
> "When they first started producing their kinky clothes, I had a feeling
> the revolution was starting." It was. She joined the revolution herself
> and opened up a boutique for Woolland's. . . . This young designer
> is the new type of Briton. Talented, determined, willing to get her
> ideas through. She says individuality and simplicity count in Britain
> now . . .

to the art-critic:

> "The artist is no longer a functional member of society. He has lost
> his usefulness. So he withdraws more and more, because he can feel
> that he is not needed."
> Charles Spencer makes many such statements about art and artists.
> They are not complex statements, but simple, logical ones. His ap-
> proach to art is simple, logical . . . Charles Spencer is typical of today's
> new Briton. He is intense, aware, always eager for a new experience.
> He says it is this attitude that makes Britain such an exciting place
> to live.

The suspicion will naturally arise that such advertisements were
written in a spirit of make-believe: in which, for instance, an art
critic could happily be quoted as talking about artists "withdrawing"
more and more, in a society which was paying as avid attention to
its young artists as any in history.

But, make-believe or no, part of the success of these advertisements
was that they so accurately reflected the tone and values of so much
"straight" contemporary journalism. It was on occasion difficult, particularly in the color supplements, to distinguish advertisements from
editorial matter—as, for instance, from a feature in the *Observer*
magazine introducing an unknown actress, with a close-up picture
and layout almost identical with the vodka advertisements, under a
heading that ended "At 22, Karen Fernald is already the most passionate professional of them all." This make-believe style of advertise-

ment-journalism, always centered around the same kind of "hard," "clean," "irreverent" virtues, even began to appear in books—such as *Private View,* a lavish production, with spectacular photographs by Lord Snowdon, written by two journalist-art critics and purporting to tell the story of "how the creative dynamism of British art came to dominate the international scene." Its tone was one of almost unrelieved congratulation, full of such capsule descriptions of artists as "A *passionate* talker among friends, a *forceful* debater in public, a *warm-hearted* and *generous* teacher . . . Harold Cohen combines all these qualities in his painting." Or, of David Hockney, talking of his "native *shrewdness,*" "his *astuteness* . . . combined with *satirical opportunism,*" the *"tough, dry, resilient* side to Hockney's pictorial sense"—and "young artists from the provinces" who

> bring to London a *built-in, edgy, sceptical* intelligence and a particular *awareness* of fashion . . . which give . . . to their work . . . a marked *irreverence* towards prevailing standards.*

Now, it might have been thought that this dream, full of "crisp, straightforward" photographers driving about London in their "simple, uncluttered" Rolls-Royces, and "tough, sceptical, irreverent" pop artists in gold lamé coats from Cecil Gee, was merely something cooked up by journalists and advertising copy writers. And certainly, as the year wore on, the interest shown by impressionable journalists in the New Aristocrats' "unconventional" doings became even more obsessive. As was shown, for instance, early in November, when the news from Melbourne that Jean Shrimpton had "shocked" race-going Australians by wearing a shift dress that stopped four inches above the knee, provided national headlines for a week.

But, in fact, there were signs that the New Aristocrats had themselves been quite as much carried away by this extraordinary make-believe as anyone. It was perhaps no longer surprising to find interior decorator Hicks suggesting to newspaper readers that they should build themselves a "rumpus room," decorated with "punch" and

---

* Throughout this book italics in quotations are mine unless otherwise stated.

furnished with such "down to earth" gadgets as a TV set "covered with Perspex so that you can see all the works."* Late in the autumn, however, there appeared from a fashionable publishing house, to a good deal of public acclaim, what was described as *David Bailey's Box of Pin Ups*. This was a box designed by Mark Boxer containing thirty-six photographs by Bailey of the "people who in England today seem glamorous to him." The list, which was virtually a Debrett guide to the New Aristocracy and their circle, included: 2 actors, 8 pop singers, 1 pop artist, 1 interior decorator, 4 photographers, 2 managers of pop groups, 1 hair dresser, 2 photographer/designers, 1 ballet dancer, 3 models, 1 film producer, 1 dress designer, 1 milliner, 1 discothèque manager, 1 creative advertising man, 1 "pop singer's friend," and the Kray brothers from the East End who could only be described as "connected with the underworld."†

It was not just Bailey's cold, hard, black photographs that gave to the enterprise the air of having been conceived in a spirit of make-believe, but, even more, the captions.

Here are some extracts:

Lord Snowdon's . . . attitude to life is essentially *theatrical* [and] shares in the stage's cosy *classlessness* . . . he has a *quick responsive* mind . . . he wants his own photographs to be *"exciting"* (his strongest term of praise) . . . *important, impulsive, nervously energetic,* he is fascinated by every form of mechanical *gadget*.

David Hicks . . . has a *polished* look, like a well-cared-for piece of furniture, *smooth, shiny, cold* to the *touch* . . .

Michael Caine is an anti-actor . . . exactly right for 1965 in his triumphant *classlessness*.

* *The Sun,* 1 December 1965. "A room like this," suggested Mr. Hicks, with an apparently straight face, "would be perfect for all that junky rubbish which one doesn't like to throw away, but which doesn't look right in the sitting-room; things like penny-farthing bicycles, and those old GPO red wicker delivery barrows."

† Although it was not at this time public knowledge, the Kray twins were in fact the leaders of the most notorious criminal gang in London, as was revealed at their trial in 1969, when they both received sentences of life imprisonment on a double-murder charge.

The Kray Brothers are an East End legend . . . to be with them is to enter the atmosphere (*laconic, lavish, dangerous*) of an early Bogart movie, where life is reduced to its *simplest* terms yet remains ambiguous . . .

As this recital proceeded, with its references to "nervously alert, baby-faced tycoons" and art directors who had "laid out their lives like a magazine feature," nothing became so striking as the unreality of it all: an impression reinforced by Bailey's photographs, showing their subjects not just in strange, theatrical poses (such as the pop singer P. J. Proby as a crucified Christ), but even in fancy dress. It was as if they were playing a part in some private pageant; all narcissistically self-conscious, yet each dependent on the others to prevent him in isolation from looking ridiculous.

Was this perhaps all that the "most swinging" group in the "most swinging city in the world" amounted to—just the leading players in some gigantic public charade, for which as dress designers and hair stylists, actors and photographers, pop artists and interior decorators, they themselves provided costumes, props and "crisp, uncluttered" stage sets? Was the whole phenomenon in fact some sort of hallucination, a collective dream to which for some particular reason at that particular time it suited a large part of English society in some way or another to subscribe? Certainly if it was some sort of dream, that would account for the peculiar importance at its center of the discothèque—the ultimate "dream environment" where, to the strange, garish costumes and the darkness theatrically broken by flashing spotlights of pink or violet or orange, could be added the final dimension of violent, hypnotic, electronically distorted noise. "At its best," claimed the *Pin Ups* caption writer, "the Ad Lib was not so much a nightclub, more a happening; an unself-conscious, spontaneous celebration of the new classless affluence." The "new classless affluence" —it was like the repetitious chant of some manic pseudo-religion, that could only be "celebrated" in a mass of all-embracing sound.

If it was a dream, however, then like most dreams there would be a time when it would find it hard to stand up to reality.

In July 1965, advance publicity began to circulate for a new magazine to be published later in the year by the Thomson Organisation. It was to be an entirely reconstructed version of the old *Tatler and Bystander,* which in nearly a hundred years as a society paper had established itself as one of the familiar minor institutions of English life; it was to be renamed *London Life*; and its editorial director was to be Mark Boxer.

London Life, as its first advertisements in the trade press had it, was to be not so much "switched on"—the vogue word of the summer—as "essentially in-touch," a new phrase carefully minted for the occasion. It was not clear from the advertising copy with what the new magazine would be "essentially in-touch"—except that it would be "as eclectic as the subjects it treats and the whole London scene will be there: creators, originators, fashion, photography, food news, architecture, scandals, the arts"; that it would be "entertainment itself," "deeply enjoyable," "as rich, many-sided, eccentric as London," and that its staff would include several of the New Aristocracy and their circle.

London Life was the first real attempt to make tangible the elusive image of "Swinging London." It was backed, to the tune of several hundred thousand pounds, by the most successful press empire built up in England since the war—and personally blessed by Lord Thomson of Fleet himself, with the simple expression of faith, distributed in a glossy folder to every advertising agency in London, "It will be a success."

It was not. Indeed the sorry and vacuous little end-product to the months of advance publicity, when it finally arrived on the streets of London on 7 October, was obviously a failure of such dimension that Lord Thomson must have wished he had done nothing more than leave the old *Tatler* to continue undisturbed on its modestly profitable career. No one was unduly surprised when, a few weeks after the magazine's launching, it was discreetly announced that the editorial staff would no longer include Mark Boxer and his "swinging" colleagues. Or that after months of dwindling circulation, the Thomson Organisation would cut its losses and close the magazine down.

Now it may be thought that, measured against the sweep of history, these petty delusions, this obsession with passing fashion, this importance attached to a peculiar form of façade by what was still, despite all the fuss, only at root a metropolitan minority, were of little significance. There were after all, although one sometimes might not have guessed it from the British press, other things happening in the world of 1965 beyond Jean Shrimpton's visit to Australia or Lord Snowdon's tour of America with Princess Margaret; there were even events of interest in England itself other than the failure of *London Life,* or what the *Observer* reported as the "shot in the arm" recently given to our "conservative furniture and interior design ideas" by "dynamic insistence on black and white patterns and sizzling colours."

There was, for instance, the shot in the arm given to the Conservative Party by its election of a dynamic new leader.

On 22 July, the former Prime Minister Sir Alec Douglas-Home brought to an end his eighteen-month "interregnum" as Conservative leader. During the five-day campaign to elect his successor, the first election of its kind the Conservative Party had held, the national press came out almost unanimously in support of the eventually successful candidate, Edward Heath. Here are some of the phrases that were used to describe him at that time:

Mr. Heath . . . a man of *action* . . . *young, determined, reserved, tough-minded* bachelor.

Sunday Times

He is *aggressive* in thought and speech, a *tactician* but also a *man of action.*

Daily Mail

Mr. Heath . . . *tough, energetic.*

Daily Sketch

17

Mr. Heath . . . *tough, ruthless.*

Daily Express

Ted Heath . . . the more *aggressive* and *dynamic* leader.

Chairman of the Bow Group

DYNAMIC MR. HEATH IS LEADER

Headline in *Bristol Evening Post*

Mr. Heath is *abrasive* and has the *energy* of a *powerhouse.*

Daily Mirror

Mr. Heath and Mr. Wilson . . . an *abrasive* pair.

Sun

Heath . . . the more *abrasive* man.

Twentieth Century

The *abrasive* Mr. Heath.

Evening Standard—twice in one edition

For several weeks the build-up continued, always with the same insistence on "toughness," "energy," "youth," "efficiency," "professionalism," and, above all, "classlessness." "Do you appreciate," breathed a *Sunday Times* interviewer, "that you are the first Tory leader with wall-to-wall carpeting?" The *Weekend Telegraph* even went so far as to publish a picture of Mr. Heath carefully posed with his master-builder father outside their "ordinary terrace house" in Broadstairs, with the caption "Ted Heath . . . had no interest in exploiting his class-origins to win votes." As was to be expected, the color supplements in particular went to town on the new Tory leader: the *Weekend Telegraph,* in a profile, mentioning his:

> *hard, direct stare* . . . slightly *harsh* voice . . . a *tough, restless* man . . . with no *taste* for small talk. . . . Deviousness *irritates* him . . . *ceremonial* rather *bores* him, heavy emphasis on *tradition irritates* him and *convention* often *irks* him . . .

And it was not just Mr. Heath himself, with his *"astonishing* capacity for hard work, great *grasp* of detail and *prodigious* memory," his Albany flat furnished in *"impeccable* taste," his *"ruthless* dieting," and his *"fierce* desire to see Britain more *competitive,"* who came in for such generous journalistic appraisal. There were also his young assistants, "a group of young Tories," as the *Observer Magazine* put it, "from very different backgrounds, but all sharing the same pre-occupation with efficiency, personal and political," and who in the months before their leader's promotion had been at his right hand during the Conservative Party's "long policy rethink," following its election defeat in 1964:

> Ted Heath likes to gather people, younger people, around him. He summons them on the telephone. They come to breakfast with him at his chambers in Albany. Like Kennedy he is very intelligent, but no intellectual. But he *ruthlessly* uses intellectuals and experts to advise him, to *feed* him with *facts* . . . it is part of the *technique,* the *computer mind* at work.

More and more, as these eulogies continued, with their succession of grainy, wide-angle photographs of Heath's young lieutenants self-consciously posing in their "extravagantly, almost senatorially furnished" flats or their down-to-earth, classless Highgate gardens, alongside such "efficiency" symbols as multiple telephones and portable television sets, the more a pattern emerged. Behind one or two immediate differences, such as the heavier emphasis on "efficiency" and the references to President Kennedy, it was to a great extent the pattern of that same collective "dream image"—"young," "classless," "irreverent," "crisp," "superbly professional"—that gilded the New Aristocracy and the heroes of "Swinging London."

Curiously enough, the first chink of reality to be opened in this particular dream came on 16 August from the normally loyal *Daily Telegraph.*

In an article soberly headed "Tory Policy Under Mr. Heath," a leading young Conservative journalist bluntly asked:

> Does his mastery of detail conceal a mind arid of principle and deficient in imagination? . . . The main worry of those who are most attached to him is that he will take refuge in details instead of concerning himself, as a leader should, with the grand perspectives of

policy. . . . He must learn to select, to stop grubbing around among the minutiae. In his speeches he must remember the adage "Stand up, speak up, shut up," and not go on so long. His very delight in organisation is itself a danger . . . etc. etc.

It was some time before the trickle of doubt really began to turn into any self-respecting stream. There was Heath's opening performance as the new Leader in the Commons, generally agreed to be "disappointing." There was a somewhat curious tour of the Highlands of Scotland, only witnessed by a handful of sheep and hand-picked Conservative supporters, more disposed to be flattered by his presence than critical of his performance.

But with the opening of the autumn political season, the trickle turned into a torrent. At every turn Heath took, it seemed he was making some blunder. When on 6 October he finally produced his new policy statement, the fruit of the "long rethink" undertaken so ostentatiously under his aegis, it was dismissed by those newspapers which had been so quick to hail the "dynamic" new leader, as little more than a rehash of old platitudes, thickly interspersed with meaningless references to "pacemakers," "incentives," the need for "competitive efficiency" and a "new dynamic" and a future which would, under Mr. Heath and his Kennedy-style aides, be somehow "vigorous."

It was hardly surprising that barely three months after Heath's election, as one respected commentator put it in the *Spectator*: "in their less guarded moments, Conservative MP's . . . can be heard asking 'Have we all made a terrible mistake?'" After reciting some of Heath's more publicized blunders, the commentator concluded that "he was, in short, oversold."

At the Conservative Conference, despite the customary standing ovation that was conceded to Heath by delegates for whom the truth that their new leader was a flop would have been too hard to bear, a noticeably warm welcome was reserved for the discarded and anachronistic Sir Alec. As the winter wore on, with Heath not only failing to score off Harold Wilson but failing to give any lead to his Party over the Rhodesian crisis, with the Young Conservatives passing resolutions that their Party leadership seemed "too complacent," it was obvious that the question of the Party leadership was by no means happily resolved.

It seemed a long way from those bright days, less than six months before, when the "abrasive, classless, tough-minded" Mr. Heath, with the "energy of a powerhouse," had bedazzled the press and so many millions besides.

But in the Britain of 1965, the failure of Mr. Heath to measure up to his "image" was no more an isolated phenomenon than the failure of Mr. Boxer's *London Life* to measure up to its colorful advertising. For the peculiar collective dream that had come to dominate England by that summer was only the most obvious outward expression of the extraordinary transformation that, in the late fifties and early sixties, had come over the whole tone and atmosphere of English life.

Chapter Two

Awakening toward a Dream

And e'en while fashion's brightest arts decoy,
The heart distrusting asks, if this be joy.

OLIVER GOLDSMITH
The Deserted Village

Awakening toward a Dream

England exploded, didn't it? I don't know when . . .

PAUL MCCARTNEY
London Life, 4 December 1965

One, two, three o'clock, four o'clock rock,
Five, six, seven o'clock, eight o'clock rock,
Nine, ten, eleven o'clock, twelve o'clock rock,
We're going to rock
Around
The clock tonight . . .

Words of popular song, 1956

Nobody has ever been able to make up his mind precisely
what the "Chelsea Set" was but I think it grew out of
something in the air which developed into a serious attempt
to break away from the Establishment.

MARY QUANT
Quant on Quant, 1966

Anyway, by this time I had met Walter Flack, the property
millionaire. And here was a real character. Walter had a
million pounds in the bank and a laugh for every one of
them.

MANDY RICE-DAVIES
The Mandy Report, 1963

What I think is clear is that what Lawrence is trying to
do is to portray the sex relationship as something essentially
sacred . . . as in a real sense an act of holy communion.

THE BISHOP OF WOOLWICH
giving evidence in Regina v. Penguin Books Ltd., 1960

I got off my stool and went and stood by the glass of that tottering old department store, pressed up so close it was like I was out there in the air, suspended above the city, and I swore by Elvis and all the saints that this last teenage year of mine was going to be a real rave. Yes, man, come whatever, this last year of the teenage dream I was out for kicks and fantasy.

COLIN MACINNES
Absolute Beginners, 1959

Anyone who looks at the evolution of English social history over the twenty years following the Second World War must be struck by the profound change that took place in and around the year 1956.

During the ten years between 1945 and 1955, the outward character of English life, like that of almost every country in Europe, was shaped above all by the memory and aftermath of the war. Through the years of austerity and rationing which lasted, in one form or another, until 1954, the long struggle to economic recovery made Britain a grey, serious and—with the passing of the brief burst of radical fervor which attended the coming of peace and the Labour election victory of 1945—basically a conservative country. Thoughts of a lighter and happier time, even when a limited prosperity began to return in the early fifties, were directed primarily not forward to some imaginary future but back into the past, the past of a lost pre-war—and nothing reflected this underlying mood more clearly than the prevailing fashion of the late forties and early fifties, the nostalgic long skirts and flowing lines of the New Look, which had arrived in Britain early in 1947, just when the initial mood of post-war optimism was finally dissolving in the harshest winter of the century.

Out of this comparative placidity, however, at the end of 1955 Britain suddenly entered on a period of upheaval. Within twelve months it was outwardly marked by a trail of signs, storms, and sensations: the coming of commercial television, the rise of the Angry Young Men, the Suez crisis, the coming of the rock 'n roll craze, and even, after a period of comparative quiescence, the beginnings of a crime wave.

This particular period of upheaval lasted for about two and a half years. When it was over, Britain was a changed country. In common with other countries of the West, she had entered on the whole of that transformation which has since become such a dominant factor in the lives of all those who have lived through it. Its major ingredient has been a material prosperity unlike anything known before. With it has come that host of social phenomena which initially, in Britain and Western Europe, were loosely lumped together under the heading of "Americanization"—a brash, standardized mass-culture, centered on the enormously increased influence of television and advertising, a popular music more marked than ever by the hypnotic beat of jazz, and the new prominence, as a distinct social force, given to teenagers and the young.

Above all, with the coming of this new age, a new spirit was un-leashed—a new wind of essentially youthful hostility to every kind of established convention and traditional authority, a wind of moral freedom and rebellion. Reflected in innumerable ways, from the lan-guage of advertising and the teenagers to the new kinds of buildings that from the mid-fifties on began to rise in London and many other cities, there took place a pronounced shift of focus from the past to a sense that society was being carried rapidly forward into some nebu-lously "modernistic" future.

There is scarcely any country which has not been affected by this new spirit in the years since 1956—but on few has its impact been so far-reaching as on Britain. In this chapter and the next, we shall be looking at one general aspect of this change. In doing so, we shall see, I hope, that what happened to England in and around 1956 was, in essence, and despite its modern gloss, something which has hap-pened in various ways to many other societies at different times down the ages—and something which provides us with the key to everything with which this book is concerned.

Of course no great social transformation takes place overnight, with-out giving signs and omens of its approach for many years before. Any process of social change takes place around certain focal points; around groups or individuals which, as it were, catch the infection of change before the majority, and from which the new mood and ideas fan out into society at large. In this narrative, we shall come across many such "centers of change"—sometimes individuals, more often groups, such as those running a certain theatre or magazine,

26

and even quite large groups, such as those of a particular generation at a particular university. Throughout our story, it will be these focal points, however statistically unimportant they may seem measured against the mass of society as a whole, which command our particular attention. And indeed the first centers of change, the first scattered signs of the transformation to come, arose in English life long before 1956.

One was the appearance some years after the war, in some of the poorest slum districts of South London, of the first "Teddy Boys" who, with their more sinister cousins the "cosh boys," soon became one of the minor curiosities of post-war England. In view of the later widespread assumption that the "teenage phenomenon" was nothing more than a by-product of affluence, it is worth emphasizing that these earliest fashion-conscious teenagers were so far from being affluent that in many cases, in order to pay for their elaborate dress, they had to resort to petty larceny.

Just why this vogue should have arisen; why, in the late forties and early fifties, the slum boys of South London should have adopted as their uniform the long "Edwardian" coats and tight trousers which had originally been adopted for a short while by young men-about-Mayfair at the time when the New Look was introduced, will forever be a mystery. But it was also clear from their studied poses, their deadpan expressions and curious hairstyles, that another major influence in arousing their self-consciousness was the "tough" dream world portrayed by Hollywood gangster films and Westerns.

A second omen of what was to come was another minority cult bound together not so much by dress as by music. The craze for reviving the traditional jazz styles of the twenties, which had spread from America during the war, and which by the late forties was established in a number of West End clubs, suburban pubs, and provincial dance halls, flourished on a very different social level from that which had given birth to the Teddy Boys. Most of the traditional jazz fans, with their reverence for the legendary Chicago of the twenties and a long-lost New Orleans waterfront, were middle class. One minor post-war phenomenon was the sharp rise in the number of entrants, mainly from all levels of the middle class, to art schools; and there was a strong link between these art students and the traditional jazz cult, which also attracted a significant number of somewhat self-consciously unconventional former public school-boys, such as the Old Etonian Humphrey Lyttelton (himself also a former art student) and George Melly. Only three things did the revivalist jazz fans have in common with the Teddy Boys of South London—their youth (even though most of the musicians themselves were in their late twenties or thirties), their sense of apartness from conventional society, and their reverence for a particular Romantic image of America.

A third, rather more general indication of what was to come was provided in 1951 by the Festival of Britain Exhibition. Against the drab background of a city of bomb-sites, peeling paint, and still boarded-up windows, the Exhibition was deliberately conceived as a look into the Britain of "tomorrow." Today it is hard to recall the first impact of those startling technological constructions in metal and glass, that "modernistic" world of concrete piazzas, abstract sculptures, and brightly colored plastics—for many of them were de-signed by the same young architects who were to be the creators of the office blocks, the high-rise flats, and pedestrian precincts that were the commonplace of the New England of the future.

A fourth, less public omen was the gathering at the Institute of Contemporary Arts in 1952 of a small group of young artists, archi-tects, designers, and critics to hold regular discussions on a number of things which were just beginning to exercise a curious fascination for them—things which hitherto would hardly have been considered as falling within the artistic purview, such as the mass media, ad-vertising, pop music, science fiction, violence in the cinema, and car styling (it was after one of the meetings of this "Independent Group" in 1954, spent in looking at blown-up projections of advertisements, that one member of the group, Lawrence Alloway, coined for such things the term "pop art").

In the England of the late forties and early fifties, these indications were very much exceptions to the climate of the time. The Teddy Boys, the jazz fans, the Independent Group, were only tiny minorities, the Festival of Britain soon nothing but a fading memory. But they were symptoms that, even in those bleak post-war days, there was already a handful of people in Britain who were beginning to catch glimpses of a very different world—an enticing, far-off New World, of shining buildings, gaudy advertisements, chromium-plated cars, flashing lights, and pulsating, thrilling music, a world of untold freedom and excitement. As yet the glimpses were fragmentary: to each of these little minorities, as to the young teenage girls who at different times in the early fifties greeted such visiting American pop singers as Johnnie Ray and Frankie Laine with an unfamiliar form of mass hysteria, had been given sight only of a small part of the vision. But as the years went by, it came ever more clearly into focus —as when, in 1955, one of the members of the Independent Group returned from America with a trunkful of new magazines, such as *Playboy* and *Mad*. From then on, according to a member of the group they began to look on America as:

> the source of a new and unexpected inspiration, as a romantic land with an up to date culture, a hotbed of new sensibility . . .*

In the early fifties, a similar subconscious awakening, particularly among the young, was going on in many countries in Europe. As the war receded, there were increasing signs that the easier times which lay ahead would not be just a return to the prosperity and standards remembered from pre-war days but, thanks to technology, a quite different age. Year by year, new inventions were appearing—the first jet airliners, the long-playing record, transistors, new drugs, new methods of processing foods, new methods of producing foods, even the first computers. And there were two other inventions coming into prominence in the early fifties which, although they were both several

* Jasia Reichardt, *Art International*, February 1963.

decades old, were shortly going to have a great influence in changing the face and character of English life: the first, the motor car—the numbers of which on Britain's roads had already doubled in the first ten years after the war to three million; the second, television.

By the middle of the decade, in short, as prosperity went on increasing, people were beginning to forget the past and turn their imaginations, with ever-rising expectations, to the future. By 1955, there was an unmistakable restlessness in the air, engendered by this promise of a new age, which was reflected in the growing consciousness of youth and the young. This new awareness was shown, for instance, in the stir which surrounded the publication in France in 1954 of *Bonjour Tristesse*, labeled as a "cynical" and even "immoral" first novel by a girl in her late teens, Françoise Sagan. It was shown in the same year by a new Italian film, Fellini's *I Vitelloni*, which attracted attention with its portrayal of the boredom and search for excitement by teenagers in a small town. It was shown even more in America, where there was already beginning to be widespread discussion of the growing "teenage problem," of teenage lawlessness and violence (reflected in 1955 for instance in the film *The Wild Ones*, starring Marlon Brando as the leader of a gang of motorcycle-crazy, leather-jacketed hoodlums) and where, even before his death in a car crash in 1955, there was growing up the cult round the young film star, James Dean, the "Rebel without a Cause." In England by 1955, variations on the "Teddy Boy Look" had long since spread upward and outward from the slums, as a kind of general working-class teenage uniform, into many areas of London and even out into the provinces. In the West End of London the first Espresso coffee bars were appearing, giving the young a distinctive and "contemporary" meeting place. One or two of the traditional jazz bands were also winning a wider following through the "skiffle groups" which they had formed, singing a crude form of urban blues to the monotonous accompaniment of guitars and washboards. Then, in September 1955, disturbances were reported among Teddy Boys at a number of South London cinemas which had been showing a violent new American film *The Blackboard Jungle,* featuring a brief appearance by Bill Haley and his Comets, playing Britain's first fleeting introduction to rock 'n roll. In the same month, the arrival of commercial television, in the London area, brought with it a strain of garishness and Americanization that to English viewers (still well under half the population) was quite new. From that time on, the subterranean vision began to break the surface.

Over the next two years, the new mood infecting Britain's youth became front-page news. 1956 was the year of the Angry Young Men, of *Look Back in Anger,* of Colin Wilson, nicknamed by the press the "coffee bar philosopher." It was the year in which the antics of the group of young aristocrats, debutantes, and hangers-on, known to the gossip columnists as "the Chelsea Set," broke into the headlines. In August and September, as was also happening in America and parts of Western Europe, the film *Rock around the Clock* provoked a series of riots much worse than the slight disorders of the previous year, in the most violent of which a mob of three thousand Teddy Boys rampaged through the South London streets for several hours, leaving a trail of broken shop windows and overturned cars. By the end of the year, Britain's first home-grown rock 'n roll idol, Tommy Steele, a 19-year-old former seaman from Bermondsey, was already a national celebrity within weeks of his début in the basement of a Soho coffee bar.

Behind the headlines, in fact, over these two years 1956–1957, were forming the outlines of the whole of that independent teenage subculture which from now on was to play an increasingly prominent part in English life—centered around its three basic pillars of dress, beat music, and an aggressive nonconformity to everything except its own values.

In November 1955, two art students, Mary Quant and her friend Alexander Plunket-Greene, an amateur jazz trumpeter educated at the public school of Bryanston, opened their first *Bazaar,* a boutique selling "whacky," "off-beat" clothes to their friends and like-minded

31

young people, in the King's Road, Chelsea. The following year, a 19-year-old grocer's son, John Stephen, came down from Glasgow to open his first clothes shop for a more working-class teenage clientele, which was moved shortly afterwards to Carnaby Street in Soho. And on a wider front, nothing more clearly indicated the influence of this blossoming youthful obsession with fashion than the speed with which, in 1957, the waistless, twenties-style sack dress and the new knee-length "short skirt" were able to sweep away the last remnants of the New Look.

Even more dramatic was the great rock 'n roll mania which in 1956, with its non-electronic shadow, the craze for skiffle, swept the country in a matter of months, extending the popularity of semi-amateur music-making over a much wider and predominantly younger section of the population than had ever been covered by the traditional jazz cult. Up in Liverpool, one of the thousands of skiffle groups formed at this time was that which, over the next five years, was to evolve into the Beatles. By the summer of 1957, as record sales reached a level they were not to see again until 1963, the performances of Elvis Presley, Little Richard, and their British imitators dominated the hit parade.

But of all the contributions of the rock 'n roll craze, by far the most significant was one which was only incidental to the music itself, really little more than an attitude of mind. For it was with the rhythmic urgency of rock music that there also arrived from America, borrowed from the self-consciously "alienated minority" of the jazz and Negro underworld, that curious use of language to express and conjure up the heady, almost indefinable state of being "hep" or "in the groove"; a state that amounted to a compulsive psychological condition, a sense of being involved in some mysterious projection of excitement; and that also carried with it an equally powerful, equally indefinable sense of aggression against all those outside the enchanted circle, the grown-up, conventional, and "boring" world of the "squares." For the avant-garde of the teenagers in 1956 and 1957, it was as if they had been caught up in an iridescent bubble, bringing for all those inside it a vision of eternal youth, freedom, and excitement. But over those who remained outside had fallen a thick veil, which made everything they did or thought important seem suddenly incomprehensible, "out of date," contemptible and grey.

By the late fifties, as the British became taken up with the revolution being brought about in their lives by the unprecedented abundance of affluence, by the nationwide arrival of television, and by change on every side, the teenagers, with their odd crazes, slang, and dress, still seemed to be little more than members of a rather mysterious, independent underworld. To some of the older and more established sections of the community, this new force, with its curiously institutionalized forms of rebellion, its declarations of moral emancipation, its search for "kicks" (and the first stories of drug-taking in Soho coffee bars) admittedly seemed positively threatening. Certainly nobody could deny the increase which had taken place since 1956 in every form of youthful crime and violence; expressed not only in such sporadic outbreaks as the Notting Hill race riot of 1958, when Teddy Boy gangs from all over London gathered to pick fights with the local colored immigrants; or the riots which broke out at several jazz concerts in the summer of 1960, culminating in September in the breaking up of the Beaulieu Jazz Festival; but also in such solid evidence as that of the Home Office statistics which showed that, between 1954 and 1958 alone, the number of young people convicted annually of crimes of violence had risen from 745 to 2,051 (the figure for 1938 had been only 147).

Already there were some older members of society, however, who viewed this new phenomenon neither with hostility nor even concern. Most notable among them, as a group, were the "liberal intellectuals," many of whom were beginning to see an image of powerful attraction in the rebelliousness, the disregard for authority, and the frantic search for thrills. One of the more conspicuous of such early admirers was the middle-aged (and middle-class) writer Colin Mac-

Innes, whose novel *Absolute Beginners* (1959), an awestruck, highly romanticized account of the amoral adventures of a working-class teenage photographer, was ecstatically received by many other "liberal intellectual" critics and journals, ranging from the *New Statesman* ("breezes like a breath of chlorophyll through the times we live in") to Kenneth Allsop in the *Daily Mail* ("boy, a real gasser").

Of course "youth" in the most generalized sense was, by the late fifties, becoming an almost universal symbol for the sense of innovation and awakening that was affecting every part of society—as, for instance, through the bright young stereotyped faces which played so important a part in the powerful new presence of advertising, with its insistence on a ubiquitous image of vitality, in which youth was identified with excitement, novelty, and change.

Another sign of the new age equated with vitality in these years was the marked increase in public concern with sex. Partly this new preoccupation, in the press and public discussion at any rate, was a reflection of the widespread relaxation of conventional morals by the young which had been accelerated by the upheaval of the mid-fifties. As early as 1956, in his review of *Look Back in Anger,* Kenneth Tynan had singled out Jimmy Porter's "casual promiscuity" as one of the ways in which he was typical of Britain's post-war youth. And undoubtedly promiscuity among the young of all classes did become even more widespread in the years after 1956, as was shown, if in nothing else, by the sharp rise in the illegitimate birth rate, particularly among teenage girls.

But the new prominence of sex in the late fifties was not just a concern with the realities of sex; even more, it was a preoccupation with the idea of sex, the image of sex, the written image, the visual image, the image that was promulgated in advertisements, in increasingly "daring" films, in "controversial" newspaper articles and "frank" novels, the image purveyed by the strip-tease clubs and pornographic book shops that were springing up in the back streets of Soho and provincial cities, and the image that, mixed with that of violence, was

34

responsible in the years after 1956 for the enormous boom in the sales of Ian Fleming's James Bond stories. Indeed it was the image of sex, making the necessity to be thought sexually experienced so compulsive in the teenagers' drive to conformity, that was largely responsible for the increase in actual promiscuity among the young. And in no way was this subtle confusion between the image and reality of sex so clearly portrayed as in the manner whereby, like the new image of youth, the cause of moral freedom was taken up after 1956 by the liberal intellectuals.

Of all sections of society, the progressive intellectuals gave the "sexual revolution" and the "New Morality" the most fervent welcome. As they proclaimed the need for a new "honesty" and "realism," and the need for "emancipation" from "Victorian, bourgeois morality," they believed that, in the wake of contraception and feminine emancipation, a new attitude to sex was becoming possible. Yet the form which their public battle adopted was almost entirely for the freedom of the image of sex, a fight against any restraints in portraying or discussing sex in the theatre, in the cinema, or in print, in discussing sexual matters, or in using certain sexual words in conversation. It was in the respectable name of sociological inquiry that, in May 1959, the intellectual magazine *Encounter* earned a good deal of réclame by publishing an account of the lives of London prostitutes, by Wayland Young; but in fact the article, entitled "Sitting on a Fortune," was almost entirely titillatory, using suggestive and "candid" quotations which even the most sensational mass-circulation newspapers could never at that time have envisaged printing. In the same year, it was the liberal intellectuals who, in the name of literature, mostly warmly welcomed the publication of *Lolita,* the story of a middle-aged man's sexual obsession with a twelve-year-old girl; it was the liberal intellectuals who welcomed Roy Jenkins's new Obscene Publications Act (designed to exclude works of art from the penalties that should still be incurred by mere "pornography"). The following year it was the intellectual world which rallied to the defense of Lady Chatterley when she was indicted for pornography. It was the Bishop of Woolwich who argued that the sexual act was one of "holy communion," and that Lawrence (although describing a love affair that was adulterous) had shown "quite astonishing sensitivity in the beauty and value of all organic relationships." In the following weeks and months the progressive intellectual press, the *Guardian,* the *Spectator,* and the *Observer,* in the name of "honesty" and "realism," dared to print the offending Lady Chatterley words out of their Lawrentian context. But it was not entirely the progressive intellectuals who then besieged the bookshops to buy 2,000,000 copies of the Penguin *Lady Chatterley* in a year.

Some time in 1958–1959, a revealing thing happened. In a way in which it had never been used before, the word "image" began to pass into journalistic and conversational currency. The new usage was introduced, as so much that was new to England, from America, in this instance from the American advertising industry. In Britain, where the term really became familiar around the 1959 General Election, it was originally used in reference to politics, to make articulate the growing awareness, in the age of television and opinion polls, of that vague, largely subconscious impression on which people judged politicians and political parties.

But the word "image" floated into the general consciousness at this time for a reason deeper than its application to politics alone—as was shown by the way its use quickly spread to describe other things, such as the appeal of television personalities, or different models of motor cars. For if there was one bond which linked the different aspects of the changes which had come over English life since 1956, it was the extent to which so many of them contributed to the presence in society of a new body of eye- and mind-catching imagery —the images of television and advertising, the subtler omnipresence of beat music, the visual imagery of eye-catching clothes, the bright lights of the new supermarkets, the glossy packaging of food.

As early as 1956 itself, the power of this new presence had been reflected in an art exhibition at the Whitechapel Gallery, largely under the influence of the Independent Group from the I.C.A., which had caused a stir among the rising generation of art students equivalent to that aroused in the theatre by *Look Back in Anger.* The exhibition, which included huge blown-up reproductions of advertisements and film stills, was dominated by what in retrospect appeared as Britain's first "pop" painting: a work by Richard Hamilton entitled *Just What Is It That Makes To-day's Homes So Different, So Appealing?* It showed a "dream couple," a he-man from the Charles Atlas advertisements and an ill-clad strip-tease dancer, set in a "home" furnished with such gadgets as a television set and a tape recorder, a painting on the wall taken from a comic book called *Young Romances,* and out of the window, the winking neon of a cinema advertisement. Indeed the exhibition as a whole was deliberately designed as a "dream environment," in which the spectators could wander and lose themselves: its title was *This Is To-morrow.*

By the late fifties, the sense that Britain was moving into the future on a tidal wave of change was to a great extent stimulated and kept in being by "images" of one kind or another—as was shown in the importance of "modern" design, for everything from the new glass-and-concrete office blocks beginning to rise on the lines first glimpsed at the Festival of Britain, to the covers of paperback books; and in the way that, in order to surround their products with an aura of up-to-dateness, television commercials were more and more given to using such suggestive contemporary imagery as sports cars speeding down streamlined motorways, as often as not to the atmospheric accompaniment of a pounding modern jazz sound track.

As the fifties neared their end, there were signs that this attraction to the image of modernity was entering on a new and more exaggerated phase.

The emergence of this new phase may be clearly traced, almost month by month, in the pages of a fashion magazine which, over the next two or three years, was to play a minor but significant part in the English revolution. The *Queen* was a long-established society paper which, in February 1957, had been bought by an Old Etonian in his mid-twenties, Jocelyn Stevens. He was shortly joined by two of his contemporaries at Cambridge in the early fifties, Mark Boxer, who became his layout editor, and Anthony Armstrong-Jones, who was already making a name for himself as a striking and unconventional photographer. For the first eighteen months under its new régime, the *Queen* had changed little—but by 1959 it was beginning to give more space to bold, black photography, its layout was becoming more adventurous, and its attitude toward the "Establishment" and society self-consciously irreverent. Then, just before the 1959 General Election, in a special issue celebrating the "consumer boom" that was shortly to give Harold Macmillan a parliamentary majority of 100 seats, Stevens and Boxer found a new approach and style. "BOOM" read their cover. Boom went Boxer's layout inside, irregular blocks of print dropped in the middle of large white spaces. Boom went the prose, in a breathless, disconnected rush:

> Nearly two thousand million pounds is pouring out of pockets and wallets and handbags (the gold mesh one above costs five guineas from Jarrolds) and changing into air tickets and oysters, television sets and caviar, art treasures and vacuum cleaners, cigars and refrigerators. Britain has launched into an age of unparalleled lavish living. It came unobtrusively. But now you are living in a new world. Turn the page, if you want proof that you are living in a . . . BOOM.

The *Queen* had discovered Affluence. It had also discovered Youth. In its last issue of the fifties, Colin MacInnes interviewed two teenagers.

> So over to you Alex and Jean, while we ancients the wrong side of 25 keep our palsied fingers hopefully crossed. For the prospect of seeing, in the next decade, what kind of men and women the first wave of teenagers of the 1950's turn out to be, is perhaps the greatest fascination.

In the same issue appeared a feature entitled "A Bad Year for Dodos," with drawings by Mark Boxer. Among the "Dodos" it had been a bad year for were "the Duke of Marlborough, Evelyn Waugh and the Archbishop of Canterbury." "Judges and Generals," it went on, "are the very stuff which Dodos are made of."

The coming of the new decade spurred the *Queen* and its headlines to an even greater frenzy: "Facing the Crazy Sixties," "The Sixties Face," "Keeping Pace with Pace," "The Tense Present." There was something about the very sound of "the sixties" which seemed to convey modernity. And here, fortnight by fortnight, as the designs of Mary Quant began to rival those of Norman Hartnell and Hardy Amies on the fashion pages, in the articles on teenagers and "The Communicators," in the general air of mockery toward everything that was old, conventional, or established, and above all in the new style of photography, was the essence, the very "image" of the new decade.

What in fact was happening in 1960, as reflected in the pages of the *Queen*—as also in the early *nouvelle vague* films which were just reaching London from France—was that the bubble of compulsive up-to-dateness, that psychological state which, in its most virulent form, had hitherto been confined mainly to the world of the teenagers, was now spreading out over a wider area. All the different manifestations of the change that had come about since 1956 were being swept up into a collective image of modernity, a vision of bright lights and speed and vitality, in which every individual ingredient was simply part of the whole. In the old rock 'n roll days of 1957–1958, the teenagers had only applied their vogue words, "hep" or "in the groove," to things of their own world, a record, a pair of drainpipe trousers, a singer. But now new vogue words were coming into currency, such as "cool," which could be applied by their users to anyone and anything redolent of the new up-to-dateness, from a new film to a new motorway. Similarly, the aggression of the teenagers toward the "squares" had been confined mainly, in time-honored adolescent fashion, to the grown-up world of those who "didn't understand": but now this collective aggression was spreading out toward all those who were not part of this new world.

Another term beginning to gain currency at this time was that supreme expression of blessed contemporaneity, "with-it," a phrase which was never defined, but everyone who used it instinctively knew the meaning. He who was "with it" was "with" the image of the age—jazz, speed, irreverence, new architecture, the whole progressive attitude— while he who was not "with it" was against "life" itself, dull, reactionary, and old. And this image of cool modernity which was so strongly projected in the *Queen* and in another restyled glossy magazine, *Man about Town* (later *About Town*), was a reflection of something that, in London, in the early sixties, was happening to a large section of young, smart, affluent, middle-class society.

In the early years of the English revolution, between 1956 and 1958, the most conspicuous impetus for change had come up, through the Teddy Boys, the rock 'n roll craze, the Angry Young writers, from the lower reaches of society. But the new ambiance of the glossy magazines represented the onset of a period in which, for two or three years at the beginning of the sixties, the real avant-garde of the revolution was drawn from the upper-middle-class young, in their twenties and thirties. For such people in 1960 and 1961, a new world was opening up: of Mary Quant and John Stephen clothes, of decayed terraces in newly fashionable Islington, of bistros and "unconventional" little restaurants opening up all over Chelsea and Kensington. It was this newly "hip," newly "aware," newly trendconscious group which, in the summer of 1961, brought over the Twist from France, and for whom, in the autumn, London's first discothèque was opened, the Saddle Room in Park Lane. It was this young, upper-middle-class world which, at the same time, by joining The Establishment Club, seeing *Beyond the Fringe,* and buying the first yellow-paper copies of *Private Eye,* helped to launch the craze for "satire." And it was this world which, in 1960 and 1961, the *Queen* and *Man about Town* both reflected and guided.

When in 1959 Colin MacInnes picked a young working-class photographer to be the hero of his *Absolute Beginners,* he had chosen more appropriately than he could have guessed. For now, two years later, at the heart of this new upper-middle-class world of glossy magazines and advertising agencies, a group of such photographers were becoming, in some ways, the most influential representatives of the time. The group of young working-class photographers from the East End, David Bailey, Terence Donovan, and Brian Duffy, whose work followed that of Anthony Armstrong-Jones into the pages of the *Queen* and *About Town,* had been heavily influenced like almost all the image-makers of the English revolution, by an American model—in their case, the style of such photographers as Irving Penn and Richard Avedon. They were captivated by visual tricks, by new lenses, by new ways of distorting light and shadow. To the advertising copy writers, the layout editors, the fashion designers trying to capture the image of the moment, the photographers were a perfect ally. Thus it was that their increasingly refined technical expertise, their wide-angle lenses and flattened-up telephoto images, their new degrees of down-to-earth "realism," became used interchangeably between advertisements for candy-striped shirts or speeding sports cars against the backdrop of towering office blocks and probing editorial inquiries into social conditions in the Black Country—until the whole world through their viewfinders had been reduced to the same grainy, pacy, ever more "realistic" dream.

Even so, at the end of 1961, it was a dream which still affected only a tiny proportion of the population. The combined circulations of the *Queen* and *About Town* at their highest were only 120,000, and the great majority of these readers belonged to one small class in London alone.

But the steady spread of affluence and the increasing tempo of change was creating a rising appetite for new excitement throughout

England. 1961, for instance, was the year when the Betting and Gaming Act launched a new gambling boom, from betting shops to the bingo craze. A revolution was taking place in the mass-catering trade, where the big chain-restauranteurs were beginning to discover the delights of opaline-lit decor and dishes such as *scampi* and menus that read like gourmand's pornography, with chips never less than "Crispy Golden Brown," and vegetables always "Tender Young Spring Fresh." The bright lights were indeed reaching the provinces —and not just the bingo palaces and strip-tease clubs and steak houses, but the Chinese restaurants and French films and the taste for Spanish holidays. Which is why, when Mr. Roy Thompson decided at the end of 1961 to add a color supplement to his *Sunday Times,* he considered that the ethos of the glossy magazine was sufficiently in keeping with the times to be ready for a mass-circulation audience—and that his editor should be Mark Boxer from the *Queen.*

The first issue of the *Sunday Times* color supplement appeared on 4 February 1962. Its cover was decorated with eleven pictures of a girl in a grey flannel dress, inset with one of a footballer. It bore the headline "A Sharp Glance at the Mood of Britain," while a sub-headline announced "a new James Bond story by Ian Fleming." In small print on the inside, it was revealed that the grey flannel dress was designed by Mary Quant, the girl was Jean Shrimpton, and the photographs had been taken by David Bailey.

Most of the contents were devoted to short profiles of "People of the '60's." They included Mary Quant and Alexander Plunket-Greene —"What do you need to be of the sixties? First, you should be under 30. Second, you should be in tune with your times . . ." Another was Peter Blake, foremost of the young "pop artists" from the Royal College of Art, whose paintings had been the avant-garde sensation of the previous year. Blake was described as having brought "a new urban realism into British art," and was shown in a crudely painted self-portrait, dressed in blue jeans and carrying a copy of the teenage fan magazine *Elvis.* Other "people of the '60's" included a profes-

42

sional footballer, described as "good-looking, shrewd, self-deprecating," "a football perfectionist," and " a product of the New Wave"; a young electronics industrialist, described as "tough, fluent, incisive"; and a sociologist at the London School of Economics, a "27-year old milkman's son from Liverpool" who, under the heading "Don on the 8:40," was quoted as saying, "We'll never get an adequate system of education until someone takes a damn great hammer to the idea of Oxbridge as a glorified finishing school."

Apart from the James Bond story, full of violence but for once without sex, another article, as a sop to the provincial audience, was a grainy "photo-feature" on the city of Lincoln, paying particular attention to its jazz clubs, its art students, its coffee bars, its electronics factory, its go-ahead young repertory company, and its dynamic young architect.

All in all, the first edition of the *Sunday Times*'s supplement was a perfect expression of the "dream image" of the time. The revolution which it represented was far from over: in one sense, indeed, it was only just beginning. But from the clues laid down in this chapter's preliminary survey, we can now turn to a wider examination of what it was that had overtaken English society in the mid-fifties.

Chapter Three

The Cult of Sensation

Go, go, go, said the bird: human kind
Cannot bear very much reality.

The Cult of Sensation

The activities of our age are uncertain and multifarious.
No single literary, artistic or philosophic tendency predom-
inates. There is a babel of notions and conflicting
theories. But in the midst of this general confusion, it is
possible to recognise one curious and significant melody,
repeated in different keys and by different instruments in
every one of the subsidiary babels. It is the tune of our
modern Romanticism.

ALDOUS HUXLEY
The New Romanticism, 1931

Romanticism comes from the fear of looking straight into
the eyes of truth.

LEO TOLSTOY
quoted by Maxim Gorky

The great object of life is sensation, to feel that we exist,
even though in pain.

LORD BYRON
in a letter to his future wife, 6 September 1813

Never was an age more sentimental, more devoid of real
feeling, more exaggerated in false feeling than our own
. . . the radio and the film are mere counterfeit emotion all
the time, the current press and literature the same. People
wallow in emotion, counterfeit emotion. They lap it up,
they live in it and on it . . . and at times they seem to get
on very well with it all. And then, more and more, they
break down. They go to pieces.

D. H. LAWRENCE
Apropos of Lady Chatterley's Lover, 1929

"You must take another road," he answered, when he saw me weeping, "if you wish to escape from this savage place. Because this beast which makes you weep, does not allow anyone to pass by her, but so entangles them that she kills them; and she has a nature so perverse and vicious, that her craving appetite can never be satisfied, and after feeding she is even hungrier than before."

DANTE
Inferno

Just as few adolescents can ever believe that their parents have been through the same stages of attitude and development before them, so one of the more frequently recurrent fallacies has been people's belief that their own age is without precedent, that some new order is coming to birth in which all the general assumptions previously made about human behavior are becoming somehow outmoded. In few ages has this belief been more prevalent than our own.

In fact there were few ingredients in the bubble of excitement which welled up in Britain, America, and other countries in the years after 1956 which have not in essence appeared in various guises in many other societies and times. To take the most obvious example, the "revolt of youth" against tradition and their elders has been a repeated theme, as we can see from that much-quoted remark by a thirteenth century monk:

> The world is passing through troublous times. The young people of today think of nothing but themselves. They have no reverence for parents or old age. They are impatient of all restraint. They talk as if they alone know everything.

Again, widespread immorality and promiscuity are hardly innovations of the twentieth century, even when elevated into some new moral system. It is hard to believe that Juvenal was not writing of D H. Lawrence and the intellectual enthusiasts for *Lady Chatterley's Lover* when he decried

> high flown moral discourse from that clique in Rome, who affect ancestral peasant virtues as a front for their lechery.

However "modern" any attitude may seem, counterparts can generally be found in many other ages. Even that phenomenon which we so particularly associate with our own time, the division of society into the "with it" and the "squares," is hardly unfamiliar. We find the same language used: the term "square," for instance, in its contemporary sense, was a coinage of the 1770's, when it was used to describe those who still affected square-toed shoes after they had gone out of fashion; and in the plays of Thomas Otway, written in seventeenth century Restoration London, we find the words "swinging" and "swinger" used exactly as they are used today, to denote the lively, "swinging" handful who recognized no conventional moral restraint, and were in revolt against the boring majority who did not know what life was about.

In all matters relating to human nature, in short, it is wise, before assuming that any manifestation of behavior or belief is new, to consult historical parallel. As Tolstoy tartly observed of Vera Berg in *War and Peace,* when she talked of "our days," she used the term

> as people of limited intelligence are fond of doing, imagining that they have discovered and appraised the peculiarities of "our days" and that human characteristics change with the times.

The most obvious and immediate historical parallel to the climate of English life in the fifties and sixties is to be found, of course, in the nineteen-twenties—particularly in the twenties of Scott Fitzgerald's "Jazz Age" America. There was not a single important feature of the upheaval in the fifties and sixties, as we have seen it so far, that did not in the twenties, in one way or another, have its counterpart— whether it was the prominence of youth, the frenzied dance crazes, the short skirts and exhibitionistic dress, the self-assertive towers in architecture, the rigidly conformist rebellion against "convention" and "Victorian" morality, or just the all-pervasive sense that society was somehow moving rapidly into an unprecedented age. Obviously in both periods these were symptoms of essentially the same social and psychological phenomenon—a similarity that was borne out even in some of the means whereby the general excitement was urged on, such as the syncopated rhythms of jazz (associated, as Fitzgerald wrote in his essay *Echoes of the Jazz Age,* with "a state of nervous stimulation not unlike that of big cities behind the lines of war").

In fact, these sources of "nervous stimulation" were one of the central ingredients of the whole phenomenon. The twenties might not have achieved the sophistication of some of the techniques we have seen in the fifties—the strip-tease clubs, the "exciting" photography, the sex in advertising, the electronic amplification or rock 'n roll—but certainly life in the twenties provides us with the same spectacle of an age plunging into a fever of verbal, visual, and musical titillation.

One particularly revealing technique was that which we saw in the *Queen* magazine's glorification of "the *tense* present," "the *crazy* Sixties," "keeping *pace* with *pace.*" Forty years before we can find this same use of language to create a sense of excitement in the business letters described by Sinclair Lewis in his *Babbitt* (1922), which were written with *"pep"* and *"punch"* and *"kick"* in Zenith, the *"Zip* City, *Zeal, Zest* and *Zowie!"* Or again, consider these two passages—the first from that Ian Fleming short story which appeared in the first issue of the *Sunday Times* color supplement:

> He *strained* his eyes, taking in the *squat flash eliminator* at the *muzzle,* the *telescopic sight* and the *thick, downward chunk* of *magazine . . .* "Kalashnikov" he said *curtly.* "Sub machine gun. Gas operated. Thirty rounds in 7.62 millimetre."

And the second from a story by Ernest Hemingway, whose literary style was formed in the twenties:

> He turned his *heavy head* and *swung away* towards the cover of the trees as he heard a *cracking crash* and *felt* the *slam* of the *.30–06 220-gram solid bullet* that *bit* his *flank* and *ripped* in *sudden hot scalding nausea . . .*

In each instance we can see that words are being used not so much to convey meaning as, by their sound and association, to work the reader up and carry him away, by arousing his subconscious mind with a constant series of little thrills and suggestive images ("slam," "squat," "chunk").

The most interesting thing about this technique—which certainly by the sixties had come to form the basis not only of thrillers, pornography, advertising, and a great deal of journalism but even much of what passed for serious literature—is that it can only achieve its effect if the reader's conscious judgment has been more or less willingly suspended, and his mind allowed to slip into a trance-like state —or he will see the trick for what it is and regard it as merely absurd. It is an indication in fact that there exists in human beings a state of mind quite different from the "normal," which is characterized by a suspension of objectivity and a desire to be "carried away." And obviously, in discussing a condition of general excitement which relies so heavily on titillation of every kind, if we can isolate and analyze that state of mind, we may well have found the central key to what we are describing.

For the moment, however, and if only to demonstrate that it is not only the nineteen-twenties that provide us with a close parallel to the atmosphere of our own times, let us look back briefly at a third period of history.

Consider, for instance, this famous passage, discussing what its author described as "this degrading thirst after outrageous stimulation":

A multitude of causes, unknown to former times, are now acting with a combined force to blunt the discriminating powers of the mind, and, unfitting it for all voluntary exertion, to reduce it to a state of almost savage torpor. The most effective of these causes are the great national events which are daily taking place, and the increasing accumulation of men in cities, where the uniformity of their occupations produces a craving for extraordinary incident, which the rapid communication of intelligence hourly gratifies. To this tendency of life and manners, the literature and theatrical exhibitions of the country have conformed themselves. The invaluable works of our elder writers . . . are driven into neglect by frantic novels, sickly and stupid tragedies, and deluges of idle and extravagant stories . . .

This was Wordsworth writing in 1800 (in the Preface to the Second Edition of *Lyrical Ballads*) of the age of the "riotous" and "shocking" Waltz, of notorious drunkenness, opium eating and gambling fever, of sexual promiscuity, low-cut dresses, and male dandyism; an age of acute fashion-consciousness and an age too when, as in the nineteen-twenties and sixties, a great many people had the sense of being swept into the future on a heady tide of modernity. In the words of William Hazlitt, from his lecture *On the Living Poets* (1818):

> There was a mighty ferment in the heads of statesmen and poets, kings and people. According to the prevailing notions, all was to be natural and new. Nothing that was established was to be tolerated . . . authority . . . elegance or arrangement were hooted out of countenance . . . everyone did that which was good in his own eyes. The object was to reduce all things to an absolute level; and a singularly affected and outrageous simplicity prevailed in dress and manners, style and sentiment. *A striking effect produced where it was least expected, something new and original, no matter whether it was good or bad, whether mean or lofty, whether extravagant or childish, was all that was aimed at* . . . the licentiousness grew extreme . . . it was a time of promise, a renewal of the world.

Nothing indeed was more expressive of that "mighty ferment" than the great fever which, from the 1760's onwards, had swept through the artistic imaginations of one country in Europe after another; that was associated at its most extreme with such names as diverse as Byron and Goya, Rousseau and William Blake, Thomas Chatterton and the Marquis de Sade; and with such qualities as a rebellion against every kind of convention, an exhibitionism and a fanatical belief in self-expression, a cult of youth and an extravagant hero-worship (as of Byron or Napoleon), and an unwearying pursuit of the exotic, the novel, the perverse, and the odd. Of all the symptoms of this fever, none was more revealing, in our present context, than—from the Gothic novels to the poetry of Byron and Shelley— its particular use of language. Compare with our extracts from Fleming and Hemingway above, for instance, this passage from Shelley's *A Vision of the Sea*:

> . . . where the *hum* of the *hot blood* that *spouts* and *rains*
> Where the *gripe* of the *tiger* has *wounded* the *veins*
> Swollen his *rage, strength* and *effort*; the *whirl* and the *splash*
> As of some *hideous engine* whose *brazen teeth smash*
> The *thin* winds and *soft* waves into *thunder.*

As a catalogue of "striking effects," of suggestive imagery and violent sounds working themselves into a frenzy that is ultimately quite meaningless (e.g. "the hum of the hot blood"), our twentieth century exponents could hardly have done better. But then there is nothing in which we see the fever of our own times so clearly fore-shadowed as in the dreams, the delusions, and the excesses of the late eighteenth and nineteenth century phenomenon known as Romanticism.

The age which gave birth to that eruption of Romanticism was one of profound social and political change. It is a commonplace that such periods of upheaval, when the certainties of more stable times are lost and the very structure of society and all that framework of the familiar which gives men a sure subconscious foundation seems to be dissolving, should fire men's imaginations, arousing them to the intense mental activity that has represented their attempt to reestablish a relationship with the world and with reality. But it is also at such times that for many people, even for whole classes and nations, a hold on reality becomes hardest to achieve. Unbalanced by change, they display, like an uncertain adolescent, all the symp-toms of insecurity. They become self-conscious, and feel an acute sense of isolation from the world. They seek, often quite unwittingly, not to harmonize themselves with the rest of society but to assert themselves. They base their hopes on nebulous dreams and visions. Confused by change, they either turn their backs on it and take refuge in nostalgia or throw themselves headlong into it, accommodating themselves to disorder by surrendering entirely to the exhilaration of its forward rush. And all these forms of unhappy adjustment are in fact symptoms of the same fundamental condition. They are all different manifestations of escapism or neurosis. That is to say, they can none of them provide more than the elusive image of security because they are based only on unreal, subjective projections of the mind. They are, in short, the results of trying to resolve an insecurity through what we may call the dream or fantasy level of the mind. And it is with the working and structure of fantasy that this book is primarily concerned.

One of the most familiar forms of fantasy, and one which indicates the two basic principles on which all fantasy operates, is the daydream. Daydreams are based firstly, although this is sometimes disguised, on self-centered wishful thinking—or some form of self-gratification or self-assertion. Walter Mitty-like, we imagine ourselves successful in love or receiving public acclaim. And secondly, they are based on a succession of mental "images," the peculiarity of which is that, like those of night dreams, they are restless and elusive and cannot be pinned down. Daydreams can therefore no more than any other form of fantasy be regarded as truly "satisfying"—but only as titillation by means of fleeting mental thrills or sensations.

Nevertheless, we all of us have a "fantasy-self," a part of our mind that makes up and is receptive to fantasies, and conscious fantasies and daydreams are only its most conspicuous projections. Our capacity for seeing the world in terms of make-believe reaches down into the depth of our subconscious minds—and may, if it is aroused and not recognized or disciplined, come to influence and color a large part of our daily thoughts, actions, and attitudes. At all times that it does so, it is possible to distinguish in its operation the two elements we have singled out in the daydream.

But first we must establish the technical property which gives to fantasies their hold over the human mind. The basic condition of anyone whose fantasy-self is aroused is that he has abandoned the certainties of "reality" and surrendered his mind to the figments and possibilities of imagination. As we saw earlier, in the passages from Fleming and Hemingway, the whole essence of fantasy images is that they act not by clear statement but by suggestion—exciting the mind with hints and innuendoes in the same way as the elusive, half-formed images of the daydream. It is in fact this very elusiveness which gives to fantasy its hypnotic power. Just as pornography and strip-tease mesmerize by holding out the suggestive image of something that is in fact unattainable, so all fantasy images excite the mind by the fact that they are incomplete and cannot be properly resolved. They tantalize and egg on the imagination in the same way as an object only seen indistinctly, because it does not provide the brain with sufficient information clearly to make it out, may tease and excite our minds into thinking it larger and more awesome than in fact it is. "Such tricks hath strong imagination" in the words of Theseus, to body "forth the form of things unknown," that "in the night, imagining some fear, how easy is a bush supposed a bear."

So important a part must this singular effect play in any analysis of the workings of fantasy that we may perhaps describe such a phenomenon as a "nyktomorph" or "night shape."* For it is the nyktomorphic effect which, whether in art or in life, causes the projections of fantasy to assume an importance and attraction beyond the bounds of reason or reality. A man whose fantasy-self is aroused is a man whose mind is continually excited by half-formed images and cloudy possibilities—whether the excitement be pleasurable, as

---

* Trusting in Horace's dictum that "new and recently coined words will win acceptance if they are borrowed from Greek sources and drawn upon sparingly."

in the case of some imagined self-indulgence, or unpleasant, as in the case of a mind churning with fears and anxieties.

It is the nyktomorphic effect, to take one familiar example, which makes a half-clothed figure, because it "leaves something to the imagination," more "erotic" than a naked one. It is the nyktomorphic effect which, in times of war or other disturbance, leads people to lend credence to the most incredible of rumors based on a suggestive playing on their fears. It is the nyktomorphic effect which accounts for the way in which exposure through the distorting media of television, journalism, and the cinema can blow up the usually rather colorless and insecure personalities of film actors, television celebrities, or pop singers into "dream figures" of inexpressible glamor. And, of course, it is the power of indeterminate imagery to excite sensations and shadowy possibilities which gives its force to all kinds of Romanticism in art, not to say the avant-garde plays, films, pictures, sculpture, and music of the twentieth century. With the addition of a few such suggestively incomplete words as "measureless" or "sunless," for instance, the otherwise straightforward image of a stream flowing underground may be conjured into a passage as powerful as:

> Where Alph the *sacred* river ran
> Through *caverns measureless* to man
> Down to a *sunless* sea . . .

And if, in fact, one were to remove from Romantic poetry all such mechanically nyktomorphic stimuli as:

nameless, infinite, weird, magic, mysterious, strange, faery, curious, ghostly, enchanted, phantom, gloom, wraith-like, dream-like, shifting, nebulous, unearthly, lurking, thrilling, trembling, haunting, obscure, mad, tempestuous, ghastly, fearful, dread etc.

what was left of a great many widely respected poems would be no more interesting and a good deal less meaningful than the London telephone directory. For the very nature of such poetry, if we can

55

forget for a moment that it is "art" and consider it merely as a psychological manifestation, is that it has passed beyond considerations of mere meaning into an illusory realm in which the only thing that matters is the evocative power of the image and the degree of excitement that it may arouse.

But such auto-suggestive illusions may as easily be worked up out of nothing, whether personally or collectively, in life as in art. And without a proper appreciation of their working and power, it would be difficult to understand almost any of the more conspicuous social and political phenomena of our times—from the importance of advertising, fashion and the mass-entertainment industry to the rise of such dream-based mass movements as Communism and Fascism.

However nebulous these emanations from the dim subconscious may seem, all fantasies in fact obey certain clear rules. And in order properly to appreciate them, we must go back and examine in turn those two elements which, as we saw from the daydream, are basic to every fantasy.

The first is the element of self-consciousness, leading to a desire for self-gratification or self-assertion. Every fantasy begins primarily as the projection of a lone individual, isolated within himself, and wishing to lose himself in a dream—and in almost all fantasies, this takes the form firstly of a focus or force with which he can, in some way, identify himself. Thus James Bond begins as the subconscious projection of Ian Fleming's fantasy-self, and in turn provides a similar focus of identification, as he moves irresistibly through his world of violence and sexual indulgence, for millions of readers and cinema-goers. The modern entertainment industry is almost entirely concerned with producing daydreams and daydream heroes with which its audiences can in this way identify. But in many instances, this central focus onto which the fantasy-self can fasten is by no means so obviously personal. It may be the musical line of jazz, even a horse in a race or, most commonly of all, some group in society or cause.

56

In his essay *The New Romanticism,* Aldous Huxley drew a clear distinction between what he described as the old Romanticism of the nineteenth century, with its archetypal hero the lone individual, at odds with society and struggling for total freedom; and the New Romanticism of the twentieth century which, as far as he could see, was exactly the reverse—glorifying these are only two sides of the same coin. On the one hand, all the ingredients of the old Romanticism are as much present in the twentieth century as they were in the nineteenth. James Bond is only the same old lone Romantic hero in modern guise. The archetypal hero of twentieth century literature and mass entertainment has been, just as much as in the nineteenth century, the lone protagonist at odds with his environment—all the way from the dream heroes of the Westerns and the Superman comics, through Charlie Chaplin's "Little man," Osborne's Jimmy Porter, and Colin Wilson's "Outsider" to the lost heroes of the nightmares of Kafka and Orwell. The old self-assertive qualities of non-conformity, youth, and rebellion have been far more extensively glamorized in the age of T. E. Lawrence, Scott Fitzgerald, and James Dean than ever in the age of Lermontov and Byron.

At the same time, however, there is no dream so powerful as one generated and subscribed to by a whole mass of people simultaneously—one of those mass projections of innumerable individual neuroses which we may call a group fantasy. This is why the twentieth century has equally been dominated by every possible variety of collective make-believe—whether expressed through mass political movements and forms of nationalism or through mass social movements, such as the teenage subculture based on dress and music.

Any group fantasy is in some sense a symptom of social disintegration, of the breaking down of the balance and harmony between individuals, classes, generations, the sexes, or even nations. For the organic relationships of a stable and secure community, in which everyone may unself-consciously exist in his own separate place and right, a group fantasy substitutes the elusive glamor of identification with a fantasy community, of being swept along as part of a uniform mass united in a common cause. But the individuals making up the mass are not, of course, united in any real sense, except through their common dress, catch phrases, slogans, and stereotyped attitudes. Behind their conformist exteriors they remain individually as insecure as ever—and indeed become even more so, for the collective dream, such as that expressed through mass advertising or the more hysterical forms of fashion, is continually aggravating their fantasy-selves and appealing to them through their insecurities to merge themselves in the mass ever more completely.

Most important of all, every group fantasy is collectively self-assertive; that is to say, it subsumes all the individual desires for self-assertion into a collective fund of psychic aggression. In fact, just as every individual neurotic feels the need firstly for a dream to escape into, secondly for a dream projection to identify with, and thirdly for the illusion of self-assertion, so every collective neurosis displays these characteristics writ large—the common dream which binds its members rigidly together, the dream heroes who attain their hypnotic glamor by embodying and acting as projections of the group neurosis, and the common fund of aggression, whether expressed toward the rest of society in general or just some other group in particular. To Nazism, the single most virulent group fantasy of modern times, the supreme dream hero was Hitler; the foci for group aggression were, on the one hand, the Jews and the Communists inside Germany, and on the other, the non-Aryan outside world. In more recent days, of the gigantic group fantasy which overtook China in 1966–1967 known as the "Cultural Revolution," the dream hero was Mao Tse-tung; the foci for aggression were again both "subversives" within the country and also, virtually, the rest of the outside world.

This was the phenomenon of mass psychology which was portrayed in an extreme version by George Orwell in his *1984,* in which he showed both the ritual homage paid to the image of Big Brother, and the ritual hatred expressed at the image of the internal subversive

Goldstein, and the shadowy enemies with whom his country was perpetually at war. But in fact the pattern Orwell described was that of every group fantasy; exactly the same that we can see, for instance, in the teenage subculture of the fifties and sixties, with its dream-hero pop singers and its enormous psychic aggression against the world of the "squares," or that of the left-wing progressive intellectuals, with their dream heroes such as D. H. Lawrence or Che Guevara and their ritual abuse of the "reactionaries," from Ian Smith to the Lord Chamberlain.

In itself, however, the conformist mass imposing pressure to sweep along all its members as one organism has been a familiar aspect of human behavior ever since the first army, bound together by dreams of conquest, marched euphorically off to war. There is nevertheless one general respect in which the twentieth century has contributed to the generation of individual and group fantasies on an unprecedented scale. Obviously no single development in history has done more to promote both social disintegration and unnatural conformity than the advance and ubiquity of machines and technology. Not only must the whole pressure of an industrialized, urbanized, mechanized society tend to weld its members into an ever more rootless, uniform mass, by the very nature of its impersonal organization and of the processes of mass-production and standardization. But in addition the twentieth century has also provided two other factors to aggravate and to feed the general neurosis; the first being the image-conveying apparatus of films, radio, television, advertising, mass-circulation newspapers and magazines; the second the feverishly increased pace of life, from communications and transport to the bewildering speed of change and innovation, all of which has created a profound subconscious restlessness which neurotically demands to be assuaged by more speed and more change of every kind.

There is also another very important sense in which machines and technology have come to influence man's fantasy life. For machines

and gadgets and the sense of the forward thrust of technological progress have themselves, as much as the crowd or mass movement, come
to provide the subconscious imagery of those impersonal, self-assertive
forces with which men, through their fantasy-selves, can identify.

Once again, this romanticism of machines has both its individual
and its collective aspects. On the one hand, for instance, we can see
the extraordinary importance accorded by so much contemporary
fantasy to the gun and the motor car, both of which come to be
regarded on a fantasy level as extensions and aggrandizements of the
self. It is the gun, with its image of untold power, that transforms
the heroes of so many thousands of Westerns, thrillers, war films,
and strip cartoons (not to say children's games) into imaginary
supermen. And it was this, of course, that completed the image of
James Bond as the romantic dream hero of the technological age;
for it was his guns, his cars, and his gadgets that extended him into
a super-human embodiment of self-assertion, able to conquer anyone
and anything.

On the other hand, the romanticism of machines and technology
also has its more impersonal aspect. Just as the disorder of constant
violent change, for the very reason that it does as much as anything
to make man rootless and insecure, is neurotically glorified for its
own sake to make it acceptable; so technology, which renders man's
environment ever more impersonal and oppressive, becomes the focus
for fantasies of limitless freedom and omnipotence. Man excites himself, in his literature, his films, and his daydreams, with the powerful images of aeroplanes, tanks, space ships, imaginary cities. On
television, he transforms the world of science into a dream world by
the accompaniment of electronic music. He adjusts himself to his
increasingly artificial and mechanical environment by creating a
dream of "exciting" skyscrapers with their mechanically patterned
windows, "thrusting" motorways, vistas of glass and metal and concrete throbbing with a mechanical pulse and giving off an aura of
inhuman excitement in which he can lose himself, swept along on

a nyktomorphic sense of progress and modernity into a science fiction future that is nothing more than a creation of his own mind.

It is by no means only the romanticism of technology, however, which makes fantasy impersonal, mechanical, and inhuman. Nothing, for instance, could have been more impersonal and inhuman than the dream worlds conjured up by some of the nineteenth century Romantics, of tempests and wild mountains and nature rude and unconfined, of desolate ruins, vampires, stereotyped pale consumptive women, and cosmic struggles between great abstract ideas such as "Liberty" and "Tyranny." For as the neurotic loses touch with human reality and comes to see his fellow men purely in terms of appearances and externals as they relate to himself, so all fantasy tends to reduce the world to abstracts and stereotypes. By its very nature fantasy is in this sense "inhuman" because it can only see the world in terms of unreal images. Which leads us back at this point to the second of the two basic elements of the daydream.

Because it is only kept in being by suggestion and innuendo, every fantasy requires a constant supply of new images and sensations for the illusion of self-gratification or self-assertion to be sustained. There is no point in identifying with James Bond unless there is a steady provision of pretty girl-images and violence-images to keep the focus of the dream gratified. And here we come to another of the most important ingredients in the nature of fantasy: that every image falls into, or is polarized between, two basic categories. The first, which we may call the image of "life" or vitality, is associated with such ideas as freedom, change, rebellion, improvisation, youth, sex, the future, and the self. And the second, which we may call the image of "order" or stability, is associated with such ideas as security, tradition, harmony, authority, age, marriage, the past, and the community.

The importance of this polarization cannot be overestimated. For what it means is that all images, regardless of what they may appear to represent on the surface, on the level at which they actually affect and excite our minds, do so in fact only because they suggest the general idea either of "vitality" or of "order" (or a combination of both).

If we consider, for instance, so exemplary an expression of fantasy as the imagery of mass advertising, we can see at once that a great many advertisements, associated with pictures of pretty girls, burning flames, jet airliners, boats rushing along in water, speeding cars, sunshine dancing through trees, or running children, and such words as:

crisp, hard, tough, colorful, instant, drastic, ice-cold, compact, high-speed, energy etc.,

are built up, regardless of the product they are selling, out of a general suggestion of life, youth, movement, and excitement. Apart from the name and purpose of the product itself, they are nothing more than indiscriminate collections of vitality images. On the other hand, another large group of advertisements, associated either with pictures of mothers, children, cosy firesides, and family scenes, and such words as:

gentle, soft, silky, relaxing, creamy, eases, luxurious, liquid, slow, mild, caressing etc.,

or with pictures of men in uniform, people in evening dress, old leather books, old buildings such as cathedrals, stately homes or thatched cottages, and such words as:

fine, rich, matured, golden, quality, aroma, elegance, sophisticated, trust, satisfying etc.,

are build up out of order, calm, reassurance, and trustworthiness. The fundamental appeal of any advertisement can, in fact, be summed up as either "It's New, Exciting, Thrilling, and Sensational!" or "It's Established, Proven, Relaxing, and Reliable."

Once we understand this polarity between life and order, between freedom and security, the whole nature of fantasy opens up in a new way. Whenever a man can be said to have lost touch with reality, it can be seen that he is doing so either by a mechanical pursuit of the outward image of order, pattern, or discipline, without the balancing life of true feeling or understanding; or by a pursuit of the image of freedom and excitement, unanchored to reality by the perspective of order and discipline. To take but a few examples of each: obviously a Hollywood film sentimentalizing marriage or religion; a right-wing colonel who is obsessed with discipline and the glories of the past; a scholar or scientist who becomes preoccupied with the endless minutiae of facts, footnotes, and statistics; bureaucracy, with its tendency to blind reliance on established practice, regulations, high-sounding jargon, and the trappings of a rigid hierarchy: all these, in their different ways, provide examples of "orderly" fantasies. Similarly, the rebellious Romanticism of a Byron or a Shelley, the vicarious sex and violence of James Bond, the visions of total moral freedom of a progressive intellectual, are all examples of "vitality" fantasies.

Nowhere does this polarization show more clearly than in a society which, like most societies at all times, is in a state of flux. As a society loses its organic homogeneity, lines of stress appear between its component groups—between class and class, between generation and generation, between rulers and ruled. Two things then happen. First, as each group becomes more conscious of its own identity, so it tends to project a group fantasy embodying its dreams of self-assertion and its aggression against other groups. Obviously the group fantasies of the "underprivileged," of the lower classes, the young, the rising ethnic group, tend to be "vitality" fantasies (making up what we may call the basic "left-wing" fantasy) associated with change, revolution, vigor, freedom, and the future. While the group fantasies of the established order, which feels itself to be threatened by this new aggressive force and reacts with aggression of its own, the upper classes, the older generation, the dominant racial group, take the form of "orderly" fantasies, associated with stability, law and order, discipline, resistance to change, and the better days of the past.

Secondly, however, another subtler polarization takes place, apparently in the opposite direction—whereby the rising lower classes in fact long for the respectability of the higher groups, and the established groups are fascinated by the "vitality" of the others. One illustration of this process has been the history of the British Labour Party, with its alliance between upper-middle-class Socialist intellectuals, often more defiantly "left-wing" than their proletarian brethren, and potentially right-wing trade unionists and members of the lower classes who have risen in the world. Another has been the fantasies thrown up by the relationship between the white and black races—providing an excellent example of both sorts of polarization, the whites either "reactionary" or over-liberal and hypnotized by Negro "vitality," the Negroes either defiantly rebellious or seeking to become over-respectable according to a white standard.

Clearly almost all the forms of fantasy we have so far seen in this narrative, whether in the England of the fifties and sixties or in the Romanticism of the nineteenth century, have been vitality fantasies. And it is in fact through one of their most obvious characteristics that we can at last consider the true nature of the sensations whereby fantasies are gratified.

The very word "sensational" conjures up the meaningless superlatives of cinema publicity, and the idea of anything odd, extravagant, or unexpected. Again, one of its most familiar uses is to describe a certain type of journalism, where it is associated with a brash, irregular layout, intended to catch the eye, pin-up photographs, an emphasis on crime and scandal, and above all a superficial presentation of the news which relies heavily on such words as:

> clash, storm, shock, row, crush, rebels, slam, probe, grab, routed, soars, plunges, lashes out, slaps down, crash, breakthrough, breakdown etc.

All these words (as in our examples from Fleming, Hemingway, and Shelley) make their impact by conjuring up a subconscious mental sensation of disorder or violence. Their very essence lies in the subconscious shock or thrill that may be derived from sensing a sudden violation of tranquillity or order.

Turning from violence to that other great standby of sensational journalism, novels, plays, and so forth—love and sex—we find that here too it is not order or tranquillity which gives off an aura of life and excitement, but the thrills of "romance," "love at first sight," and violations of order such as adultery, prostitution, transvestism, homosexuality, or incest. In every way and by every permutation, the image of love and sex must, in order to excite sensations, be a disturbance of ordered normality—from the suggestive allure of "forbidden" decadence and corruption which has been so consistent a theme of a certain kind of Romantic poetry, down to the way in which, at the height of the mania surrounding the Beatles in 1963–1965, the pitch of hysteria among their audiences was reserved for the moments when, at the climax of a song, the four young men moved their voices into a girlish falsetto register.

Whatever form of vitality fantasy we choose to consider, whether social, political, personal, or artistic, we find the same story: that the essence of the sensations on which it feeds is that they are, in some way, violations of order or the image of order—and that, for this purpose, any image or convention of order will suffice. It may be a violation of the social order, represented by such symbols of authority and tradition as the Monarchy, the police, bishops, judges, schoolmasters, or parents. It may be a violation of the natural physical order: perversions of which, such as giants, dwarfs, freaks, and monsters, have excited men's fantasies in legends and on fairgrounds since time immemorial. It may be a violation of aesthetic order: providing visual thrills derived from unusually angled photographs, speeded up or slow motion film, the visual tricks and unnatural juxtapositions of surrealism, the optical illusions of Op Art, or the suggestively disordered glimpses and fragments of *collage*; or the musical thrills derived from violations of the conventional sense of key and harmony, ranging from the chromaticism of Wagner's "music of the future" to the "blue notes" and "flattened chords" (or discords) which provide sensations in jazz. Or it may even be a violation of the order of sanity itself: as we can see in the consistent Romantic preoccupations with dreams and madness, the appeal of hallucinogenic drugs or the teenage subculture's use as terms of approbation of such words as "wild," "rave," and "crazy."

Whatever form it takes, a vitality fantasy is thus not simply a dream which pursues the elusive image of life, freedom, and excitement, but actually derives its lifeblood from the very act of contemplating disorder. Vitality fantasies are in fact active "disorderly" fantasies. The sensation of violation, of rebellion, becomes an end in itself. The anarchist "needs" order to give him the illusion of freedom in escaping from it; the progressive novelist or playwright "needs" bourgeois convention in order to make his impact by offending it. We are confronted, in fact, with that neurotic condition which, at its most extreme, was described by the nineteenth century Romantics as "cosmic protest" or, in the context of the teenagers of our own time, "rebellion without a cause." One of the commonest symptoms of someone whose fantasy-self is aroused is a sense of constriction or social claustrophobia—whether it be labeled tyranny or merely boredom—coupled with the longing to break out, to escape into some dimly sensed "heightened reality"; a desire for self-assertion which inevitably involves rebellion and which, if necessary, will create or at least exaggerate beyond all reality its own images of order—such as the all-purpose image of "Victorianism," or the indiscriminate application of the term "Fascist"—in order to provide it with a focus for its aggression.

But what is this "heightened reality" for which they long—the teenagers, the Romantic poets, the congenital radicals, the addicts of drugs or romantic fiction—if it is not simply the shadowy, suggestive world of nyktomorphs? Which brings us back to where we started. For the hypnotic appeal of a nyktomorph—like the optical illusions of Op Art—lies in the fact that it is an image that is in some way unresolved or unresolvable, an image that is *incomplete*. And all these violations of order are exciting in the same way, like the images of decaying ruins which so fascinated the early Romantics, precisely because they are images which are in some way incomplete; they are nyktomorphically suggestive because they excite the brain with discords and an elusive vision of restless, "swinging," thrilling disorder, which it cannot properly resolve.

So far we have treated orderly and disorderly, right-wing and left-wing fantasies as though they were polar opposites. But the closer we look, for instance, at certain aspects of vitality fantasies—such as the mechanically regular rhythms of jazz, or the painstaking attention to surface detail of surrealist painting, or even simply the orderly conformity imposed on its followers by any left-wing group fantasy —the more clearly we see that a certain kind of neurotic or mechanical order, pattern, and discipline is integral to disorderly fantasies as well. Indeed the very ease with which a left-wing fantasy such as Russian pre-Revolutionary Communism could, on coming to power, so swiftly develop many of the characteristics of a right-wing fantasy —such as a colossal bureaucracy, anti-Semitism, slave camps for the nonconformists, and a violent hostility to modern art—shows that the dividing line between one form of fantasy and the other is by no means firm or clear.

On the other hand, we find a virulent right-wing fantasy such as Nazism displaying many of the characteristics of a left-wing fantasy, such as its cult of youth and vitality. The cult of technology, although primarily a right wing fantasy with its roots in the excitement of power, similarly displays all the symptoms of a vitality fantasy in its worship of change, movement, and the future. While even the most apparently reactionary orderly fantasies feed on the sensations which derive from contemplating violence and disorder, as may be seen from the language with which certain right-wing fantasists excite themselves into a frenzy at the image of left-wing or progressive disorderliness:

shocking, filth, blasphemy, vile, obscene, repulsive, hooligans, louts etc.

Ultimately, in fact, the two kinds of fantasy can only be regarded as two sides of the same coin—not least because ultimately they both gratify themselves through the same fundamental violation of organic order, the assertion of the self.

At any time of violent change, in short, when what we may call the collective fantasy of society as a whole becomes excited, we shall find that it is made up of both left-wing and right-wing fantasies, each exacerbating and feeding each other's hostility; each feeding on the potent half-truth that, since the other is wholly wrong, they themselves must be wholly right; and yet both fundamentally part and parcel of each other. For however different they may appear on the surface, all fantasies are in the end rooted in the same basic, perverse, self-assertive, aggressive instinct. If carried far enough, all fantasy evolves into an obsession with sex or violence, which are merely the two extreme expressions of the self-assertive urge. It is true that, throughout history, right-wing fantasies have tended to be concerned more with the rightness of power and the wrongness of sex, while left-wing fantasies have been concerned more with the wrongness of power and the rightness of sex.* But in the end, as we have seen so clearly in America during the years of the Vietnam war, the anti-war, pro-sexual-freedom, left-wing fantasists and the pro-war, anti-sexual-freedom, right-wing fantasists are only complementary symptoms of the same basic disturbance.

And if this fundamental identity of sex and violence needs to be spelled out any further, we have only to hark back once again to the way in which, for James Bond, the gun becomes a symbol of virility, just as aggressive weapons have always been—from the spear to that

---

* Compare, for instance, the way in which the sixteenth century witch-hunters constantly accused their victims of holding sexual orgies or intercourse with the devil, with the way in which progressives of our own time cannot imagine the administration of any form of discipline or authority without its giving a perverse pleasure or a "power complex" to the administrator. Recall also, however, the way in which the Russian Communists who, before the Revolution, were theoretically all in favor of free love, switched some years after coming to power to a fervent support of the institution of marriage and brought in laws making it harder to divorce.

symbol of national virility in our own time, the ballistic missile: phallic symbols uniting in human fantasies the ultimate vitality images of sex and aggression.

Having thus reached the roots of fantasy, only one of its characteristics remains to be discussed—and that, in many ways, the most important; our starting point being that, by its very nature, no fantasy can remain static. The essence of fantasy is that it feeds on a succession of sensations or unresolved images, each one of which arouses anticipation, followed by inevitable frustration, leading to the demand for a new image to be put in its place. But the very fact that each sensation is fundamentally unsatisfying means that the fantasy-self becomes progressively more jaded. In the words of W. B. Yeats, "We have fed the heart on fantasies, the heart's made brutal by the fare." Thus, in order to achieve the same thrills, it demands larger and larger gratifications. Short skirts must get shorter, the gambler must increase his stakes, the heroin addict must step up his dose— simply to achieve the same degree of excitement. And so we arrive at the fantasy spiral.

Whatever pattern of fantasy we choose to look at—whether in life or in art, whether the evolution of a James Bond film or a strip-tease act or a revolutionary movement or a piece of music such as Ravel's *Bolero* or a trend in fashion—we shall find that it is straining through a spiral of increasingly powerful sensations toward some kind of climax. But unlike such a mental pattern as, for instance, a Beethoven symphony, in which each ingredient plays its part in working for an organic and satisfactory resolution of the whole, a fantasy pattern based on a whole series of images which are themselves unresolved cannot by definition resolve everything that has gone before. What happens therefore is simply that, in its pursuit of the elusive image of life, freedom, and self-assertion, the fantasy pushes on in an ever-mounting spiral of demand, ever more violent, more dream-like and fragmentary, and ever more destructive of the framework of order. Further and further pushes the fantasy, always in pursuit of the elusive climax, always further from reality—*until it is actually bringing about the very opposite of its aims,* the dream producing the nightmare, the vision of freedom producing the slavery of the gambler or drug addict. But still the climax cannot and must not be reached, for it is on the very edge of the climax that ultimate titillation is to be found. Skirts may rise and necklines fall, but they must never in the name of suggestiveness go the whole way. The blue note may teeter in unbearable tension on the very edge of harmony, but must never get there. The nyktomorph, in short, must never quite be resolved. For the climax, like the final disaster in a nightmare which always coincides with waking up, is the "explosion into reality."

There are times, however, when the dream does "explode into reality." The dream hero is not always James Bond plucked by a miracle from the final disaster or the girl saved in the nick of time from the path of the oncoming train. In many artistic fantasies, such as Scott Fitzgerald's novel *The Great Gatsby* (1925) or Vladimir Nabokov's *Lolita* (1955) or Francois Truffaut's film *Jules et Jim* (1961), we can trace the identical pattern of an initial dream-like excitement slowly souring into a nightmare inconsequence which culminates in an apparently senseless explosion of destructive or self-destructive violence. Catherine, the heroine or "dream focus" of *Jules et Jim,* having become progressively more insane, finally beckons her lover Jim into a car and, with studied deliberation, drives both him and herself off a bridge. Humbert Humbert, finally deprived of his Lolita, hunts down his sinister *Doppelgänger* Quilty and murders him in a manner which can only lead to his own self-destruction— while Lolita dies in childbirth. Gatsby "the mysterious," the supreme and most subtle Romantic hero of twenties literature, floats full of bullets in his own swimming pool. It is at such moments that the cult of sensation has shown its true face: that with the "explosion into reality" every fantasy, if pushed far enough, must inevitably bring about its own self-destruction; and that behind the glittering dream of life and vitality hides nothing less than the death-wish. And

70

it is, in fact, in artistic works such as these that we can see laid out in all its stages, and with almost mathematical precision, one of the most familiar and basic patterns in human experience. It is the pattern of any attempt to resolve insecurity through pursuing a dream-focus or fantasy—when carried through to its only possible ultimate resolution.

The "fantasy cycle" has five stages.

The first is the *Anticipation Stage*—of "vital" energy, sensing constraint, looking for a dream-focus, a cause, a release. Jules and Jim, the young students, living a gay life in pre-First-War Paris, yet lacking direction. Humbert Humbert, the middle-aged *roué* living with his secret obsession for twelve-year-old "nymphets," yet lacking a Lolita. When Jules and Jim find their shared obsession with the dream-focus Catherine and Humbert his in Lolita, there begins the second stage . . .

. . . the *Dream Stage*. This is a period of rising excitement when, as in a daydream, everything seems to be going right, every need is gratified. Jules, Jim, and Catherine embark on a hectic, three-cornered idyll, ending up in a white dream-house by the sea. Humbert marries Lolita's mother, but she is conveniently run over, and he is thus as Lolita's guardian, able to enter into the thrilling "forbidden" relationship with her and to embark on their year-long sexual odyssey round the motels of America. As the straining for an unattainable resolution increases, however, the heady delights of anticipation are flecked more and more with frustration, which eventually leads to the third or . . .

. . . *Frustration Stage*. The First War brings Jules' and Jim's idyll to an end, the trio are separated, and by the time Jim catches up with Jules and Catherine again after the war (they having in the meantime married), all is obviously not well. Similarly Humbert and Lolita end their wandering and settle down at Beardsley in increasing disharmony. But still the drive to climax continues—and as the fantasy craves for more and more violent sensation, so the Frustration Stage passes into the fourth or . . .

. . . *Nightmare Stage,* the reverse of the Dream Stage, in which everything goes increasingly and unaccountably wrong, and marked by a steadily more violent and shadowy sense of menace. In the film of *Jules et Jim* this sense of an approaching doom is reflected in haunting mists, dark forests, a growing melancholy interspersed with febrile outbursts of fey gaiety, by Catherine's becoming increasingly mad, by the strangely threatening presence of the mysterious Albert, and by the plot's becoming increasingly confused. In *Lolita,* the plot becomes equally inconsequential and confusing, Humbert becomes increasingly aware of the threatening presence of the mysterious Quilty stalking them across America in a nightmare parody of their earlier dream-odyssey, he goes steadily out of his mind and eventually is deprived of Lolita herself. In each instance, the Nightmare Stage is resolved in the only way possible—it turns into the fifth and final stage . . .

. . . the *Death Wish Stage,* or "explosion into reality."

Many of the ramifications of these last few pages will only begin to come clear at the end of this book and beyond. But in these five stages or moods of fantasy, we have, in fact, not only uncovered the pattern of innumerable films, novels, plays, and stories, the basic Romantic legend (as in Tristan and Isolde, Romeo and Juliet, Frankenstein, Werther, and Doctor Faustus), in which the pursuit of some kind of defiance or violation of order winds to its self-destruction; but also the framework in which any kind of uncontrolled subconscious activity may be analyzed. The essence of any form of fantasy, after all, whether it be a daydream or a night dream, a pop song or a plan for the Greater Germany, is that it is something which forms, as it were unbidden, in the subconscious. And what could seem less restricted than the world of dreams? Yet these patterns produced by the subconscious obey strict rules, and indeed express only a limited range of emotions and thoughts. The basic range of fantasy emotions is polarized between, on the one hand, excitement and anticipation, and on the other, oppression and frustration. They are all of them, like the great Romantic emotion of nostalgia, a fixing of the mind on something unattainable, unresolvable, or inexplicable. Or, as Hazlitt wrote of the poetry of Shelley, all fantasy is as

> astrology is to [the certainties of] natural science—a passionate dream, a straining after impossibilities, a record of fond conjectures, a confused embodying of vague abstraction a fever of the soul, thirsting and craving after what it cannot have, indulging its love of power and novelty at the expense of truth and nature, associating ideas by contraries, and wasting great powers by their application to unattainable objects.

As for the importance of the five basic moods of fantasy in themselves; if we look, for instance, at such a spontaneous effusion of the subconscious as the words of popular songs, we shall see that a great many of them merely reflect the state of one of the first three stages of the cycle; that is, they describe either love or excitement anticipated in the future ("We're going to rock around the clock tonight"), the Dream Stage of love that is actually being enjoyed ("You're Walking On Cloud Lucky Seven") or the Frustration Stage of love thwarted or lost ("Empty Bed Blues"). If we look at the plot of any James Bond story, we shall see that it runs through the first four stages of the cycle, culminating in the Nightmare Stage of his near-destruction; but that then, by dint of the fact that he is basically fighting for "our side" against some evil conspiracy, and therefore on a fantasy level still represents "moral order," a false happy ending is interposed; the audience, as it were, waking up from the nightmare just before it explodes into the final reality of his death. And if we need further confirmation of the inner logic of this pattern, we have only to look at the course of the piece of music mentioned some pages back, Ravel's *Bolero*. Here is a composition based nakedly on the rising spiral of sensations; the same tune, almost indefinitely repeated, rising louder and louder through a Dream Stage toward what? In what possible way could Ravel resolve this model fantasy pattern? If we examine the closing bars we

73

can see that the momentum of his music left only one course open. Eventually, as the pursuit of the elusive climax becomes desperate, Ravel at last changes key (Frustration Stage). This only makes the music even more frantic and the piece accordingly falls into a series of raging discords (Nightmare Stage), culminating in the only possible way it could, by falling to pieces in cacophony and thus destroying itself.

But the five-stage fantasy cycle is also the basic pattern followed by a form of art greater than any we have analyzed so far. The adventures of James Bond or Humbert Humbert, after all, are fantasies described from the subjective viewpoint of the hero; they can only be "enjoyed" by the reader who identifies himself, to some extent, with the self-gratification of the central figure. But the fantasy cycle is also the pattern of the great classical or Shakespearean tragedy; the pattern of hubris followed by nemesis, described from an objective and profoundly moral viewpoint. In our times, the very word "moral" has come to take on a subjective, self-assertive coloring: if I describe something as "immoral" it is assumed that I am in some way asserting my ego, and, since morality is purely a relative matter, one man's idea of what is moral is as good as another's. But to the ancients, to Shakespeare, morality was objective, observable, subject to unchanging rules: certain courses of action were inevitably followed by certain consequences. To Shakespeare and the Greeks, their tragedies were not just fantasy patterns that came unbidden into their brains, but a pattern endlessly observed and reflected in nature, in history, in real life, and in some of the most profoundly sensed myths of the human race. Othello, Macbeth, Mark Antony were all men who in some way offended against the laws of order, nature, and society, pursuing a chimera of jealousy or power or passion until they were drawn ineluctably to its ultimate consequence.

Whichever of Shakespeare's tragedies we consider, we can clearly decipher in its unfolding the five stages of the fantasy cycle. In *Macbeth,* for instance, the Anticipation Stage of the first act culminates in the witches' holding out to the successful general the promise that he would be Thane of Glamis, Thane of Cawdor, and King of Scotland—a particularly stark example of fantasy finding its focus. The Dream Stage of the second act shows Macbeth hailed as Thane of Cawdor and then, as the fantasy wins increasing hold over him, plotting and achieving the murder of Duncan. "Thou hast it now— king, Cawdor, Glamis all" as Banquo begins Act Three—but already with Banquo's suspicions, the Frustration Stage is setting in. "We have scotched the snake, not killed it" frets Macbeth himself—as he is led up, step by step, to the murder of Banquo, the vision of Banquo's ghost, the second, ominous and far less satisfying visit to the witches and then, as his desperation to secure his position runs ever faster out of control, to the killing of Lady Macduff and her children. By Act Four, stalked by the threat of approaching armies and the even more sinister witches' prognostications, Macbeth is firmly into his Nightmare Stage. And in the fifth act, with the suicide of Lady Macbeth, the surreal approach of Birnam wood and his own killing by Macduff, Macbeth's fantasy finally destroys itself in the Death Wish Stage.

The same basic pattern may be discerned not only in each of Shakespeare's tragedies—but also in those of Sophocles, Aeschylus, and every other classical tragedian. For the tragic form is not something that has arisen by chance, but is a beautifully, one must even say scientifically, exact portrayal of the pattern of any great disturbance in the natural or civil order, winding inevitably to its climax as the disturbance of fantasy destroys itself and the balance and order of nature and society are again restored. Unlike *Lolita* or *Jules et Jim* or *Bonnie and Clyde* which are fantasies of identification, pursued from within by the fantasy-selves of both author and audience, the classical tragedies are observations of the same pattern from the level of "reality." And nothing is more revealing of the gulf between the two levels on which Romantic and classical tragedies are conceived than the mood prevailing in the wake of their respective climaxes: compare, for instance, the way in which in so many fantasies the Death Wish Stage is followed by a brief coda expressing the pointlessness of it all, representing the post-climactic guilt feelings and depression of onanism—as in Humbert Humbert's pious wish that Lolita might have been an ordinary child, untouched by all that he had done to her, or the closing passage of *The Great Gatsby*:

> Gatsby believed in the green light, the orgiastic future that year by year recedes before us. It eludes us then, but that's no matter—tomorrow we will run faster, stretch out our arms further . . .

with the definite satisfaction expressed at the conclusion of so many Shakespearean tragedies that, although the times have been "out of joint" and so much "amiss," order and peace have now, however tragically, been restored—often coupled with the quite explicit language of order and thanksgiving itself:

> . . . come, Dolabella, see
> High order in this great solemnity.   (*Antony and Cleopatra*)
>
> Within my tent his bones tonight shall lie,
> Most like a soldier, ordered honourably.   (*Julius Caesar*)
>
> Our Peace we'll ratify; seal it with feasts:
> Set on there! Never was a war did cease,
> Ere bloody hands were washed, with such a peace.   (*Cymbeline*)
>
> Now civil wounds are stopped, peace lives again,
> That she may long live here, God say Amen!   (*Richard III*)

The climaxes of Shakespeare are altogether "satisfying," because in everything that leads up to them we have recognized the unfolding of a natural law, as sure in its operation as the law of gravity. We have recognized that, like the eddies which spin and dissolve in the flow of a great river, all fantasies, all disturbances in order must ultimately long for and bring about their own destruction—in order that the steady flow of society and nature may be preserved.

It is in fact in real life even more than in art that a realization of the true nature and patterns of fantasy can help us to understand all sorts of curiosities and phenomena that would otherwise be inexplicable. It helps us to understand, for instance, the curiously self-destructive urge that eventually comes over so many gamblers, alcoholics, drug addicts, or criminals—whose subconscious drive to sensation leads them to bigger and bigger crimes, to greater and greater risks until it seems that they are almost asking to be caught. It helps us to understand how so many record-seekers come to an untimely end, like Donald Campbell or John Cobb, or explorers, or mountaineers, or revolutionaries, or racing drivers, like the thirty-five or more leading Grand Prix motorists who have killed themselves in crashes since the war. It helps us to understand how acts of violence, such as rioting, crimes, or vandalism, can be undertaken in a dream-state, in a condition of excited fantasy, with no more thought of the real consequences than has a motorist wrapped in the dream environment of his car, his fantasy-self excited by the exhilaration of speed or alcohol, before he explodes into the sudden "reality" of a tree. Indeed for a vivid picture of an "explosion into reality" and its aftermath, it would be hard to better that given by a social worker quoted by Mr. T. R. Fyvel in his book *The Insecure Offenders,* in describing the extraordinary change in demeanor of members of teenage gangs, when they have been brought up against the sudden "reality" of arrest by the police:

> They even look physically smaller—they were really only infants, suddenly finding themselves completely helpless . . . they didn't know how to put it into words, but what seemed to me the worst was the sudden awareness that their fantasy strengths were no use to them.

Even more important, it helps to explain why so many dream figures and Romantic artists and heroes seem otherwise unaccountably to destroy themselves or to die violently. It can hardly be complete coincidence that even of such figures mentioned in this chapter alone, Ernest Hemingway should have shot himself, James Dean died in a car crash, Scott Fitzgerald drank himself to death at the age of forty-four, T. E. Lawrence died in a motorcycle crash at the age of forty-seven, Byron died at thirty-six (with his brain, according to the autopsy, showing the wear of a man of ninety), Shelley drowned at thirty, and Lermentov was killed in a duel at twenty-seven. Nor can it be coincidence that so many other dream figures and embodiments of collective neurosis should have come to untimely ends, whether such film stars as Marilyn Monroe (committing suicide at thirty-six), Jayne Mansfield (killed in a car crash at thirty-nine), Jean Harlow (dead of drugs at twenty-six), and Rudolph Valentino (dead of disease at thirty-one), or such famous jazz musicians as Charlie Parker (dead of drugs at thirty-four), Billie Holiday (dead of drugs at forty-four), and Bix Beiderbecke (dead of drink at twenty-eight), or such painters as Van Gogh, the suicide, Jackson Pollock, the pioneer of action painting killed in a car crash, and Modigliani, who died of a combination of drugs, alcohol, and venereal disease at the age of thirty-five. Their very genius itself, and the peculiar neurotic brilliance with which they shone for others, were in fact nothing more than expressions of the sickness (in the most general sense) by which they were also ultimately destroyed.

Similarly, a grasp of the workings of group fantasies, and of the way that fantasies and neuroses can afflict societies, opens out vistas of understanding on a much more general scale. We can begin to see in a new light, for instance, the patterns of nationalism and revolt; how it is that nationalist movements become increasingly violent; how it is that every unsuccessful rebellion, from Spartacus to Pugacheff, from the Peasant's Revolt to that of the Hungarians in 1956, should have run through the pattern of the fantasy cycle, from the dream stage of early successes to eventual self-destruction; and how it is that such apparently successful revolutions as those of 1789 or 1917 should have become progressively more violent and out of hand until they ultimately destroyed almost all of their original leaders, let alone, as the dream of freedom turned inevitably into the reality of tyranny, their original dream intentions.

We can see why it was that such a figure as Napoleon, after initially sweeping all before him, had in the end, by the insatiable nature of the collective psychosis of which he was the embodiment, to overreach and destroy himself. We can appreciate more clearly how it was that the collective excitement and rising expectations of Jazz

78

Age America should have spiralled dizzily toward the explosion into reality of the Wall Street Crash and the Great Depression. And only through a grasp of the power and workings of fantasy does it begin to be possible to understand such a phenomenon as Nazism, and the way in which the group fantasy of which Hitler was the embodiment was bound to "escalate" its desire for self-gratification until it had run through all the stages of the fantasy cycle to the appalling self-annihilation of 1945.

In the light of the nature and structure of fantasy, for instance, such academic controversies as the recent one over whether Hitler did or did not "plan" the war in advance are seen to be irrelevant. From a properly objective point of view, the only fact that matters is that the madness which gripped Germany in the thirties was a group fantasy, obeying the rules. The only value of such "evidence" as Hitler's wild dreams of conquest in *Mein Kampf* or the details of the Hossbach Memorandum of 1937 lies in the extent to which they are evidence of an unfolding dream state. What should really matter to the historian is the inner logic of the fantasy itself, and the establishment of the various stages through which it unfolded: of which one may say that the period of the twenties marked the Anticipation Stage, up to the point of focus of the years 1930–1933; the period up to the conquest of France in 1940 marked the Dream Stage; the failure to subdue Britain, leading to the demand for even greater sensation in the invasion of Russia, marked the beginnings of the Frustration Stage, which reached its height with the battles of Stalingrad and El Alamein; leading into the Nightmare Stage of 1944, with forces closing in on Germany from three sides; and the whole cycle culminating in the Death Wish Stage of Germany's collapse and Hitler's own suicide in 1945.

The full workings of fantasy in society are, in fact, both so complex and yet so simple that they can only be fully appreciated and understood by looking at their evolution in detail, in one society in particular, over one particular period of history. Only thus is it possible to appreciate fully the way in which fantasy works like a disease; the way in which all forms of fantasy are highly contagious, feeding on and attracting each other; and the way in which a society or an individual infected by one form of fantasy is all the more susceptible to others.

Which is why we must now, at last, return to the history of England in the fifties and sixties. For we can now see that what in fact happened to England in and around 1956 was simply that, at every level, and in every way, the collective fantasy-self of English society became excited. The "bubble of excitement" welling up in England over the years after 1956, of which in the last chapter we superficially traced the preliminary course, was nothing more nor less than a gigantic "vitality-fantasy," of which the rise of the teenage subculture, the cult of youth, the "New Morality," the "New Wave" in English theatre and films, the crime wave, the overall euphoria of change, and the sense of being carried into a modernistic future, were all different individual symptoms. Equally, the extraordinary infectiousness of the imagery of America, seen in everything from the supermarkets to the adoption of an Americanized vocabulary, from rock 'n roll to the introduction of one-armed bandits, was a recognition of the fact that, owing to the accident of America's having pioneered so many of the techniques of a modern mass society, the American Dream had grown up throughout the twentieth century into the most powerful "vitality image" in the world—and it is therefore the example of America which any country wishing to escape into the modern dream must follow.

Why was it that in the mid-fifties Britain embarked on such a collective fantasy? To a large extent, of course, it was due to the emergence from the shadows of the post-war period, and the inevitably devastating psychological impact of the "affluent revolution"; the profoundly unsettling effect of prosperity and technological change, combined with the presence of a mass-communications industry which, through television in particular, was better placed than ever to express that fantasy.

There were many other societies, however, which in the same period were subjected to these new strains. Why was it then that the impact of this revolution, which affected every industrialized country, was in Britain to be so particularly far reaching? Why was it going to be Britain that would produce the Beatles and Carnaby Street and television satire and the James Bond films, why London that would end up acclaimed as "the most swinging city in the world"? The answer lies in the fact that no breeding ground for fantasy is so fertile as a society in a state of disintegration and flux, a society in which the basic certainties which derive from a reasonably stable social framework are themselves breaking down. The reason why Britain was so uniquely vulnerable to the winds of fantasy was simply that, in Britain as nowhere else, two different revolutions were going on at the same time, each at every point and level feeding and exacerbating the other.

In the years after 1956, Britain not only witnessed the revolution brought about by the coming of affluence, but also the last stages of the breakup of her empire and of a class structure which had been peculiarly identified with it. Thus the social structure, the class system, and all the framework which might otherwise have provided a more determined bulwark against the new forces making for disintegration were already gravely weakened by a set of circumstances which had nothing to do with affluence. From 1956 onwards, these two revolutions—the affluent and the social—became one. At every point where the influence of one revolution would provide a challenge to the social structure, as in the rebellion of the young against the old and traditional, the other revolution would redouble the force of that challenge, by identifying the old and traditional with the already crumbling upper-class order and Britain's half-rejected past. At every point, the friends and enemies of one revolution would reinforce and merge with the friends and enemies of the other. With all this in mind, we can now return to take a closer and much wider look at the history of English society in the fifties and sixties.

Part Two

Chapter Four

The Dream before the Storm

As the saying goes: *sic transit gloria mundi.* Now it is an enormous and powerful state, and suddenly everything may go to pieces!

LEO TOLSTOY
quoted by A. B. Goldenveiser

I am sure that this, my Coronation, is not the symbol of
a power and splendour that are gone but a declaration of
our hopes for the future.

Queen Elizabeth II, Coronation Day
Broadcast, 2 June 1953

The probability is, I suppose, that the Monarchy has
become a kind of ersatz religion. Chesterton once remarked
that when people cease to believe in God they do not
believe in nothing but in anything.

MALCOLM MUGGERIDGE
New Statesman, 22 October 1955

Q. "Have a photograph of Queen Victoria?"
A. "No thanks, I'm trying to give them up."

Archetypal *Goon Show* joke, middle-fifties

It is ruling classes which set cultural patterns and for
more than a century the dominant culture of Europe has
been that of the well-to-do middle classes, the *haute
bourgeoisie.* It was a culture that went with those great
English social inventions: the gentlemen's club . . .
amateur sport and the long week end . . . In all its aspects
. . . this bourgeois way of life was also a minority culture
from which the lower class majority of the population was
. . . excluded. It is this bourgeois minority culture . . .
that has been crumbling. What we are now entering
instead is a social era based on mass-participation.

T. R. FYVEL
Encounter, June 1955

Today it is hard to believe that, as late as 1947, the Union Jack still flew over more than a quarter of the human race, and the peoples of a fifth of the world's land surface looked to London as the center of their government. Even in 1950, after the liberation of India, Burma, and Pakistan, Great Britain was still the center of a mighty empire, set in all five continents. Her political and military influence was supreme throughout the Middle East. She was still the second exporting nation of the world, and along with the United States and Russia, one of the three richest. At home, either in the countryside where many farms were still ploughed by horses, or in the towns, where the bicycle was still the most complicated form of personal transport that the vast majority aspired to, the English way of life was still, in its outward forms and customs, unlike that of any other country. At all levels, despite considerable American incursions through the cinema and dance music, the Englishman's culture was still to a great extent homegrown and unique—its most powerful single element the British Broadcasting Corporation, still very much the creation of its stern founder Lord Reith, and of which a later Director General, Sir William Haley, wrote in 1950 that its greatest obligation was to act as:

a bastion against the tide seeking to submerge values in a disintegrating world.

Yet, at the turn of the new decade, despite her position in the world and her comparative cultural self-sufficiency, England's mood could scarcely have been bleaker. Five years before, in the first joy of peace and the dawn of Labour's great election victory, the country had been caught up in a flood of optimism. On every side there had been talk of building a "New Britain." Under the twin banners of Socialism and Democracy, government and people had been going to march together into a new future, casting aside the evils, the egotism, and the stagnation of the past in the prospect of a bright horizon of peace and prosperity. And for eighteen months or so, in a frenzy of legislation, blueprints, and hope, the dream had lasted.

But already by the time of the great winter crisis of 1947–48, with its power cuts, its coal rationing, and its dark and frozen nights and days, a different reality had begun to emerge. The taking into state ownership of the coal mines, the gas and electricity industries, the railways, far from ushering in a new age of industrial peace and prosperity, had appeared to leave those industries even more discontented and inefficient. By 1948, the momentum of the great burst of radical legislation had faltered. As the country's economic difficulties not only failed to disappear but actually worsened, many of the blueprints of 1945–1946 became faint memories of a lost age. Murderous wars and civil wars sprang up over the settlements of empire in India and the Middle East. By the end of 1949, the brave dream of 1945 had been extinguished.

Almost five years after the war, the "New Britain" was still—with the substitution of dingy prefabricated housing estates for the blackout—the grey and seedy land of Graham Greene's wartime novels; or even that grim present which in 1948 George Orwell had projected into an even grimmer future to make a recognizable proportion of his *1984*. In a land where spivs and snoek and government snoopers were still the staple fare of cartoonists and comedians, rationing and shortages were almost as bad as ever. The egg ration at the beginning of 1950 was one per person per week, the butter ration three ounces. The economic crisis, in the wake of an enforced devaluation of the pound, was turning into a seemingly endless nightmare. Abroad, the Cold War was at its height; Russia had just exploded her first atom bomb, and the Korean War, to add to the Berlin crisis of the previous year, was about to begin. Looking around the world at the beginning of the new decade, the *Economist* could find only one consoling thought in a picture of universal gloom and despair:

> Each of the recent decades has turned out to be very different indeed from what watchers at its birth expected.

Over the first two years of the fifties it seemed that only the *Economist*'s blackest prognostications were to be borne out. By 1951, the cost of living was rising by 1 percent a month. The Government, with its majority reduced at the election of 1950 from nearly 200 to less than 10, was hanging by a thread. In less than a year it had lost two of its outstanding figures by the fatal illnesses of Stafford Cripps and Ernest Bevin. In the London of that summer, where trams still clanked down the Embankment and only the ragwort and willowherb provided a touch of color on mile after mile of dusty bomb sites and boarded-up windows, the Festival of Britain seemed a last defiant echo of the People's Revolution that had failed. It was against this background that, in October 1951, the country turned back to its old leaders. With a Commons majority of 17, Winston Churchill was returned to Number Ten—at the head of a Government even more upper-class in composition than those of Baldwin and Chamberlain before the war. The strange conservative interlude of the early fifties had begun.

Slowly the grey nightmare passed away. Harsh measures, including the raising of the Bank Rate to what was regarded as the almost shocking level of 2½ percent, its highest peacetime figure since 1932, eased the pressure of the economic crisis. Step by step, the mountainous structure of rationing and controls was dismantled. By the summer of 1953, the glittering Coronation of a new young Queen, marked in a suitably imperial gesture by the conquest of Everest, was a symbol that during the years of hardship the old traditions had merely been sleeping. People were once again dressing for dinner and for Ascot. Mr. Churchill was suitably invested at Windsor in all the splendor of a Knighthood of the Garter. Readers of the popular press were regaled with news of Sir Bernard and Lady Docker, with their yacht *Shemara* and their gold-plated Daimler. Debutantes once again danced away June nights on the river, to the strains of Tommy Kinsman and the splash of champagne bottles thrown by their braying escorts. Unmistakably, British society seemed to be returning from a long dark night to sunnier and more normal times.

In the early years of the fifties, this impression might have been confirmed by the most thoughtful observer, whether pleased by his suspicion or no. Indeed he might well have been forgiven for thinking that the long dark night which Britain was leaving behind had in fact been one lasting much longer than just the years of war and the austerity of the forties.

For a glance across the expanse of history would have shown that, since well before 1800, the main lines of conflict in English society had been drawn over two things: on the one hand, social and political recognition of the huge new groups thrown up by the industrial revolution—firstly the new bourgeoisie, latterly the lower-middle and industrial working classes; and on the other hand, the acquisition, maintenance, and eventual liberation of the greatest empire the world had ever seen.

Now, in the early fifties, it seemed that both these sources of conflict had been virtually eliminated.

The great tide of class struggle appeared finally to have petered out on the sands of the Welfare State. The new classes were now being so rapidly assimilated into the old system that it was already a matter of course that not only should many of their members go to Oxford and Cambridge, but that they should go on to occupy many of the senior and most influential positions in English life—in the judiciary, in the civil service, in politics, and in business.*

And yet, despite or perhaps because of this assimilation of new blood, as the dust of the post-war revolution settled, the old order stood basically unchanged. The social structure and great institutions of English life were now apparently more secure than ever—capped by a New Elizabethan monarchy which seemed everything the new

---

* As for instance, Sir Oliver Franks (Bristol grammar-school), British Ambassador in Washington 1948–1952; Sir William Haley (left school at 14 to become a ship's wireless operator), Director-General of the BBC 1946–1952, then Editor of the *Times;* Ernest Bevin (ex-farm laborer), Foreign Secretary 1945–1950.

age of mass communication and equality could desire; providing both the pageantry, for which over 20,000,000 people could watch the Coronation on BBC Television, and the human details, whereby the former Royal Nanny "Crawfie" could win half a million readers overnight to the circulation of *Woman's Own*.

At the same time, all the political parties seemed agreed not only that Britain should continue with the "responsible" liberation of her empire: but that in doing so she would retain her old greatness in a new form, as a moral force in the world, and as the leader of a Commonwealth to which all nations would look with respect and admiration. As one observer wrote in 1954:

> For the first time in history we see an empire dissolving with dignity and grace. The rise of this empire was not an edifying story: its decline is.*

It was an irresistible vision, hardly marred by news of distant new forces stirring in the world, of "isolated" troubles in Cyprus and Kenya and Malaya, in Persia and Egypt. And what need had Britain to consider closer cooperation with the countries of shattered Europe, then rebuilding and huddling together against the world's new icy blasts under their Schumann Plan and their first faltering steps toward West European unity? For Britain had her own conception of an ordered international progress—in which she still took her place at such international conference tables as those of Geneva in 1954 and 1955, as one of the "Big Three."

It was not only in the field of politics that Britain seemed to be reviving. In 1954, for instance, it seemed only right that a young upper-middle-class Englishman, Roger Bannister, should on 6 May be the first to run the four-minute mile. The following October all England cheered as Bannister's Oxford colleague Chris Chataway raced past the Russian Kuc for the world 5,000-meters record; yet another

* Arthur Koestler in the second volume of his autobiography *The Invisible Writing*.

triumph for the British tradition of the "gentleman-amateur"—for, as the sporting press was not slow to rub in, Chataway was never a man to allow his training to stand between him and a glass of beer.

They were years too when Britain's inventive genius seemed to be reviving undimmed—to continue in the spirit that had given to the world television, penicillin, radar, and the jet engine. If her first atom bomb had only been exploded in 1952, the year when America had already reached the H-bomb, then the press at least was full of the blessings that would ensue from Britain's lead in the peaceful applications of atomic fission. While the great aircraft industry, with its constant flow of new projects—the Viscount, the Vulcan, the Valiant, the "Whispering Giant" Britannia, and, above all, the Comet—was by any standard a world-beater. Maybe the Comet itself, the world's first jet airliner, was to run into disaster, with two crashes from clear Italian skies in 1954: but what matter all America's technology when, as late as 10 March 1956, British genius could still wrest back from her the world air speed record—giving her all three major speed records, in the air, on land, and on water.

In 1953 and 1954 and the first months of 1955, the fact that it should be under a largely upper-class Conservative Government that Britain was so smoothly moving forward, only completed the picture. So placid was that picture that, after its sharp rise in the forties, even the crime rate was falling. As Sir Robert Jackson, head of the C.I.D. at Scotland Yard from 1953 to 1963, was later to put it:

> In 1953 London's crime level was the lowest since the war, and the following year it fell even lower. I was taking command, it seemed, of a victorious army.*

And in the center of the picture, as the last relics of rationing and Socialist controls were stripped away, there stood revealed the central arch of Conservative economic "freedom": the belief that, left more

* *Sunday Express,* 16 January 1966.

or less to itself, the economy might boom indefinitely, and the pound be preserved as one of the two major international currencies of the world. There could be little wrong with a Britain in which the Chancellor of the Exchequer, R. A. Butler, could confidently predict that the standard of living would be doubled in only twenty-five years; or even in which the great shipbuilding industry, second to none and unhampered like its German and Japanese competitors by the needs of post-war rebuilding, was fulfilling the longest order book it had ever known.

In such an atmosphere, the Labour Party, bereft of ideas, sunk in its own internal squabbles, obsessed with the paranoid circumstances of its defeat in 1951, might well have seemed, after only fifty years, to have fulfilled its role in British politics. And in May 1955 it was no surprise when, after Sir Winston had handed over the Premiership to Sir Anthony Eden, the Conservatives more than doubled their majority at the General Election.

The same mood of an old upper and upper-middle-class order safely restored dominated almost every area of national life. In an essay on "British Intellectuals" in the May 1955 issue of *Encounter,* Edward Shils, an American sociologist, began a section headed "Rediscovering the Old School Tie":

> Look at the British intellectuals now . . . how rare has become the deeply critical voice. Not long ago I heard an eminent man of the Left say, in utter seriousness, at a University dinner, that the British constitution was "as nearly perfect as any human institution could be," and no one thought it even amusing. Who criticises Britain now, in any fundamental sense, except for a few Communists and Bevanite irreconcilables? There are complaints here and there and on many specific issues, but—in the main—scarcely anyone in Great Britain seems any longer to feel that there is anything fundamentally wrong.

Mr. Shils went on to discuss the "cultural domination" of the "London-Oxford-Cambridge triangle," the "vindication of the culture associated with the aristocracy and the gentry," and, in the course of a brief survey of contemporary novelists, the fact that "we do not find the working classes treated at all."

The same was true of the British cinema which, since the heyday of Michael Wilding and Anna Neagle's romanticism and the Ealing comedy in the late forties, had become increasingly dominated by the stiff-upper-lip wartime heroics of Kenneth More, Richard Attenborough, Jack Hawkins, and John Mills. It was true of the theatre, dominated by the tinkling pianos and nostalgia (despite their role also as harbingers of the returning mood of the twenties) of *The Boy Friend* and *Salad Days,* by Terence Rattigan and American musicals, and by what a new young critic on the *Observer,* Kenneth Tynan, called in 1954:

> our drama's prevalent *genre,* the Loamshire play. Its setting is a country house, in what used to be called Loamshire but is now, as a heroic tribute to reality, sometimes called Berkshire. Except when someone must sneeze, or be murdered, the sun invariably shines. The inhabitants belong to a social class derived partly from romantic novels and partly from the playwright's vision of the leisured life he will lead after the play is a success—this being the only effort of the imagination he is called on to make. Joys and sorrows are giggles and whimpers: the crash of denunciation dwindles into "Oh, stuff, Mummy!" and "Oh, really, Daddy!" And so grim is the continuity of these things that the foregoing paragraph might have been written at any time during the last thirty years.

This particular heart cry, typical of many that Tynan was to utter over the following two years, concluded:

> The theatre must widen its scope, broaden its horizon . . . we need plays about cabmen and demi-gods, plays about warriors, politicians and grocers—I care not, so Loamshire be invaded and subdued. I counsel aggression because, as a critic, I had rather be a war correspondent than a necrologist.

But of course the very fact that Tynan should be crying out for plays in the "living vernacular," that Shils should be so caustic about the "unification of the intellectuals with the other groups of the ruling elite" were signs that beneath the placid, successful, monarchy-loving, conservative face of England in 1955, not all was quite as it seemed.

It was nothing more, in fact, than a dream—a mildly Bourbon interlude after the years of austerity and war, as artificial a bout of nostalgia as the long skirts of the New Look which had first reflected it. The nostalgia was partly, as was shown by the spate of war films, for the heady days of wartime spirit, when everyone had felt their place in the framework of national purpose. Its motto, however, and its highest expression of praise, whether for the revival of Ascot or the return of bananas, was "It's just like pre-war"—referring sometimes, it might have been suspected, not even to the war that had recently ended, but to one long before.

But it was more than just a harmless dream—it was a dam against reality. Against the reality that imperial Britain was still declining in the world, that the upper class and bourgeois dominated structure was crumbling—and that the rising new classes were in fact far from being quietly assimilated into the old order. And it was the very height and strength of the dam which ensured that, when it was finally breached, the explosion should come with such bitter violence. For building up behind it, in particular, were the frustrations and anticipations of four powerful forces—four groups which between them were going to create almost all the atmosphere, the crises, and the changes in the England of the next ten years.

In the course of this narrative we shall single out a comparatively small number of people, only about two hundred in all, who among them symbolized the revolution that took place in English life between 1955 and the late sixties. Obviously this tiny minority only rose to prominence because they were the outward representatives of much deeper social movements—and indeed the interesting thing about these people was the extent to which they fell into certain very clearly defined groups, the groups which, as English society fragmented and lost its coherence, would be most notably vulnerable to insecurity and therefore attracted to the glamorous escape offered by the collective fantasy.

(1) *The Young Urban Lower Class**

The first of these groups was the young urban lower class. Indeed we can be even more specific, for all but a handful of the members of this class who were to play a prominent role came either from twelve out of Britain's fifteen largest cities, or from the industrial areas of South Wales; and of those twelve cities, the most notable were those of the Midlands and the North, Birmingham and Nottingham, Leeds and Leicester; the huge unfashionable hinterlands of South and North London; and, above all the great seaports, such as Liverpool, Glasgow, and the East End of London, where large religious and racial minorities, such as the Jews and the Irish, created an added conflict of tradition and identity.

For years there had been a steady trickle of people from such backgrounds into the fields of entertainment, literature, and journalism—such as Charlie Chaplin, Alfred Hitchcock, Stan Laurel, Vera Lynn, Noel Coward (all from South and East London), Neville Cardus (Manchester), J. B. Priestley (Bradford). But the social upheaval brewing in 1955 was on a larger scale than anything which they individually had represented.

Now the traditional framework and attitudes of the lower classes were beginning to disintegrate, as the imagination of the young was

---

* Before we go any further, I had better define the sense in which I shall be using the somewhat confusing terminology of class. On some occasions I shall use the full, more or less conventional categorization of upper class (to mean aristocratic), upper middle class (to denote professional or public school background), middle and lower middle class, and working class. At other times, which I hope will always be clear from their context, I shall use merely a more general division of society into upper class, meaning roughly all those educated at public schools, and lower class to indicate the rest.

opened up by National Service, by art and drama schools, technical colleges and universities—and of course by the new prosperity itself, giving a sense of being on an ever-rising escalator.

It was this group which would provide the stage armies of the future, the "teenage market," the pop fans in their anonymous millions, the Mods and Rockers—just as it had already provided their first foretaste in the Teddy Boys of South London. It was this group too which would provide the individual heroes of New England, symbols of a class revolution—the working-class writer, the pop singers and actors, idols who would eventually command the attention of the whole nation. With the "explosion" of 1956, this social upheaval would be launched with the arrival of such diverse figures as John Stephen (Glasgow) and Mary Quant (South London), John Osborne (South London) and Colin Wilson (Leicester), Tommy Steele and Marty Wilde (both from South London).

An important part of this social upsurge, so important that it deserves special consideration, was the "emancipation" of another powerful group within the urban lower class—the immigrant communities of the previous seventy or eighty years, the Irish, the Italians, and, above all, the Russian and Polish Jews—all of whom had predominantly settled in the poorer parts of those same great cities and seaports, Glasgow and Liverpool, the East End and the cities of the North of England. It was these groups which, as they emerged from their own racial and religious framework, would more than any feel a lack of inner security, and the need to prove themselves and find new identity in an alien society.

The Central and Eastern European Jews, in particular, had long been improving their position in English society, as had been so clearly symbolized ever since the twenties by their emigration from the East End to the respectable suburbs of North West London. The more prominent among them broke out in the ways that have become familiar from the history of the same movement in America: either by adventuring into glamorous, egotistical occupations dominated by the image of "vitality"; by entering the entertainment world or the more speculative sides of big business; or by pursuing security in those professions which provided a new framework of tradition and stability, such as learning or the law. In fact many of the Jews who were going to play such a prominent role in the years after 1956 had begun their careers before the war: such as Charles Clore (East End) and Jack Cotton (Birmingham) in the property business, and the Grades and the Bernsteins, who were to become dominant in commercial television. But already they were being followed by a young generation, and on a much wider scale; for instance, of the 130-odd people whom it is estimated were to become millionaires through the property boom of the late fifties and early sixties, well over half were Jewish, and others were to play a numerically disproportionate role in fields ranging from ownership of the new supermarkets to the new drama.

Two other immigrant groups which were to play their own, less obvious part in the years after 1956 were the Italians and the Irish—the Italians, in particular, through the affluent revolution in the restaurant business. And as for the Irish, even though their influence on the next ten years might not seem so apparent, it should not be underestimated. For it was out of the large Irish-descended minority in Liverpool that there were to emerge three of the four Beatles: John Lennon, Paul McCartney, and George Harrison.

(2) *The Oxbridge "Intellectuals" and the Upper-Class Young*

To this "invasion" from below, the upper classes were by no means going to show an impenetrable front. For the recurrent pattern of the twentieth century's social changes (as has indeed been true of almost all revolutions down the ages) is one of intimate cooperation between members of the crumbling old order and of the rising new —each fascinated by the powerful image of the other: the insecure lower or less "established" group longing for the style and "stability" of culture and breeding, the insecure upper group mesmerized by the life and vitality of the *arriviste*.

The upper classes in England had in fact been losing faith in their traditional values, and bourgeois self-confidence had been crumbling, for over half a century. The process was already well under way by the time the first middle-class anti-imperialists and "guilty" middle-class Socialists helped to found the Labour Party at the beginning of the century. The alliance between middle-class Fabian intellectuals and working or lower-middle-class Socialists and trade unionists (of which the marriage between Beatrice Potter, the upper-class daughter of a director of the Great Western Railway, and Sidney Webb, a lower-class London Jew, was a microcosm) was indeed to provide a pattern for such "Old-New" liaisons which, through political, artistic, and business partnerships, not to say marriage, was to become one of the most consistent themes of the age. And in later years, from the Bloomsbury "revolt" in the decade of the First World War and the beginnings of that "Café Society" in the twenties, in which aristocrats and film stars could meet on all but equal terms, to the great upper-middle-class intellectual swing to the left in the thirties, the process begun with the early Fabians had accelerated.

By the early fifties, the desertion from traditional bourgeois loyalties of class and morality that had been symbolized by Aldous Huxley and George Orwell had not come to a halt. The loss of faith in their own class values which had led Huxley, Bertrand Russell, and Lady Ottoline Morrell to fall with such excitement on the working-class vitality of D. H. Lawrence, and such impeccably upper-middle-class Cambridge undergraduates of the early thirties as Donald Maclean, Kim Philby, and Guy Burgess to embrace the vitality of Russian Communism, had not suddenly been reversed. It had merely gone underground.

And now, with such straws in the wind as Kenneth Tynan's plea for plays in the "living vernacular" it was once again emerging. For one of the great centers of change in this movement had been the

university of Oxford—the Oxford of the twenties, for instance, that
had produced such "class rebels" as the prominent Labour politician
Hugh Gaitskell, Cyril Connolly, Old Etonian champion of twentieth
century literature, and Claud Cockburn, the Communist who had left
The Times for the *Daily Worker* and had ended up in 1935 running
his anarchic political broadsheet *The Week*; even more, the Oxford
of the thirties, which had shown such fascination with the causes
of the "proletariat" in the years of Depression and the Spanish Re-
publicans after 1936, and which had later contributed so much to the
victory of the new, largely intellectual-dominated Labour Party in
1945. By 1955, many of these Oxford graduates of the thirties were
in the House of Commons, spread in positions of increasing influence
across all three parties—from the Labour Party's Harold Wilson, the
son of a Yorkshire chemist, and Roy Jenkins, the son of a South
Wales trade union leader, to Edward Heath, the builder's son who
was shortly to become Chief Whip of the Conservative Party, and
the young Etonian, Jo Grimond, who was already Chief Whip of
the tiny and enfeebled Liberal Party.

In Kenneth Tynan, the illegitimate son of a millionaire chain-store
proprietor, Sir Peter Peacock, an even later Oxford generation was
beginning to surface—for he had been a prominent member of the
generation that had been up at Oxford in the years just after the
war—and that had been even more aggressively democratic and
(to quote a phrase of Tynan's own) "unposh" than their own thirties
predecessors. Thrown together in the years which had begun in that
heady, optimistic dawn of Labour's "New Britain," from every kind
of social background, the more aggressive of them were self-consciously "classless" and "progressive"—and the fervent atmosphere
of those years, which lingered on at Oxford at least until the turn of
the decade, had sent many of them out into the world with almost
as evangelistic a sense of mission as had been shown by that other
"Oxford Group" led in earlier years by Frank Buchman.

By 1955, in fact, Tynan himself (King's School, Birmingham) was
by no means the only member of this "New Oxford Group" begin-

ning to make his mark. There were some, such as the young Labour MP Anthony Wedgwood Benn, who had chosen the traditional Oxford road of politics. Others had chosen less familiar paths—such as the two ex-grammar school boys, Kingsley Amis (South London) and John Wain, both of whom had gone out to lecture in provincial universities and had caused a considerable stir with their first novels: Amis' *Lucky Jim* (1954), describing the fantasy life of a young Red-brick university lecturer, having been acclaimed in particular as the promise of something quite new in English literature. There was a whole host of the New Oxford Group who had been attracted to television and journalism. Still others had chosen the theatre and film world for their platform, men like Peter Brook, Tony Richardson, and Lindsay Anderson, the son of a major-general in the British Army.

The influence of these intellectuals over the England of the next ten years was to be incalculable. But there was another sense in which the New Oxford Group would be linked not only with their post-war contemporaries up at Cambridge who, although less prominent as a group, displayed many of the same general attitudes—but also with the whole of the generation up at Oxford and Cambridge in the ten years after the war—including for instance Jocelyn Stevens, Anthony Armstrong-Jones, and Mark Boxer.

This generation was to be placed in a curious position in the years after 1956. On the one hand, they would not be old enough, like their predecessors of the Wilson Heath generation of the thirties, to take over the commanding positions of English life. On the other, unlike the post-1956 generation and their non-Oxford contemporaries, they were not going to play the leading roles in England's social revolution either. Somehow they were a generation which "missed out." Yet, as Tynan's *cris de coeur* as dramatic critic showed, in 1955 they were as explicitly eager for a revolution as anyone. Their eagerness for excitement, drama, and make-believe was vividly shown by the way so many of them were drawn to the glamorous world of "communications," of the theatre, journalism, television, films. Indeed it was here above all that their role was to lie—in promoting England's revolution, as it were vicariously, through their control over the communications industry. Even if they were not, like the Wilsons, John Osbornes, and Beatles, to play the leading roles themselves, it was they who were to act as the public relations officers, the midwives of the New England. It was they who, as directors, critics, and commentators, through the respectable Sunday newspapers, the glossy magazines, the color supplements, were above all to promote the cult of youth, of dynamism, of sexual freedom, and of lower-class vitality. And like the Athenians who were ever eager to acclaim "some new thing," it was they who would most truly be worthy of description as neophiliacs.

It was by no means only among the younger generation, however, that in 1955 a new spirit was stirring. There were also two others, older groups in society who were to make their own contribution to the mood and history of the next ten years.

(3) *New Generation in the Unions*

The trade union movement in 1955 was beginning to find itself in a position unique in its history. As the country moved into unprecedented prosperity, the unions' two traditional preoccupations, full employment and the right to basic wages, could suddenly be taken virtually for granted—leaving them in a position of potentially irresponsible power. At the same time, a new generation of leaders was coming forward. The older generation, which had ruled the unions back to the war years and beyond, was departing. It was soon clear that some of their successors, notably the aggressive Frank Cousins, who less than a year later was himself to take over the leadership of the Transport Workers, were no longer interested in the warnings of the older generation that "increased productivity" would be needed to support a constant flow of wage claims.

The birth of this new era was marked, from the closing months of

1954, by a wave of strikes and industrial unrest, the worst since the war—ranging from the month-long dock strike of December, costing millions of pounds in exports, to the national newspaper strike of April 1955 and an all-but-complete standstill on the railways for the first two weeks of June. The new union leaders were flexing their muscles—and over the next ten years, there would be few patterns in national life more familiar than the round of threats, urgent consultations, and appearances of grave-faced union leaders on television, carried away by a self-important charade that often seemed to have little connection with economic or any other kind of reality. The hunger for drama and excitement that was an end in itself would by no means be limited to the fantasy worlds of teenagers, artists, and intellectuals.

But the new attitude of the union leaders in the middle fifties only represented a much wider and deeper mood in society as a whole. For not the least of the ingredients in the great collective fantasy would be the need for ever-rising wages, regardless of the remorseless tide of inflation that would follow. It is a characteristic of societies on a wave of material improvement that they should generate an illusion of betterment outstripping reality, the difference between their appetites and their achievements being measured by a steady fall in the value of money. To this rule the British were to be no exception—thus bringing on themselves, with ever-gathering seriousness, a succession of economic and financial crises which would be their inevitable "explosions" into economic "reality."

(4) *The Old Guard Betrayed*

For each of these first three groups, the future in different ways seemed welcoming. But for the last of our four groups, the growing desire for self-assertion in 1955 stemmed from exactly the opposite reason—from a desire to reassert the values of a vanishing past. To the middle and upper classes, this new world into which England was moving was not so tolerable. To the declining *rentier* class, the retired officers and NCO's of imperial rule, the crumbling gentry, the brigadiers and business people who couldn't find servants any more, or found it harder and harder, year by year, to keep up old standards, the new prosperity of the fifties was a cruel fiction. To them, the power of the unions meant only one thing—inflation. The new younger generation, with its independence and its money, seemed even more of an irritant than any younger generation usually seems to its elders. And for the growing frustration and aggression felt by this class, there was one great subconscious outlet—in identification between their own decline in Britain and the decline in the world of their country which they so recently, it seemed, remembered great.

By the mid-fifties, in fact, there were many signs that, for the Conservative right-wing, those "distant forces" stirring in the great world were beginning to outrun the liberal dream by which the remains of empire were to be freed, as "soon as they were ready." The extremist League of Empire Loyalists founded in October 1954 by a former Beaverbrook journalist may have been tiny—but it was a symptom of the times. In Kenya, where African nationalism was on the march, the worsening Mau Mau troubles could not have fed the Right Wing's suspicions more ominously. As for Cyprus, which, since Britain had been forced to agree to evacuation from the Suez Canal Zone, would soon become the main base controlling her last great sphere of influence, the Middle East—on 28 July 1954 the Minister of State for the Colonies had gone so far as to say that such a prized possession could "never" be granted full independence.

For the Old Guard, bewildered by an increasingly strange world, tired of "being pushed around," whether by trade unionists or foreigners, patience was beginning to wear thin.

These then were the forces standing in the wings. Beneath its still comparatively placid and united surface, English society was beginning to fragment. And looking back to 1955, we can see many omens of the country's changing mood, none of particular importance in itself, but all adding up to a new sharpening of spirit, a sense of excitement on the wind.

There was, for instance, the growing popularity of *The Goon Show,* which had been running on BBC radio since 1952, with its surrealistic comedy based on the parodies of upper-class voices by a team including the young actor Peter Sellers, on lunatic sound-effects, and on the fascination of its chief script-writer, Spike Milligan (South London), for "cardboard cutouts of the British empire" and the more ludicrous aspects of such imperial bric-a-brac as pith helmets and "Mukkinese Battlehorns." There was the vogue for the novels of Angus Wilson (Oxford 1930's), for what Edmund Wilson described as his "tart and trim little pictures of the English upper-middle-class, shaken in its self-sufficiency and stinging itself to death." There was the controversial editorship of *Punch* by Malcolm Muggeridge, that world-weary and quizzical figure who had risen years before from a lower-middle-class household on the fringes of South London, to go to Cambridge and later become a friend of George Orwell; and whose *Punch* (which he edited from 1953–1957) had been the only journal, with the exception of one veiled editorial in the *Sunday Times,* to break through the barrier of "good taste" that had shrouded the growing senility of Sir Winston Churchill during his last, patriarchal years of office.

By September 1955, portents were abundant. There was the eagerness with which intellectual circles seized on the ironic phrase "the Establishment," revived in the *Spectator* by Henry Fairlie (New Oxford Group) to disparage the social influence which in his view had been used to cover up the tracks of the Burgess and Maclean affair. Indeed the White Paper on the defection of the two Foreign Office officials, which had prompted Fairlie's article, was in itself a sign that behind the outwardly secure and still impressive façade of the upper-class Establishment, everything was not as it seemed. A further symptom of the death-watch beetle eating its way through the social structure was provided in the same month by the excitable discussion fomented by a celebrated article in the September issue of *Encounter* by Miss Nancy Mitford, as to what social usages were "U" and "Non-U"—hardly evidence of a secure framework in which everyone knew his place, and perhaps in its way as revealing a comment on the new pressures at work as the decision a few months earlier by the thirteenth Duke of Bedford to become the first great English aristocrat to market his "stately home" and his social position as if they were show business assets.

In September also, there was the quite unexpected commercial success at the Arts Theatre of a new, experimental play, *Waiting for Godot,* written by Samuel Beckett, directed by a recent Cambridge graduate Peter Hall, and unlike anything yet seen in the early fifties—the impenetrability of which not only had critics and audiences delightedly groping for meaning in something that by definition had none, but struck a rich chord in the subconscious by its all-pervading mood of nebulous anticipation. Even *Waiting for Godot,* however, was not so portentous a symptom of the spirit beginning to awaken in the theatre as a decision taken at about the same time by the Queen's cousin Lord Harewood and the poet Ronald Duncan: that in the coming year they would revive the old English Stage Company at the Royal Court Theatre in Sloane Square, with the special intention of discovering new plays.

Still in that same month of September, there were more violent harbingers of the country's changing mood. In the neighborhood of various South and East London cinemas there were the first embryonic teenage disorders attendant on the showing of *The Blackboard Jungle.* After three years, there were the first signs also of a small but sudden rise in the crime rate—marked notably by a sharp increase both in crimes of violence, and in a hitherto relatively unfamiliar class of crime, such as mail-van robberies and bullion thefts, requiring both careful organization and a vivid and dramatic imagination. At the same time too there was the coming, on 22 September, of commercial television.

In a previous chapter we have seen the arrival of commercial television in the closing months of 1955 as the first real indication of the explosion which, over the next two years, was to bring with it super-markets and coffee bars, the revolt of the young, and a complete change in the prevailing social climate. In fact the battle of a tiny pressure group to establish the new medium, and to break the BBC monopoly over British broadcasting, had hung over English life for some years—provoking bitter opposition ranging from that of the traditional Establishment and the Church ("for the sake of our children" the Archbishop of York had declared "we should resist it") to the Labour Party's claim that it would be "a national disaster." The violence of this opposition had been an implicit recognition of just what a major innovation in English life was involved. And indeed in retrospect, it can be seen that this new arrival, the first taste of the values of affluence, was one of the two or three major turning points in post-war English social history.

By October 1955, there was no question that the placid interlude of the early fifties was coming to an end. Already in July had come the first breach in the "central arch" of Conservative Freedom—when a run on the pound had awakened the financial establishment from their dream that they could preserve sterling as an international currency, while at the same time the economy at home was inflating by leaps and bounds. Now in October, the Chancellor, Mr. Butler, who only a year before had been blithely talking about the standard of living doubling in twenty-five years, was forced to introduce an emergency Budget. The central arch had collapsed. Conservative Freedom didn't appear to work, after all.

On 22 October there appeared in the *New Statesman* an article by Malcolm Muggeridge. Inspired largely by the speculation surrounding Princess Margaret and Group Captain Townsend, then at its height, it was headed "Royal Soap Opera," and opened with the words:

> There are probably quite a lot of people—more than might be supposed —who, like myself, feel that another newspaper photograph of the Royal Family will be more than they can bear. Even Princess Anne, a

doubtless estimable child, becomes abhorrent by repetition. Already she has that curious characteristic gesture of limply holding up her hand to acknowledge applause. The Queen Mother, Nanny Lightbody, Group Captain Townsend—the whole show is utterly out of hand, and there is a much greater danger than might superficially appear that a strong reaction against it may be produced . . .

It was doubtful whether language as strong as this had been used about the royal family since Victorian times. But one of the more curious features of the piece was that almost all of the correspondence it aroused was entirely favorable. The old myths were suddenly losing force. At every level of society, new insecurity was at work, a hunger for sensation that was as vaguely defined as Godot but was somehow felt to be on the way. If there was one sign that marked the beginning of the new age more than any other, it was that, at the beginning of the year, the leaders of the two major political parties had been Sir Winston Churchill and Clement Attlee, aged eighty-one and seventy-two respectively. By the year's end a new generation, over twenty years younger, was in power—Eden, aged fifty-eight, and Hugh Gaitskell, elected leader of the Labour Party on 14 December, a mere forty-nine. But even so, as products respectively of Eton and Winchester, they could hardly have been more typically members of Britain's traditional ruling caste. The age that was just beginning was going to see far greater changes in English life than merely the succession of one generation by another. Mr. Tynan was indeed about to get his "war."

Chapter Five

Finding the Focus

For each age is a dream that is dying or one that is
coming to birth.

A. W. E. O'SHAUGHNESSY (1844–1881)

Assume the miracle: assume the advent of a masterpiece.
There it crouches, a pink-eyed, many-muscled, salivating
monster. Who shall harness it?

KENNETH TYNAN
Observer, 1954

Oh heavens, how I long for just a little ordinary enthusiasm. Just enthusiasm, that's all. I want to hear a
warm, thrilling voice cry out Hallelujah! (*He bangs his
breast theatrically*) Hallelujah! I'm alive!

JIMMY PORTER
in *Look Back in Anger,* 1956

EDEN GETS TOUGH . . . LET THE CRYBABIES HOWL!
It's GREAT Britain Again.

Headline, *Daily Sketch,* 1956

IT'S OUR H-BOMB!

Headline, *Daily Express,* 1957

BAN THE BOMB!

London streetcry, 1958

There have been few years in this century which have marked so considerable a watershed as 1956. The restlessness that had shown itself in English life toward the end of 1955 was only in fact the symptom of a much wider stirring that was beginning to affect many other countries, in every part of the world. Everywhere old frustrations were coming to a head and new energies seeking release. All over colonial Africa and the Middle East, nationalist movements were gathering force. In Western Europe, the association of "The Six" was moving toward the establishment of the Common Market in March 1957. Countries such as Western Germany and Japan were rising as phoenixes from their ashes of ten years before. In America, where 1956 began with the Negro boycott of the buses of Montgomery, Alabama, led by the Rev. Martin Luther King, Jr., the civil rights movement was entering a more militant phase. In both America and Russia, the idea of launching satellites into space, which even two years before would have seemed a science fiction dream, was rapidly approaching reality. And there were great events afoot in the Communist bloc, venturing forth at last from the dark night of Stalinism, with the full emergence of Khrushchev and Bulganin, the first denunciations of the Stalin cult, and the beginnings of the cultural "thaw." While even if the tensions of the Cold War were now unimaginably less than they had been three years before— illuminated for Britain in particular by the celebrated visit in April 1956 of the new Russian leaders—there were also ominous signs that the new Communist era was not to be without its violent birth pangs. As the year went on, a murmur of discontent was to rise from Poland and Hungary. There were also unfamiliar strains appearing in the societies of the industrialized West, as the fruits of prosperity itself—particularly the increasing self-consciousness and aggression of the young, and the garish and egotistical blandishments of the approaching affluence that was now only just round the corner.

Throughout the world, in short, mankind was emerging from the shadows of the forties and turning its imagination toward the future. In all parts the pattern of change was essentially the same—the underdogs, the underprivileged, the young, the colonially occupied, all those who could see themselves as oppressed, were becoming fired with the same bright vision of a new world—a world of freedom and excitement, to be achieved through revolt against the established order. But for few countries (possibly unhappy Hungary) was the shock of entering that new age to be so dramatically manifest as for Britain.

For Britain, quite apart from rock 'n roll, Angry Young Men or other domestic excitements, the year 1956 was to be dominated above all by one thing—the disaster of the Suez War, the final "explosion into reality" of that make-believe that, despite the twilight of empire, despite the rise of America and Russia, still nothing in the world had really changed.

In most things that were happening to Britain, the history of the next two years was to be the history of a dream coming to birth. But before it could do so, in the catastrophe of Suez and all that in the wider terms of English society it stood for, there had to be written the closing stages of a dream already in its death throes.

As Britain stood on the threshold of 1956, it might have seemed outwardly that the position she had won in the world through centuries of empire still stood—diminished certainly, shaken perhaps, but more or less intact. Yet the mood in which the country entered the new year, particularly in political circles, was one of unease. The standing of the still comparatively untried Eden Government was low. In the wake of the emergency budget, the cost of living was steadily rising, and the Old Guard in particular were showing increasing restiveness. From the very first week of the year there was sniping in the right-wing press at what was painted as the Prime Minister's lack of purpose; on 3 January, widespread attention was aroused by a call in the conservative *Daily Telegraph* for what the author, the paper's Deputy Editor, described as "the smack of firm government"; there was a joke current that "the sooner Sir Anthony retires and makes way for Sir Winston the better"; and on 7 January, Eden even took the unusual step of issuing an official denial to rumors of his impending resignation.

As an embodiment of Britain's dying imperial dream and the mounting urge of the Old Guard for some desperate act of national self-assertion, it would have been impossible to conceive a more suitable figure than Sir Anthony Eden. Quite apart from his background and the obsession which had been dinned into his subconscious in the late thirties that Britain must never again allow herself any policy that could be painted as appeasement, for half a generation he had stood almost entirely in the shadow of Churchill. It was hardly surprising that Eden's insecurity and need to prove himself, when the moment came, should have been overpowering.

In the early months of 1956, that moment was approaching. On 2 March, on top of the terrorism that in Kenya, in Malaya, and in Cyprus seemed to be eating away the remains of the empire, on top even of the agreement into which Britain had virtually been forced two years before by the new Republican Government of Egypt that she would by the summer of 1956 evacuate her main Middle Eastern military base on the Suez Canal, came the news that the Government of Jordan had dismissed Sir John Glubb, known as Glubb Pasha, the British Commander of its army. This act, comparatively trivial though it might have seemed, struck at the heart not only of Britain's prestige in the Middle East but even more of that Arabian romanticism which, since the days of T. E. Lawrence, had acted like a drug on English upper-class consciousness. As we have it on the authority of Mr. Anthony Nutting (in his book *No End of a Lesson*), it was from that moment that the Prime Minister became obsessed with the need to try his strength against President Nasser (whom he regarded as mainly responsible for the sacking of Glubb) as if it were the chief end of his government.

Seven days later, in the island of Cyprus, the Government's patience ran out. Archbishop Makarios and three of his lieutenants were arrested, and flown to exile in the Seychelle Islands, five thousand miles away. The "smack of firm government" had at last been heard. And from the citadels of the Old Guard, from Cheltenham and Tonbridge and Bournemouth, came an almost audible sigh of approval.

It was against this background that in May 1956, from a quite different quarter, the hunger for sensation that had been brewing up in England for the past year broke fully into the open. The occasion was the first night of the English Stage Company's second production at the Royal Court Theatre, John Osborne's *Look Back in Anger*. Today it is hard to recall the shock with which this play broke on the theatre audiences of 1956, even ones which might have been slightly prepared for it by the riddles and stark sets of *Waiting for Godot,* or the "social realism" of Arthur Miller. Everything provided a shock of novelty, including the "Kitchen Sink" set of a dingy flat in "a Midlands city," complete with ironing board and off-stage lavatory. But the chief shock lay in its social message. It was in this context, rather than anything merely theatrical, that the almost legendary importance to be accorded to *Look Back in Anger* in later years was born: from passages like this one, in which Jimmy Porter, Osborne's lower-class hero, was talking about his wife's brother:

> Have you ever seen her brother? Brother Nigel? The straight-backed chinless wonder from Sandhurst? . . . well, you've never heard so many well-bred commonplaces from beneath the same bowler hat. The Platitude From Outer Space—that's Brother Nigel. He'll end up in the Cabinet one day, make no mistake.

Heavy-handed though such language may seem today, the real shock when it was first heard lay in the fact that, in one outburst, Osborne had broken through all that stifling atmosphere of socially deferential conservatism which had settled over Britain since the early fifties.

The 26-year-old son of a commercial artist, Osborne had his roots in that almost independent city within a city, the wide arc of anonymous, predominantly working and lower-middle-class London that stretches along the banks of the Thames, from Fulham round to Bermondsey and the East End. Like the Teddy Boys, also from South London, Osborne's Jimmy Porter wore a neurotically aggressive exterior; and like them he was hungering for sensation, for "good brave causes," for the "warm thrilling voice" crying out "Hallelujah!" But whereas the Teddy Boys of 1956 could find their release only in the wave of rock 'n roll riots of August and September, in the destruction of cinema seats and car windscreens, Osborne and Jimmy Porter found theirs in flinging abuse at the entire upper-class dominated order of English society—at Bishops and Generals, at "posh" Sunday newspapers and posh West London addresses, at Brother Nigel and Edwardian colonels and above all at everything which was represented by Porter's upper-class wife Alison.

Osborne's elevation of the figure of Alison, so central to the play, into a kind of all-purpose order image, symbolizing upper-class society, was particularly interesting. It was revealing, not only because, despite its effectiveness as a dramatic device, the marriage between Jimmy and Alison was on the face of it so implausible, but much more in the fact that this pattern, of lower-class boy dominating upper-class girl, was to become familiar in the fantasy projections of lower-class writers in these years. Originally, as Osborne made clear, Alison had been swept off her feet by the image of Jimmy's vitality— "everything about him seemed to burn"—just as he had been attracted in turn by her apparent stability and order—her "wonderful relaxation of spirit." This subconscious reflection of the mutual attraction of the classes (and particularly the self-projection of a virile lower-class honesty sweeping away bourgeois hypocrisy and pretension) had already played an important part in another fantasy by a lower-class South London writer two years before, in the book which many people soon came to associate with the general spirit of *Look Back in Anger,* Kingsley Amis's *Lucky Jim.* It was essentially the same pattern that was to appear again the following year in John Braine's best-selling *Room at the Top*. And of course it had already appeared over twenty-five years before in that archetypal fantasy of lower-class vitality raping the image of a crumbling upper-class order which had lost confidence in itself, Lawrence's *Lady Chatterley's Lover*.

Sure enough, even before *Look Back in Anger* opened, to the rapturous acclaim of its largely upper-middle-class audiences and the almost unanimous welcome of the upper-middle-class "quality" press,* the insecure upper classes and Oxford intellectuals had already come rushing to collaborate with this shining image of new vitality; for not only, as a founder of the English Stage Company, was one of the play's sympathetic sponsors the Queen's cousin, the seventh Earl of Harewood; but the manager of the Royal Court, the man who had first fallen eagerly on the play and who was to be the *éminence grise* of the "renaissance" in the English drama, was George Devine (Oxford, 1930's), the son of a public school headmaster. The play's producer, Tony Richardson, had admittedly come from a similar class background to Osborne, but was a typical member of the New Oxford Group. While the play's most enthusiastic champion was to be that other prominent member of the New Oxford Group, Kenneth Tynan, welcoming at last the "pink-eyed salivating monster" for which he had been picturesquely waiting so long. At last, he cried, *Look Back in Anger* presents:

> post-war youth as it really is, the instinctive leftishness, the surrealist sense of humour . . . the casual promiscuity, the sense of lacking a cause worth fighting for . . . the Porters of our time deplore the tyranny of "good taste" . . . they are "classless."

* It was to become part of the legend of *Look Back in Anger* among its more aggressive supporters that its reception from the press had been almost unanimously hostile: e.g. Penelope Gilliatt, writing in *Life* on 13 June 1966: "Apart from Tynan and Hobson, the rest of the press treated it like a bad smell." In fact the only national dailies to greet the play with unqualified hostility were the *Daily Mirror* and *The Times*; while the majority of the daily and weekly press was relatively enthusiastic, if not actually rapturous (e.g. the *Daily Express* "It is intense, angry, feverish, undisciplined. It is even crazy. But it is young, young, young.")

Just as in the play itself, Jimmy and Alison, lower class and upper, could only come together and find refuge in a fantasy they both shared—the make-believe game of "marvelous squirrels" and "super bears"—so the entire incident was an exact subconscious projection of what was already happening and what, in the years to come, was increasingly to happen to English society as a whole.

Less than three weeks after *Look Back in Anger*'s opening, that same May saw the advent of another center of change in the London theatre, this time in the heart of the East End itself. The Theatre Workshop company, built up around the "lower class vitality" of Joan Littlewood (South London) to bring plays to the people, in self-conscious defiance of the "upper class" commercial theatre of the West End, had in fact been in existence in various forms for ten years. But it was significant that for her first real success, Miss Littlewood should have had to wait until May 1956—and for an entirely new kind of play, Brendan Behan's *The Quare Fellow,* full of "living vernacular" and written by a drunken anarchic Irishman, who had once done a spell in a Liverpool prison for juveniles for gun-running with the Irish Republican Army.

An even more illuminating insight into the country's mood was provided four days later, with the third intellectual sensation of the month, the launching of Colin Wilson's turgid pseudo-philosophical work, *The Outsider.*

Mr. Wilson struck a chord of public interest on two levels. Firstly, he himself became almost instantly what the popular press wanted as a symbol of the new mood infecting Britain's youth. With his scruffy appearance, his background as the son of a Leicester shoe factory worker, his history of working in coffee bars and sleeping in the open on Hampstead Heath to save rent, and above all his willingness to cooperate to the full with the machinery of publicity, he became for more than a year a national figure—of a kind which he himself implicitly recognized in one of his notebooks, printed early in 1957 over a whole page of the *Daily Mail,* when he wrote:

How extraordinary that my fame should have corresponded with that of James Dean, Elvis Presley, Bill Haley, Lonnie Donegan.

But even more interesting than this aspect of his fame was the tremendous vogue for his book itself among a large section of the intelligentsia, led once again by the Oxford intellectuals, but this time of an older generation, such as Cyril Connolly and Philip Toynbee, who reviewed the book respectively in the *Sunday Times* and the *Observer*.

From time to time there appear certain works, of which differing examples were to be provided over the next ten years by the writings of the Bishop of Woolwich, Marshall McLuhan, and Herbert Marcuse, which enjoy a sudden intellectual vogue by gesturing with vast nyktomorphic significance toward something that is sensed to be of great importance to their age. It is an ingredient in the appeal of such books that they should be so clumsily and obscurely written that their message emerges only in fitful Delphic gleams. To their admirers, such oracular obscurity is justified as the price for receiving profound insights from those few spirits courageous enough to explore beyond the confines of conventional thought. But viewed from outside, it can be seen that the real achievement of such writers is not that they have clarified and explained the confusions of the age, but that they have articulated and made worse-confounded some particular aspect of its neurosis, in a form which many other people find suggestively attractive.

Such a work was *The Outsider,* a rambling survey of some of the more conspicuously neurotic and self-destructive misfits of the past three hundred years, such as Van Gogh, Nijinsky, and T. E. Lawrence. The real appeal of *The Outsider* in 1956, as with Jimmy Porter, was that it provided a glamorous cloak for the neurotic's self-importance and sense of isolation, at just the moment when so many of Britain's intellectuals and young people felt the need for such an identification. Like *Look Back in Anger,* it reflected a vio-

118

lent subconscious desire to break out from an insecurity that had suddenly become claustrophobic. In Wilson's case, the chief cause of the claustrophobia was identified as the "spiritual *malaise*" of the whole age, if not of the human condition itself. In fact, however, behind the opacity of his language and his apparently erudite parade of quotations, it is interesting to note that Wilson's underlying message was that he looked forward to the birth of some new, semi-religious philosophy of "vitalism." Like Jimmy Porter and the rock 'n roll hungry teenagers, he was in fact suffering from nothing more than a powerful, ill-defined longing for sensation.

Already by the end of May 1956 it was abundantly clear that, for all the violence of language of the "Angry Young Men," they were hardly beating their fists against a stoutly self-confident brick wall. There were obviously large parts of the wall waiting to give way at their slightest suggestion, and other parts already caving in without any prompting.

Nevertheless, even now, the young and avant-garde, whether lower class or upper, were still only a small minority. There was still one major part of the wall that overshadowed everything, undermined but intact. The intellectuals and the teenagers were not the only groups in that uneasy summer which were beginning to hunger for violent sensation. There was that other group, still more powerful and with emotional roots at every level of English life, stretching up to the Government and the Prime Minister himself, for whom, as month succeeded month, the year was proving one of intolerable strain.

The Suez Crisis, which dominated the last half of 1956, provides us with the first example in this narrative of a complete fantasy, unfolding through all the five stages of the cycle.

The long "anticipation stage" stretched back two years or more. During the first half of 1956, in the months following the sacking of Glubb Pasha and the exiling of Makarios in March, there were further signs of the waxing impatience of the Old Guard. In June, a full-page advertisement in *The Times* announced the formation of a new "right-wing ginger group," the People's League for the Defence of Freedom, organized by Edward Martell, an eccentric former Liberal, with the support of a regiment of retired service officers and declining gentry, to fight "Trade Union tyranny and arrogant bureaucracy." For those who had cheered the deportation of Makarios, patience was wearing yet thinner. Their center might be giving way, their left in retreat; only one course, it seemed, remained open —to attack.

The most recent act of "imperial retreat" had been the withdrawal of the last British troops from the Suez Canal Zone. A month later, the British and American governments announced the cancellation of their offer to finance President Nasser's Aswan Dam. On 26 July, as the climax to a two-and-a-half-hour speech to a nationalist rally in Alexandria, the Egyptian President announced that the Anglo-French Suez Canal Company would be forthwith taken into Egyptian hands. From that moment on, the aggressive dreams of the Old Guard found their focus; all the resentment, the agony, and the frustration of a class and empire so long in decline were concentrated through thirteen late summer weeks toward their last great cathartic act.

From the outset, the attitude adopted toward the "little Egyptian upstart" by the Prime Minister and his supporters was one of absurdly theatrical defiance.* And already, in the closing days of July, as the first ramshackle British forces were moved to the Mediter-

* On 30 July Eden was asked in the Commons the whereabouts of two destroyers which had recently been sold to Egypt by Britain. "I do not know where they are" was his steely reply, "but I think we can leave it to the Royal Navy. It will take care of them, wherever they are." In the war films of the previous few years, John Mills and Jack Hawkins had not looked duffle-coated out from so many cardboard bridges in vain. In fact, the destroyers were still in Portsmouth Harbour, where they were quietly handed over to the Egyptians a few weeks later.

ranean, there was no doubt what role they imagined themselves to be playing—or rather replaying. On 31 July, *The Times*—which throughout the crisis was to act under the direction of Sir William Haley as the Old Guard's chief rallying point—abandoned its usual courtesy of prefixing "Colonel" or "President" to the name of the Egyptian leader, but referred to him simply as "Nasser." In the Commons two days later, even Hugh Gaitskell, despite his later *volte face,* compared President Nasser not only to Hitler but also, for good measure, to Mussolini as well.

August and September, passing in a rising clamor of threats and international consultation, marked the height of the "dream stage." During August alone, no less than eleven of *The Times*'s first leaders were devoted to the subject, under such titles as "A Hinge of History," "Resisting the Aggressor," "Straight Issues," and, on 27 August, the celebrated clarion call "Escapers' Club," which concluded:

> Doubtless it is good to have a flourishing tourist trade, to win test matches and to be regaled by photographs of Miss Diana Dors being pushed into a swimming pool. But nations do not live by circuses alone. The people, in their silent way, know better than the critics. They still want Britain great.

On 12 September the Prime Minister assured the Commons: "The Government is not prepared to embark on a policy of abject appeasement." Nothing more clearly reflected the mood of many of his followers than the *Daily Sketch*'s celebrated headline: "Let the Crybabies Howl! It's GREAT Britain Again."

As the weeks passed, the momentum of this giant collective dream increasingly demanded more than the torrent of speeches, letters, and editorials that were filling every newspaper. As late as mid-October and the Conservative Party Conference at Llandudno—with the Old Guard in full cry, cheering not only Anthony Nutting's assurance that "we shall not flinch," but also a number of lip-smacking calls for the retention of capital punishment—the dream still masked the frustration welling up from beneath. But during the last two weeks in October plans for more positive action were at last determined. With the Israeli invasion of Egypt on the morning of 29 October, the last two stages of the fantasy had begun.

Over the following eight days, which were to culminate in the chaotic Anglo-French landings at Port Said, it seemed as if English life would be shaken to its foundations. As the British and French governments issued their "ultimatum" to the combatants and their air forces began the bombing of Egyptian airfields—to the background of the rebellion raging in Hungary—the political atmosphere of London was plunged into hysteria. Rumors flew at an intensity that would only be equaled in the Profumo days of 1963; that the Prime Minister was sobbing, shouting, and sweeping telephones to the floor in rage; that nineteen members of the Foreign Office, some in the most senior positions, had gathered in a Pall Mall club and threatened mass resignation; that forty Conservative M.P.'s led by Mr. Butler himself, were about to withdraw their support from the Eden Government. And almost as if to add credence to rumor came the news of the first actual resignations (seeming, as they always do in such circumstances, to be the precursors of many more); of Anthony Nutting himself, of William Clark, Eden's press secretary, and of Sir Edward Boyle (New Oxford Group).

In the House of Commons, a series of emergency debates was conducted in almost unending uproar. Shouts of "traitor," "Nasser's little lackey," "every country but your own," catcalls, boos, and jeers echoed in mounting crescendo, leading in one case even to the suspension of the House.

Fleet Street too was split down the middle—ranging from Eden's fanatical supporters, such as the *Daily Sketch, The Times,* and Lord Beaverbrook's *Daily Express,* which declared on 1 November that Eden had acted to "safe-guard the life of the British Empire" and to "keep Britain Great," to an at times equally fanatical and hysterical array of opponents, led by the *Daily Mirror,* the *Manchester*

Guardian, and the *Observer* which, on 4 November, proclaimed that it "had not realized that our Government was capable of such folly and crookedness."*

On the same day, Sunday, 4 November, the "nightmare stage" of the Suez fantasy was complete. With the newspaper front pages uneasily divided between Suez and Budapest, which had been re-entered by Russian tanks the day before, thirty thousand people gathered in Trafalgar Square for the biggest political demonstration in Britain since the war. It was followed by a march ten thousand strong down Whitehall to Downing Street, where the demonstrators were charged by mounted policemen amid the puff of exploding smoke-bombs. On television that night, Hugh Gaitskell appealed to Conservative M.P.'s to desert their leader and to form a new Government immediately.

The following day came the actual invasion of Egypt—and the "explosion into reality." At last the full consequences of what they had done were brought home to the Eden Government—as they were hit by a wave of shock and censure from almost every country in the world, a major financial crisis, including the heaviest run on the pound since 1951, and the threat from Moscow that unless Britain and France desisted from their aggression at once, London and Paris would be showered with nuclear rockets. Within thirty-six hours the whole gigantic charade had ground to a halt in the cease-fire. And it was at this point, just as the crisis reached its very peak, that a most remarkable thing happened. For, from the start of the crisis back in July, as all the opinion polls agreed, there had never been a majority in the country to support military action; but now, as the full enormity of what Eden had done began to dawn, there was a marked swing to his support. It was as if a thick protective veil had fallen

---

* This particular editorial, which cost the paper an estimated 30–40,000 readers, marked the full emergence of the change which had been taking place in the character of the *Observer* under its Old Etonian editor-proprietor, the Hon. David Astor (Oxford 1930's); more than any other paper in Fleet Street, it was to reflect over the following years the general attitudes of the New Oxford Group—several members of which were on its staff, including Kenneth Tynan.

between the majority of Englishmen and the reality they could not bear to face. The dreadful orgasm had been achieved—and from now on, as after some gigantic national act of onanism, the greater part of the population never wanted to think about the matter again.

And thus it was that the great Suez "crisis" petered out—with the limping of one sick Prime Minister off into the wings of history. The flow of the nation's politics resumed apparently almost unbroken. No Governments fell, no other heads rolled; even the vicious flurry of anti-Americanism in which the Tory right-wing sought to expiate their unspoken feelings of disaster was soon left to die away. As a new year dawned, bringing with it, after a consummately smooth demonstration of one of the most time-honored of Establishment rituals, a new Prime Minister, Harold Macmillan, the Conservative Party began once again to lift its head. And almost the first act of the new Cabinet, as if to console itself for the shattering of one illusion with another in some ways even greater, was to give the new Defence Minister, Duncan Sandys, the go-ahead to prepare a new national defense policy—centered to an unprecedented extent on nuclear weapons. In the years to come, the social consequences of Britain's decision to place so much store by her "independent nuclear deterrent," and to become the first country in NATO no longer to demand that her young men of eighteen should do National Service, were in many ways to be even greater than its political and military repercussions.*

Outwardly it seemed that little had changed. Deep in the national psyche, however, was the knowledge that a very real watershed had been passed. Attitudes to the outside world and to authority, the relations between class and class, England's fundamental view of herself —a whole complex of sentiments and assumptions that had been

---

* Without this decision, for instance, it would have been unlikely that the world would have seen the rise of the Beatles; for the years 1961–1963, when they would have been eligible for military service, were just those when the foundations of their fame were being laid.

built up over hundreds of years—had been irreparably undermined. The dam had burst.

Over the next eighteen months, taking shape on the lines sketched out in 1956, there emerged the foundations of the New England of the future. The mood of a restless "anticipation stage" that had been so characteristic of 1956, particularly among the teenagers and the young intellectuals, spread in 1957 and 1958 throughout English life, ranging from television to politics. For the Old Guard, 1957 was to be a year of particular confusion as they cast round bewilderedly for a new cause—in particular the power-symbol of Britain's new H-bomb—while in the autumn they were to find a rallying point in fighting back at attacks on the aura surrounding the monarchy, by Malcolm Muggeridge and a young journalist member of the New Oxford Group, Lord Altrincham. Indeed the autumn of 1957 provided the first setback for the New England, in the exploding of the bubble reputation of Colin Wilson, when his second book, *Religion and the Rebel,* received almost unanimously contemptuous reviews, including one or two from those who had previously been most conspicuously enthusiastic.

But by and large, in the early months of 1957, the nyktomorphic promise of the New England seemed set nothing but fair. Few things are more revealing of an underlying shift in mood than a major innovation in women's fashion—and from February 1957 onward, the craze to raise hemlines from calf-length to the knee spread across England in a matter of months. It was to be a year of crazes, from skiffle groups to the hula hoop. After an already sharp rise the previous year, the sales of pop records reached the highest level they were to see until 1963. The popular press became fascinated by the antics and rags-to-riches success of the strange new breed of gold-lamé-clad rock 'n roll idols, still looking for the most part like gilded Teddy Boys, with names such as Marty Wilde and Terry Dene and Wee Willie Harris, almost all of them products of the Soho coffee bar, the *Two I's*. But the new wind was by no means blowing only through fashion and pop music. In the first months of the year, it became apparent that the arrivals of the previous year, Osborne and Wilson, Tynan and Tony Richardson, had been the outriders of a new generation, now suddenly emerging as novelists, playwrights, actors, directors, film-makers, and journalists in all directions.

On 25 January, for instance, the traditionally conservative *Spectator* (now owned by a member of the New Oxford Group, Ian Gilmour) launched a new political column, written under the pseudonym of "Taper" by the 29-year-old Bernard Levin. Over the next few months, with its mixture of formal irony, informal abuse, and satirical or merely insulting nicknames for leading politicians (such as "Sir Reginald Bullying-Manner" for the Attorney General Sir Reginald Manningham-Buller, "Sir Shortly Floorcross" for the increasingly unenthusiastic Labour frontbencher Hartley Shawcross, or "Marshal Bigmouth" for his least favorite among M.P.'s, Harold Wilson), Levin's weekly eye-witness account of proceedings in the Palace of Westminster became a major talking point.

Another phenomenon of the time was the establishment as household names of a new type of young, university-educated "television personality," such as Robin Day, Ludovic Kennedy, and Christopher Chataway, all of whom had begun their careers as newsreaders on Independent Television News and had been at Oxford just before or after the war. Nowhere was this increasing prominence of television, following the introduction of commercial competition, to have more drastic effect than inside the BBC itself, still generally dominated by a consciousness of the great role played by Sound Radio during the war—and in a year when, for the first time, almost as many people were watching television as listening to the wireless, there was no innovation so significant as the launching on 18 February of a new, early-evening magazine program *Tonight*. It was symbolic that the new program, with its earnest lack of respect and "satirical" interludes, should originally have been put out from a tiny studio in Kensington, far from the centers of the BBC empire.

For its producer, again a member of the New Oxford Group, Donald Baverstock, and his young team, again largely dominated by Oxford graduates, had little appreciation of the staid values which had governed BBC policy for forty years. They were "excited" by television in a way that inside the BBC was new; "irreverence" was one of their key words; and they wanted to make *Tonight* a kind of "tabloid of the air," "probing," opinionated, and "pulling no punches."

Neither Baverstock nor Levin were, however, what the popular press described as "Angry Young Men"—that heterogeneous collection of critics, playwrights, novelists, and quasi-philosophers who still remained an exclusive mixture of the young urban lower class and members of the New Oxford Group, and whose numbers in the aftermath of Suez seemed to have swelled to legion. Still at their forefront was John Osborne, whose second major play, *The Entertainer,* staged at the Royal Court in April, was directly inspired by the Suez crisis—portraying the decadence of Old England even more vehemently than *Look Back in Anger,* through the guise of a broken down old music-hall comedian who was also conveniently made the product of a public school. Once again, the play was received rapturously by many of the supposed representatives of Old England itself, as was poignantly demonstrated by the fact that it was England's leading "Establishment" actor Sir Laurence Olivier who at his own request played the title role of Archie Rice.

The hysteria aroused by the Suez episode had in fact marked the final breach between the right-wing fantasy of the Old Guard and the left-wing fantasy of the new avant-garde. On the one hand, the chauvinism of the Old Guard, although it would never again be quite so powerful as it had briefly been in the summer and autumn of 1956, found new excitement in such images as that of Britain's nuclear weapon, tested for the first time in May to the accompaniment of such headlines as the *Daily Express*'s "It's Our H-Bomb!" On the other hand, the avant-garde were working up their image of a complacently self-confident upper class holding unbroken sway over every aspect of English life into an increasingly unreal caricature. Nowhere was this unreal violence so clearly expressed as in the self-conscious essay by various Angry Young Men, published toward the end of 1957 under the title *Declaration*. John Osborne's own contribution, entitled "They Call It Cricket," was one long tirade against "royalty religion, the national swill," the "waffling cant" of the "well-off and mentally under-privileged" who "rule our lives," the "moral funk" of the Church, full of bishops sounding like "bewigged old perverts at Assizes." His fellow contributors, who included Colin Wilson and three members of the New Oxford Group, gave scarcely less imaginative vent to their fury, ranging from the "claustrophobic" upper-class snobbery of English films to the "pusillanimity" and "cowardice" of other members of their own generation.

And the irony of it all was that the "revolution," for which Tynan, Lindsay Anderson, and so many of the New Oxford Group had eagerly been waiting, was now taking place almost faster than they could take in. At the very moment Anderson, for instance, was caustically declaring that "a young actor with a regional or cockney accent had better lose it quick . . . for where are his chances of stardom?", at least one such actor, Albert Finney, the son of a bookmaker from Salford, was being discovered in repertory in Birmingham; another, Peter O'Toole, the 23-year-old son of an Irish immigrant from Leeds, had already been drawing theatre audiences for some time to the Bristol Old Vic. *Room at the Top,* the story of a young working-class executive's ruthless rise to success in business and love, by John Braine, a librarian from neighboring Bradford, was one of the year's best sellers. One of the successes of the following year was to be *Saturday Night and Sunday Morning,* an idealization of the "vitality" of working-class life in Nottingham, by another lower-class novelist, Alan Sillitoe.

But it was above all in writing for the theatre that 1957 seemed like the beginning of a new renaissance, England's social upheaval having suddenly thrown up a flood of aspiring playwrights from every point along the class spectrum. Almost all of them, however, fell into one of two categories. In the first, and by far the largest, were the tough-sentimentalizations of "lower-class vitality," full of "living vernacular," by such writers as Shelagh Delaney, a 19-year-old mill-hand also from Albert Finney's Salford. The second category, of which Harold Pinter (East End Jewish) was eventually to be the chief example, was that of playwrights concerned almost entirely with pure fantasy.

Whatever was to happen to this "unending stream of new talent" in future years, at least in 1957 the fantasy was rising hot and strong. There was at last "excitement" in the air. For the New Oxford Group, in that heady dawn, there seemed little doubt that the millennium was at last arriving. In August, for instance, the young Lord Altrincham (New Oxford Group) was sufficiently emboldened by the new atmosphere to write in his magazine, the *English and National Review,* that the speeches written for the Queen by her "tweedy entourage" were "a pain in the neck," and that her public personality was that of

a priggish schoolgirl, captain of the hockey team, a prefect and a recent candidate for confirmation.

By the following year, the ethos of change seemed firmly enough established for Kenneth Tynan to issue a confident situation report:

The ivory tower has collapsed for good. The lofty, lapidary, "mandarin" style of writing has been replaced by prose that has its feet on the ground . . . Britain's angry young men may be jejune and strident, but they are involved in the only belief that matters: that life begins tomorrow.

There was hardly an aspect of national life that was not touched by the ferment of 1957. After sharp rises in 1956, the figures for illegitimacy, suicide, violence, and all sorts of crime rose even higher. Industry was hit by more than twice as many strikes, both official and unofficial, as in any year since the war. And if the ferment in national politics was to see nothing like the stormy peak of Suez, the outlines of a new age were taking shape that was to govern the course of

English politics for the next seven years. In the early months of the year, the Government's popularity continued to sink. But despite the groggy state of the Conservatives, the Opposition seemed less capable than ever of taking advantage of its opportunities.

As it entered even further into the confusion about its role and future that had characterized it throughout the fifties, the Labour Party was beset by every sort of claim as to which way it should go. Two of these claims were particularly significant. The first, though unofficial, was the vociferous movement of young intellectuals who, roused by Suez and Hungary, and grouped around a new magazine, the *Universities and Left Review,* and a Soho coffee bar, *The Partisan,* described themselves as the New Left. Beginning with general discontent against Establishments everywhere, particularly that of American capitalism, which was soon to crystallize in an emotional opposition to the H-Bomb, they represented the first political expression of the spirit which had underlain Jimmy Porter's hunger for "good brave causes," of the kind which had been virtually absent from Britain since the days of the Spanish Civil War. The second, more relevant to the long-term future of the Labour Party itself, was the movement centered initially around a member of the New Oxford Group, Anthony Crosland, whose book *The Future of Socialism* had been published the previous year, to drag the Party away from its obsession with nationalization, and into a kind of post-Socialist compromise with capitalism.

In the years to come, both of these seeds were to bear considerable fruit—but in the meantime, of infinitely greater importance were the subtle changes which were coming over the Conservative Party.

Outwardly the Conservatives were still in disarray. The Party had been through a traumatic shock, and the new Prime Minister, apparently aloof, was still largely an enigma. But already there were signs, such as the readiness with which in March, after bringing back Archbishop Makarios from exile, he accepted the resignation of the extreme right-wing imperialist Lord Salisbury, and his promotion of a new and socially broader-based group of Ministers, that the Conservative Party and Government of Harold Macmillan would be very different from those of Sir Winston and Sir Anthony.

Even so, it was not from the Labour or Conservative Parties that the new hunger for change and excitement that was running through the country first burst onto the political stage. One of the more striking phenomena in English politics over the next five years (out of all proportion to its gain in votes) was the dramatic revival of the tiny third party, the Liberals. By 1957, the Liberals (who had last formed a government between 1905 and 1916, and declined ever since) only held 5 of the 630 seats in the House of Commons. But in 1956 they had elected a young and attractive leader in Jo Grimond, a radically minded, rich Old Etonian. At a time of rapid social change, when both the major parties seemed to be frozen in the social and ideological postures of an age that was receding into the past, the Liberal Party was ideally placed to embody the political mood of a new era. With its glamorous new leader, and yet its great tradition to provide balancing respectability, poised midway across the class and political spectrum, the Party began in 1957 to pick up surprising new support in all parts of the country, and to make a number of recruits from the glamorous ranks of young television personalities. And over the next five years, on a vague but aggressively radical program, they were to provide the vanguard of that hunger for "a new politics" that was eventually to transform the character of both the major parties (and that indeed, as we shall see, formed something of an English counterpart to the same radical temper which in America found expression in President Kennedy's New Frontier).

The winter of 1957–58 was one of unrest in many parts of the world. It was dominated, perhaps, by the news on 4 October of the launching of the first Russian sputnik—the psychological impact of which was enormous, particularly on America where the economic boom of the fifties had run into the sharpest recession since the war, resulting in a winter-long indulgence in national self-examination. In

France, the winter was to be one of unbroken political crisis, centered over Algeria, and culminating the following May in the downfall of the Fourth Republic and the coming to power of General
de Gaulle. But for Britain, too, it was to be an unusually turbulent
winter, marked by rows, storms, and political sensations. A major
financial crisis in September, followed by the highest peacetime bank
rate since the eighteenth century and steadily rising unemployment,
gave further impetus to the declining popularity of the Macmillan
Government. In January, the Prime Minister brushed off the unprecedented resignation of all three of his Treasury Ministers after
a dispute over the rise in government spending as nothing more
than "a little local difficulty"—but even such equanimity must have
been shaken when, in February and March, the reviving Liberal
Party came from nowhere to bring about the loss of two Government
seats in Parliamentary by-elections, achieving swings of votes on a
scale far greater than anything since the Labour election victory of
1945.

Did this new-found volatility of the electorate (aided by the first
major incursions into British politics of those two new forces, television and opinion polls) herald a new era of political instability,
even the breaking down of the familiar two-party system? Certainly
such an interpretation might have been confirmed also by another
political event of the winter, the sudden rise of a somewhat hysterical
national debate over the threat to mankind of the hydrogen bomb.
Within months, a campaign launched in the left-wing weekly *New
Statesman,* under the aegis of such prominent intellectual figures as
Bertrand Russell and J. B. Priestley, had gathered such a volume of
support that by the Easter of 1958 a national protest movement had
been promoted—the first major extra-Parliamentary political movement in Britain of its kind since the hunger marches of the thirties.

The first result, over Easter weekend, was a demonstration in
Trafalgar Square, directly inspired by the great Suez rally of eighteen
months before, followed by a march to the nuclear weapons center
at Aldermaston, forty miles from London. For the purposes of

gathering support along the route, the march was, of course, pointed in the wrong direction (although in later years it would be reversed). On Easter Morning, it therefore petered out in a somewhat aimless crowd of five-thousand-odd assorted pacifists, Young Communists, venerable liberals, bearded anarchists, and duffle-coated students, milling about in the mire of a Berkshire meadow. Nobody involved seemed to have a very clear idea of what the Campaign for Nuclear Disarmament stood for, except that it was "against the Bomb." But already they had found one common factor that was to unite them in the years to come—the little badge that bore "a strange device," the dream symbol that no mass movement based on fantasy can be without. And already in that Berkshire meadow, as in the first militant civil rights demonstrations in America, were being laid the foundations of that phenomenon of stereotyped youthful protest which, by the sixties, would become perpetuated in sit-downs, sit-ins, and demonstrations against almost any manifestation of order or authority, long after the Bomb itself was more or less forgotten.

One spur to the self-importance of the Aldermaston Marchers had been the fact that, while they were passing through London, the powerful trade unionist Frank Cousins had been sighted eyeing the marchers with what appeared to be some sympathy from the roadside. A month later, Mr. Cousins threw the capital into near chaos by bringing his bus workers out on strike for seven weeks. In some mysterious way this strike was the last act in the turbulence which had seized the country since the previous September. It marked more, however, than just the end of one winter of unrest. On the opinion polls in that early summer of 1958 there was a sudden flood of support back to the Conservatives, the first for well over two years. The fire of the Liberal Revival in the wake of its successes of the winter seemed to have died to a mere glow, as fast as it had flared up. The fever of the rock 'n roll craze was dying away among the teenagers. Even the Angry Young Men were suddenly muted, and

John Osborne, described by Kenneth Tynan as a "dandy with a machine gun," was quietly settled in an expensive house in upper-class Chelsea, preparing to become a film tycoon. It might even have seemed that the impetus of that revolution in English life which had begun in September 1955 was dying away.

In fact, of course, the revolution was only just beginning. The up-heaval of the previous two and a half years had been merely the shudder as the process of change in English life moved into a new and higher gear. At every level of society the appetite for new excitement had been whetted. A hundred seeds had been sown that would now begin to germinate, evolve, and work their way to the surface: not least in a little book entitled *British Economic Policy since the War,* directly inspired by the financial crisis of September 1957 and written during that winter by Andrew Shonfield (Oxford, late 1930's), the Economic Editor of Mr. Astor's *Observer.*

The real trouble with Britain, Mr. Shonfield argued, lay in her poor rate of economic "growth," brought about by too much importance being attached to such international status symbols as saving the pound and military spending overseas, and by the "conservatism" and "complacency" of both managements and trade unions. What was wanted, he concluded, was a "realistic" reappraisal of Britain's role in the world, and the freeing of her economy from "restrictive" influences. Then, with a "Five Year Plan" to "release a *dynamic* movement of production against the traditional forces of resistance," Britain's economy might once again leap forward in the "atmosphere . . . of a frontier boom town."

Mr. Shonfield's book was a serious attempt to get to the root of some of Britain's recurrent economic and political difficulties. Nevertheless, almost more relevant to the future was some of the imagery he employed, above all his use of that ominous word "dynamic."

Chapter Six

Too Good to Be True

We have plunged down a cataract of progress which
sweeps us on into the future with ever wilder violence the
farther it takes us from our roots. Once the past has been
breached . . . there is no stopping the forward motion. But
it is precisely the loss of connection with our past, our
uprootedness, which has given rise to the "discontents" of
civilisation; and to such a flurry and haste that we live
more in the future and its chimerical promises of a golden
age than in the present, with which our whole evolution-
ary background has not yet caught up. We rush
impetuously into novelty, driven by a mounting sense of
insufficiency, dissatisfaction and restlessness. We no longer
live on what we have but on promises, no longer in the
light of the present day, but in the darkness of the future,
which, we expect, will at last bring the proper sunrise. We
refuse to recognise that everything better is purchased at
the price of something worse . . .

C. G. JUNG
Memories, Dreams, Reflections
(written in the late fifties)

BOOM for brokers, decorators, dress designers
BOOM in cars, champagne, art treasures
BOOM in lavish living . . .

> Headlines from BOOM issue of *Queen,*
> 15 September 1959

The class war is obsolete.

> HAROLD MACMILLAN on television after
> Conservative election victory, 9 October 1959

At the gates of the new decade, the main peril, blinding
our eyes to what we could achieve, seems almost to be
smugness.

> The *Economist,* in leading article
> "Farewell to the Fifties," 26 December 1959

Somehow the wind is beginning to change. People—not
everyone by a long way, but enough to disturb the
prevailing mood—seem to seek a renewal of conviction, a
new sense of national purpose.

> PROF. ARTHUR SCHLESINGER, JR.
> on "The New Mood" in American politics,
> *Esquire,* January 1960

This is our message for the Sixties—a Socialist-inspired
scientific and technological revolution releasing energy on
an enormous scale.

> HAROLD WILSON to the Labour Party
> Conference at Scarborough, October 1960

A dogged resistance to change now blankets every segment
of our national life. A middle-aged conservatism, parochial
and complacent, has settled over the country.

> ANTHONY CROSLAND,
> *Encounter,* October 1960

"What's Wrong With Britain?"

> Title of *Picture Post* article, March 1947

The dying down of the unrest that had ruffled the country since 1955 was dramatic. By no means its least manifestation in the early summer of 1958 was a rise in the popularity of the Prime Minister. In barely two months, between the beginning of May and the end of June, public approval for Harold Macmillan on the Gallup Poll rose by thirteen points, from 37 percent to 50 percent—and went on rising —without any specific explanation, apart from the marginal effect of a successful broadcast on television. But the real reason for the change in the country's mood ran deeper. If the country's appearance in those summer months was one of comparative calm, it was by no means a return to the placid conservatism of the early fifties. As the sound and fury died away, there stood revealed a different England—febrile, on the make, settling into a new and faster tempo of life. Three years before, reserves of nervous energy had been awakening, groping for a focus. Now that focus had been found.

Of all the new outlets for nervous energy one was becoming more apparent than any. Twelve months before, in a speech at Bedford, on 20 July 1957, the Prime Minister had remarked:

> Indeed, let's be frank about it; some of our people have never had it so good.

In later years this quotation from the Democratic Party's campaign slogan of 1952 was to be damagingly distorted to the Conservatives' discredit. But in the summer of 1958, that was still far ahead. Only then, and still, it must be remembered, only four years after the end of food rationing, was it beginning to dawn on the people of Britain that they had embarked on the greatest spending spree in their history: a prosperity of a different dimension from that brief pre-war burst in the late thirties. The golden age of Macmillan's England had begun. As it moved into its stride, there would be few who would remember that, in his speech at Bedford, the Prime Minister (warning of the dangers of inflation) had gone on to say:

What is beginning to worry some of us is "Is it too good to be true?", or perhaps I should say "Is it too good to last?"

The eighteen months just beginning were to see as great a change in the surface and character of English life as any in her peacetime history. Of all its manifestations, none was more symbolic than the two which were above all to typify Macmillan's England—the boom in consumer goods and the boom in property.

By the last two years of the fifties, the property boom which had been unleashed in London by the relaxation of building and rent controls, was accelerating by leaps and bounds. Between 1958 and 1959, deals in property shares rose from 16,000 to 102,000. The value of ordinary shares in property companies was to rise in the next four years by almost eight times. By 1958–1959, the first giant glass-and-concrete office blocks were beginning to rise above the London skyline. It was in 1959 that the first of the rising property magnates became household names, notably Mr. Jack Cotton from Birmingham who, less than four years before, had said "There's one thing I cannot stand and that's the press," but who now began regularly to court publicity with such flamboyant press conferences as those in which he announced his plans for the development of Piccadilly Circus, and for the building of the world's largest office block, the Pan American building in New York.

But even the triumphant march of Mr. Cotton, which was to culminate in 1960 in the merger of his interests with those of two other increasingly well-known figures, Charles Clore and Walter Flack, to make up the world's largest property company, was only the tip of a gigantic iceberg. Already the developers were changing not only the face of London, but the towns and cities of the provinces, with schemes as large as that announced in September 1959 for the replacement of the whole of the city center of Birmingham. While away from the headlines, and in the wake of the Rent Act of 1957, murkier fortunes were being made by such men as the later notorious slum landlord and racketeer, Peter Rachman.

138

The second aspect of these years was the boom in consumer goods and personal prosperity. Between 1956 and the end of 1959 the country's hire purchase debt rose faster and by a greater amount overall than at any other time before or since. Expenditure on advertising too was rising at its fastest rate (although even by 1958 it was only reaching the proportion of the national income that it had been). It was hardly surprising that the country sensed itself, after the dark years that lay behind, taking off into a dazzling future. They were the years when the cut-price washing machines of John Bloom (East End Jewish) began to raise his empire on the flood-tide of hire purchase and when the boom in American-style supermarkets was getting under way. 1958 was the year in which the first parking meters and traffic wardens appeared on the streets of London, to cope with the private cars which had already doubled in number since 1955. It was the year in which the jet age opened with the coming into service of the Boeing 707's and Comet IV's. It was the time too when Britain first really became aware of the growing numbers of colored immigrants who, ever since the war, had been flocking from the poorer parts of the Empire into the poorer areas of London and the cities of the North and Midlands.

But above all, new money was pouring into tills, pockets, and bank accounts at every level of society. In three years, thanks to television, the impact of advertising had increased by a measure it could never repeat. The jingles and slogans of commercial television had saturated the consciousness of the nation, even coming to replace age-old nursery rhymes in children's games. Deep Freeze had arrived and TV Instant Dinners and Fish Fingers and Fabulous Pink Camay. With so many bright new packages on the shelves, so many new gadgets to be bought, so much new magic in the dreary air of industrial Britain, there was a feeling of modernity and adventure that would never be won so easily again. For never again would so many English families be buying their first car, installing their first refrigerator, taking their first continental holiday.

And from America, from the title of Professor Galbraith's book published in Britain in November 1958, came the word which a year later had become the everyday journalistic commonplace to describe this new state of things. Britain had entered "the age of affluence."

Borne along on the general surge, the tentacles of social change spread out, thriving, multiplying, consolidating. Particularly was this true among the young, of every class. Never before had the young been so prominent. From the eager young faces in television commercials to leading articles on the Aldermaston marchers, there was everywhere emphasis on youthful energy, youthful enterprise, youthful idealism. The new, half-wary, half-admiring obsession with teenagers was a symptom of the feeling, as yet barely defined, that youth had glamor and power, that England was moving into a new, mysterious age to which the young alone had the key.

1958 was the year in which Colin MacInnes was discovering the brittle teenage underworld of *Absolute Beginners*: and in which Anthony Armstrong-Jones foreshadowed the future with a book of impressionistic photographs of *London* which for the first time made the grimy East End and the imperious Mall look like part of the same "dream city." In the gossip columns of the *Daily Express* and the *Daily Mail* it was the heyday of the Chelsea Set and huge photographs of black-stockinged runaway heiresses and the search for "kicks," before that particular Chelsea dream began to curl at the edges, before some of the *jeunesse dorée* ended up in prison and others were forced to flee the country for meddling in the romance of another and more dangerous underworld. Through an avant-garde minority on either side, the upper- and lower-class young were beginning to mix as never before. Increasingly they were meeting not on that guilty, self-conscious basis with which George Orwell had taken the road to Wigan Pier, but in the new "classless" middle ground of jeans and modern jazz, of "hip" and "cool," of casual Americanized clothes and casual Americanized speech that foreshadowed the pop culture to come. And for those smart young graduates from the older universities who might once have entered the Foreign Office or administered the Empire or drifted into teaching, it was now becoming more than ever fashionable to aim at the "young" and "classless" world of "communications"—at advertising, journalism, or, best of all, the glamorous world of television.

For television it was a golden age. The novelty and excitement that had attended the birth of commercial television and Donald Baverstock's *Tonight* had now spread throughout the industry, which was at last developing away from sound radio with pictures into seemingly limitless regions of its own. On the BBC it was the heyday of the serious "prestige" programs—*Panorama,* John Freeman's *Face to Face* interviews, *Tonight* itself. February 1958 had seen the launching of *Monitor,* the Sunday night arts program introduced by Huw Wheldon, which was soon to reach a regular audience of over 2,000,000 with its deferential, never critical Instant Culture, predating the Sunday color magazine by four years. Meanwhile commercial television, with its dream-world advertisements, its soap opera serials, and its give-away quiz shows, was introducing an element of glossy vulgarity and fantasy that British broadcasting had never known.

For the new English theatre, still centered on George Devine's Royal Court and Joan Littlewood's Theatre Workshop, the years 1958–1959 were equally golden. By 1959—the year in which, as the *Annual Register* records, "the youth movement in the British theatre took definite and unmistakable shape"—the stream of new talent was rising faster than ever. Some of the new dramatists were cast in more conventional mold—such as Robert Bolt (Manchester Grammar School) and Peter Shaffer (Liverpool Jewish and post-war Cambridge). But most of them fell into the now familiar patterns— either, like Arnold Wesker, romanticizing lower-class vitality; or else, like Harold Pinter, concerned with pure fantasy; in Pinter's case, of plays threaded with nightmare menace, and the unresolvable uncertainty of trying to "communicate" as in a dream, in which no one's identity is ever quite established. 1959 was also the year in which Shelagh Delaney's *Taste of Honey* became a West End success; and in which there also appeared from Joan Littlewood's

141

Theatre Royal perhaps the most successful glamorization of lower-class vitality of all, the musical *Fings Ain't Wot They Used T'Be,* a sprawling fantasy of Soho low-life that sprang from the archetypal East End union of Lionel Bart, hitherto song writer to Tommy Steele, and Frank Norman, a scarred ex-convict with a "colorful" fund of criminal slang.

If the social revolution begun in the theatre three years before now seemed within sight of total acceptance, already the burning brand was being carried into a new field. The British cinema in 1958 and 1959 was in commercially dire straits. Studio after studio had closed under the impact of television, audiences were down to half their post-war level and still falling. By 1958, with such films as *Ice Cold in Alex, Carve Her Name with Pride* and *Dunkirk,* the tradition of "stiff upper lip" epics looking back to wartime greatness was on its last legs.

Far from the traditional centers of the film industry, however, a rescue force was at hand—as in Italy and France—consisting of a new generation of film-makers whose ambition was to make a new kind of film expressing the spirit of the times. The first portent in the English cinema appeared in the commercially successful *Room at the Top* (1959), hardly made outside the established framework of the film industry, nor even a "working class" film, but widely praised for its "social realism," and introducing to English films a "hard," "realistic" style of photography which included loving shots of back-to-back slums and poignant close-ups of puddles in the street.

The real impetus behind the "revival" was to come from the company set up in 1958 by John Osborne and Tony Richardson as Woodfall films—linked closely with the so-called "Free Cinema" group launched in 1956 by Richardson, Karel Reisz (post-war Cambridge), and Lindsay Anderson. Already during the year, both Anderson and Reisz had made short documentaries confirming the direction in which their interests lay—Anderson's showing the first Aldermaston March and Reisz's *We Are the Lambeth Boys* being a picture of South London teenagers. Nevertheless, the new company's "stagy" production of *Look Back in Anger* (1959) directed by Richardson, although widely acclaimed at the time, and introducing many of the cinematic clichés which later Woodfall Films were to make so familiar (such as the "pub scene," the "graveyard scene," smoke enveloping railway bridges, and characters running to give the sense of pace), gave only a limited foretaste of the vogue which lay ahead.

If all this ferment of youthful promise and rising expectation seemed like the dawn of a new era, it was not without indications of a more destructive fantasy beneath. It is a rule of fantasy that somewhere, sometime, even if not immediately apparent, every dream must have its corresponding nightmare—and the greater the dream, the greater the nightmare. And certainly in 1958, beneath the dream into which English society was moving, there were premonitory glimpses of the nightmare that was to be its price. In the late summer, there was the eruption of racial violence, beginning on the evening of 23 August with an ugly race-riot involving several hundred people in Notting- ham. The following weekend the street fighting began again—and spread even more savagely to Notting Hill, where for two nights running, teenage gangs congregated to roam the streets with bicycle chains in search of colored immigrants. The crime rate, particularly of crimes involving violence, rose at alarming speed, bringing the total number of crimes during the year to 40 percent above the total of only three years before. And already there were some, such as Richard Hoggart, a don of working-class origins in Leeds, whose book *The Uses of Literacy* published the previous year had painted a vivid picture of the breaking up of the traditional, closely knit urban working-class culture, who were prepared to see a darker side to the rising affluence.

But by and large in 1958 and 1959 the violence and bitterness of Suez and Angry Young Men had died away. The old barriers, after all, were obviously falling or already down. The Tory Old Guard, which at the time of Suez had loomed so large, seemed increasingly a marginal political irrelevance. In every walk of national life, from politics and journalism to the arts and social behavior, it seemed that the liberal, progressive, "classless," and affluent New England could hardly be emerging faster. Even those institutions which might have been regarded as most impervious were succumbing. In 1958, the House of Lords had admitted Life Peers, including women. In 1959, the Royal Academy Summer Exhibition, long notorious for its artistic conservatism, had admitted its first abstracts, and the "Kitchen Sink" paintings of John Bratby (South London). In the Church, there was the appointment as Bishop of Southwark of Mervyn Stockwood, a prominent Aldermaston marcher and vocal member of the Labour Party, while his friend John Robinson, an even more "radical" theologian, became Bishop of nearby Woolwich. In the popular press much publicity was given to "go-ahead" young vicars who thought to win themselves larger congregations by experiments with "rock 'n roll masses" or coffee bars in the crypt, and in the East End, a Rev. Shergold set up a youth club for "Rockers," under the auspices of the Eton College mission, joining his members in wearing black leather jackets and riding powerful motorcycles. Within a year, in 1960, another august establishment institution, the Royal Shakespeare Company, would be appointing as its new Directors those two young radicals of the theatre, Peter Brook (New Oxford Group) and Peter Hall, the director of *Waiting for Godot*.

Yet the fact remained that by and large, for all this torrent of change, and behind this increasingly garish façade, the great central institutions of English society—the Establishment, the Monarchy, the public schools—seemed to have survived as impregnable as ever. The bright young *Spectator* might in 1959 be running a wistful series of articles on "What is Radicalism?" The young historian Hugh Thomas (Cambridge, early 1950's), who had resigned from the Foreign Office after Suez, might be compiling a book of polemical essays under the title of *The Establishment*. But already their search for a cause seemed dated, a vestigial throwback to the black days of Jimmy Porter and Eden's War. For despite youthful irreverence and social emancipation, the country was now politically dominated by one man—the 64-year-old "Edwardian" father-figure of Harold Macmillan, uncle by marriage of a Duke and presiding over a Cabinet a third of which consisted of fellow Old Etonians.

On 3 November 1958, the cartoonist Vicky moved from the *Daily Mirror* to the London *Evening Standard*. In a world increasingly shadowed by the H-Bomb and the ambiguities of affluence, Vicky's simple progressive moralities were now finding their most confident touch. One of his favorite motifs was the nightmare jungle of the property speculators; another, the floral-hatted Tory ladies and moustached neo-Blimps of the Old Guard, eternally baying for violence. But it was on 6 November, just three days after joining the *Evening Standard*, that he unveiled his most successful creation—Supermac, the wonder Prime Minister, whose prestidigitation enabled him to get away with anything. Despite the irony, it was the implied if unwilling admiration which stuck.

For England in that "dream stage" of new prosperity, Macmillan was an ideal shepherd. The country wanted political calm—he gave it the image of wise and unflappable authority. In a meretricious age he was an actor with an unashamed touch of fraudulence, his most familiar public mannerism, the smile with tongue in cheek. Politically shrewd, highly literate but by no means averse to a racy Americanism, he had established a personal sway over the House of Commons, his Party, and eventually the country, unequaled since the wartime Churchill. And above all, while his country was still in painful adjustment to its reduced place in the world, with his constant posing on the world stage, his white-fur-hatted visit to Moscow, his striving toward the "Summit," he played out a kind of charade of past greatness that by its very self-parody made the final adjustment easier for the country to bear. It was only appropriate that it should have been a founder member of the CND who christened him "Supermac"; just as it was one of his outwardly most scornful opponents in the Commons, Nye Bevan, who called him "Macwonder." For by 1959 Macmillan had become a "dream symbol" to

145

friends and opposition alike. The essence of a dream symbol being that it carries no "value"; it is merely an image that for the time being is hypnotic, both for those who profess to dislike it and spend a disproportionate amount of their time explaining why, and for those who find it irresistible until such time as they become bored and seek another.

For the time being, nothing could touch him. Not the colonial troubles which broke out in Nyasaland in early 1959, nor the 620,000 unemployed in the early months of the year. Even the troubles in Cyprus, which had provided the previous year with a growing *obbligato* of distant violence, were now brought to a miraculous end. The summer of 1959 was the finest of the century. And as England basked through cloudless months and the "consumer boom" reached still greater heights, the troubled mood of 1955–1958 seemed far away indeed. For Supermac the omens for the coming election in October could not have been happier. The country had truly "never had it so good." And as if to rub in the moral to his own Cabinet, he passed round copies of the *Queen*'s "Boom" issue at one of their last pre-election meetings.

The election campaign was, like so many, described as "dull," and there was much talk in the press of "apathy." There was also, for the first time, widespread and self-conscious use of the new jargon of advertising men and market researchers, particularly of the word "image." The Labour Party, like any group of politicians far from office, fell back on the vain comforts of a mild paranoia—weakly protesting at the "immorality" and uneven spread of affluence, and the unfairness of the Conservatives' unprecedented £1,000,000 advertising campaign. Even so, their own campaign, with its series of *"Tonight*-style" television broadcasts (under the aegis of Anthony Wedgwood Benn) and its glossy pre-election pamphlet *The Future Labour Offers You,* compiled by the staff of the *Daily Mirror* with the aid of Mr. Harold Wilson, and full of references to "the age of the Sputnik," the "age of automation and atomic power," "scientific progress," and "Tory stagnation," was itself tinged with many of the latest tricks of mass communications make-believe.

But the slogan "Life Is Better under the Conservatives" was invincible. On 8 October, the Government was confirmed in power with its majority again doubled—the first time that any Party had increased its representation at four successive elections. It seemed like the millennium—and for months and even years ahead, many commentators were to assume, almost as a law of nature, that the Conservatives would be in power for several elections to come. On the Monday after the election, much attention was paid to the *Daily Mirror*'s symbolic and somewhat ostentatious dropping from its masthead of the once-proud slogan "Forward with the People"—which had stood there since two months before Labour's great victory of 1945.

When, in its last issue of 1959, the *Economist* looked back on the decade which ten years before had seemed so dismal in prospect it was filled with complacent amazement. Britain had been lifted from the shadows into what seemed a new promised land of peace, progress, and abundance. Could ever the future have looked more golden?

Yet in some profound sense, the election had been a landmark. It had been a final recognition that the age of affluence had arrived, altering the whole nature of England's political and social life. The *Daily Mirror*'s post-election gesture had been typical of the mood—as was to be its introduction of a City page, to acquaint its 13 million largely working-class readers with the mysteries of the stock market. Altogether the notion of progress and modernity, the social pressures to change and get "up-to-date" were beginning to take on a new, more self-conscious, more desperate tinge.

Already this more febrile note had been sounded during the election itself, with the evidence, for instance, that the Liberal revival was far from dead; with Jo Grimond flying the country by helicopter and urging an end to the "sterile Party stalemate" and for Britain to "get into Europe" and titillating the middle-class fancy to be daring and respectably "progressive" with his call for "a new radicalism" in politics.* It was sounded even louder in the Labour Party's election post-mortem—the dispute being conducted almost entirely between the Party's Oxford-educated intellectuals. On the one side were such old-guard Oxford Socialists of the thirties as Michael Foot, Barbara Castle, and Richard Crossman, the erstwhile Bevanites clinging blindly to the dogmas of their youth. On the other were the increasingly frantic "modernizers," such figures as Anthony Crosland, Douglas Jay, and Hugh Gaitskell himself—who chose to make the symbol of his campaign the revision of the sacred nationalizing Clause Four of the Party Constitution: their cry was to drag the Party "kicking and screaming into the twentieth century" (even though it had only been founded in 1900), rid it of its "cloth cap image," to spend more money on advertising and even, perhaps, most desperate of all, to change its name—to something more smoothly consonant with the findings of market research.

As we have seen in an earlier chapter, as England stood on the threshold of the "crazy sixties" it was by no means only in politics that such straining after a headier pace was beginning to show. There was, for instance, the rising tempo of London's social life. It was the time when, as we have seen, the new-style *Queen* began to reflect and articulate the spirit of the times, with its new hectic headlines, its cult of the teenagers and the contempt for age and convention exemplified by its feature "A Bad Year for Dodos." There were signs too of a stronger "beat" and a new mass excitement returning

---

* The Liberal vote of over 1,500,000, double that of 1955, had been significantly high in a number of "new middle class" suburbs, such as Finchley, Cheadle, and Orpington—areas like those where, in America, John Kennedy was to do particularly well in the presidential election of a year hence. One Liberal manifesto of the time contained such phrases as: "Many of you are *irritated* and *bored* by politicians . . . the truth is that these [Labour and Conservative] politicians are *out of date* . . . with a *young, practical leader* in Jo Grimond the *new* Liberals have brought *excitement* back into the political scene . . . *realistic* . . . *progressive* . . . *relevant* . . . *exciting* etc."

to pop music, partly through the growing craze for a processed traditional jazz, that in the summer of 1960 was to be associated with huge, excitable mobs of fancy-dressed "ravers" and several outbreaks of rioting. Early in the new year, the *News of the World* provided a reflection of the new moral climate in its serialization of the memoirs of the actress Diana Dors. These *histoires,* which could still in 1960 be widely regarded as somewhat "shocking," dwelt in particular on the voyeuristic taste of her former husband Dennis Hamilton for two-way bedroom mirrors—one of which he had installed at their Thames-side house near Cliveden, and another in his London mews cottage. Among Hamilton's acquaintances, both of whom were later at different times to install their girlfriends in the same mews cottage, were the property speculator Peter Rachman and Stephen Ward, the fashionable osteopath.

These were all signs of the times—as was the evidence in the first week of the new decade that the members of the Campaign for Nuclear Disarmament were also beginning to hunger for more violent sensation, with a demonstration at Harrington air field which ended with seventy-nine of the demonstrators imprisoned in Leicester gaol. As the *Economist* commented:

> For the first time since the days of the militant suffragettes a group of people are actively seeking to be sent to prison as a means of political protest.

Indeed the CND had come a long way since the first march of two years before. Its annual Easter pilgrimage was becoming a national institution, its closing rally in 1959 having drawn almost fifty thousand people. Still at the head of the movement were the old faithfuls: Bertrand Russell, left-wing Socialist politicians, and progressive priests. But behind them were not only the leavening of earnest idealists, but also a strange and growing assortment of adolescents, beatniks, students, and ravers, many of whom were confessedly stringing along with the CND "just for a giggle" and because it was becoming a teenage craze to wear the badge and "belong."

All this acceleration beneath the surface was, in short, something much deeper than a passing political tremor; it marked the symptoms of a returning unrest that was eventually to prove far more violent and prolonged than that of four years before—that was to hang and form in the air for a time, without being really noticed.

It was a mood, in fact, which in 1960 extended far outside England, and that was already manifesting itself most prominently in America, where it had already begun to show as far back as the middle fifties, with the popularity of such books as *The Organization Man, The Man in the Grey Flannel Suit, The Hidden Persuaders,* the paperback version of David Riesman's *The Lonely Crowd,* and *The Power Elite,* all in different ways attacking conformity, the complacency of the Eisenhower years, the power of Madison Avenue, the big corporations, and the Pentagon, the collective constituents of America's conservative Establishment. It had been vividly expressed in 1958 in Professor Galbraith's *The Affluent Society,* with its scorn for the "conventional wisdom" of Eisenhower's America, the years of the "bland leading the bland." It had shown in the protest against social conformity of the "Beat" movement, and in the new wave of American satirists and "sick" humorists, such as Mort Sahl and Lenny Bruce. And nowhere was this sense of a new age more clearly crystallized than in an article written for the January 1960 edition of *Esquire* by Professor Arthur Schlesinger, Jr., under the title of "The New Mood in Politics," with its castigation of the fifties as a decade of "passivity," "acquiescence," and "torpor," while now, he claimed, increasing numbers of Americans "were waiting for a trumpet to sound," in the hope that the sixties would be:

> spirited, articulate, inventive, incoherent, turbulent, with energy shooting off wildly in all directions. Above all, there will be a sense of motion, of leadership and of hope.

Already when, on 3 February 1960, Harold Macmillan made his famous "Wind of Change" speech in South Africa, he was speaking for the temper of the times more starkly than he could have imagined. Even in Africa itself, of which he was speaking, events were moving faster than anyone could have judged; when he spoke the Sharpeville massacre was only six weeks away, the first assassination attempt on Dr. Verwoerd only two months, and the beginning of the long drawn-out catastrophe of the Congo, only five. While as for Britain's own still very substantial African empire, the young Conservative Bow Group was later in the year to be criticized as irresponsibly "radical" for suggesting that Kenya alone should be given independence as early as 1970.

Curiously enough, another cause of disquiet in Britain in the early months of 1960 was the economic boom. For, as the year progressed, it was becoming evident that the country was running up its largest balance of payments deficit since the last days of the Labour Government. Furthermore, the restlessness was spreading to the trade unions, which through 1959 had been quieter than at any other time of Conservative rule. In February, a national rail strike was only bought off at the last minute by the personal intervention of the Prime Minister; and the subsequent wage demands from other unions not wishing to be left behind introduced the certainty that further inflation would follow.

Economic observers were only too aware that the "crisis," when it came, would be the fourth of its kind and possibly the worst in a decade. Even normally self-confident businessmen were losing their trust in established ways—and as these jitters increased, so many of the ideas which had first been crystallized by Andrew Shonfield in his *British Economic Policy since the War* began to pass into general currency. The "conservatism" of the trade unions in particular had become so widely accepted, that it even became the subject of two of the year's most successful films, *The Angry Silence* and *I'm All Right Jack*. The more technical catch-phrases of "investment" and "growth" were clutched at by businessmen and leader-writers alike. Both economists and politicians in 1960 began to gaze around the world in search of images of success and "dynamism." They became hynotized by the miracles of the German and Japanese shipbuilding industries, which were now leading the world because back in the early fifties they had invested in new plants. They were hypnotized by the miracle of the French who, only four years before, had seemed more down and out than Britain, but who now appeared to have recovered their self-respect under President de Gaulle and to be enjoying a "planned" boom. And above all they were hypnotized by the miracle of the Common Market itself, which at its foundation three years before they had largely ignored and which, even as lately as the election campaign, had, except by the Liberals, hardly been mentioned. But now, for many of the anxious, the vision of "Europe" suddenly began to loom as the dream solution to all Britain's economic troubles.*

Not that Britain's troubles were a matter of economics alone. In April, the virtual abandonment of Blue Streak finally undermined any plausible pretense she might have to be an independent nuclear power. And in May, with the sensational collapse of the Paris Summit Conference, at last so painfully achieved, Macmillan's own dream image as world statesman and bringer of peace began its long fade into reality. Grain by grain, beneath the edifice of Supermac's proud tower, the sands were shifting. By midsummer, only nine months after his great election triumph, the mind of the Prime Minister too was beginning to turn to thoughts of some large and historic gesture by which his country, his Party, and above all perhaps his Premier-

---

* As might be expected, and as a foretaste of their domination of the "What's Wrong With Britain" cult that was to emerge later, the European "dream" was particularly attractive to many members of the New Oxford Group. On 30 July 1960, the magazine *Time and Tide,* then enjoying a brief progressive revival under the ownership of the Rev. Timothy Beaumont and the editorship of John Thompson (both members of the New Oxford Group), published a typically vehement call by Lord Altrincham for Britain to join Europe and abandon the Commonwealth, that *"verbal gimmick," "vain dream,"* "of all the *relics* that *gather dust* and *resist* the daylight in *Britannia's mansion* . . . perhaps the most *pernicious"* and which had not turned out to be "the *dynamic* association of like-minded states I had hoped it would become."

ship might ultimately be saved. Already on 11 June, one of the leading journalistic proponents of Britain's entry into Europe, the *Economist,* had observed:

> Slowly, tentatively, like a bather in a chilly sea, the British Government is screwing up its courage to decide whether to attempt a full-scale plunge into Europe. By its step by step advance, it has already immersed enough of its body to take a traditionalist's breath away.

When, in a Government reshuffle on 27 July, Mr. Macmillan raised the 14th Earl of Home from comparative obscurity to become his Foreign Secretary, the press was too much amazed at what the *Daily Mirror* described as "the most reckless political appointment since the Roman Emperor Caligula made his favourite horse a consul" to observe the importance of Mr. Edward Heath's appointment as Home's second-in-command—with special responsibility for Britain's relations with the continent of Europe. Indeed, the new appointments were more portentous than they could have seemed at the time. For they also included, apart from Mr. Selwyn Lloyd's move to the Exchequer, the promotion to the War Office of John Profumo (Oxford, late 1930's).

Thus by the summer of 1960, the surface calm was already flecked with unease. For the time being, however, in a summer which had begun almost as fine and cloudless as that of the year before, such speculations and manœuvers and subterranean rumblings were still only distant portents. Despite a gentle rise in Bank Rate, the great economic boom was still at its height, while Britain's social transformation roared on.

In London, that point where the hereditary attitudes of the upper- and upper-middle-class young were most obviously crumbling into a new freedom, the smart, quasi-bohemian demimonde that was to be associated with Chelsea bistros and the *Queen* magazine and John Michael shirts from the King's Road was becoming increasingly prominent.

A landmark in its emergence had been, on 13 January, the marriage of Lady Pamela Mountbatten, a cousin of the Queen and daughter of the last Viceroy of India, to Mr. David Hicks—a thirty-year-old interior decorator, educated at Charter-house and the Central School of Art, whose flamboyant and highly colored "designs for living" were soon to establish his reputation in the drawing rooms of Kensington and Chelsea. Only five months later, an even more significant landmark was the Royal Wedding, surrounded by all the pomp of Westminster Abbey, of Princess Margaret to *Queen*'s bohe-mian photographer Anthony Armstrong-Jones. England and society had traveled a long way since those days only five years before when Princess Margaret had been more or less forbidden to marry a dashing (if divorced) officer of the Royal Air Force. Amid the national rejoicing, only the *Economist,* once again, allowed itself a word of warning:

> A wise Court, in Bagehot's view, is one "which stands aloof from the rest of the London world, and which has but slender relations with the more amusing parts of it . . . for the light nothings of the drawing-room and the grave things of the office are as different from one another as two human occupations can be" . . . the task of all concerned is to show that the English social revolution is by now old enough and wise enough and flexible enough to treat this sort of problem as a challenge to be met.

Also at last emerging into its own, in the same year that the French *nouvelle vague* and Antonioni's *L'Avventura* first arrived in England, was the "neo-realist" movement which over the next three years was to dominate the English cinema. One of the most widely hailed films of 1960 was Karel Reisz's version of *Saturday Night and Sunday Morning,* produced by Osborne and Richardson's Woodfall Films. Once again, it was the young, upper-middle-class intellectual world that acclaimed this new image of "lower class vitality"—and perhaps the film's most enthusiastic greeting came in an almost absurdly excited review from the film critic of the *Queen,* the Old Etonian Francis Wyndham (Oxford, war years):

With *Saturday Night and Sunday Morning,* the British cinema really has grown up at last: indeed one might argue that this is the first British film ever made. It is about working class life today . . . *fresh, sharp* vision . . . *exciting* . . . *exciting* etc., etc.

It was the first harbinger of the series including *A Taste of Honey, The Loneliness of the Long Distance Runner, A Kind of Loving,* and *Billy Liar* (both written by Keith Waterhouse and Willis Hall) that between 1960 and 1963 was to create a new, sexually and socially "frank" and "honest" image for the English cinema.

It might seem strange that, at the very moment when the image of "lower class vitality" was thus entering on an even more powerful vogue, the revisionists in the Labour Party should be seeking to emancipate their Party from a supposedly fatal identification with the working class. Perhaps the clue to the paradox was contained in the fact that Karel Reisz's "neo-realistic" style of film-making was to serve him to equally good purpose in making television commercials, his "hard" and "realistic" photography and "exciting" choice of angles being equally effective whether used to glamorize the smoky skyline of Nottingham or a bowl of cornflakes sparkling in the sun. For the truth was that Woodfall's picture of industrial England had as little to do with the vision of Keir Hardie or Orwell's road to Wigan Pier as Teddy Boys or supermarkets. Albert Finney's portrayal of Arthur Seaton, with his cupboard full of suits and his aggressive egocentricity, was as much part of the new English social revolution as the hero of Colin MacInnes's *Absolute Beginners* or the clothes of John Stephen, at that time just opening his fourth shop in Carnaby Street; a dream projection of that "sixties" modernity, based on a "tough" and youthful fantasy, which the Labour Party so conspicuously lacked.

In view of the later dramatic reversal of the images of the major parties, it is now curious to recall the extent to which in 1960, as was shown by their sweeping successes in local elections and their gain of a seat from Labour in the first by-election of the new Parliament, it was Mr. Macmillan's Conservative Party which was most firmly identified with the changing face of British life. In a Penguin Special, *Must Labour Lose?* the market researcher Mark Abrams found, in the early months of the year, that:

> Labour Party supporters see the Conservatives as exercising a much greater attraction for ambitious people, middle class people, young people, office workers and scientists . . . the image of the Labour Party . . . is one which is increasingly obsolete in terms of contemporary Britain . . . today's young people are more likely to be Conservative than Labour.

It might have seemed that the Labour Party was almost the only element in Britain not being carried along on the accelerating tide.

In the autumn of that year, the discontents which had been plaguing the Labour Party throughout the fifties finally came to a head in the stormiest episode British politics had known since Suez.

The only remote parallel in recent politics to the Labour Party's crisis in 1960 was the temporary take-over of the Republican Party by the followers of Senator Goldwater at San Francisco in 1964. The equivalent to the Cow Palace Convention was the Labour Party's annual Conference held at the seaside resort of Scarborough. The part of the Goldwaterites was played by a number of the leading trade unions, on which the Labour Party depended for the greater part of its financial support.

What gave the episode its similarly unreal, and in retrospect almost incomprehensible, character was the fact that, during the summer of 1960, the leaderships of these trade unions were suddenly swept, as by a virus, with a sudden conversion to the neutralist policies of the Campaign for Nuclear Disarmament. For the CND, 1960 had already seen support swelling on a greater scale than ever before. Even so, the chance that they might actually take over one of Britain's two major parties was one which, at the beginning of the year, would have seemed inconceivable. The explanation, however, was simple. For it was not so much a newfound preoccupation with the peace of the world and the perils of the hydrogen bomb which had suddenly overcome the trade union leaders (headed by Frank Cousins)—as a sudden determination to bring down the man they identified with all the Labour Party's troubles, the upper-middle-class intellectual Hugh Gaitskell.

By the time of the Conference, held in a highly explosive atmosphere at Scarborough in October, the anti-Gaitskell faction had gathered sufficient support to force through a motion on Britain's defense which, if taken seriously, would have meant committing any future Labour Government to a virtually neutralist foreign policy—giving up the H-Bomb and withdrawing from NATO and all her military alliances. The highlight of the Conference was a speech delivered by the grim-faced Gaitskell, promising that he and his friends in the Parliamentary Labour Party would "fight, fight and fight again" to restore sanity to "the party we love." Among those who ostentatiously failed to rise during the standing ovation which followed was one of the Labour leader's closest Parliamentary colleagues. In the words of Bernard Levin, in the *Spectator*:

> "I am afraid," said one who had been close to Mr. Gaitskell throughout the crisis, "that we must be prepared for Mr. Wilson to behave very badly when the vote is over."

For some members of the CND, the triumph of Scarborough was only incitement to even more violent sensation. Before the month was out Bertrand Russell announced the setting up of a new CND splinter group, the Committee of 100. It marked the final breach between those members of the movement who still thought it could best win support by demonstrating quietly and "responsibly," and those, more representative of the spirit of the times, who longed for more dramatic gratification. Among the new Committee of 100's members were John Osborne, Lindsay Anderson, Vanessa Redgrave (an actress who was later to marry Tony Richardson), the novelist

John Braine, and Shelagh Delaney. In furtherance of the cause of international peace, these artists and intellectuals now pledged themselves, "if necessary," to large-scale breaches of the law of the land.

For the Labour Party as a whole, however, the experience of Scarborough had been something of an "explosion into reality." When the Parliamentary Party reassembled in the autumn, Mr. Harold Wilson did indeed "behave badly," by making a bid to replace Mr. Gaitskell in the customarily uncontested leadership election. But already the fever was dying down, and Gaitskell was confirmed in office by 166 votes to 81.

There had nevertheless been one development at Scarborough, almost obscured by the Conference's central drama, that was eventually to prove of even greater significance. Little attention had been paid to the Conference's acceptance of a new document on Party policy, largely drawn up by Peter Shore (Liverpool and post-war Cambridge), the young head of the Party's research department, and modishly titled *Labour in the Sixties*. For the first time, the document suggested an orientation of the Party's appeal away from traditional Socialism and towards a regrouping around the bright images of economic "growth" and, even more important, the "scientific revolution." There was no Labour leader in whose subconscious this language struck such a thrilling chord as the man who, back in the fifties, had once described Labour's party organization as being still "at the penny-farthing stage in the jet-propelled era," and who had been fascinated by the suggestive jargon of technology ever since he had been President of the Board of Trade back in the late forties— Peter Shore's official superior as Chairman of the Labour Research Department, Harold Wilson.

With the Labour Party thus stricken, and his own Party girding itself to meet the country's long-term problems on a radical and dramatic scale, it might have seemed in the autumn of 1960 that, despite his setbacks earlier in the year, Harold Macmillan was still riding high. Nevertheless at this moment the first portent appeared that the increasingly aggressive hunger of a certain type of young politician and journalist for "change," "action," and political excitement was turning into something that could not be met just by measures alone, however radical. It was becoming a need which went much deeper—for something that no "Edwardian" father figure in his sixties could provide, however imaginative or shrewd. The first full-dress statement of this new mood appeared in an article in *Encounter* in October 1960; its author was Anthony Crosland, now returned to the Commons as Labour MP for Grimsby; and the article contained such significance for the future of English politics, both in its message, and even more in its use of language, that it is worth quoting at some length:

> A *dogged resistance to change* now *blankets* every *segment* of our *national life*. A *middle-aged conservatism, parochial* and *complacent,* has settled over the country; and it is hard to find a single sphere in which Britain is *pre-eminently* in the *forefront*. Our production and export performance is *almost the poorest of any advanced industrial country;* and in individual industries one constantly finds that the only *dynamic* firm is controlled by an American, a Canadian, an Irishman or a refugee. The trade union movement shares with the Labour Party a *profound conservatism of outlook.* Our Parliament and Civil Service . . . are in need of *drastic modernisation.* Oxford and Cambridge [and] much of our technical education are equally *backward.* We cling to every *outmoded scrap* of *national sovereignty,* continue to play the *obsolete* role of an *imperial* power, and *fail to adjust* to the *new dynamic* Europe. Our *deplorable* post-war architecture and city planning demonstrate a *failure of nerve* in the face of *contemporary cultural problems* . . . our transport system is no more *antiquated* than our licensing laws, our attitude to homosexuality, British football or the Labour Party constitution.
>
> No doubt we still lead the world in certain *traditional* spheres—merchant banking, classical scholarship, trooping the colour or sailing the Atlantic single-handed. But wherever *innovation* is required, we see a *frightful paralysis of the will* . . . *complacent ignorance* . . . *colossal resistance to change* . . . *complacent, sluggish, hide-bound* . . . *ossified,*

middle-aged, stagnant, complacent, class-conscious conservatism etc., etc., etc.

Here was the creed which over the next three years was to become the dominant force in English politics. In a previous chapter, we have seen how, between 1960 and 1962, the young upper-middle classes became the pace-makers of the English revolution: and in no respect was this more true than in the flowering of the cult of which Crosland's article was the perfect expression. All the key words and phrases were there. On the one hand, "complacent," "sluggish," "stagnant," "obsolete," "resistance to change," "paralysis of the will," and "failure of nerve." On the other, "drastic," "modernisation," "innovation," "change," and, above all, "dynamic." It was the chant of the neurosis that could be summed up in the years to come under the all-purpose phrase, "What's Wrong With Britain." And it was only a month after Crosland's article appeared that this growing hunger for "dynamism" was to find its dream hero, shining like the sun itself. For it was on the same restless surge in the United States, on a tide of such slogans as "We must get America moving," "a Tory country is a tired country," and "the need for dynamism," that on 8 November John F. Kennedy was elected President.

In President Kennedy, the general longing for youth, for toughness, for efficiency, for nonconformity, and for excitement that since the middle fifties had been welling up in the collective subconscious of America, Britain, and Europe found its supreme focus. As Norman Mailer, the leading philosopher of "hip" America, excitedly proclaimed in *Esquire,* "Superman Comes to Supermarket." Not since the youthful Napoleon, had any man so captured the dreams of half the world.

The influence of the Kennedy "image" and of the trappings of Kennedy-ism on the climate of British politics was to be enormous. Even now, within weeks of his election, an opinion poll showed that this fresh wind blowing from across the Atlantic had almost erased the general anti-American feeling that, only two months

before, had been expressed by 47 percent of the British people. But
in late 1960, it was still to be some time before the full impact of
the "New Frontier" and "whiz kids" and the "Hundred Days," and
of the "bright, crisp Kennedy style" really began to sink in on British
political life. In the weeks following his election, only one group saw
itself mirrored in the Kennedy image. The "new" Liberal Party,
with its "relevant" policies, its "new young leader," and what even
sober political commentators were now learning to describe as its
"slick, well-oiled machine," saw the new President's election as a
projection of their fondest dreams. One Young Liberal Association
even sent off a telegram congratulating Kennedy on being elected as
"Liberal President." And it was certainly true that, in a group of
by-elections falling shortly afterwards, the Liberals once again im-
proved their vote coming in second place in no less than four out of
six; even if it was not now the Conservatives they were overhauling,
but Mr. Crosland's dilapidated Labour Party.

There was a further respect in which the advent of the new President was to influence English life, less obvious but in the long run
almost equally powerful—and that was the way in which the aura of
Kennedy-ism was to prove the final catalyst in the emergence of a
new style in English journalism. The first example of the style, which
was closely related to and flourished in the same journals as "What's
Wrong With Britain-ism," appeared in the *Observer* of 19 March, in
an article by Michael Davie (New Oxford Group), inaugurating a
series entitled "Washington on the Move." The piece was appropriately headed with a quotation from Kennedy himself: "The Presi-
dency needs someone creative and dynamic." The New Frontier
Washington it portrayed was a dynamic dream world, painted in
such phrases as "intense vigor," "cracking pace," "mind bubbling with
questions." Everyone described had to be built up with some image
—"tall and determined . . . with a square-cut face," "a heavy faced
man." In addition to the stereotyped epithets and the larger than life
characters, another characteristic element was the use of trivial detail,
and of "tough," throwaway anecdotal asides:

"Hell," said one old hand this week, "the people still think it's Christmas."

Over the following months and years, this mechanically make-believe use of language, indiscriminately transforming the commonplace into a preconceived image of the remarkable, was, particularly in the *Observer,* the *Sunday Times,* and their respective color supplements, to become the most distinctive journalistic reflection of the spirit of the age.

And so, with the inauguration of the new President, began 1961. The tenor of the coming months and years was foreshadowed in the murder, three days before Kennedy's inauguration, of Patrice Lumumba, the most striking figure to have emerged out of the chaos in the Congo. All over the world in the early months of 1961 the process of change was becoming more heady and more violent. On 15 March, Dr. Verwoerd announced that South Africa was leaving the Commonwealth. On 12 April, the day after the beginning of the trial of Adolf Eichmann in Israel, the Russians launched the first man into space. Five days later, as the climax to Kennedy's first Hundred Days, came the disastrous and abortive invasion of Cuba. Four days after that came the news of the Generals' revolt in Algeria. In May, the battle for Negro rights in America moved into a new, aggressive phase with the first invasion of the southern states by the so-called Freedom Riders. And from the Dominican Republic, with the assassination of President Trujillo, came the news of the second killing of a national leader in five months.

In Britain, the incipient turbulence of 1960 was quickening. As inflation worsened, even the Prime Minister's son, Maurice Macmillan (Oxford, late 1930's), Conservative MP for Halifax, complained on 6 February that for years the country had looked to the Government for economic leadership in vain. In the same month, Bertrand Russell's new Committee of 100 for the first time showed its strength, with an albeit peaceful "sit-down" of four thousand demonstrators outside the Ministry of Defence. Also in February, at the annual exhibition of Young Contemporaries, the movement which had been germinating among young British artists finally surfaced in a bright shower of the dream-images of pop art. The sociological significance of this event was as considerable as its promise of a major new artistic fashion; for whereas the stream of new novelists and playwrights was showing signs of drying up, the pop artists represented a younger generation from those same areas and social backgrounds as had produced the writers of the fifties. They marked the advance guard of a new generation emerging in English life that was the first to have spent its formative years in the new, more prosperous, Americanized and image-conscious atmosphere of the years since 1955.* Meanwhile, in the same early months of 1961, the What's Wrong With Britain movement and the clamor for "dynamism" gathered way in newspapers, magazines, and even books. A Penguin Special, *The Stagnant Society,* by a journalist, Michael Shanks (New Oxford Group), sold 60,000 copies, while another, *What's Wrong with the Unions,* launched a whole series under the all-embracing title *What's Wrong with . . . .* The vogue was almost entirely the creation of the New Oxford Group (although in the *New Statesman,* Mr. Wilson, catching the whiff of the times, published his own, rather more conventionally phrased "Four Year Plan" for Britain) and the clamor was particularly strong in those newspapers where the New Oxford Group was by now strongly entrenched, such as the *Observer* and the *Sunday Times,* under the guidance of its new Political and Economic Editor, William Rees-Mogg. It was also catching on with the glossy magazines, *Queen* and *About Town,* who could now throw in alongside their photographs by David Bailey and Terence Donovan, such headlines as "Wanted—A Minister of Planning" and "A Shot in the Arm," featuring the "tonic men for a country half-asleep," photo-

---

* At about this same time, of course, the "pop art" movement was coming to the surface in America, with the first major successes of Jasper Johns, Robert Rauschenberg, the British painter Richard Smith, and others.

graphed against a background of thrusting hypodermic syringes and a cartoon of fading Britannia. It was no accident that it was just these papers which were on the crest of a wave of young, upper-middle-class popularity, with their antennae out for any new excitement that happened to be in the air, whether joining the Common Market or candy-striped shirts, economic "growth" or features on leather-jacketed "ton up kids."

Even if their impatience occasionally led them into flights of fancy which were obviously wild, certainly the message of the "What's Wrong With Britain" journalists was clear enough. Britain was being "strangled" and "suffocated" by "complacency," "inefficiency," "outworn attitudes," "archaic institutions," the "class system," and "amateurism." The remedies, only too obvious, were "dynamism," "professionalism," "ruthless competition," "tough-mindedness," "more research," "more investment," "more roads," "monorails to speed Britain's traffic," more tough ruthless professionalism in every direction. But for all the chunky phraseology that Messrs. Rees-Mogg, Crosland, and their *confrères* were given to, the fact was that it all remained amazingly vague. For all the fearless assaults on "complacent managements," rarely if ever was such a complacent management actually named. For all the talk about the need for "classlessness" and an end to the "top jobs always going to the man with the right tie and the right accent," it almost always came from top journalists with the right public school and university background. And certain passages of the litany began to appear again and again—such as the charge, invariably unspecified, that "too much British sales literature is going to South America written in English" —like incantatory runes, all part of the same dynamic dream.

Every collective dream demands not only a focus for its aggression, however, but also dream-figures to which it can pay homage. Such was the inherent unreality of the whole exercise that most such objects of sycophancy had to be at a convenient distance from everyday familiarity—abroad, for instance, like the Common Market or the New Frontier dream world of Kennedy's Washington. But there were rare occasions when such stray suns were to be found in the English heaven—one such in 1961 being BBC Television.

There were two chief reasons why BBC Television should have developed such an aura at this time. The first, as part of the growing obsession with the apparatus of image-making, was simply that the internal workings of television, as the newest and most powerful of all the media, were beginning to exercise a special glamor as such— particularly in the minds of certain newspaper journalists, who were only too aware of the extent to which this Big Brother had already stolen the limelight. The second, more specific reason was the extent to which the "new" BBC itself, under its progressive new Director-General, Hugh Carleton-Greene (Oxford, 1930's), could be painted as the very image of "dynamic" vitality, in contrast to its stuffy, Establishment days before commercial competition.

Despite the fact that the BBC had by now entered the battle for ratings almost as unashamedly as its commercial rivals, the pride of the "What's Wrong With Britain" press were the three big "prestige" programs (all of which had in fact been well established before Mr. Carleton-Greene took over in 1960); *Panorama,* Huw Wheldon's *Monitor,* which was praised for instance by the *Observer* for the "purism" which had given the program its:

> *attack* and *dignity* . . . Wheldon has drawn around him a *gifted young team* who show a certain *stylistic perfectionism,*

and *Tonight,* the "irreverence" of which had been so successful that Donald Baverstock had already been promoted to the post of Assistant Controller of Television Programmes. In the *Spectator,* summing up the BBC's prospects, Peter Forster (New Oxford Group) described Baverstock as "marvellously dynamic," "entirely televisual," and "a self-propelled dynamo," and forecast that

> the practical future of BBC–TV probably depends on the axis of power recently formed between Stuart Hood and Donald Baverstock.

He had little doubt in 1961 that that future would be bright indeed.

Despite this mounting frenzy, the face of England's prosperity remained unbroken. In his April budget, the Chancellor of the Exchequer Selwyn Lloyd even granted a major concession to the most prosperous section of the community by raising the surtax level from £2000 to £5000. As spring turned into early summer, the dream bubble of Macmillan's England welled ever larger.

On 14 April, Mr. Paul Raymond, the proprietor of Soho's most luxurious strip-tease club, was charged with keeping a disorderly house. The Chairman of the London Sessions told him:

> Your establishment and others have been vying with each other to see what degree of disgustingness they can introduce to attract members from all classes who are only too ready, out of curiosity or lust, to see the filth portrayed in this establishment. This, I think, is the fourth or fifth case I have had, and this is by far and away the worst.

Mr. Raymond was fined £5000. But in London's new moral climate, it was a losing battle. The Revuebar stayed open—and the strip-tease clubs continued to proliferate. On 1 May, the second part of the new Betting and Gaming Act came into force—adding betting shops to bingo to make up what still no one foresaw would turn into a gigantic gambling boom. At the same time, another in a succession of major spy cases, this one involving the double-agent George Blake, broke into the headlines—and it was perhaps a measure of these strained new times that on 3 May Blake was sentenced to the longest term of imprisonment ever awarded by a British court.

The Conservatives were still well ahead of Labour in the opinion polls—as they had been since the summer of 1958. In the local elections in May they won a landslide total of 442 seats, the Liberals coming up fast behind with gains of 200 (their eighth year of net gains in succession), while the Labour Party lost over 600. But like a river that appears to speed up its flow the nearer it approaches the edge of a waterfall, the revolution with which Harold Macmillan had but two years before so firmly identified his Party, now seemed to be rushing on almost out of control.

It is a familiar pattern of history that, on the eve of revolutionary crises, the established order veers erratically between liberal concessions, and recklessly reactionary steps which seem calculated to cast it in the most unfavorable light, and to hasten its own destruction. Certainly by the summer of 1961 there were signs that Mr. Macmillan himself was beginning to draw back from the world his Government had played its part in bringing about—as in his Government appointments he showed an increasing preference for hereditary noblemen, subconscious links with a more gracious and ordered past. Following his elevation of the Fourteenth Earl of Home, the previous summer he had on 28 October appointed his nephew, the Eleventh Duke of Devonshire, to be an under-secretary at the Commonwealth Office. Another of his relations, his son's brother-in-law David Ormsby Gore, heir to the barony of Harlech, he was shortly to appoint as Ambassador to Washington. There were already two other Earls and a Marquess in the upper reaches of Government. And when, on 1 July 1961, Lord Cobbold stepped down as Governor of the Bank of England, he was replaced by the Third Earl of Cromer.

All of this, of course, only fired the "What's Wrong With Britain" journalists to new frenzy, particularly when they could contrast it with the dream picture from across the Atlantic of glamorous whiz kids and intellectuals drafted in at all levels to serve on the New Frontier. A particular cliché of the "What's Wrong With Britain" writers became nostalgia for the war-time days when such academics as Hugh Gaitskell and Oliver Franks had been called in to aid the Civil Service, expressed in such articles as that by the psephologist David Butler (New Oxford Group) in the *Daily Telegraph* of 9 May 1961, entitled "Too Little Change at the Top." A special target was the "stuffy" and "tradition-bound" Civil Service, which they pictured as being staffed largely by aging and upper-class classical scholars from ancient public schools and Balliol. In fact, as established by an analysis published in 1960, nineteen out of the thirty most senior Civil Servants had been to grammar or other non-public schools, while very few had been classicists. But increasingly in

English life such realities were coming to be disregarded in favor of the preconceived image. And it was true that Mr. Macmillan's preference for aristocrats—again regardless of the fact that many of them justified their appointments by their performance—could hardly have been better calculated to confirm the New Oxford Group's most fondly held prejudices. Indeed, at the beginning of July 1961, it was possible not only to portray Britain as firmly dominated by a hereditary Establishment—but also, that she was more so dominated than at any time in the previous sixty years.

The month began with yet another crisis in the Middle East, the threat by Iraq to invade the tiny sheikdom of Kuwait, from which Britain bought 40 percent of her oil. On 2 July, the British Government began an airlift of 6000 soldiers into the Kuwait desert. Although the invasion threat never materialized, the operation was from a British point of view far from a success. Troops fainted in dozens from the sweltering heat and in London the operation's direction was marked by constant rivalry between the Ministry of Defence and John Profumo's War Ministry. On Saturday 8 July, in the middle of a sultry weekend, Profumo left the strain of the crisis, which was already dying down, to join a weekend party at Cliveden, the Thames-side seat of Lord Astor. It was late that evening that he met the Soviet Naval Attaché, Eugene Ivanov, and Christine Keeler, who were spending the weekend at the nearby cottage rented by Stephen Ward.*

* The consequences of this event were later to be so blown out of proportion that it is in order at this point to provide a short summary. During August 1961, the War Minister conducted a brief affair with Miss Keeler, meeting her on a handful of occasions, at the same time as she was having an equally irregular affair with the Russian *attaché* Ivanov. By the end of 1961, relations between Profumo and Miss Keeler had come to an end. There had been no orgies, no wild parties—just an unimpressive little private liaison, lasting not more than a few weeks. Why then was this little episode to become two years later the focus of a scandal attracting worldwide attention, and the center of a crisis which virtually spelled the end of the Conservative Government? The answer cannot simply be that Mr. Profumo had been running a security risk (although perhaps he had), or that he had broken the Seventh Commandment, in what was, after all, an increasingly permissive age (even Mr. Gladstone, that pillar

Meanwhile, throughout the month, it became apparent that the economic storm was on the point of breaking. The growing jitters about Britain's financial position had finally exploded in the heaviest run on the pound since 1949. On 25 July, the Government mustered all the paraphernalia to meet a major crisis. Machinery was set up to give the country for the first time some sort of "French-style" economic planning. A White Paper announced that, with an eye to "drastic" modernization and reform, inquiries would be set in train into two of Britain's most blatantly "inefficient" and "nineteenth century" industries, the railways and the mines. And on 31 July, Mr. Macmillan himself at last unveiled his Grand Design, his boldest gesture and his last throw—that Britain would be applying for membership of the European Economic Community.

From that moment on, the atmosphere of English life began to pass into a new and more hysterical phase.

---

of Victorian rectitude, claimed that eleven out of the twelve Prime Ministers he had known were guilty of adultery), or even that he was eventually to lie about his liaison to the House of Commons in March 1963. The real reason for the prominence of the Profumo affair was that by 1963 it became, almost by chance, the vehicle and focus for a much deeper and wider movement of social and political resentment, directed at the whole idea of an upper-class, Conservative Establishment which in 1963 was to enter its death-throes.

Chapter Seven

Every Dream Must Have Its Nightmare

"We are come to the place where, as I said, you would
see the wretched people who have lost the good of the
intellect" . . . here sighs, cries and deep wailings resounded
through the starless air, at first bringing tears to my eyes.
Strange tongues, horrible outcries, words of pain, tones of
anger, voices deep and hoarse . . . made a tumult which
echoes for ever through that tainted air, like the whirlwind eddies of desert sand.

DANTE
Inferno

Every Dream Must Have Its Nightmare

Macmillan, Kennedy and Khrushchev are the wickedest
people in the history of man.

BERTRAND RUSSELL, September 1961

If the intellectual has any function in society, it is to
preserve a cool and unbiased judgement in the face of all
solicitations to passion.

BERTRAND RUSSELL,
from his essay in *I Believe,* 1940

The ranks are drawn up and the air resounds with the
armourer's hammer. When battle is joined one can only
hope that blood will be drawn.

JONATHAN MILLER, on the forthcoming
opening of *The Establishment* club,
Observer, 1 October 1961

I'm one of those who feel that sex is a thoroughly good
thing, implanted by God. I'm not one of those who
belong to the generation who thought it was a sort of
smutty thing that you only talk about hush-hush.

DR. COGGAN, Archbishop of York,
talking to Adam Faith, BBC *Meeting Point,*
28 January 1962

The Liberals—oh yes, that's the new with-it Party, isn't it?
Young Surrey housewife to Liberal
canvasser, shortly after Orpington
by-election, March 1962

I expect I'll be dead by the time I'm thirty. We all will.
It's the strain, you know.

"A typical teenager in the sixties,"
profiled in *Queen,* 17 April 1962

From time to time, it would seem, some spirit of disorder grips the human race. An outbreak of hysteria in one country or area is matched by others. In the same weeks or months, international crises break out, politicians rant, bankers panic, teenagers riot. As Carl Jung wrote in his essay on "Archaic Man":

> A calf is born with two heads and five legs. In the next village a cock has laid an egg. An old woman has had a dream, a comet appears in the sky, there is a great fire in the nearest town and the following year a war breaks out. In this way history was always written from remote antiquity on down to the eighteenth century. This juxtaposition of facts, so meaningless to us, is significant and convincing, to primitive man. And, contrary to all expectation, he is right to find it so. His powers of observation can be trusted. From age-old experience he knows that such connections actually exist. *What seems to us a wholly senseless heaping up of single, haphazard occurrences—because we pay attention only to singular events and their particular causes*—is for primitive man a completely logical sequence of omens and of happenings indicated by them. It is a fatal outbreak of demonic power, showing itself in a thoroughly consistent way.

So alien to us is this comprehensive way of looking at human affairs, with our distrust of detailed "pattern-making," that I must just re-emphasize the lines above italicized. The particular strange occurrences listed by Dr. Jung may seem a trifle far-fetched or even trivial to our present way of life. But I am sure no one can dispute—to take an example on the grandest scale—that the years before the First World War were marked throughout industrial civilization by a peculiarly widespread unrest—expressing itself not only in political and industrial disorders, the rapid growth of socialist and communist movements, and the rising hysteria of the international arms race, but also in a remarkable acceleration of technical advance and in a series of revolutionary new departures in the arts. Can anyone doubt that the wars and rumors of wars of those years before

1914, the spate of assassinations, even such violent artistic innovations as Cubism, Futurism, and the music of Stravinsky, may be looked on in one sense as all having been symptoms of a mounting collective disorder, a psychic epidemic which eventually manifested itself in world war—in short, in Dr. Jung's phrase, a "fatal outbreak of demonic power"?

Similar waves of disturbance are familiar throughout history, and on a comparatively tiny scale we have already caught something of such coincidence of unrest in the years 1956–1958. We must also recognize, however, that such peaks of the fever chart in human affairs are not just cyclical, periods of comparative calm alternating with periods of disorder indefinitely, but that each outbreak of aggressive energy may be part of a much wider pattern. We have already seen, for instance, that the unrest of 1956–1958 was in many senses an awakening from the aftermath of the Second World War; the dawn of Khrushchev's Russia, and of affluence in the West, the emergence of the new unity in Western Europe, the beginning of the space race, the re-emergence of the battle for Negro rights in America, the upsurge of nationalism in Africa, Asia, and the Middle East. In 1960 and early 1961 we have seen the process of change becoming more violent—in the Africa of the Congo, in Kennedy's New Frontier America, in the spread of moral "emancipation" and the rising frenzy of youthful "revolt." All over the world by the middle of 1961, different patterns were working themselves out in parallel and increasing tempo. It would be impossible fully to understand any particular one without taking some account of the others. For the fact is that it was by no means in Britain alone, or for that matter in the worlds of politics and finance alone, that the midsummer months of 1961 recorded a rise in temperature sufficiently dramatic to be accounted the onset of a climacteric.

The world was suddenly full of troubles as though July had been a Pandora's box; fighting between Tunisia and France; more fighting in the Congo between the United Nations and Katanga; in

August Mr. Nehru's invasion of the small Portuguese enclaves on the coast of India, as a prelude to the full-scale invasion of Goa four months later; and above all, the ugliest crisis in the Cold War since Korea.

As lately as the beginning of June, Kennedy and Khrushchev had met in Vienna in at least outward amity—despite the feverish glare that seemed to attend all the activities of the new President. In the following weeks, however, there began to open a major breach between the two powers over the future of Berlin and East Germany. On 9 August Khrushchev announced that Russia was now capable of making a 100-megaton bomb. Four days later the East German frontier was sealed off and the building of the Berlin Wall began.

Still the tension mounted. Khrushchev announced that Russia was about to resume nuclear testing. America replied likewise—and was swept by a panic craze to build fallout shelters.

Away from it all in Scotland, where he was golfing at Gleneagles, Harold Macmillan on 26 August dismissed the crisis as "got up by the press." But the rising anxiety of many of his compatriots was not to be assuaged so easily. In the leader columns were appearing such phrases as "stumbling closer to the brink," or "How close is the world to the nightmare of nuclear war?" On 28 August the pro-CND *Tribune* cried:

> Today every inhabitant of this planet must contemplate the day when it may no longer be habitable.

On the same day *Tribune* published a letter from John Osborne in the South of France, headed "A Letter to My Fellow Countrymen":

> This is a letter of hate. It is for you my countrymen. I mean those men of my country who have defiled it. The men with manic fingers leading the sightless, feeble, betrayed body of my country to its death. You are its murderers, and there's little left in my own brain but the thoughts of murder for you.

I fear death but I cannot hate it as I hate you . . . my hatred for you is almost the only constant satisfaction you have left me. My favourite fantasy is four minutes or so non-commercial viewing as you fry in your own democratically elected hot seats . . .

There is murder in my brain and I carry a knife in my heart for everyone of you. Macmillan, and you, Gaitskell, you particularly . . .

Till then, damn you England. You're rotting now, and quite soon you'll disappear . . . I write this from another country with murder in my brain . . . knife carried in my heart . . . all I can offer you is my hatred . . . sour offal . . . etc., etc., etc.

In London, the Committee of 100, which had been growing increasingly wilder in its language and more anarchic in its methods, announced that on 17 September it would hold its biggest-ever demonstration in Trafalgar Square. Such was the atmosphere of the time that permission to use the Square was refused.

The refusal could not have been better calculated to feed the Committee's increasing paranoia. It was announced that the demonstration would go on—and on 7 September, the day before the most nearly successful of all the attempts to assassinate General de Gaulle, Bertrand Russell and three of his supporters were arrested and imprisoned for incitement to riot. From prison the 89-year-old philosopher, who was now wont to compare Kennedy and Macmillan with Hitler, issued a statement to the world:

Kennedy and Khrushchev, Adenauer and de Gaulle, Macmillan and Gaitskell are pursuing a common aim, the ending of human rights. You, your families, your friends and your countries, are to be exterminated by the common decision of a few brutal but powerful men.

It was language on a par with his followers' dismissal of all policemen as "fascists"; and four days later, on the evening of 17 September, the police struck back. Over 6000 demonstrators and bystanders were gathered in the Square in an atmosphere of simmering tension. As the evening wore on and midnight approached, it began to seem as if nothing was going to happen after all. The press and a large number of onlookers began to trickle home. And then, with carefully staged suddenness, police wagons appeared from all sides and, amid ugly and sometimes violent scenes, 1314 people were arrested—including various celebrities like John Osborne. It was the largest mass-arrest in English history. On the same night the Secretary General of the United Nations, Dag Hammarskjöld, on his way to Katanga, was killed in a mysterious plane crash in the Northern Rhodesian bush.

By October the world's attention was once more focused on Moscow, where Khrushchev announced that Russia was about to explode the most powerful bomb ever made. From the United Nations came a desperate plea to desist. Meanwhile, at the twenty-second Communist Party Congress, the denunciation of Stalin was resumed more fiercely and publicly. As Stalingrad was transformed into Volgograd, the world learned also that the strains detected for some time between Russia and China might be welling up into an open breach. But to the West this could hardly be a promise of future comfort when, on 30 October, it was announced that the spectacular series of Russian tests had culminated in the greatest artificial explosion in history, as 57 megatons went up in the Arctic and radioactive dust settled for months in every part of the world.

Against this background the atmosphere of English life was beginning to take on an altogether more fevered flush. The aggression of the unilateralists and the Trafalgar Square Rally were by no means the only signs of new hysteria in the air. On Merseyside, the two-year-old "trad boom" had given way at the Cavern Club to a new and wilder teenage hysteria over the pounding guitars and black leather "Rocker gear" of the Beatles. By early autumn, as the first long low E-type Jaguars roared in the Chelsea night and dress-conscious young men were swept by the craze for candy-striped shirts, the Twist was bidding fair to become the biggest dance sensation

since the Charleston. There was also the arrival of "satire." Nothing
more clearly indicated the sudden change which had come over the
country during the summer of 1961, than the emergence that autumn
of what later became known as the "satire industry." When *Beyond
the Fringe* (much of which had actually been written in the fifties)
had first arrived in London on 10 May, it had been wildly, if rather
curiously, acclaimed by Kenneth Tynan in the *Observer* as "the fun-
niest revue that London has seen since the allies dropped the bomb
on Hiroshima." But Tynan's warmest enthusiasm, as that of most
other reviewers, had been reserved for the whimsical clowning of
one of the four members of the cast, Jonathan Miller. To the others
he had devoted little more than a paragraph, including the lines:

> Mr. Moore satirizes folk singers, fashionable composers and the col-
> laboration of Peter Pears and Benjamin Britten . . . Cook does a num-
> ber of things . . . including the Prime Minister casually tearing up a
> letter from an Old Age Pensioner.

During that eventful summer, however, as *Beyond the Fringe* mushroomed into the success of the theatrical year, so Tynan's one throwaway reference to "satire" bloomed into a description of the whole
show; just as the sketch he had almost dismissed, featuring Peter
Cook's immensely tired, broken-down Macmillan, talking on television of his visit to the "young, vigorous" President Kennedy, became almost its centerpiece. By October, "satire" was the rage of
progressive young upper-middle-class London. In Soho, Peter Cook
and his friend from Cambridge of the late fifties, Nicholas Luard, an
Old Wykhamist and former Guards officer, had opened "London's
First Satirical Nightclub," *The Establishment,* to a torrent of publicity. The first amateurish, yellow-paper copies of the magazine
Private Eye were beginning to circulate in the bistros of Kensington
and Chelsea. Between them they were to bring back into English
life a strain of public insult and personal vilification which, although
foreshadowed in the late fifties by such things as Bernard Levin's

Taper column and some of Peter Sellers's sketches, it had not known
for many years.*

The emergence of the satire movement in fact marked a new stage
in the social revolution. Like the pop artists (and the pop singers yet
to come) the satirists—who were mainly in their early twenties—
formed part of a new generation coming to the surface in English
life, one young enough to have been molded by the garish, anarchic,
and youth-conscious atmosphere of the late fifties, following the
watershed of 1956. It was noticeable, for instance, that like the pop
artists, the satirists were heavily influenced by the imagery of the age;
a great deal of their material was concerned with parodies of television
shows and advertising, the clichés of journalism, the jargon of trend-
setters and the glossy magazines. But at the same time, like the
New Oxford Group, the satirists came almost entirely from the older
universities (in this instance, particularly from Cambridge); in social
background, like their predecessors, they were an almost exact balance between upper class and lower, Old and New. And to a large
extent the underlying message of the satirists was simply that of the
"What's Wrong With Britain" journalists—only carried to a newly
irresponsible, unreal, and more destructive level, particularly in their
violent attacks on "Establishment" figures, on Royalty and judges
and Conservative ministers and upper-class accents and the class system, on Britain's pretensions still to be a great nuclear power and,
above all, on the "decrepitude" of the father figure Macmillan himself. Indeed what they saw as the "upper-class charade" was only
the most blatant symbol, to *Private Eye* and *The Establishment* in
particular, of a decay that was beginning to affect the whole of
English society. Like the Committee of 100, the satirists were the first
expression in society of a darker longing for sensation, chaos, and

* Another powerful influence on the British satirists was the success of various
new American satirists in the years just before, like Mort Sahl, Lenny Bruce, and the
cartoonists of *Mad*. Indeed, *Private Eye* was directly inspired to produce its captioned
cover photographs by an American magazine cover showing a smiling President
Kennedy proudly exclaiming, "I got my job through the *New York Times!*"

178

collapse—without even the dream of "dynamism" to provide hope of a remedy.

By the closing months of 1961 the political scene had undergone a radical transformation. The first signs of the new mood had appeared in the immediate wake of the July economic crisis and the Government's announcement of its bid to join the Common Market. For the first time in three years the Conservatives had fallen behind the Labour Party on the opinion polls. Not only had the Government's attempt to restrain wage increases, the so-called "Pay Pause," set off widespread unrest among the unions, but the Common Market issue, with its unspoken abandonment of the ideal of the British Commonwealth, had also touched off a violent revolt among the Conservative Old Guard, one of whom described the Prime Minister as "a national disaster" almost before he had had time to complete his initial statement. But despite the fall in Conservative standing, it was not so much a reflection of positive gains by the Labour Party as of startling new support for the Liberals.

As the autumn moved on, it became apparent that the Government was in trouble much deeper than that of any mere temporary unpopularity. In the life of any Government, however safe its majority, there comes a moment when the social movements of which it was once the expression turn inexorably against it. Up to that moment, however many mistakes it makes, however damning the criticisms that may be leveled against it, however unpopular it may become, it can sail on serenely. However much it may in fact be out of control of events, it outwardly seems to be riding on top of them. But after that moment, every mistake it makes becomes magnified; indeed blunders multiply as if feeding on themselves; and both outwardly and inwardly the Government appears to be at the mercy of every wind. It was that moment which the Conservative Government reached in the autumn of 1961.

In no respect was the Government's powerlessness more sharply demonstrated than by its frailty before an issue which had suddenly blown up—that of colored immigration from the Commonwealth. A tiny pressure group in the Conservative Party, mainly in the Midlands, had been campaigning for some years for curbs on immigration. But the whole tradition of the Conservative Party, not least that of the imperial-minded Old Guard, had lain against such a move in the name of the ideal of Commonwealth. Even after a sharp rise in the number of immigrants to 60,000 in 1960, an undersecretary at the Home Office had, in February 1961, been able to declare quite flatly that the Government refused:

> to contemplate legislation which might restrict the historic right of every British subject, regardless of race or colour, freely to enter and stay in the United Kingdom.

Even as late as October, when the flow of immigrants, particularly from India and Pakistan, had doubled the figure of the previous year, the Government still seemed resolute against an increasingly violent campaign in which many Conservative Associations were now beginning to find a subconscious outlet for their sliding morale.

Three weeks later the Government published its Immigration Bill, placing the first serious curb on free entry from the Commonwealth. Typical of the bitter dismay with which the new measure was greeted was the *Daily Mirror*'s front page headline on 2 November: "Britain's Race Law—This Is an Outrage." In the fires of this new criticism, coupled with progressive disintegration of the Pay Pause, the morale of the Macmillan administration began to show its first signs of collapse. A malaise began to affect its control of the simplest matters. Even Government business in the Commons seemed to be getting pointlessly tied up, and much criticism was leveled at the new Party Chairman and Leader of the House, Iain Macleod, who, when he had been appointed on 13 October, had been almost unanimously acclaimed as the Party's "white hope," "Crown Prince," and "Macmillan's most likely successor." Indeed the succession to Macmillan was for the first time beginning to arouse considerable speculation: and as 1962 began, an apparently inconsequential call by a right-wing MP for the Prime Minister's resignation sounded a distracted cry in the gathering night. Long gone now were those palmy days of "Supermac," barely two years before, for whom nothing could go wrong.

In the country at large unrest continued to deepen. Back at the beginning of December, the Committee of 100 had threatened an even more sensational demonstration than that in Trafalgar Square —a mass "take-over" of eight heavily guarded nuclear airbases. But in the event it was only evidence that the September martyrdom had been the cue for a final spiral into total unreality. The Committee announced in advance that at least fifty thousand people would turn out for the invasion. When the day came, there were less than six thousand. The operation was a fiasco, and in February six of the ringleaders were imprisoned. Later in 1962, even Bertrand Russell was to join a rush of resignations from the Committee, and from this point on, in the words of a chronicler of the movement, it was increasingly to develop:

> a quasi-outlaw character, defiantly challenging the authorities on a wide range of subjects, few of which [had] anything to do with the Bomb.*

More serious, as the new year opened, was the still swelling antagonism to the Pay Pause. Throughout a wet and windy January postal services were thrown into chaos through a "go-slow" by the Post Office workers. On January 29, a one-day tube strike, leading to the worst traffic jams in London's history, reinforced another fashionable ingredient in the "What's Wrong With Britain" litany, that London was becoming "strangled" by overcrowding and that the country's population was too much weighted toward the South Eastern corner of the island. Later in the year the *Economist* was to suggest, partly as a joke, that the center of British government should

* George Thayer, *The British Political Fringe.*

be moved to a new and shining "Brazilia" on the Yorkshire moors but many people were disposed to take the proposal seriously. It was no coincidence that the newly imagined "excitement" and "vitality" of provincial England, and particularly of the industrial North, was playing an increasing part in the restless fantasies of the London-centered, predominantly upper-middle-class "What's Wrong With Britain" press: for it was part of the pattern that "excitement" and "dynamism" were invariably only to be found elsewhere. And it was no coincidence that when a handful of young university graduates employed by the BBC had been looking for the right locale for *Z Cars,* their new "tough," "realistic" police, crime, and working-class television serial, they should have gone North on their search, and picked as its setting the "raw" and "vital" city of Liverpool.

And so we return to the point where so many pages ago we left off —the week in February 1962 when the *Sunday Times* produced its first color supplement, with its Jean Shrimpton-Mary Quant cover and its "Sharp Look at the Mood of Britain," its James Bond short story, and its articles on "People of the 60's." It was a perfect embodiment of the neurosis of the times, as, in the same week, greeting the news that Mark Boxer's latest recruit to his color supplement's staff, Lord Snowdon, had enjoyed £85,000-worth of repairs at public expense to his residence in Kensington Palace, was the sharpest and most widespread criticism of the Royal Family since 1957. Faster and faster hurtled the roller coaster—and it was hardly surprising that the larger the collective daydream swelled, the more violent grew feelings of frustration and aggression.

It is one of the paradoxes of this period, the full irony of which was not to emerge until several years later, that halfway through 1962, when it was being almost daily castigated for its "complacency" and "inertia," the Macmillan Government was in fact in the thick of the greatest burst of radical activity since the years immediately after the war. The application for membership in the Common Market, the attempts to provide machinery for closer economic planning and income control, the establishment of seven new universities altering the whole structure of British higher education, the tremendous acceleration of the colonial emancipation program, not to say the setting in train of major reforms of the railways and coal industry, all marked a major reversal of previous Conservative policy, and a concentration of change which has no parallel in the fifties and sixties.

Of course the explanation of the paradox is that both the clamor for change and the actual reforms of the Macmillan Government were products of the same accelerating tide. The demands for "dynamism" and "modernization" were merely the mountain of froth thrown up on its surface. And by 1962 this froth of expectation had long since parted company with the reality of what the Government was doing. The first serious test of just how far the Government's growing unpopularity had already gone was in March, when, incredibly, one of the safest Conservative seats in the country, the London suburb of Orpington, was lost in a by-election to a young Liberal candidate. The Liberals' Orpington triumph, and the even more incredible moment two weeks later, when a major opinion poll showed them leading both the other two parties in popular support, was nevertheless something of an "explosion into reality" for the Liberals—for never again was their revival to see such heights, and from then on, despite further surprisingly good results, their support was to enter on an almost continuous decline.

Indeed, over the following months, as the Conservative vote in by-elections continued to sink to ever lower levels, there were for the first time signs of a positive accession of support to the Labour Party. By midsummer, even a senior Cabinet minister could speak openly in a newsletter to his constituents of the nation's lack of "a sense of purpose." In June, despite the fact that Labour leaders were once again being jeered at public meetings by mobs wearing the CND badge, the Labour Party won its first by-election since 1958. While in the mammoth *Anatomy of Britain* by Anthony Sampson (New Oxford Group), the still rising chorus of "What's Wrong With Britain" journalism produced the best-selling book of the summer. On 13 July, following yet another by-election in which the Conservatives had been driven to the bottom of the poll, the country's mounting hysteria at last broke through the Prime Minister's hitherto imperturbable facade of "unflappability." In a sudden panic move, he sacked seven of the older members of his Cabinet, replacing them with the "youngest" and "toughest" team he could assemble. The only effect of the move was to emphasize his own increasing isolation and to set off a further wave of unrest.

The summer of 1962 was wet and miserable, with widespread flood damage. Traditional summer sporting events took place under grey skies, with the constant threat of renewed torrential rain. For almost a year the country's economy had been running down, while the figures of unemployment edged steadily upwards. The crime rate had also begun to rise at unprecedented speed, after a comparative slackening off in its rate of increase that had lasted since 1958. In dance halls and converted cinemas, the bingo craze launched by the previous year's Gaming Act was now raging. Meanwhile, the great building and property boom of the late fifties was reaching its peak.

1962 was the year in which the value of property shares, at £800 million (an increase of £700 million since 1958), reached their highest level. The year saw the opening of more glass-and-concrete towers than ever before, including the Shell Building on the South Bank of the Thames, almost as high as St. Paul's Cathedral and the largest office block in Europe. But for the first time there were signs of strain in this gigantic boom—not least among the three partners in the world's largest property company, City Centre. Since their merger with Mr. Charles Clore two years before, both Jack Cotton and Walter Flack had been showing increasing symptoms of *folie de grandeur*. According to one account:

> as 1961 and 1962 wore on, the strain of the internal strife in City Centre began to sap the health of both*

* Oliver Marriott, *The Property Boom*.

and in neither case was such professional strain eased by the increasingly hectic pace of their private lives.

Throughout the year, on television and in the press, the cult of the teenager had been drifting further into fantasy. In January, in a BBC *Meeting Point* program, the Archbishop of York had attracted considerable attention by conducting a somewhat unhappy dialogue with the pop singer Adam Faith, bewilderedly reaching for a kind of hearty vernacular in which to communicate, throwing around such words as "bloke" and "chap," conceding that he would be "all for" rewriting the hymns so that young people might "understand" and declaring that:

> All youngsters should think out a faith strong enough for this life and for the world to come. Religion is jolly relevant to this life.

It was by no means only the middle-aged who paid such baffled homage to this new power. In an article in a special issue of *Town* devoted to youth, Ronald Bryden (Cambridge early 1950's), formerly the drama critic of the *Spectator,* conducted a survey of what he described as "these future rulers of ours," attempting to assess "what kind of masters they're likely to make":

> We know that they'll be bigger than us . . . healthier than us . . . they'll probably feel the cold less . . . The new generation will demand something more than the ninety-odd miles of modern motorway. They will expect air as clean as Pittsburgh's or Dusseldorf's . . . They will see no reason why we shouldn't follow European experiments with monorails, hydrofoils and district heating . . .
>
> They will be cleverer than us . . . they're going to be classless. Their clothes already are. So are the things and places they like most— Whimpey [*sic*] Bars, bowling alleys, the M.I.: all too new to have any connotation of upper or lower, in-group or out-group. When they come to furnish homes they'll pick "contemporary" design with none of the connotations antiques carry of a bygone, aristocratic taste . . . etc., etc.

The satire movement, although still almost entirely confined to London, flourished apace. The circulation of *Private Eye,* which in

April had been bought by *The Establishment,* was rising by the late summer towards 20,000. It was also in April that *The Establishment* itself enjoyed its hours of greatest notoriety, with the visit from America of the "sick" comedian Lenny Bruce—whose tormented meanderings through a drug addict's nightmare packed the club nightly for three weeks. To George Melly in the *New Statesman* Bruce's compulsive flow of obscenity and blasphemy earned him the title of "evangelist of the New Morality"; while in the *Observer* Kenneth Tynan wrote:

> At times Mr. Bruce drawls and mumbles too privately, lapsing into a wealth of Yiddish . . . one also wishes he had read more; during his opening performance he referred to Dylan Thomas as if he thought he was an Irishman. But at the end he had broken through frontiers of language and feeling that one had thought inviolable; and Jonathan Miller, who watched the performance in something like awe, agreed with me that if "Beyond the Fringe" was a pinprick, Mr. Bruce was a bloodbath.

Even without such an example, it was hardly surprising that, as 1962 progressed, there should be signs in the home-produced satire movement itself of the familiar spiraling demand for more violent gratifications. *The Establishment* team itself was increasingly falling back on "daring" four-letter words, blasphemy, and violent abuse, without the palliative of wit; in the club itself there were several outbreaks of violence. *Private Eye* too was showing signs of the progression, as its layout became increasingly harsh and bold, its personal abuse more shrill (as, for instance, its full page in June 1962 describing the Home Secretary R. A. Butler as "a flabby faced old coward") and its images more nightmarish—as in its grotesque cartoons by William Rushton and Gerald Scarfe, or in such articles as that describing the "death by hanging" of Lord Russell of Liverpool. Nor perhaps was it surprising that there were some who had initially fallen on the satire movement in euphoria, but who were now beginning to find out, once the initial shock had worn off, they remained unsatisfied. For despite the satirists' own straining after new sensation, the whole idea of "satire" had for many people, such as Tynan and Melly, simply become a nyktomorph, associated with vague, half-formed images of Jonathan Swift, George Grosz, and Berlin in the twenties—touching off deep in their subconscious minds suggestive thrills of destruction and violence which could never be made manifest.

When in 1918 he observed that a whole series of his German patients were relating dreams containing what he described as "Wotanistic imagery," Carl Jung began to conclude that individual dreams might provide a clue to movements in the collective subconscious, fore-shadowing future developments in the conscious world. And, of course, particularly in the twentieth century, there are few more revealing windows on the dream-life of the age than artistic activity —books, plays, and films above all. Certainly the films released in 1962, particularly some of those from the continent, such as Antonioni's *La Notte,* Alain Resnais' *Last Year at Marienbad,* and Truffaut's *Jules et Jim,* had a darker, more fragmented and nightmarish quality than anything that had come before—even though they were nothing compared with the films actually made in 1962 which would not be released until 1963. But in England it was more the theatre which seemed to be sinking down through the subconscious into a more obscure and violent fantasy world.

Of the by now established new playwrights, only Arnold Wesker, whose *Chips with Everything,* a cardboard allegory of the class war, was the year's biggest commercial success, seemed still on safe, familiar ground. John Osborne followed *Luther,* his historical parable of frustration, heavily laden with imagery of constipation and excretion, with two short plays for the Royal Court which showed him desperately groping for new sensations. The first, *The Blood of the Bambergs,* a clumsy satire on a wedding of a photographer and a princess, was described by John Russell Taylor in *Anger and After* as "easily the feeblest work [he] has yet allowed to reach the stage." The second, *Under Plain Cover,* directed by Jonathan Miller, was the story of a couple whose married life could only be kept together by their constant acting out of sado-masochistic fantasies and by their shared obsession with knickers.

But in some ways the greatest theatrical interest of 1962 was aroused by a series of new plays at the Arts Theatre. Typical was *The Knacker's Yard* by Johnny Speight, an East End dockworker's son, which was set in a squalid boarding house at which there arrived a "mysterious and sinister" figure called Ryder, whose nightly plea- sure (to quote Russell Taylor again) was

> ritually slashing a series of voluptuous nude pin-ups with a razor on a little patriotic altar of Union Jacks. All of which, plus his large col- lection of handbags, seems to suggest that he must be the Jack-The- Ripper-like killer in the neighbourhood etc., etc.

After many twists of the dream-nightmare, the hero ended by gassing himself. Another of the Arts series, and the first of an experimental season put on by Peter Hall and Peter Brook's Royal Shakespeare Company, was David Rudkin's *Afore Night Come,* which in similar fashion ran through all the five stages of the fantasy cycle to "a grue- somely compulsive climax involving a ritual murder beneath the poison sprays of a pest-control helicopter." A third, Fred Watson's *Infanticide in the House of Fred Ginger,* ended equally gratuitously in the killing of a child. The "nightmare stage" had been more or less familiar in British drama since Pinter's *The Birthday Party* in 1958. Only now had the "death wish stage" become not only explicit —but a commonplace.

It is one of the characteristics of a bad dream that "anything can happen," that events either absurd or charged with menace occur quite haphazardly, and that, not infrequently, they appear to be leading uncontrollably toward disaster. It was into such a dream that England itself appeared to be moving in the closing months of 1962.

The malaise which had infected the Government's handling of even the simplest events now turned into an almost willful invitation to catastrophe. Within only five days of the "July purge," for instance, the new Home Secretary, Mr. Henry Brooke, found himself in trouble with the first of a whole series of personal cases which were to dog him over the coming months—and which as much by his apparent incompetence as by any actual inhumanity were to transform him into the most hated holder of his office since Joynson Hicks in the twenties.

Even stranger was the sequence of events between September and November in which Mr. Profumo attempted to deceive an opposition military affairs expert, George Wigg, over the findings of a secret army report on the Kuwait fiasco. Up to the eve of a Commons debate on defense Profumo let Wigg think that together they were going to "ventilate" the unfavorable findings of the report, since they might redound to the War Office's advantage in its rivalry with the Ministry of Defence. But when the debate arrived, Profumo denied all knowledge of the report, leaving Wigg looking foolish.*

Meanwhile, by the early autumn, the Common Market negotiations in Brussels, Macmillan's last hope of a miracle, were moving into their final stages—but inexplicably dragging out as if scripted by Kafka, hours and even days being taken up by discussion of the tariff on Indian tea or Australian kangaroo meat. Day after day the newspapers were full of immensely detailed supplements, explaining exactly what joining the Common Market would entail—but few of the public thus became any the wiser. At the Labour Party Conference in Brighton, Hugh Gaitskell finally led his Party into downright opposition to the venture; not on the grounds that it was impracticable, but, in the voice of the most diehard Conservative, because it would involve betraying the Commonwealth and "a thousand

* Wigg was later to play an important part in unearthing the Profumo-Keeler affair, and thus in fostering the consequent crisis.

years of history." While at the Conservative Conference at Llandudno a week later, Harold Macmillan finally won over the majority of his Party to the most radical step they had ever undertaken. Many of the delegates supported him like zombies, wearing lapel buttons bearing the one word "Yes," as if to re-emphasize their desperate unanimity. And *Private Eye* immediately set an extract from Macmillan's speech to a backing of hysterical screams and twanging guitars, to make a best-selling record—in the same month of October that the Beatles, still only locally known in their home town of Liverpool, first joined the fashionable beat of the Madison in the charts with their first English record *Love Me Do*.

In those last months of 1962 it was not only England, with its satirists and screaming teenagers and "What's Wrong With Britain" masochists and its new fashion for black leather boots, black leather coats, and black stockings, that seemed determined to shake itself into oblivion. At the end of October, the whole world was hypnotized by what appeared later to have been the most dangerous crisis in its history. For a full week, as Khrushchev and Kennedy played their game of cosmic "Chicken" over Cuba, the world teetered on the brink of disaster. In the same week, the world's two largest nations, India and China, inched toward open war, in the snows of the Himalayas.

In England, forced to look on at the Cuba crisis stupefied and powerless, it was the final twist to a hysteria now bubbling beneath the surface. From *Private Eye* came a strip cartoon of Kennedy blowing up the world with the words "I had to earn a place in history somehow." From the Committee of 100 came a chaotic demonstration in Grosvenor Square, imploring anyone who happened to be listening within the darkened American Embassy to take his "hands off Cuba." A few hundred yards away, off Wimpole Street, Stephen Ward was, as we have it on the authority of Miss Rice-Davies, "in a state of tremendous excitement and tension, almost bordering on hysteria," convinced that unless, with his friend Ivanov, he could set up a Summit meeting, "it could mean the end of the world."

Appropriately, these weeks provided both the press and television with the final catalyst for a style of news projection which was to play its own part in reflecting and exacerbating the hysteria of the next twelve months or so. In the *Observer,* the *Daylight* column began its account of the Cuba crisis with the sentence:

> An hour before President Kennedy was due to broadcast in Washington on a matter of "urgent national importance," Adlai Stevenson stepped into a high-speed lift to the thirty-eighth floor of the United Nations building in New York . . .

The column thus launched in the Sunday press what was to be called the "blow by blow" style of journalism, originally perfected by *Time* in the thirties, and more recently popularized by *The Making of the President,* published in Britain a few months earlier. At the same time, television found its own version of the "blow by blow" style in the frenziedly cut *ciné-vérité* film clips, urgent music, and clamant narrative of Granada's current affairs program *The World in Action.*

Looking back on those weeks around the Cuba crisis, one can see event after event that was to have bearing on the denouement that was approaching. In October one of the most glittering of the success stories of Macmillan's England had shown its first signs of turning sour, when the name of the washing machine millionaire John Bloom made headlines in connection with a night-club proprietor's murder of his wife, with whom Bloom had been having an affair. In November Peter Rachman, slum landlord and former lover of both Christine Keeler and Mandy Rice-Davies, died a mysterious death in Edgware Hospital. In the defense debate of 23 November, the War Minister incurred the undying enmity of George Wigg— just twelve days after an anonymous voice on the telephone had warned Wigg in Worcestershire that, in his constant vigilance over security, it might well repay him to "Look at Profumo."*

It was also in the aftermath of Cuba that there came the first rumblings of serious trouble over the Vassall case, the beginnings of a climax to almost two years of spy fever. As early as May 1961, when George Blake had received his record prison term, it had been apparent that the forces of authority were becoming increasingly rattled by this continual evidence of instability at all levels of Government. Now hysteria was unleashed, firstly in the press which, unable to remain content with the evidence brought out at Vassall's trial, reveled for days in rumors of further ramifications. Even such a responsible journalist as John Freeman (Oxford, late-1930's), the Editor of the *New Statesman,* attempted to make the flesh of *News of the World* readers creep with hints of the existence of a powerful "Mr. Big." The recklessness of Fleet Street, however, was matched by that of the politicians, including Macmillan himself—who allowed a Junior Minister to resign the day after a White Paper had apparently cleared him of any sinister link with Vassall.

It was appropriate that these same weeks should also see the beginnings of a climax to that other expression of fascination with spies that had been typified in the late fifties and early sixties by the cult of James Bond. The curious way in which the Bond phenomenon had become a shadow to the history of the age had been given a further twist in March 1961 when an American magazine had claimed—erroneously, as it later turned out—that one of the most fervent Bond readers was President Kennedy. Partly aided by this

---

* During the year, a number of people in London had come to know about the Profumo-Keeler liaison in August 1961 through the indiscretions of Stephen Ward, Miss Keeler's friend. The first very oblique public reference to the affair had been made in a humorous article in the *Queen* magazine in July, by Robin Douglas-Home, nephew of the Foreign Secretary. The next important step in its coming out into the open was an incident that took place a few weeks later, on 14 December, when a West Indian, Johnny Edgecombe, was arrested for firing a number of shots at the mews house occupied by his friend Miss Keeler and Mandy Rice-Davies. His trial the following March—when Christine Keeler as an important witness fled the country rather than make a public appearance—gave the popular press its first opportunity to make public insinuations involving her name with that of Mr. Profumo.

revelation, in 1961 and 1962, the sales of Bond books on both sides of the Atlantic had soared. Now, by the end of 1962, with the arrival of new authors such as Len Deighton (North London) and John Le Carré (Oxford, early 1950's), a Foreign Office official, "spy literature," like satire, seemed to be turning into an industry. It was also in November 1962 that, with the arrival of James Bond on the screen, played by a former Carnaby Street model and Royal Court actor Sean Connery (Glasgow), the record-breaking *Dr. No* marked the beginning of a turn in the British cinema away from "Northern Realism" and indeed "naturalism" of any kind toward an altogether more colorful and sensational kind of fantasy. The real explanation for this new popularity of spy stories, in fact, was not so much that they were a reflection of the increase in real life, as a more subtle reflection of the *Zeitgeist*. They provided, in fact, the perfect vehicle for "dream-nightmare" stories in which no one's identity was certain, in which self-assertive lone heroes could wander at will, in any disguise, through any social milieu, and in which acts of violence and promiscuity, vaguely condoned by the fact that the heroes were always fighting for "our side" against "the enemy," could take place at any time, without any need for elaborate explanation.

If films and books, the press and television were each finding their own ways of reflecting the *Zeitgeist,* all their innovations paled beside the reaction of the BBC. For the new "liberal" BBC, under the Director-Generalship of Mr. Carleton-Greene, acclamation had reached its peak during 1962. The young men, such as Donald Baverstock and Michael Peacock, now in positions of considerable seniority, were almost automatically described by the *Observer* and other journals as "whiz kids" or "Young Turks." In recommending that the BBC should be given a second television channel as soon as possible, the Royal Commission on the Future of Broadcasting, under the Chairmanship of Sir Harry Pilkington, had dismissed the commercialism of ITV in terms so scathing that some dispassionate observers wondered whether the Commission had observed any of the changes which, since the introduction of competition, had come over the BBC itself.

On 24 November, the BBC launched the program which marked its final breach with the standards laid down by its founder Lord Reith. Although it was on the air for barely eight months, *That Was The Week That Was* was destined to become almost overnight the most successful television series in British history. In a sense it was a final drawing together of almost all those threads which had been working for "revolution" and sensation in the England of the previous seven years. Through David Frost, the perfect "classless," mass-medium-synthetic version of the Cambridge satirists, his colleague William Rushton, the *Private Eye* cartoonist, and the editor of *Private Eye* as one of its chief scriptwriters, it brought the destructive force of the satire craze to a mass-audience. Other contributors included Bernard Levin, various new playwrights and "Northern Realist" film-scriptwriters, and even, on occasion, Kenneth Tynan. Above all, it was the climactic achievement of the "marvellously dynamic" Donald Baverstock, who fathered the show, and whose *Tonight* empire had brought forth its creator and producer Ned Sherrin. *That Was The Week,* watched as an obsessive ritual by millions of people, with its huge team of writers earning comparatively astronomic sums for mass-producing personal abuse and bitter attacks on every kind of authority, was the satirical fantasy itself finally turned inside out. If some of its material was witty and original, particularly the surrealist sketches by the cartoonist Timothy Birdsall (Cambridge, late-1950's), much of it was amateurish, juvenile, and completely stereotyped in attitude. Its success, like its very existence, was due to the extraordinary nature of the times. But even in the first few weeks of its run, those times were to become more extraordinary yet.

On 21 December Harold Macmillan, in conference with President Kennedy in the Bahamas, was informed that the American Skybolt missile, on which Britain's deterrent force had been depending ever since the collapse of Blue Streak, had been canceled. Macmillan's troubles were now reaching unimagined depths. At the end of November, the Government had lost two out of a group of five by-elections in Conservative seats, including one through the intervention of a widely respected local figure standing in protest against the Government's Common Market policy, which the Conservatives had only lost before in the Liberal landslide of 1906. Furthermore, when on 15 December Macmillan visited General de Gaulle at Rambouillet, he was given the first serious inklings that his Common Market policy itself, the last hope, was in danger.

Piece by piece, the frail edifice with which old England had sought to console herself for the ending of three hundred years as a great, imperial power in the world, was crumbling. The Commonwealth, the independent deterrent, membership of a greater Europe—all were myths and dreams, fading like an insubstantial pageant into reality. On 6 December, the comment of the former American Secretary of State, Dean Acheson, that "Britain has lost an empire and not yet found a role" raised only a brief petulant cheep from the British press: for the truth was too obvious to be denied.

At the beginning of December a thick fog began to settle over England. In its first week it killed 340 people in London alone. Among the more prominent invalids was Hugh Gaitskell, who went into hospital with what appeared to be nothing more than a bad attack of influenza. On Boxing Day, the fog was joined by heavy falls of snow. It was already colder than at any time since the winter of 1947.

The nightmare was moving into its final phase.

Chapter Eight

1963—*The Year of the Death Wish*

In the most high and palmy state of Rome,
A little ere the mightiest Julius fell,
The graves stood tenantless and the sheeted dead
Did squeak and gibber in the Roman streets.

Hamlet I, 1

There are two years, the seventh and the ninth, that
commonly bring great changes in a man's life, and great
dangers; wherefore 63, that contains both these numbers
multiplied together, comes not without heaps of dangers.

Levinus Lemnius

Stephen Ward . . . had an extraordinary sense of humour
and loved creating a sensation.

CHRISTINE KEELER
News of the World, 9 June 1963

"Their physical appearance" said my friend, who is a
Liverpool housewife, "inspires frenzy. They look beat up
and depraved in the nicest possible way."

MAUREEN CLEAVE on the Beatles,
Evening Standard, 2 February 1963

The popular morality is now a wasteland. It is littered
with the debris of broken convictions. A new concept is
emerging, of sexual relationships as a source of pleasure.

PROFESSOR GEORGE CARSTAIRS
BBC Reith Lectures, 1962–63

I do not live among young people fairly widely.

HAROLD MACMILLAN, House of Commons,
17 June 1963

The Queen of England has been booed tonight and I am
furious.

HENRY BROOKE, Home Secretary,
10 July 1963

Frank J. Wilson, a former chief of the American Secret
Service . . . states in his autobiography . . . that the threat
to the President's life at that time could be gauged as
higher than in any recent years. The total of threatening
and abusive letters received in the year he was shot dead
reached the "staggering and frightening high" of 32,000.

Sunday Telegraph book review,
April 1966

The events and character of 1963, certainly in Britain and to a limited extent in the rest of the world, have no parallel in our times. Although all of its twelve months were in a sense for the British a climax to the events of the previous seven years, its own climax was the one event so shocking that there is scarcely anyone who cannot remember the exact circumstances in which he or she first learned of it—the assassination of President Kennedy on 22 November.

For Britain, the months that preceded this event, with the Profumo affair, the collapse of the age of Macmillan, the unforeseen changes of leadership in both the major parties, the greatest peacetime robbery in history, and, as the final expression of all those new forces which had been rising to the fore in English society, the simultaneous emergence of Harold Wilson and the Beatles, marked the peak of the fever chart which had been rising steadily since 1955. But these climactic events in Britain itself took place against a backdrop of extraordinary events in the rest of the world—including a long series of major natural catastrophes, the violent overthrow of a whole series of governments, and the murders of four heads of state in different parts of the world, each one an embodiment for his country of the dreams of a new age.

The extraordinary nature of the year was heralded and heightened for Britain by three months of the worst winter recorded in over 200 years, bringing havoc and paralysis to almost every field of human activity. Over London, the fog hung like a shroud, combining with the snow to give the city an air of ghostly unreality. In the *Spectator,* the cartoonist Timothy Birdsall suddenly found a nightmarish new extension of his style to greet the New Year. A huge, pocked, and monstrous specter, carrying a bunch of balloons covered with all the inane slogans of a newspaper new year and wearing a tinsel tiara labeled "1963," leaped from out of a desert landscape onto a tiny bewildered human figure with a shout of "Hello, hello, hello, hello, hello, hello, hello."

On 8 January, President Nkrumah narrowly missed death in the first of the year's many attempts at political assassination. Five days later, President Olympio of nearby Togo actually was assassinated, in the first of the year's many *coups d'état.*

On the same morning in London, the Sunday newspapers announced that Hugh Gaitskell's health was "improving." The following day, just as the Common Market negotiations appeared to be moving to their climax, President de Gaulle staggered the world by the uncompromising finality of his objections to Britain's entry, almost all of which would have been equally valid at any time since the discussions had begun. On the same day it was announced that Hugh Gaitskell had taken a sudden turn for the worse. Within four days he was dead, of a rare chest disease, at the age of only fifty-six. Two weeks later, the talks in Brussels petered out, in an atmosphere of bewilderment, acrimony, and frustration. Britain's European "dream" was over, and she was more than ever alone in an increasingly perplexing world.

Already, on 25 January, when the year was only barely begun, *Time* magazine published a long and widely-quoted survey of the calamities, scandals, and disappointments piling up in English life, under the heading of "Britain's Troubled Mood." In an article on the "gulf between the generations" in the *Sunday Times,* Godfrey Smith (New Oxford Group) wrote:

> How *flavourless,* how *eerily unnatural* a society would be where the child's notion of morality, his views on life and death . . . *meshed smoothly* with those of his parents.

It was obvious that his own moral sympathies lay with the "child" rather than its "parents," and he went on to quote with approval (as the kind of thing that was likely to divide one generation from another) the scene in *Beyond the Fringe* in which a young pilot was sent off by his commanding officer to commit suicide over Germany because "we need a futile gesture at this stage, Perkins. It'll raise the whole tone of the war."

Another advertisement of the time was for a new nightclub, to be started by Nicholas Luard of *The Establishment* in partnership with Lord Timothy Willoughby D'Eresby, the heir of an earldom and a prominent member of the old Chelsea Set of the late fifties, with all the glitter of high decadence:

> WIP'S—piranhas—WIP'S—vodka—WIP'S—sharks and caviar and russian roulette—WIP'S—smoke and darkness—WIP'S—faces—WIP'S opens late february london's sharpest nightclub.

In February, the great freeze, the fog, and the snow continued. Along the Tyne and the Tees and the Clyde the shipyards fell silent. All over the "raw" and "vital" North the dole queues lengthened, as the unemployment figures rose to 900,000, by far their highest level since the crisis winter of 1947. England, it was commonly remarked, was once again "two nations," as she had been at the height of the Depression thirty years before.

It was from this bleak and ghostly land that the Queen and the Duke of Edinburgh set off on a Royal Tour of Australia and New Zealand that, in the wake of the Common Market negotiations, was to be in places received almost coldly. In the *Sunday Pictorial,* the Labour MP Woodrow Wyatt (Oxford 1930's) spoke for much of the country when he wrote:

> Everybody is asking . . . what is Britain's role in the future? . . . everything seems such a muddle.

In a fever of intrigue and counter-intrigue, Harold Wilson was elected Leader of the Labour Party; for those at the center of the struggle it was a peculiarly heady few weeks, and not a few of them, having read *The Making of the President,* now saw themselves in fantasy re-enacting the glamorous scenes in "smoke-filled rooms" of 1960.

Another advertisement appeared for:

WIP'S—piranhas in the darkness above london's skyline—WIP'S— black velvet and the new faces—WIP'S—music strong and hard and moody—WIP'S WIP'S WIP'S opens on 19 March.

It was about this time that, as their second record *Please Please Me* reached the top of the hit parade, the world outside Liverpool was becoming dimly aware that the still virtually unknown Beatles were no ordinary pop group—and indeed that pop music itself was beginning to exert some peculiar fascination, expressing the spirit of the times. In the *Evening Standard* on 2 February, Miss Maureen Cleave (Oxford, mid-1950's) wrote a piece headed "Why the Beatles Create All That Frenzy," and quoted Paul McCartney as saying:

Our humour is based on anything that other people don't laugh at— death, for instance, or disease. It sounds dreadful if you write it down, but it's the cruel stuff, the cruellies that make us laugh.

But, for the time being, an even more immediate source of national sensation was in the offing. For, as February drew to its close, rumors were already beginning to race around the dinner tables, the Commons corridors, and the newspaper offices of Fleet Street that, in the wake of the Vassall hysteria, yet another major scandal was brewing, this time of such proportions that it might "bring down the Government."

The freezing weather continued well into its third month, until gales and torrential rain in mid-March turned the snow into thick grey slush. On 7 March, the High Court sentenced two reporters to prison for refusing to disclose the sources of highly colorful stories they had printed at the time of the Vassall affair. The extravagant bitterness and self-dramatization of many journalists knew no bounds. The breach between Mr. Macmillan and much of the popular press was complete; and the "revenge" they were eagerly looking for was already close at hand.

The London air was now thick with rumors about the War Minister, about call-girl rings and official secrets and orgies at Cliveden involving "some of the highest names in the land." As the month progressed, the Profumo affair bubbled ever nearer to the surface, urged on by the desperate indiscretions and urge for sensation of Stephen Ward. With each new turn of events, from the sentencing of the West Indian, John Edgecombe, to seven years' imprisonment and the flight from the country of the "key witness" in the case, Christine Keeler, to a near-mutiny in the Brigade of Guards stationed near Windsor, the heart of the British Army, the insinuations of the popular press grew ever broader.

Eventually, late on the evening of 21 March, the boil reached the bursting point, with the all but open accusations of three Labour MP's, George Wigg at their forefront, on the floor of the House of Commons. The nightmarish scene which followed, as Profumo was roused from his bed to be interrogated by five of his fellow Ministers in the middle of the night, gave rise to his first Parliamentary statement the following morning, denying that any impropriety had taken place between himself and Miss Keeler. But never was boil more messily lanced. Never was there the slightest chance that the truth would not sooner or later emerge. In fact, the only people who believed Profumo's disclaimer were those who wanted to believe it. And in the mood of 1963, in London at least, they were few and far between.

The image of authority seemed to be collapsing on all sides. On March 26 a mob of five thousand unemployed from the North of England massed angrily in Parliament Square, finally making a nearly violent attempt to break into the Palace of Westminster itself. In a by-election in Swansea, the Conservative candidate came in fourth, behind even a so-called "People's Party Independent," and polling only 7 percent of the votes. The first of a chaotic series of debates in the House of Commons brought into the open the strange case of Chief Enahoro, the latest and most prolonged of the series of administrative and moral confusions centering around the head of Henry Brooke at the Home Office.

In no way was the disintegration of authority more subtly and profoundly reflected, however, than in a book published in March which was to sell more than three-quarters of a million copies, and which finally brought to a head all the doubts and insecurities which had recently been afflicting many leading members of the Church of England. The sensational impact of *Honest to God* derived from the fact that it was written by a senior member of the Church itself, the "radical" Bishop of Woolwich. Indeed the Bishop himself proudly bandied about the word "radical" and even "heretical" to describe his own views, together with a great deal more of that familiar language, talking of "the wind of change" having turned into "a gale," pouring scorn on the moral attitudes that were sufficient for "our Victorian grandparents," claiming the doctrine that "marriages are made in heaven" to be "simply the metaphysic of a pre-scientific age" and describing the Sermon on the Mount as "a series of flash-light pictures." In a chapter on "The New Morality," the Bishop swept aside the Ten Commandments, the doctrine of natural law, and the entire framework of the Church's traditional teaching, with the rousing declaration that:

> Relativism, utilitarianism, evolutionary naturalism, existentialism have taken their stand, quite correctly, against any subordination of the concrete needs of the individual situation to an alien universal norm.

In an article rather more obviously intended to set the Thames on fire, published by the *Observer* on 17 March and entitled "Our Image of God Must Go," he wrote:

> Few people realise that we are in the middle of one of the most *exciting* theological *ferments* of the century . . . *suddenly* . . . *new* ideas about God and religion, many of them with *disturbing revolutionary*

implications, are *breaking surface . . . radical . . . dangerous . . . immensely exhilarating . . . exciting . . .* in the *world of the H-Bomb* etc., etc.

In fact, the true message of *Honest to God* was one which we have already seen in *Look Back in Anger* or in the rage of the nuclear disarmers against the "Fascist" police force—that is to say, the subconscious projection of a false image of order and authority in order to provide an Aunt Sally for feelings of aggression and superiority. The "nursery picture book" idea of God, which the Bishop so confidently painted as having done service for all believers before "man's coming of age," and which he claimed had been "destroyed" by the "coming of the space age" had nothing to do with the idea of God expressed in the Old or New Testaments, let alone by millions of believers of all religions down the ages—but was only the same superficial caricature which had, quite understandably, been rejected by every one of Bishop Robinson's agnostic predecessors.

The Bishop of Woolwich had last been in the headlines for his defense of *Lady Chatterley's Lover* in 1960. This case more than any other single incident had paved the way for Britain's later reputation as one of the most "permissive" countries in the world. By now, three years later, the full consequences of this trend to greater freedom in discussing sexual matters was just becoming fully apparent. In the words of a startled *Time* magazine:

> On the island where the subject has long been taboo in polite society, sex has exploded into the national consciousness and national headlines. "Are We Going Sex Crazy?" asks the *Daily Herald*. "Is Chastity Outmoded?" asks a school magazine for teenagers. "Are Virgins Obsolete?" is the question posed by the solemn *New Statesman*. The answers vary but one thing is clear: Britain is being bombarded with a barrage of frankness about sex.

The second consistent theme of the British press at this time, remarkable as one looks back through the files, was the language of "crisis"—crisis of every conceivable kind: "The Crisis of Complacency," "Crisis in the Classics," "Moment of Truth for the Tories," "The Uncertain Planemakers . . . Convulsions have marked the progress of Britain's aviation industry. The latest crisis is the most crucial." So ran, for example, the *Sunday Times*—and through it all, more violent than ever, What's Wrong With Britain prose still urged "The Need for Dynamism," "The Importance of Making Ourselves Efficient," and the plaintive cry (from a book review) "Why, oh why did Britain never drag herself into the twentieth century?"

On 27 March, the Chairman of British Railways, Dr. Beeching, produced the first full-dress statement of what might happen to an "obsolete," "nineteenth century" industry if it was subjected to all the "ruthless," "stringent," "drastic," "dynamic," "competitive" "rationalization" for which the What's Wrong With Britain fantasists hungered. His proposal that half the stations and a third of the track on Britain's century-old railway system be closed down was the first official recognition (apart from the building of the first handful of motorways) of just what a revolution the previous fifteen years, along with an eightfold increase in car ownership, had brought about in Britain's transport methods. For more than a hundred years, the puffing locomotive, emitting its clouds over the countryside or filling Victorian termini with billowing steam, had been something of a national symbol to the country where railways began. Now that railway age, with the replacement of steam by diesel and the recognition of the superiority of the motor car, was to be brought abruptly to its end. In the words of the *Annual Register*:

> The outcry from a nation of train lovers (and car owners) was hysterical. All of a sudden, it seemed, everyone had something to lose.

It was not long, however, before the *Sunday Times*'s new *Insight* team were able to find contemporary imagery to make Dr. Beeching's proposals not just palatable—but even "exciting" and at one with the mood of the times. "Inside Beeching's Abbatoir" ran the headline—and under a picture of the moustached but otherwise remarkably unsinister British Railways Chairman:

In a room filled with maps of the *doomed* railways, the doctor controls their *extinction* as *firmly* as he proposed it.

In April and May, as winter gave way to a watery spring, the nightmare drifted into an interlude of painless disintegration and even farce. The rumors surrounding the names of Profumo, Keeler, and Ward began to coalesce with those now percolating down from Edinburgh, where behind locked doors the Duke of Argyll was suing his Duchess for divorce, until, with memories of the Vassall case thrown in, a boundless fantasy emerged, in which not only every member of the Government but the entire upper class of England seemed to have been caught up in an orgy of model girls, perversions, and fancy dress sexual frolics.*

For the satirists, granted the sensational potential of the fact that all this could still be referred to only by suggestion and innuendo, it was a high noon of excitement. *Private Eye* was able to portray Harold Macmillan, in a parody of Gibbon's *Decline and Fall,* as the decrepit Emperor lounging amid dancing girls and prancing homosexuals, while the Empire crumbled around him. *That Was The Week,* with its *leitmotif* of suggestive references to Christine Keeler, neared the end of its first season with an audience risen to over twelve million, although some of the program's original supporters were becoming increasingly uneasy at its growing reliance on sexual innuendo and desire to shock.

As the weeks went by, however, it became increasingly difficult to distinguish between the exaggerations of the satirists and the mounting absurdities of "reality" itself. The disintegration of the Government's morale grew daily more complete. As the Enahoro affair staggered to its messy conclusion, with the Government contradicting itself, and the Attorney General even reported officially on a charge of "unprofessional conduct" by a fellow lawyer MP, an-

* Among the more lurid rumors connected with the Argyll divorce was that concerning the production of a photograph showing a naked man, whose head had been cut from the picture to protect his famous name. The so-called "headless man" was to feature in London demonology for the remainder of the summer.

other pitfall awaited the hapless Henry Brooke in the ludicrous circumstances by which Lenny Bruce, invited for a return season to *The Establishment,* had twice to be de-deported by the Home Office in three days. And when the Prime Minister, with a ghostly flourish of his old *insouciance,* called the Cabinet to Chequers for a weekend discussion on "Britain in the Seventies," the only return he received from most political observers was a stare of disbelief.

But even these marks of the Government's vanishing authority were made trivial in April by the extraordinary "Spies for Peace" episode. On 12 April, at the outset of the sixth Aldermaston March, over four thousand copies of a duplicated pamphlet were distributed to the marchers and to national newspapers, purporting to reveal the closely guarded whereabouts of all the underground bunkers from which government would be carried on in the case of nuclear war. Page after page of highly classified Official Secrets were thus broadcast for all to see. One "Regional Seat of Government" happened to be situated in a wood just off the CND's route into London, and a section of the march, the most unruly and hysterical ever held, split off from the main body to pay homage.

By the time the marchers entered London two days later a mood of complete anarchy prevailed. A sack of flour was showered over the head of the CND's Chairman, Canon Collins of St. Paul's Cathedral. The powerless authorities made pitiful attempts to arrest distributors of the pamphlet, the *Daily Mail* reporting that, as the procession wound down Regent Street, "a man was arrested for singing the secret" (a news item that was to be equaled only a few weeks later when, after more demonstrators had fed aniseed buns to police dogs outside an Essex Air base, the *Daily Express* reported that "the police then took custody of some buns"). But not one of the members of the Committee of 100 who had actually produced the document (as a result, in fact, not of treachery, but simply by the chance that some of them had happened on a bunker containing the secrets of a day when the door was left open) was ever arrested or even publicly identified.

As a final anarchic gesture, however, the episode was an epitaph of the nuclear disarmament movement itself. For although its tradition of protest, anarchy, and demonstration would live on in English life, and although even in 1963 the Committee of 100 had still, as we shall see, far from exhausted its last violent spasm, the Aldermaston March which, in six years, had become a national and almost international institution, would never take place in the same form again.

Despite this continuing fever, April and May were still the calm before the final storm. Even from abroad there was little news of fresh disaster—except for the mysterious loss of the American nuclear submarine *Thresher* with 129 souls, and from America's southern states the growing rumble of threatening racial violence, with a series of riots and bombings.

From England's teenage underworld, however, a distant scream was growing louder, as the sales of pop records began to climb as fast as in the heyday of rock 'n roll, and as the Beatles' third record, *From Me to You,* rose to the top of the hit parade and stayed there for six weeks. The Royal Academy, more anxious than ever to win itself a less "stuffy" and "conventional" image, admitted for the first time to its Summer Exhibition several examples of Pop Art. But it soon transpired that the painting which won most publicity, *Nude Reclining,* showing a crudely drawn cardinal, general, and judge, all in their robes of office, peering down at a book of pin-ups, was a *Private Eye* hoax, the work of an "Old-New" partnership between the magazine's cartoonist William Rushton and Barry Fantoni, an Italian-Jewish artist from South London.

Meanwhile, beneath the surface, the poison of scandal and rumor ran still faster. The police had been investigating the activities of Stephen Ward since the beginning of April. In May, it was announced that Nicholas Luard and another partner from the old Chelsea Set, Dominic Elwes, the son of a titled society portrait painter from a distinguished "Establishment" family, were to star Christine Keeler in a film of her life story. Toward the end of

208

May, it was reported in very small print that Stephen Ward had sent a letter to the Home Secretary on "an undisclosed matter."

In *Private Eye,* on 31 May, Timothy Birdsall drew a nightmarish panorama depicting contemporary England in the style of an eighteenth-century cartoon of debauchery and moral collapse. Against a backdrop of towering office blocks, a huge crowd carrying such banners as "Hang the Queers" was gathered in Trafalgar Square to watch the public figures of the day, each uttering a street cry such as "Come ye and stare at ye breasts of a duchesse!" "Come buy my sweet pornographie, pictures of ye famous lovinge me!" A placard proclaimed a debate between two bishops on "Is There A God?" The Royal Family were posed on a fairground platform, alongside the sign "Get Snapped with the Royals." Over it all flew helicopters showering advertising and free gifts with the cry "Buy Something Today. Buy Anything Today. It Doesn't Matter What But Buy Itte." The Prime Minister looked on and declaimed "Looke around ye my people! See what happiness I have brought ye"—and the whole cartoon was entitled "Britain Gets Wythe Itte 1963."

Three weeks later, Birdsall was dead of leukemia, at the age of twenty-seven—but not before the nightmare which had haunted his drawings for six months had finally erupted into the full light of day. On 4 June, after spending a weekend in Venice, John Profumo returned to England to admit that he had "misled" the House of Commons, resigned all his offices, and plunged English public life into the final depths of unreality.

The events of the following weeks and months had little real connection with the personal indiscretion of two summers before which was nominally their occasion. The Profumo affair was merely the focus and catalyst for the coming to a head of that revolution in the mood and character of English life which had begun to show itself in the late summer of 1955. It was the end of a trail which had had its beginnings in those first grumblings of Henry Fairlie against the Establishment and Malcolm Muggeridge against the Monarchy; a trail that had led on through the Angry Young Men and all the resentments sown by Suez, through the heyday of affluence, through all the mounting impatience with convention, tradition, and authority that had been marked by rebellious teenagers and the CND and the New Morality, through the darkening landscape of security scandals and What's Wrong With Britain and the rising aggression and bitterness of the satirists, in ever more violent momentum. And now, in that wet and windy June, the climax had arrived. Not one ingredient was missing. With Profumo's admission of guilt, all the swelling tide of scorn and resentment for age, tradition, and authority, all the poisonous fantasy of limitless corruption and decay into which it had ripened, were finally unleashed in full fury.

As the *Daily Mirror* thundered in its blackest capitals: "WHAT THE HELL IS GOING ON IN THIS COUNTRY?" Anything was possible and only the worst was to be believed. On 8 June, Stephen Ward was arrested for living on immoral earnings. On the following morning, the *Sunday Mirror*'s publication of the letter from Profumo to Christine Keeler and the beginning of Miss Keeler's own story in the *News of the World,* lifting the veil of rumor on that nyktomorphic fantasy world of the Cliveden swimming pool and Ivanov and dressing up in suits of armor, seemed merely the first confirmatory installment of an unending deluge of scandal to come. Over the following days, sensation followed sensation: in *The Times,* recalling his editorials as the voice of the Old Guard at the time of Suez, Sir William Haley lashing the decadence of a nation gone rotten with affluence, under the heading "It *Is* a Moral Issue"; wild rumors of further cabinet resignations impending; on television, Lord Hailsham losing his temper with Profumo's deceit; the news that the Home Secretary was being rushed back from the Channel Islands, to deal with a new security crisis over a letter sent him by a London solicitor, alleging that Christine Keeler had admitted trying to persuade Profumo to divulge nuclear secrets—leading to an *Evening Standard* placard all over London reading "Christine and the Atom Rockets," as if the whole thing had suddenly turned into a cartoon adventure story.

By Sunday, the frenzy of events at last found suitable expression, as the *Insight* column on the *Sunday Times* revived that breathless narrative style used by the *Observer* at the time of the Cuba crisis. Headlines packed with menace leaped from the page—"The Profumo Volcano," "The Orchestration of a Crisis." The drama of politics had been transformed into entertainment.

The following week, the hysteria was still rising. On Monday, in the House of Commons debate, with twenty-seven Conservative abstentions and Mr. Macmillan giving the most broken performance of his career, nothing so betrayed his bewilderment as those few words "I do not live among young people fairly widely." Behind the by-now familiar facade of Profumo, Keeler, Ward, Ivanov, and Mandy Rice-Davies, rumor was getting completely out of hand, people no longer content with mere exaggerations, but longing to believe any scandal about members of the Government, the Establishment, or the upper classes (however improbable). A town gone mad was obsessed with phantasms—with royal pimps and headless men and naked Ministers in masks. In *The Making of the Prime Minister,* by Anthony Howard and Richard West, Mr. Iain Macleod is quoted as recalling a visit to Mr. Macmillan in these days:

> He was in a terrible state, going on about a rumour of there having been eight High Court judges involved in some orgy. "One," he said, "perhaps two, conceivably. But eight—I just can't believe it."

At the end of the second week of the crisis, the day after commissioning from Lord Denning a judicial inquiry into the whole affair, the Prime Minister was at a garden party in his constituency. To quote Howard and West again:

> He moved like a sleepwalker around the coconut shies, the raffles and the lucky dips. As he posed for a photograph with the tiny daughter of a constituent, one of a group of young hecklers hissed into his ear "Take your hands off that little girl. Don't you wish it was Christine Keeler?"

The next morning, in the *Sunday Times,* Mr. James Margach summed up the week:

> The Conservative Party had been very close these past few days to running berserk in an outburst of tribal frenzy, drawing back just in time from offering the highest sacrifice of all to the tribal gods.

The Labour Party's lead on the opinion polls, if such a mundane measure in the midst of madness meant anything at all, was now over twenty points—then the highest ever recorded by any Party since the taking of polls in Britain began. The following week, as Stephen Ward entered the dock of the Marylebone Magistrates' Court for his committal proceedings, the press was again thrown open to a flood of sensation, new names and images to feed the fantasy: two-way mirrors; Lord Astor, the owner of Cliveden; Douglas Fairbanks Jr.; the stream of prostitutes through the witness box. Outside the courtroom the crowd, transfixed by the magic presence of dream figures, longed for they knew not what. As June drew to a close, the Government still stood amid the ruins. But nowhere had the first inklings of reality yet broken in.*

Not that the rest of the world did not have its own share of problems, crises and impending disasters. The year 1963 stands out as being extraordinary not just in Britain, but in many parts of the world. There were more *coups d'état,* more assassinations of heads of state, and more major natural disasters than in any year since the Second World War—including the cyclone in East Pakistan, which equaled the Agadir earthquake of 1960 as the worst natural disaster for a generation. For Roman Catholics all over the world, it was sig-

---

* Stephen Ward's trial, which technically had no connection with the Profumo affair, was on a charge of living off the earnings of prostitution. The evidence produced to show that he had ever done this was remarkably insubstantial. Obviously Christine Keeler and Mandy Rice-Davies had received lavish presents from their various lovers—but again there is little or no evidence that they were anything more than "good time girls" of a most traditional kind, or that any of the proceeds of their friendships with various rich men were passed on to Ward. The trial, like the affair itself, was in short a product of the gross irrationality of the time.

nificant as being the year of the death of Pope John XXIII, after four years in the Papacy which were as momentous for his Church as any in the century.

To place these things in proper perspective is beyond the province of this book, and I shall therefore only mention them to provide a backdrop for the events which more immediately preoccupied the British. One country undergoing a traumatic crisis was South Vietnam, where the riots, Buddhists suicides, and other disorders heralding the end of the Diem regime marked the closing stages of a period which had begun in 1956 with such promise. Another was Iraq, where the assassination of President Kassem marked the catastrophic end of the nationalist and republican honeymoon which had begun with the overthrow of the monarchy in 1958. A third was the United States, where for the first time began to dawn the full horror of the potential nightmare unleashed by the civil rights campaign, from its comparatively peaceful beginnings in the southern states back in 1955 and 1956.

In June 1963, after the violence afflicting several southern states earlier in the summer, the civil rights crisis took another sharp turn for the worse, with the murder of the Negro leader Medgar Evers in Mississippi, four days before President Kennedy presented his Civil Rights Bill to Congress. On 23 June, the *Sunday Times* reported, in that frenetic imagery which was becoming so familiar in its columns, on the mood of the Deep South, describing a meeting of the Ku Klux Klan:

> In a field in Alabama, a fiery cross blazes into the night. The flames eerily illuminate a gaggle of ghostly figures in white robes and hoods. From a parked truck, a speaker spouts venomous racial hate . . .

There was excitable talk in liberal circles of James Baldwin's apocalyptic forecast of the racial violence that lay ahead, *The Fire Next Time,* taking its title from the old spiritual "God gave Noah the rainbow sign, No more water, the fire next time." And it was from these appalling shadows lengthening over his country that, in the last week of June, President Kennedy briefly escaped for the ten-day tour of Europe that was to turn into a royal progress, the climax to the hold he had established over the imagination of the world. In West Berlin, he was acclaimed by over a million people. Vast crowds followed his visit to his ancestral Ireland. His visit to England, lost in its own dark clouds of crisis, was more private and discreet, including a helicopter flight to Derbyshire to visit the grave of his sister Kathleen, who had been killed in an air crash in 1948; she was the second of his family to die a violent death in the flush of youth. Even in that lonely country churchyard at Edensor, a blood plasma team stood by in a nearby spinney, lest anything should befall the most powerful of all men.

In July, Britain's nightmare continued. The tenor of the times was set by the title of the month's special issue of *Encounter,* "Suicide of a Nation?" the most pessimistic of all What's Wrong With Britain manifestos.

Not the least of the spheres in which 1963 saw something of a crisis after earlier, happier days was the property world. Now, following the suicide in March of Walter Flack, came the even more sensational downfall of the best-known of all the property speculators, Jack Cotton, who, after ejection from his position as Chairman of City Centre, died a few months later. 1963 was proving critical for the property world in other ways, ranging from the collapse of the disastrous alliance between an English company and the American speculator William Zeckendorf (which it was eventually estimated had cost the English company more than 20 million dollars), to the first realization of just how ill-fated Britain's two largest shopping precinct schemes were to be, those at the Bull Ring, Birmingham, and at the Elephant and Castle, South London, both of which had been announced in the same month in 1959 and were now nearing completion.

But it was in fact from out of the Profumo miasma that there emerged the most publicized aspect of the underside of that glittering property boom of the late fifties, in the specter of Rachmanism. With the first hints of the character and extent of the Rachman property empire, a new region was opened up in popular fantasy, the world of protection rackets and slum landlordism, where who knew what bloated white monsters might still be scuttling away from the light. The fact that Rachman himself was dead only added to the drifting uncertainty—particularly when, on 8 July, a Labour MP claimed in the Commons that he might still be alive. The fact that most of the evils directly associated with the Rachman empire had at least been mitigated by Government action as long ago as 1961 was hardly worthy of notice to a sensation-drunk public.

Other mysteries ramified. There was the strange case of Mr. Lawrence Bell, a freelance journalist, accused of impropriety with guardsmen in order, so he claimed, to "shut him up" on the Profumo affair (he was in fact acquitted). There was the even stranger case of Lucky Gordon, the West Indian singer and former lover of Christine Keeler, who in June had been sentenced to three years' imprisonment after hysterical scenes in the courtroom, and was now released by the Court of Appeal on the strength of evidence (a tape recording owned by Miss Keeler) which was never made public. And still rumor raged on, whipped up by such stunts as the *Daily Mirror*'s declaration in huge front-page headlines "Prince Philip and the Profumo Scandal," the popular effect of which was hardly assuaged, of course, by the small print beneath asserting that the spate of rumors connecting Prince Philip to the affair was "utterly unfounded."

Another ghost from the past plunged the Government into further trouble, with the admission on 1 July that Kim Philby, the *Observer* correspondent who had vanished in the Middle East in January, had indeed been the "third man" involved in the Burgess and Maclean affair of 1951. In all sorts of ways, the years 1962–1963 were marking the culmination of an era of espionage on both sides of the Iron Curtain. In many respects, the spies against Russia itself who defected or were captured during this period, such as Oleg Penkovsky, were more important than that unhappy handful of weak and insecure members of the English upper-middle class, Philby, Vassall, Maclean, and Burgess, whose treachery and secret fascination with the image of Russian Communism had provided such a significant footnote to the social history of England over the previous thirty years.

On 9 July, there began in London the most unfortunate visit of prominent foreigners to London since the day in 1849 when the Austrian General Haynau had been set upon by the workers at Barclay Perkins' brewery—the state visit of the King and Queen of Greece, which became a last focus for all the bitterness and aggression of the remnants of the Committee of 100. On 10 July Queen Elizabeth became the first British monarch for over a century to be booed openly in the streets. But even this was not an end to the episode, for among its repercussions was the "Challenor affair," the outcome of the planting of half a brick on one of the many demonstrators arrested by the hysterically zealous (and mentally unbalanced) Sergeant Challenor at the Saville Row police station.

The "Challenor affair" was a culmination of the growing strain imposed on the police in recent years, not only by the rising crime rate, but also by the mounting aggression of the youthful protest movement, whose demonstrations increasingly made the police the main target for their hostility. The reaction of Sergeant Challenor himself was a classic example of a right-wing fantasy exacerbated to the point of "explosion into reality" by a left-wing fantasy—and a left-wing fantasy that, in the following weeks, was to grow even more hysterical, when the Challenor incident was followed by two more police scandals, the first the suspension of two detectives in Sheffield for their unduly violent treatment of suspects and the second the mysterious circumstances which were alleged by *Private Eye* in August to have surrounded the death, while in hospital under police guard, of a drug-addicted artist named Hal Woolf.

On the periphery were other symptoms: the "stamp war" raging at its height in the supermarkets; the strange experience of a group of Covent Garden printers who produced as a private joke some stickers for their car windows reading "Marples Must Go," and suddenly found themselves with a national craze on their hands; the fraught imagery of a news item in the *Sunday Times*:

> The night is *silent*, the city *peaceful*. The early tradesmen move *ghost-like* in the streets. Beneath the earth *powerful stresses grind relentlessly* towards an *unredeemable climax*. At 5.17 the *shock strikes*. In a *fraction* of a *second* the ground *shakes* with a *hideous shiver* . . . substance *crumbles*. Life is *extinguished* in a *cloud* of *dust*.

All of this might seem a curiously feverish and self-indulgent way to describe the earthquake which on 26 July killed over a thousand people in the Yugoslavian town of Skopje.

Not all the month's climaxes were so "unredeemable," however, nor was all its news of scandals, hysterias, and disasters. On 16 July, for instance, came the culmination of Anthony Wedgwood Benn's eight-year campaign to allow hereditary peers to disclaim their titles —a "victory over mediaeval anachronism" that was to have consequences quite unforeseen by the eager Benn, although when the Peerage Bill finally became law, it would be he and his fellow member of the New Oxford Group, Lord Altrincham, who would be the first to take advantage of its provisions.* The end of a more momentous story came on 25 July when the seven years of growing concern at the perilous effects of fallout from nuclear tests bore fruit in the signing of the international Test Ban Treaty in Moscow. But by then few people in England, at least, had eyes for this news, or even for the headlines that recorded a further sharp deterioration in the relations between Russia and China. For on 22 July the saga of Stephen Ward had once again taken the center of the national stage. Only this time, it too, after all those months of crescendo, was approaching its own "explosion into reality."

---

* The most significant immediate result of this Act, of course, was that three months later Lord Home would be able to resign his peerage in order to become Prime Minister, as a member of the house of Commons.

It was by now irrelevant that Ward's trial had been in any strict legal sense highly suspect; that the charges were dubious; or that the "evidence" presented by that bizarre stream of girls dredged up from the depths of a world in which neither truth nor morality had any place was little more reliable than that of so many bewildered children. For the pattern now being worked out had long since departed from any ground where "truth" might be found or "justice" arrived at—into a twilight of subterranean terrors and squeaking ghosts. The trial, like the rumors themselves, was merely an infernal charade, played out around the central character, with his increasingly strained, unseeing smile. On the last day of July, Ward forestalled the inevitable verdict of the Court by taking an overdose of Nembutal. On 3 August he was dead.

Five days later, the eyes of the public were riveted by a new sensation—a high point in the crime wave which had been rising yearly since 1955—the greatest robbery in British history. At once the crime passed into newspaper mythology as "the Great Train Robbery." And as the headlines were filled for days with the computation of the haul, with mysterious happenings at Leatherslade Farm, with the finding of fortunes in Surrey woods and Bournemouth garages, "reality" was once again submerged in fantasy. Even the underworld itself was stunned by the enormity of the crime, and for several weeks was unusually quiet. A further army of rumors flooded into the void, more nyktomorphic shadows—a "Master Mind" who was a household name, perhaps even a Peer of the Realm. As over the next two months, the names and professions of the Great Train Robbers began to emerge, they read in fact almost like a cross-section of the affluent New England—a South London antique dealer, a South London hairdresser, a Chelsea racing driver, and a South London book-maker. So vast and so brazen was their crime that its perpetrators began to acquire a strange glamor, fantasy figures to be regarded with the same awe as Keeler or Rice-Davies or, increasingly, the Beatles. This was particularly true of Douglas Goody, one of the first to be arrested, and of whom an acquaintance and chronicler of the affair was later to write:

> There were flaws in Goody, however, even as a criminal. He was in it for the kicks as well as the cash . . . he seemed to believe he bore a charmed life, although those who knew him began to see signs of that death-wish not uncommon in criminals—"He almost wanted to be caught," they said.*

At about the same time came news of a terrible storm in the Mediterranean, between France and Corsica. Many lives were lost as small boats capsized—among them a fragile Criss-Craft on which, at the height of the storm, Lord Timothy Willoughby D'Eresby, the co-proprietor of the night club *Wip's,* had been attempting to cross the strait. Back in London, Willoughby D'Eresby's partner Nicholas Luard was also in trouble, as another wild venture, an expensive show business magazine launched on the early tide of profits of the "satire boom," collapsed. *The Establishment* club too was now heavily in debt; the Luard empire was declared bankrupt; and *The Establishment* which, before its brief reign as "London's first satirical night club," had been a strip-tease club, now returned to the hands of the more traditional Soho underworld as a gambling saloon, while the premises of *Wip's* were sold to become a discothèque, under the name of the *Ad Lib*.

From America came the news, on the same day as the death of Stephen Ward, of the suicide of one of President Kennedy's closest friends, the millionaire proprietor of *Newsweek,* Philip Graham. On 28 August the biggest demonstration in American history took place, as over 200,000 civil rights protesters marched through the streets of Washington in an endless stream.

During July and August, Lord Denning, the third ranking figure in Britain's judiciary, had been interviewing a train of more than 150

---

* Mrs. Peta Fordham, *The Great Train Robbery* (1965).

witnesses in order to reduce to meaningful proportion the miasma of rumor which hung over British public life. He had talked to Ministers of the Crown and professional prostitutes, policemen, and liars, Harold Macmillan and Mandy Rice-Davies. One Cabinet Minister had even submitted to medical examination to prove that he was not the subject of obscene photographs produced in evidence during the Duke of Argyll's divorce case. The episode was like some parody, whereby the judicial standards and grave procedures of a bygone age were rendered pitiful and absurd by the attempt to apply them to a new, unreal order of things.

In fact, Lord Denning's inquiry itself seemed as much a projection of the new age as a relic of more sober days. In the days before the publication of his Report on 26 September, its author apparently reveled in a glare of newspaper publicity. His report itself was racily written, with headings that would not have looked out of place in the *News of the World*: "The Man in the Mask," "Christine Asks for £5000," "Paul Mann Takes a Holiday," "The Man without a Head." For hours before its publication, shortly after midnight, a crowd of several thousand was gathering outside the Government Publications Office in Kingsway, specially opened at this extraordinary hour for the purpose. Both television channels ran late night programs, with cameras and floodlights on the scene, and the world's press men jostled in hundreds. Already the first of a series of paperbacks, the *Insight* team's *Scandal '63*, was in the best-seller lists. But at long last, as if the British public sensed that behind all the insubstantial edifice of rumor there was no more real sensation to come, the peak of the fever had been passed. While Mandy Rice-Davies dismissed the Denning Report as a "joke," and her friend Christine Keeler disappeared behind the walls of Holloway Prison for perjury in the trial of Lucky Gordon, the crowd and events rushed on elsewhere.

It was at this time that the Beatles' fourth record, *She Loves You,* went to the top of the hit parade, where it was to stay for seven weeks. The "Liverpool phenomenon" and the "Mersey Sound" were now arousing interest far beyond circles normally interested in pop music, and were attracting an increasing number of newspaper articles written in the same mesmerized tone as that of the *Sunday Times*:

> By night they *flood* out into the *raw mistral* that *rips* in from Liverpool Bay . . . the Fourmost . . . the Spidermen, the Mindbenders, the Undertakers . . . as music it is *vigorous, aggressive, uncompromising . . . exaggeratedly rhythmic, high-pitched, thunderously amplified,* full of *wild insidious* harmonies.

From South Vietnam, whence had come pictures of a further wave of public suicides by Buddhist monks, came news of violent rioting, thousands of arrests, and, from the United Nations Secretary General U Thant, the claim that the situation was "chaotic and growing worse." In the Dominican Republic, the Government was overthrown in the year's fifth military *coup,* in Brazil over 300,000 people were made homeless by forest fires and in India 200,000 by floods, and in Birmingham, Alabama, the year's racial violence came to a head with further riots, following the bombing of a Negro church, killing four little girls. In Jakarta, the British Embassy was burned down by ten thousand screaming demonstrators, while along the Indonesian-Malay frontier a guerilla war broke out that was to rage for the next three years.

In Britain, the Liberal Party, now committed to every kind of "dynamic" reform, held its largest and most excitable Assembly since the Liberal Revival had begun seven years before, under the huge banner "GO JO GO." The *Sunday Times* summed up the last day:

> The Liberal Party's symbol of a new broom . . . seemed to have assumed a new and far more menacing bristle by the time Jo Grimond sat down to a standing ovation . . . "I intend to march my troops towards the sound of gunfire," he boomed. And the troops exploded. Clapping until it hurt, young men and girls dreamed wide-eyed dreams . . .

At the month's end, *That Was The Week That Was* returned to the nation's television screens, amid a buzz of anticipation. The *Observer* gave the program a page of eulogistic welcome, quoting the proud claim of a nonagenarian couple that David Frost and his colleagues had "changed their lives." But the surfeits of the summer and their previous whirlwind success had taken toll of both cast and writers; the neurotic fires of the previous winter were burned out; and the program's first few editions were slipshod and lifeless. A new craze took over the nation's Saturday nights, on the commercial channel—a violent thriller series, *The Avengers,* starring a bowler-hatted Old Etonian actor Patrick MacNee and Miss Honor Blackman as a pair of mysterious secret agents. The show aroused particular excitement through Miss Blackman's "kinky" black leather costumes. And indeed the London-centered craze for "kinky" black boots, "kinky" black raincoats, and "kinky" black leather or plastic garments of all kinds raged throughout that autumn.

At the end of September, the American magazine *Newsweek* summed up Britain's mood:

> This has been the year of Britain's discontent, and the nation has been wallowing in an orgy of self-criticism as relentless as the one which swept the U.S. after the launching of the first Sputnik in 1957. Last week the weekly *Spectator* speculated about "a failure of nerve at the centre." The *Times* worried about sagging prestige abroad. The *Guardian* found the root of Britain's troubles in "our veneration for out-of-date institutions" while the Labour Party bewailed "the corruption of standards of public life." For the Liberals . . . "the Civil Service is a blind giant." For the Conservatives the target is "an administrative machine which has run riot." Everywhere there was disenchantment and self-denigration, and as the *Economist* put it, "the British have become, suddenly, the most introspective people on earth."

As October began, the Labour Party gathered at Scarborough for its annual Conference. Through the smoke and thunder of the summer, one image of political stability alone had bored in on the nation's consciousness—the stock figure of Harold Wilson, with his Gannex raincoat, his pipe, and his consistent air of public gravity before the unfolding of regrettable but somehow inevitable events. Never before had the Labour Party had a leader so conscious of the importance of cutting the right impression, of putting up the right facade, regardless of what lay behind. For as Wilson himself knew, his past record and reputation for duplicity gave him much to live down. Throughout the year he had assiduously polished his front of responsibility. He had played the international statesman—visiting Washington to be photographed with President Kennedy, and Moscow with Mr. Khrushchev. Even throughout the Profumo affair itself, he had been careful to concern himself only with its "security aspects."

But now, at Scarborough, in the hall where, three years before, he had sat through the ovation given his predecessor, inscrutably biding his time, Mr. Wilson faced a new test. His Party had been given an opportunity which even twelve months before would have seemed unimaginable. It was still in essence, however, the same Labour Party, the same "loose confederation of warring tribes" (as James Reston once described administrative Washington) that throughout the fifties and early sixties had seemed to have exhausted its role in British politics, without philosophy, policy, or purpose. Mr. Wilson's challenge at Scarborough was to provide and clarify for his Party those three ingredients without which no group fantasy can flourish —the dream hero, which he provided himself, the focus for group aggression, which already existed in the image of the decaying, upper-class, grouse-shooting Macmillan Government, and lastly, the common dream, which would unite all its members with the vision of a promised land. And it was at this point that the Labour Party's leader produced his masterstroke—with one lick of paint erasing all the lingering unhappiness and discord of previous years. On 1 October, in his flat Yorkshire voice, he unveiled to his followers the new vision:

223

The strength, solvency and influence of Britain, which some still think depend on nostalgic illusions and nuclear posturings, are going to depend in the remainder of this century on the speed with which we come to terms with the world of change.

"Change," "Technology," "Automation," "The Scientific Revolution"—these were the glittering slogans of the new crusade. No mention of Clause Four or nationalization or the dead mottoes of revisionism; the eyes of the faithful were lifted to new hills, misty, far off, and shining in the dawn—a "university of the air," a "crash programme" on the "fuller use of universities," the reorganization of industry so that it "applied the results of scientific research more purposively to the national production effort." How lifeless the words look printed cold on paper, particularly in the knowledge of the dismal reality into which this dream was to fade. And yet what an effect they had on those four thousand delegates. The past was over!

As for what it all meant in terms of reality, perhaps the most revealing comment came from Mr. Wilson himself, in a remark to *Time* magazine only a week later. The Labour Party, he said,

is like a vehicle. If you drive at great speed, all the people in it are either so exhilarated or so sick that you have no problems. But when you stop, they all get out and argue about which way to go.

On 9 October, after a week of headlines full of the disaster in the Caribbean following Hurricane Flora, and the breaking of the Bobby Baker scandal in Washington, which threatened to engulf American public life in its own more serious version of the Profumo affair, the Conservative Party met in a tense and gloomy mood for its Conference at Blackpool. In the morning the British press had been dominated by only one piece of news—that the sixty-nine-year-old Prime Minister's health had at last broken under the strain. After seven long years, the age of Macmillan had entered its final torment.

Already by the first day, even before it was clear whether the

Prime Minister's operation would entail his resignation, the Conference was, in the words of Alan Moorehead in the *Sunday Times*:

> living on its nerves . . . the rival groups were forming . . . and not even Chicago could have outdone the scurrying . . . the canvassing, the hourly shifting in the betting, the mood of fatal self-induced excitement.

By Thursday, when Lord Home, as President of the Conference, looked out over his half-moon spectacles and read the message from Mr. Macmillan asking that the Party should "carry on the customary processes of consultation . . . about its future leadership," it was evident, in the words of the *Insight* column, that "the Party was now going headlong into a leadership war."

That evening, as Lord Hailsham spoke to an audience of 2,500 in a local cinema, with a further thousand or so people waiting expectantly outside, there came the first hint of the hysteria that was to come; in the words of *Insight* again:

> He spoke for an hour and a half, under emotion and sometimes incoherent, until finally at 10 p.m. he said . . . "My inclination is, after deep thought, to disclaim my peerage." The rest was lost in a roar . . .

The Conservative Party had never known anything like it—nor indeed had the country. For the next two days, as the three main contenders for the leadership grappled in rivalry, the atmosphere of Blackpool was, again in the words of Moorehead:

> like a fireworks display that gets bigger and better as it goes along, and in the end no one knew where to turn for certainty . . .

Before the gaze of the electorate, the Conservative Party seemed to be tearing itself to pieces, as lost in self-destructive frenzy as the Labour Party three years before. Once again, British politics had collapsed into entertainment that could no longer be reflected in the calm measures of conventional reportage but only in the disjointed prose of "blow by blow" journalism and the hectic *ciné-vérité* of

World in Action. For a week the tempest raged while the identity of the three contenders became lost, mere "images" tossed in the tumult.

Only one man at Blackpool had, by a mere chance of office, been able to stand aloof from the chaos—the President of the Conference, the fourteenth Earl of Home. By the time that, on 17 October, Harold Macmillan came to make his last great decision as Prime Minister, and was, once again, tempted back from the vulgar and disorderly present toward an "image" of aristocratic stability and calm, he was putting the seal on a process which had begun in many minds, consciously and subconsciously, a week before. Through the night of October 17, when it first seemed that, after all, the impossible was about to happen, the younger generation of the Party leadership gathered in bewildered midnight conclave to contemplate a last-ditch stand. But it was too late. On the following morning, Harold Macmillan resigned the Premiership. Six days before, *That Was The Week That Was* had marked the departure of the one man who had been the *raison d'être* for Britain's "satire movement," with a moment of profound nostalgia—as William Rushton, cast as Macmillan, had come on from the wings to sing in broken voice "The Party's Over." The father-figure had at last been destroyed, and the satirists marked the advent of his successor with an attack of such contempt that for the first time the Director-General himself actually ordered cuts before the program went on the air. That night the BBC received more calls of protest than in any week of the program's run.

Over the last days of October, with a further stream of television interviews, television profiles, and "background" features in the press, the country accustomed itself to the strange figure who, by so many freaks of chance, had become Prime Minister. Already, in the glare of publicity, that brief mantle of authority which descended on the man unknown, was beginning to crumble. As he stripped himself of his titles and set off for the glens of Perthshire to re-enter the House of Commons; as, with remarks such as " I have lived with miners all my life," he fumbled for the trappings of a "democratic," "contemporary," image, it was already becoming clear that he had little natural kinship with the mood of the times.

It was also in October that a major landmark was established in the history of the English theatre, with the opening of the new National Theatre. Among those who had campaigned most fervently for its creation was Kenneth Tynan, whose career was now crowned by his appointment as the Theatre's dramatic adviser or "dramaturge." Once again, Mr. Tynan's inclination toward self-dramatization had led him into make-believe, for the true meaning of his high-sounding title was not mere dramatic adviser but an actual writer or creator of plays. Nevertheless there was no doubt that, in Tynan's appointment and in the establishment of the National Theatre itself, as in the Queen's creation during the year of Peter Brook and Peter Hall of the Royal Shakespeare Company as Commanders of the British Empire, the new English drama had had its full measure of official acceptance and recognition.

Toward the end of the month came the news that, on a visit to Dallas in Texas, Adlai Stevenson had been the center of a near-riot, being violently jostled and jeered, spat upon and hit on the head with a placard. On the same night, the Chief Justice of the Supreme Court, attending a dinner in New York, was barricaded in the building for two hours, while an angry crowd outside chanted "Impeach Warren." America's own year-long nightmare was not over yet.

On 1 November, the crisis in Vietnam finally erupted in open revolt, with a successful *coup d'état* by the army, the seventh during the year, and the murder of both President Diem and his brother. On 6 November, there were signs that another crisis might be blowing up over Berlin. Two nights before in London, huge crowds had blocked the streets around the Prince of Wales Theatre for several hours—but throughout the arrival of members of the Royal Family for the year's Royal Command Variety performance, the only noise audible had been a shrill, unending squeal from thousands of teen-agers, "We want the Beatles." Over the next few days, the national press completely caved in to this phenomenon, running page after page, from the *Daily Mirror*'s editorial:

> YEAH! YEAH! YEAH!
> You have to be a real sour square not to love the nutty, noisy, happy, handsome Beatles . . . rumbustious young Beatles . . . [who had taken] a middle-aged Royal Variety Performance by the scruff of their necks

to the analysis of the *Sunday Times*:

> Sexual emancipation is a factor in the phenomenon, though at a super-ficial level this may not be so important. "You don't have to be a genius," said a consultant in a London hospital, "to see parallels be-tween sexual excitement and the mounting crescendo of . . . a stimu-lating number like 'Twist and Shout' . . . but I think it is the bubbly, uninhibited gaiety of the group that generates enthusiasm."

The year-long rise of the Beatles and the new popularity of pop music generally, with record sales rising even above their previous peak of 1957, had provided a suitable *obbligato* to the year of an ever-swelling "dream." But in other fields of artistic activity, 1963 had given birth to little more than a succession of extraordinary night-mares. As windows on the collective subconscious, the somber qual-ity which had marked a number of films of the previous year had descended into even blacker depths, with a whole series of films from both Britain and Europe expressing the ultimate pitch of in-consequentiality and despair, such as *Le Feu Follet* (France), Ingmar Bergman's *The Silence* (Sweden), Antonioni's *The Eclipse* (Italy); *The Servant,* made in England from a script by Harold Pinter and portraying the corruption of an upper-class young man by his lower-class butler; and Orson Welles's version of Kafka's *The Trial,* filled with huge, dream-like buildings and endless corridors, and of which Paul McCartney was quoted as saying:

What I like best . . . was when they walked quietly through the concentration camp. It was so dead quiet, just like another world, and Elsa Martinelli in the background just necking like mad.*

Another film made during the year was *Dr. Strangelove: Or How I Learned to Stop Worrying and Love the Bomb,* a nightmare comedy set in the last hours before the blowing up of the world. Its plot was based on the characteristic nightmare situation of "inability to communicate," in this case with the pilot of an American nuclear bomber hurtling toward the Russian "Doomsday Machine," and which ended with the familiar nightmare dénouement of a sensation of falling, the bomb and the bomber's pilot slipping away together toward the world's blinding disintegration.

One of the most obvious characteristics of these films was their "blackness," the gloomy, dark photography which set off their depressing themes. This vogue for "blackness" was by no means found only in films, but could also be seen in the sets for *That Was The Week That Was,* a bare, darkened studio; in the *ciné-vérité* photography which was becoming so popular on other television programs; in the black, "kinky" leather clothes and even in the photography and harsh layout that was characteristic of the more avant-garde magazines and newspapers. The nightmarish and suicidal mood that was so clearly reflected in other ways also found its expression in many of the year's novels, including Ian Fleming's tenth and all but last installment of the James Bond saga, *You Only Live Twice,* the plot of which was set around a "suicide garden" in Japan, and which was later described by one of Fleming's most fervent admirers, Kingsley Amis, as "horrific and haunting in a way that none of the others are."

On 12 November, Hugh Carleton-Greene, Director General of the BBC, issued a statement:

* From *Love Me Do: The Beatles' Progress* (1964) by Michael Braun, to which I am indebted for various information and quotations.

The BBC announces that the present run of *That Was The Week That Was* will end on 28 December 1963 and not continue, as had originally been intended, until the Spring.

The BBC had taken its decision, Mr. Greene added, solely because the following year would be an election year, a fact which had hardly been in doubt for some time, and in no way because it had "ceased to have confidence in the TWTWTW team." In fact, it was no secret that the show's recent poor quality, combined with its straining after sensation, had made it virtually impossible to defend. In the same week, the circulation of *Private Eye* was beginning a collapse even faster than its meteoric rise, which was to take it from 90,000 down to 25,000 and the verge of bankruptcy in less than three months. The satirists' dream was over. But the mood of the country was still black and feverish. On 17 November, James Margach reported of the political mood at Westminster:

Already they're all living on their election nerves . . . emotionally tensed up in a taut election atmosphere and in danger of being carried along by the momentum.

Five days later, on the morning of Friday 22 November, the *Daily Express* carried a page of photographs of Barry Goldwater. Their headline was "The Man Who Is Gunning for Kennedy."

Just before eight that evening came the first newsflash from Dallas. The assassination of President Kennedy was the final sensation, the only possible "happening" short of major war which for the British could have out-climaxed everything else in such a year. Anything it now seemed, could happen — and already, as people groped for their reactions, the first images began to swim disconnectedly out of the darkness. The television tributes — George Brown, mumbling, aggressive, incoherent; Harold Wilson, businesslike, still unable to think outside reference to himself, laying persistent stress on the change that Kennedy's "vigor" had brought over a "tired" country; Home, formal and vacuous. For four days, Britain, like the world, was stunned, mesmerized before the flickering screen by the unfolding of the nightmare; the shooting of Oswald, the frantic crowds, the endless replaying of the amateur's blurred, chaotic roadside film, the funeral procession in Washington with so many of the disparate figures in the world pageant suddenly bizarrely brought together.

It was perhaps not totally inapposite to paraphrase the meaning of a sentence from Sir James Frazer in *The Golden Bough:*

> The honour of living for a short time in the character of a god and dying a violent death in the same capacity was not restricted to men in Mexico.

Or even that among the year's film releases had been Antonioni's *The Eclipse,* a black and drifting nightmare which had ended in a cloud covering the sun, throwing the world into a silent twilight.

For days the shock—far greater than that which could have been caused by the death of any Englishman—lay over Britain, blanketing everything. Then, into the ensuing void, the noise which had been rising all the year flooded in a deafening torrent. In the last month of 1963, it became apparent that the Beatles were a phenomenon like nothing that pop music had known before. Already in their wake there were an estimated three hundred and fifty further pop groups in Liverpool alone. But it was not only in Liverpool that this phenomenon had come to the surface. A similar underground surge was also surfacing in America, associated with such names as Phil Spector and Tamla-Motowna. It spread like wildfire through other cities in Britain, such as London itself, where in such teenage centers as *The Scene,* a Soho club for "Mods," the rhythm 'n blues of the Rolling Stones was beginning to arouse enthusiasm every bit as hysterical as anything on Merseyside.

On 29 November, the Beatles' fifth record, *I Want to Hold Your Hand,* went straight to the top of the hit parade and stayed there for almost two months. It was to become the best-selling British record ever made, selling over the next year and a half more than ten million copies in all parts of the world. Two weeks later, no less than eight out of the top twenty records were songs written by Lennon and McCartney. In a celebrated and significant moment marking the surrender of more traditional forms of culture to this new mass hysteria, the Music Critic of *The Times*, William Mann (post-war Cambridge), wrote on 27 December:

> The outstanding English composers of 1963 must seem to have been John Lennon and Paul McCartney . . . the slow sad song about "That Boy" . . . is expressively unusual for its lugubrious music, but harmonically it is one of their most interesting, with its chains of pandiatonic clusters . . . but harmonic interest is typical of their quicker songs too . . . so firmly are the major tonic sevenths and ninths built into their tunes, and the flat sub-mediant key switches, so natural is the Aeolian cadence at the end of "Not A Second Time" (the chord progression which ends Mahler's *Song of the Earth*) etc., etc.

Two days later the Beatles were described by Richard Buckle in the *Sunday Times* as "the greatest composers since Beethoven."

On 16 December, there was a one-day debate in the House of Commons on the Denning Report—but already the Profumo affair seemed like something from another age. The debate was chiefly remarkable for a polished, quietly philosophical speech from Harold Macmillan, below the gangway. It was a last echo of his old mastery. The Macmillan era was finally over. At the end of the year, as the Beatles opened for a Christmas season at Finsbury Park (for which more than 100,000 tickets had been sold in advance), the *Evening Standard* put out a special commemorative supplement. It was headed simply "1963 . . . The Year of the Beatles."

It was also the year in which, after a steep rise in 1956 and 1957, falling off a little and then sharply accelerating again in 1962, the British suicide rate had reached the highest level ever recorded.

Part Three

Chapter Nine

The Dream after the Storm

When devils will their blackest sins put on,
They do suggest at first with heavenly shows.

Othello, II, 3

The more insignificant, the lower, the emptier a
phenomenon is, once it becomes the object of suggestion,
the more supernatural and exaggerated is the importance
attached to it . . . suggestion is always a deceit, and every
deceit is an evil.

LEO TOLSTOY
Shakespeare and the Drama

"Wait till you see the Stones! They're so sexy! They're
pure sex! They're *divine!* . . . When Mick Jagger comes
into the Ad Lib in London—I mean there's nothing like
the Ad Lib in New York. You can go into the Ad Lib and
everyone is there. They're all young, and they're taking
over, it's like a whole revolution, I mean, it's exciting,
they're all from the lower classes, East-End-sort-of-thing.
There's nobody exciting from the upper classes any more,
except for Nicole and Alec Londonderry, Alec is a British
marquis . . ."

"BABY" JANE HOLZER, New York socialite,
quoted by Tom Wolfe in "The Girl of the Year,"
New York magazine, 1964

There is now a curious cultural community, breathlessly
à la Mod, where Lord Snowdon and the other desperadoes
of the grainy layout jostle with commercial art-school
Mersey stars, window dressers and Carnaby Street pants-
peddlers. Style is the thing here—Taste 64—a cool line
and the witty insolence of youth . . .

JONATHAN MILLER
New Statesman, 29 May 1964

They're young, I said, and for the first time they're being allowed
to roll about in it and have clothes and money and music and sex,
and you can take or leave any of it. No one before has been able to
do such things with such charm, such ease, such frozen innocence as
all of you seem to have . . . but there isn't much loving in any
of your kindnesses, Jane, not much kindness, not even cruelty,
really . . . perhaps just a very easy, controlled, sharp, I mean
"sharp" pleasure in discomfiture . . .

BILL MAITLAND in John Osborne's
Inadmissible Evidence, September 1964

236

Yes, I am a Mod and I was at Margate . . . it was great,
the beach was like a battlefield. It was like we were taking
over the country.

18-year old London mechanic,
quoted in *Generation X* (1964)

What I think we're going to need is something like what
President Kennedy had when he came in after years of
stagnation in the United States. He had a programme of
a hundred days—a hundred days of dynamic action.

HAROLD WILSON
Labour Party Political Broadcast, 15 July 1964

The contrast between the England of 1963 and that of 1964 is the greatest provided by this narrative. The "grand climacteric" of 1963 was the central crisis of the English revolution. The previous seven years had marked the increasing conflict between Old England and the New England that had been rising to replace it. The events of 1963 had marked Old England's downfall.

As we turn toward the second half of this narrative, two general observations may be made. I have suggested that the new climate emerging in Britain after the middle-fifties was part of a much wider pattern affecting many other countries. In all sorts of ways, the years after 1956 saw a widespread awakening from the post-war shadows, a turning to the future, with all its attendant fantasies based on change, youth, freedom, and the rising up of underdogs against the established order.

But the events of 1963 marked a "central crisis" only in the peculiar context of Britain's experience during these years. I am not suggesting that, except for one or two other specific countries, 1963 was a year of climax in the more general worldwide pattern. From now on, there was to emerge an increasing difference in the force with which this more general pattern affected Britain and other countries. Britain was never to see again quite such a height of turbulence as she had seen in 1963, but for other countries the coming years were to bring a much more terrible nemesis following the awakening of nervous energy which had taken so many forms in the late fifties and early sixties. In particular, of course, the eyes of the world would increasingly be fixed over the next five years on Vietnam and America.

The second point I wish to discuss briefly is the broad pattern of events in Britain between 1955 and 1963. The events had run exactly through a fantasy cycle. Now, it may be argued that I have here and there picked out the particular facts to suit my thesis; and undoubtedly there are a great number of qualifications which can be

238

made to the thesis (such as the extent to which the different fantasies of different groups and individuals overlap, or take place on different time-scales); nevertheless, it cannot be denied that, in the most general sense, the changes in the prevailing mood in English life in these years corresponded uncannily to the five stages of the fantasy cycle.

During the initial upheavals of 1955–1958, there was an extraordinarily widespread sense of awakening anticipation, finding its focus in all sorts of ways from the acclaim of the intelligentsia for the doctrines of Jimmy Porter, and that of the teenagers for rock 'n roll, to the excitement with which the country at large received the coming of affluence and television. This passed into a stage between 1958 and 1960 when it seemed that all parts of English society could move together into the future, both the "new groups" most obviously affected by the change and the established order, represented above all by the Macmillan Government. By 1960–1961, this unanimity for change had begun to dissolve into a phase when feelings of frustration became dominant, and when (even though the country could hardly have been changing faster) new groups, such as the What's Wrong With Britain journalists and the satirists, represented a growing clamor for much more radical changes than any so far. This had given way to the "nightmare" of 1962, when the country's mood seemed to become altogether more nervy, and when all sorts of things began to go wrong, particularly for the Macmillan Government. And this had culminated in turn in the extraordinary spirit of disorder of the central crisis of 1963.

One interesting aspect of this pattern is that, borrowing from Professor Crane Brinton's celebrated analysis in *The Anatomy of Revolution,* it can be seen in the broadest sense to be the pattern of almost any phase of violent social and political change, such as that of more obviously revolutionary upheavals. In terms of collective psychology, for instance, it is perhaps not too far-fetched to see a parallel between that initial stage of turmoil in 1955–1958 and the initial turmoil in 1789 which marked the onset of the French Revolution. This gives way to a Dream Stage, as in France in 1790 and 1791, when for a time it seems that the established order and the new forces can cooperate in a program of rapid reform and change, both being carried along on the same tide. Eventually, however, as in the rise of the Jacobins and the followers of Danton in France, and the emergence of the satirists and What's Wrong With Britain journalists in England, there appears a more extreme group of reformers who can no longer be satisfied by cooperation with the established order, however liberal and radical it appears to be. This sign of frustration quickly ushers in a more violent phase, in which the established order goes to pieces and is finally and destructively overthrown.

I am sure that for many readers, even allowing for qualification, any claim that what happened in Britain in the fifties and sixties was a "revolution" will seem wild—no heads rolled, no blood was shed, and the most conspicuous political fruit of these events at the end of 1963, at least, was that Britain had its most aristocratic Prime Minister since 1902.

Yet the real and profound change that was taking place in people's lives in this period, all over Britain, must not be underestimated— it was a much more "revolutionary" change, in some respects, than had been experienced by the average Frenchman in the 1790's. It may have been thought that the arrival of an unprecedented prosperity and a television set in the corner of the living room were somewhat pleasanter symbols of revolutionary upheaval than tumbrels rolling through the streets. Nevertheless, it was a profound change, with all the consequent new insecurities and deeper anxieties. What Britain underwent in these years was a major stage in the replacement of the remains of a somewhat conservative social order, built on a framework of traditional assumptions and symbols, by a new, more fluid, and possibly more neurotic social structure, in which no one any longer knew with certainty who he was or where he stood—and was therefore prey to egocentric fantasy compensations of every kind. Not the least consequence of such change, in which the incredible events of 1963 had played their part, was a kind of increasing suspension of belief—a general sense that, in a world where everything seemed to be changing, and all the familiar landmarks and certainties were being eroded, nothing any longer seemed quite real.

Of course, one vital point to be made immediately is that 1963 was far from being the end of the story. The events of 1963 marked the end of one cycle, and, in the tremendous sense of anticipation that was building up around, for instance, Harold Wilson and the Beatles, the beginning of another. The second half of the story, concerning itself with the fate of that New England which Wilson and the Beatles symbolized, and which at the beginning of 1964 was just emerging in all its pristine glory, was yet to come; and it was to take off in 1964 with a new "dream stage" even more detached from reality than anything which had gone before.

As 1964 opened, the aftermath of the mood of 1963 was still much in evidence. In January, conscious that the General Election might be announced any day, Harold Wilson launched into a series of major speeches across the country. In Birmingham, to wildly cheering supporters, he unveiled his vision of an "exciting new Britain." With confidence in every syllable, he tore into the tottering Government; now is the chance, he declared, for:

> *change* . . . for *resurgence.* A chance to *sweep away* the *grouse-moor conception* of Tory leadership and *refit* Britain with a *new image* . . . we are living in the *jet-age* but we are governed by an *Edwardian establishment mentality* . . . the *chill frost* of Tory leadership . . . *clammy unimaginativeness* at the top . . . *clumsy, amateurish, ineffective* and *out-of-date* . . . *conservative, nostalgic, backward-looking* etc., etc.

The alternative he offered was that of "a *breakthrough* to an *exciting* and *wonderful* period," the *"mobilisation"* of natural resources, the *"streamlining"* of institutions, the *"modernisation"* of methods. He spoke of *"hard facts"* and *"decision making."* He wanted the youth of Britain, with their *"thrusting* ability" and *"iconoclasm"* to *"storm* the *frontiers* of knowledge." He talked of the British people's *"brashness* and *saltiness* and political *irreverence, energy* and *determination,"* of the "age of *automation,* of *jet* and *space travel,"* of this *"scientific* and *dynamic* age." He twice used the word "purposive," and "purpose" alone twelve times.

In its way it was a speech even more significant than the one at Scarborough three months before. For here at last, Mr. Wilson had firmly united the two different streams of phraseology which, over the previous four years, had separately portended this growing bubble of make-believe in English politics; on the one hand, all that "jet age" vitality imagery of the "technological revolution," which had always been his own special preserve; on the other, all those clichés of "dynamism," "frontiers," "complacency," and "nostalgia," which since 1960 had been particularly associated with the cult of Kennedyism and "What's Wrong With Britain" journalism. In Swansea, a week later, he was still talking of the coming *"breakthrough,"* now *"overcoming* the *forces* of *inertia"*; while the difference between his own future Government and that of the Conservatives was compared to the *"thrust"* of a space rocket leaving its launching pad. In Edinburgh, he was back to *"nostalgia," "faded imperial grandeur,"* and *"feudal glories"*—with two mentions of "a *head of steam,"* several of *"science* and technology," and one each of *"dynamic"* and *"purposeful,"* used together in the same sentence. *"Breakthrough"* was for the first time used in reference to *"computers."* In Leeds it was a *"dynamic* approach to building methods" and a *"breakthrough* in Government methods." In Liverpool "the *confident* and *assertive new* Britain" would be achieved by *"releasing* the *energies* and *mobilising* the *talents* of the *whole* British people."

But by now not even the British people were giving such rallying-cries their undivided attention. For 1964 was a new year—with new preoccupations. In California it was the year of the topless dress, in New York it was the year of Andy Warhol and "camp culture" and "underground movies"—but in 1964 it was England that was becoming the entertainment capital of the world.

The spray thrown up by Britain's class revolution had been reaching the outside world for some years. As long ago as 1957–1958, *Look Back in Anger* had been voted the Best Foreign Play of the Season on Broadway, and in succeeding years Britain's share of the New York playbill steadily increased. In the early sixties, plays by Robert Bolt, Shelagh Delaney, Brendan Behan, and Lionel Bart had all been given long runs. In 1962 both *Beyond the Fringe* and *The Establishment* team enjoyed vast successes. And by 1963, with yet more British shows acclaimed, such as *Stop the World I Want to Get Off* by the "Old-New" partnership of Anthony Newley (East End Jewish) and Leslie Bricusse (Cambridge, early-1950's), New York critics were already beginning to talk of the "British domination of Broadway." Similarly the new British cinema had been making inroads, although it was not really until, in 1963, the black-and-white Northern Realist phase began to give way to more colorful extravaganzas such as the first two James Bond films and Woodfall's *Tom Jones,* scripted by John Osborne and directed by Tony Richardson, that British filmmakers began to register steady box office successes. Another beachhead had already been established by Mary Quant, who first started to sell in New York in 1959 and who, in 1961, made a highly successful visit with Alexander Plunket-Greene. It was also in 1961 that young British artists first made an impact on New York in the early days of the Pop Art craze, notably Richard Smith (Royal College of Art, mid-1950's)—while in 1963 another group of British artists, including David Hockney, Peter Blake, Peter Phillips, and Allen Jones (all from the Royal College of Art), were the sensation of the year's Paris Biennale. These were the foundations.

The Profumo affair and the Great Train Robbery had been the last confirmatory jolts to open the eyes of the world to the fact that Britain was no longer a country of "bowler hats, stiff upper lips and

Victorian morals." In 1964 came the deluge. From an exhibition of Hockney's paintings sold out on the day of its opening in New York to the world record of eighty-nine curtain calls given to Dame Margot Fonteyn and Rudolf Nureyev of the Royal Ballet in Vienna in October, the spray was turning into a tidal wave. Above all, of course, there were the Beatles.

In America, the state of shock which followed the death of Kennedy lasted longer than in Britain. As the hysteria died down, a gloom fell over America which was to last over two months. And then, in the first week in February, the trance was broken. The Beatles had just concluded a visit to Paris, which had turned from polite curiosity to wild enthusiasm; in England the officials at London Airport had been familiar since the previous October with the sight of up to twenty thousand teenage girls clustered like huge flocks of squealing starlings whenever the Beatles appeared there. But no one, least of all the Vice-President of Capitol Records who was actually thinking of hiring girls to scream a welcome to the Beatles at Kennedy Airport, was in any way prepared for what happened from the moment they touched down at New York on 7 February. For days the city seemed to go mad. Vast crowds of girls waited all night outside the Plaza Hotel, hoping for a glimpse or even a touch. Big stores sprouted "Beatle" window displays, containing everything from Beatle wigs to pictures of London policemen. The Beatles themselves appeared on the Ed Sullivan Show. They gave a concert at Carnegie Hall. In Washington, a party given for the quartet by the British Ambassador turned almost into a riot —leading to a question in the House of Commons about "the disgraceful behaviour at the Embassy."

When Sir Alec Douglas-Home arrived in Washington on 12 February for talks with President Johnson, his presence was hardly noticed. In March, American advance sales for the Beatles' sixth record, *Can't Buy Me Love,* were 2,000,000, a record still unbroken. On 4 April they commanded not only the first five places in the

American Top 100 but also the first two places in the L.P. charts; and that in a year in which America, like England, was enjoying its biggest record boom in history. It was the first time that any country had fought back against America's domination of twentieth-century mass culture since the first craze for *Alexander's Ragtime Band* in 1912. And the irony of it was, of course, that America's rout had been achieved with what were almost entirely her own weapons.

These events in America were nothing to what was happening back in England itself. The fever which only six months before had run riot in tracking down every new rumor about Profumo or Keeler was now given over to the frenzied pursuit of pop singers. Almost every week some new "group"—the Kinks, the Moody Blues, the Ivy League—emerged into the collective fantasy, and particularly as the rhythm 'n blues groups swam into ken, the Rolling Stones, the Animals, the Pretty Things, each weirder in appearance and manner than the last. The spectacular was followed in headlines once reserved for politicians, film stars, or Royalty. "Tottenham Sound Has Crushed the Beatles," shouted the front page of the *Daily Express,* when the Dave Clark Five (North London) briefly replaced the Beatles in their almost permanent reign at the top of the hit parade. On 11 March even the conservative *Daily Telegraph* began the weekly printing of the "Top Ten." The television channels vied with one another to produce the most frenetic "live" pop show—*Top of the Pops, Thank Your Lucky Stars, Ready Steady Go*—each complete with its glazed-eyed teenage audience, shuffling or mesmerized before the cameras. In headlines and on the fashion pages, the age of "kinky" gave way to the age of "fab" and "gear."

The "pop explosion" of 1963–1964 in fact marked the last consummatory wave of all that youthful and social upheaval which had begun back in the jazz clubs and art schools and among the South London Teddy Boys of the late forties. Once again, the majority of the pop singers came from the same cities and seaports and the same primarily lower-middle-class origins as the playwrights and novelists and pop artists*—but now members of the upper-middle and even upper classes were mixed amongst them, with the same smart or casual Cardin and Carnaby Street clothes, the same long hair and Beatle fringes, everything but the same accent—and even that distinction was submerged on their records. When the Lennon-McCartney song *World without Love* displaced *Can't Buy Me Love* at the top of the hit parade, it was sung by two Westminster public school boys, one of them the brother of Paul McCartney's girl friend. Another singer was the grandson of the seventh Duke of Wellington. How different were the pop stars of 1964 from that first wave who had risen from South London and the East End only eight years before—Tommy Steele, Marty Wilde, Terry Dene! Now they were "the new youth," products of the revolution rather than its progenitors, "classless," accustomed to the age of affluence since their early teens, even educated—to the extent that much play was made in publicity with the fact that Paul McCartney had an A-Level in English, that Mick Jagger had been briefly at the London School of Economics, or that Paul Jones (Portsmouth) of the Manfred Mann group had been, also briefly, at Oxford.

Thus had the "protest" of John Osborne and the surly aggression of the early Teddy Boys been transmuted into the scowl of Mick Jagger, the smiling arrogance of John Lennon, the shoulder-length hair and outlandish appearance of The Pretty Things. But of what significance was such flouting of convention now, when the whole of England was prepared, it seemed, to gaze in awe at this new phenomenon in its midst? In March, a little book of drawings and literary doodles by John Lennon raced to the top of the best-seller list and was described by *The Times Literary Supplement* as "worth

* For example, apart from the nucleus from Liverpool itself, there were also The Animals (Newcastle), The Kinks (North London), The Hollies (Manchester), The Fortunes (Birmingham), Lulu (Glasgow Irish), The Pretty Things (all but one, like Mick Jagger and Peter Blake, from Dartford, on the South East London fringe), Sandie Shaw (like the satirist Dudley Moore, from Dagenham, Essex) etc. Once again, as with the original jazz musicians, there was a strong link between the pop singers and art schools. Just as the pop artists had been younger than the writers, so the singers were younger still—most of them born between 1943 and 1947.

the attention of anyone who fears for the impoverishment of the English language," while by George Melly in the *Sunday Times* Lennon's artistic ancestry was traced back to "Lewis Carroll, Klee, Thurber, the Goons . . . and very noticeably, late Joyce." In April, at a Foyle's Literary Luncheon to mark the four hundredth anniversary of the birth of Shakespeare, Lennon was the chief guest of honor—and more requests for tickets were received than any time since they had so honored George Bernard Shaw. Waxworks of the Beatles were placed on display at Madame Tussaud's. They were invited to dinner by the Master of Brasenose College, Oxford, they were praised by Prince Philip, and they were even squabbled over by the politicians—when the Prime Minister praised them as "our best export" and Harold Wilson was quick to retort that the "Tories are trying to make the Beatles their secret weapon."

Amid such universal genuflection, an article in the *New Statesman* by its Deputy Editor Paul Johnson (Oxford early 1950's) entitled "The Menace of Beatlism" read with strange discordance:

> Bewildered by a rapidly changing society, excessively fearful of becoming out of date, our leaders are increasingly turning to young people as guides and mentors—or, to vary the metaphor, as geiger counters to guide them against the perils of mental obsolescence.

In England in the spring of 1964 such sour dissent was that of a lone voice indeed. For the kingdom of the teenager was at hand. And if further proof was needed of its omnipotence, it came on 28 March —when owners of wireless sets in South East England first began to pick up a mysterious new station on 199 metres. "Radio Caroline" was on the air—and the farce of the "pirate radio stations" had begun.

It was only appropriate that the most blatant rebellion against law and order in 1964 should be not a Great Train Robbery nor an anarchic demonstration in Trafalgar Square but merely the day-long unauthorized broadcasting of pop records from a rusty hulk moored ten miles off the coast of Suffolk. It was equally surprising that it had never happened in Britain before. For the Swedes, the Danes, and the Dutch had been plagued by offshore pirate stations as long ago as 1961–1962, and the conservatism of the BBC's radio monopoly, combined with union restrictions on the broadcasting of pop records, offered unusual temptation to any competition. In fact the idea of radio piracy had first occurred to a London music publisher named Allan Crawford as early as 1960; after exhaustive investigations of its legal and technical pitfalls, by the end of 1963 his "Radio Atlanta," backed by a company under the chairmanship of a City accountant and former Vice-President of the Liberal Party named Oliver Smedley, was in the last stages of preparation. But in a rash moment Crawford had disclosed his plans to Ronan O'Rahilly, the young manager of *The Scene* club—and in the heady and reckless atmosphere of the new pop underworld, such an idea was spark to tinder. Within a matter of months, O'Rahilly had not only rounded up financial support of up to £500,000 from five City millionaires, but his own ship, named after Kennedy's daughter, the *Caroline,* was ready to go on the air. The most ardent of its backers was Jocelyn Stevens of the *Queen*.

Throughout the month of April, the country—and the pirates— waited in mounting suspense to see what the Government would do. For there was no question that, under the Copenhagen Agreement of 1948, the Government was bound to do everything within its power to terminate such unauthorized invasion of the airways. Preliminary shots were fired. The Post Office cut off *Caroline*'s ship-to-shore telephone. The Customs Officials in the sleepy port of Felixstowe did as much as possible to hinder intercourse with the ship. The Foreign Office lodged a protest with the Government of Panama, where the *Caroline* was registered. The press was almost unanimously in favor of immediate and decisive action; on 2 April *The Times* had declared:

> The motive of these operations is profit, cloaked with the assertion that such vessels provide a service which the public wants. There is not a shred of evidence for this.

But within weeks a Gallup Poll provided the evidence—that *Caroline* was already rivaling Radio Luxembourg in popularity, with around 7 million regular listeners. On 1 May the new station carried its first advertisement, for the Duke of Bedford's stately home at Woburn. Four days later, when Crawford and Smedley's Radio Atlanta also began transmission, within a mile of *Caroline,* the prospect of a whole armada of pirates massed round Britain's shores elevated the problem briefly into major political importance. But slowly it dawned that the Government was paralyzed, hypnotized into impotence by the pirates as, in the words of Jeremy Thorpe, "a rabbit by a stoat." As May drew to a close, another political crisis drifted off into fantasy —as from the Pool of London, "Screaming Lord Sutch," a pop singer from North London whose career had begun in the *Two I's* coffee-bar seven years before and who had earned notoriety in 1963 by standing for Parliament in a by-election as a "National Teenage" candidate, set sail with a theatrical agent named Reg Calvert and a trawlerful of leopard-skinned acolytes, took possession of a disused army fort on Shivering Sands in the Thames Estuary and announced a round-the-clock service of Sutch classics, spiced with readings from *Lady Chatterley's Lover.* By midsummer, the Government's original firm declaration that "legal action is being considered" had dwindled into a mere reference of the matter to the Council of Europe.

By no means was all authority gone, however. Over the Easter weekend, the seaside resort of Clacton had been invaded by huge gangs of Mods and Rockers, mainly from the working- and lower-middle-class areas of London, who ran berserk through the streets, smashing deck chairs, attacking passers-by, and fighting each other with senseless fury.* A large number of teenagers were subsequently fined. At Whitsun, the violence broke out again, this time (by careful

---

* "Mods" and "Rockers" were the two general teenage styles which had evolved over the previous seven years—the former more interested in clothes (they were the chief patrons of Carnaby Street), the latter wearing leather jackets for motorcycles. The two styles, although seemingly opposed, were not wholly mutually exclusive. The Beatles had begun dressing like Rockers, but by the time of their fame in 1963–1964 had switched to the neater Mod styles.

249

arrangement) in the streets of Margate. On 18 May, Dr. George Simpson, a Margate magistrate, imposed fines of up to £75 on the dozens of rioters who were brought before him and described them as "long-haired, mentally unstable, petty little sawdust Caesars" who hunted, like rats, only in packs. His remarks and the riots themselves once more landed Britain on the front pages of the press of the world.

The summer just beginning was to be almost as fine as that of 1959. On millions of transistor radios, in the record shops (which were selling a quite unprecedented 101,257,000 records during the year), in the deafening darkness of the *Ad Lib*, which, on the ashes of *Wip's* and the patronage of the Beatles, was becoming "the world's most famous nightclub," the great "pop explosion" continued unabated. The Beatles were shortly to extend their kingdom even further as the stars of one of the year's major commercial film successes, *A Hard Day's Night*, directed by Dick Lester and scripted by the Liverpool playwright Alun Owen. The public fascination, however, was by no means limited to pop singers or Mods and Rockers. On 10 May, for instance, the *Sunday Times* color supplement launched a new group of dream-figures, in a long article by Francis Wyndham (who had now joined Mark Boxer, his old colleague from the *Queen*), under the title of "The Model-Makers":

> The London idea of style in the 1960's has been adjusted to a certain way of looking, which is to some extent the creation of three young men, all from the East End. These are the fashion photographers Brian Duffy, Terence Donovan, David Bailey. Among them, they make more than £100,000 a year, and they are usually accompanied by some of the most beautiful models in the world: they appear to lead enviable lives.

Illustrated partly by large "black" photographs of the three photographers taken by each other, partly by their photographs of "some of the most beautiful models in the world" (including Bailey's girl

The Dream after the Storm

friend Jean Shrimpton), the article was written partly in that familiar Sunday-newspaper dream-style ("With thick black hair and large bright eyes, [Bailey] is handsome, reserved, slightly sulky") and partly in the form of a "conversation" which:

> took place against a changing background; an empty bar at the Ritz; a crowded Chelsea restaurant; a party given by Mary Quant and Alexander Plunket-Greene . . . Terry Donovan's small Hampstead flat, which contains a collection of Victoriana, a pile of books on Judo and an organ. There was a regular (if occasionally somnolent) audience of extremely beautiful girls.

On another page of the same issue, which was entitled "Taste '64 a way of looking: people, places, things," was an article on "the hairdresser of the sixties," Vidal Sassoon (West London Jewish), illustrated with a photograph taken by Terence Donovan of Sassoon bending over the hair of Cilla Black (Liverpool Irish) and quoted as saying "Camus is my favourite writer . . . very few people really turn me on like he does."

Singers, photographers, hairdressers—the pop culture that would eventually make up the image of "Swinging London" was emerging, piece by nyktomorphic piece, before the public gaze—a world of youth and "style" and "Taste '64" that was bringing the *Sunday Times Magazine* at last into its own. Never before had Mark Boxer's color supplement been so attuned to the public mood—its "mini-nostalgic" features on "The Phoney Peace" and the First World War, its color spreads on "The Flavour of Brazil—Its Zest, Its Style," vying with story after story on "The Long Hair Musicians" (a long article by Francis Wyndham on "The Pretty Things"), on "Changing Faces" (full-color pictures of London Mods and their strange, new, colorful clothes), on "Design for Tomorrow":

> This year's design students are just starting their first jobs. Some are *unquestionably brilliant* . . . their work may strike *conservative* manufacturers as *brash, disagreeable* and—worse—unsaleable . . . but . . . in the long run *these kids can't miss* . . . these *young* designers have some-

251

how got the *feeling of the times*. The *undeniably fast technological pace* is going to *move* so *fast* that people won't *tolerate* machines or furniture or even rooms which are more than a few years old . . .

Forgotten now was any "Sharp Look at Britain's Mood"; even going slowly was the "down to earth" and grainy style of photography—submerged beneath a shallow, brightly colored sea of "major decorating trends" in London restaurants and snippets on *art nouveau*—or the latest craze for old posters, old tin boxes from the Portobello Road, and Edwardian-type sign lettering, copied in fiberglass at £3 a time.

This sudden vogue among teenagers and the avant-garde middle class for colorful playthings and visual "images" pillaged indiscriminately from a century of industrialized culture, whether *art nouveau* ties or grandfather clocks painted white or vests printed with slogans varying from "I love the Beatles" to "Jesus Saves," was marking the disintegration of the youthful collective fantasy into a more fragmented and inconsequential phase, in which no one "look" or fashion would prevail, but in which titillatory images could be seized on almost at random. In dress, rigid trends in fashion were already giving way to a tendency to wear any article of clothing, whether in "space age" plastics or a tattered Victorian wedding dress, so long as it was sufficiently eye-catching and bizarre. In a similar search for surface "images" that would provide a flicker of novelty, the pop musicians were already on the trail which was to lead them over the next eighteen months to using anything from lutes and string quartets to the sound of the Indian sitar.

An even more revealing aspect of this disintegration was the widespread and rapid merger that was taking place between the cultural interests of teenagers and the avant-garde intellectuals. Eight years before, there would still have seemed an almost unbridgeable gulf between the concerns of, say, the teenagers jiving to Tommy Steele in the basement of the *Two I's* coffee bar and those of the audiences for Ionesco at the Royal Court Theatre. Now, in 1964, the coalescence of one form of fantasy with another to make up a sort of overall "pop culture" was taking place so fast that, within a year or two, no one would be surprised to see the pages of the "quality" press regularly taken up with the rapturous reviews of the latest pop records, or prominent pop singers being starred in plays and films by directors of impeccable "intellectual" credentials, such as Peter Hall and Jean-Luc Godard—any more than they would be surprised to see Paul McCartney advertised as spending his leisure hours with the latest electronic fragment from the pen of Stockhausen.

As in New York at the same time, this unification of popular and avant-garde interests was taking place in 1964 on two levels. The first was simply through the increasingly dream-like and sensational character of all avant-garde culture, with the consequent disintegration of any rigorous intellectual standards of "meaning" or technical skill —a movement which the pop singers, as traders in suggestive imagery, were as qualified to join as anyone. The second was the increasingly fashionable obsession among certain of the intellectuals themselves with the imagery not just of contemporary popular culture, but of its more traditional forms, often the most blatantly commercial and intellectually vacuous, such as Superman comic strips, the adventures of Batman, old Hollywood films and so forth—the sort of things which had long been the stock in trade of the "Pop" artists.

Indeed, the "pop art" industry was almost as flourishing in 1964 as pop music itself. In the art galleries of Mayfair, such as that started the year before by an "Old-New" partnership between John Kasmin and the twenty-six-year-old fifth Marquess of Dufferin and Ava, or the Robert Fraser Gallery, run by the Old Etonian son of Sir Lionel Fraser, a City banker, the paintings of David Hockney and Peter Blake were selling as fast as they appeared. To the dream-images of Pop, the Beatle portraits of Peter Blake, the stark, dream-shapes of "Hard Edge Abstractionism," the year added a new craze—for the restless, startling patterns of Op Art, painted by Miss Bridget Riley, a product of that one-time citadel of upper-middle-class feminism, Cheltenham Ladies College.

From the art schools, still newer and younger artists poured in ever more intoxicating flow: and in the pages of the *New Statesman,* Jonathan Miller's prose style caught something of that heady summer's mood:

> Rauschenberg long gone. New Generation just finished. The gargantuan Gulbenkian still in full swing at the Tate. The New Generation at the Whitechapel pushed a consistent style—cool, "go" and very purple heart . . . here is art without lapels, sartorial almost, and in the canvases of Hoyland and Huxley, and the cheeky little toys by Marisol, downright cosmetic. "Mod," of course, is the word one is groping for, since it gets, better than the over-used "pop," the emotionally indifferent swish of these paintings, so many of which are decorative in a camp sort of way . . .

From sixty years before came the echo of a dream—the dream of H. G. Wells in *The Time Machine,* and his description of the Eloi, the "little people" of the future, "brightly clad" in orange and "chequered purple and white":

> In a flash I perceived that all had the same form of costume . . . in costume and in all the differences of texture and bearing that now mark off the sexes from one another, these people of the future were alike . . . a queer thing I soon discovered about my little hosts, and that was their lack of interest. They would come to me with eager cries of astonishment, like children, but like children they would soon stop examining me and wander away after some other toy.

There was one considerable difference between the England emerging in 1964 and that of the years immediately preceding. The element of black frenzy which had characterized the years up to 1963 had given way to a kind of faery world. The frenzy was still there. But whereas the "explosions into reality" of that former age—the Labour Conference of 1960, the mass-arrest of the Committee of 100, the Profumo affair, even in its way the Orpington by-election—

had been shattering and violent, like the surfacing of poisonous boils
—now, in 1964, they seemed simply like the popping of harmless,
brightly colored bubbles.

There was, for instance, the curious case of the BBC Second Channel. The first serious hints that all was not well in BBC Television
had come in the summer of 1962—at the very time when Donald
Baverstock and Michael Peacock had been most fervently hailed as
the BBC's "Young Turks" and "whiz-kids."

Throughout 1963, the BBC's reputation had been artificially colored by the aura of adventure surrounding *That Was The Week*.
But behind this somewhat thin "revolutionary" facade, there were
increasing signs that the whole performance of BBC Television was
becoming tired and ragged. The big "prestige" programs, in particular, *Tonight, Monitor,* and *Panorama,* were dying on their feet. In
the circular, claustrophobic corridors of the BBC's huge new glass-
and-concrete Television Centre the sound of bickering grew louder.
It was against this background that the hectic planning of the
£5,250,000 Second Channel, under the direction of the "whiz-kid"
Michael Peacock, proceeded; on 30 September 1963, under the ominously trivial "dream symbol" of two kangaroos, named "Hulla-
baloo" and "Custard," the vast preliminary campaign of advertising
began.

By the early months of 1964, in the aftermath of *That Was The
Week* public discontent with the BBC became vocal and widespread.
Under the added strain of its new channel, the Corporation was in
debt to the tune of millions of pounds. Meanwhile the advance advertising for the new service, with its promise that each night's programs would be built round a "main meal" of "education" or "comedy" or "repeats of past successes," seemed suspiciously like the
clutching at straws of men who no longer knew what they were
doing. It was announced that the audience for Channel Two would
be "at least 1,250,000." In mid-April the publicity rose to a crescendo,
with articles by all the BBC's Byzantine high command in the *Radio*

Times and the *Listener,* and even a Service of Dedication in Westminster Abbey. The last hymn of the service was "Thou, whose Almighty Word, Chaos and Darkness heard . . ."

The following evening, 20 April, chaos and darkness descended. A huge power-failure, blacking out large stretches of West London, brought the Channel's opening night to an almost complete halt. In the following weeks, it became clear that the new service was a fiasco. By June an opinion poll showed that on an average evening only 90,000 sets were tuned in. In a series of press conferences, Michael Peacock announced the dismantlement of all his original plans—while a stockpile of old American comedy shows, Westerns, and documentaries was brought in to fill the gap. Morale in the Television Centre fell even lower.

As the summer sun shone down, the economy was once again booming. From the outside world, the news of the death of Nehru on 27 May, following the departures in 1963 of Kennedy, Macmillan, and Adenauer, was a reminder that other countries too were moving into an age of unfamiliar leaders. The death of Lord Beaverbrook on 9 June, two weeks after his eighty-fifth birthday, marked the departure of one of the last two men alive who had been prominent in English politics before the First World War. The other, Sir Winston Churchill, still the Member for Woodford, was now making his last token series of appearances in the Chamber where he had sat, on and off, since the reign of Queen Victoria. And already the deaths were being reported of men who had played their part only in the New England of the fifties and sixties: on 20 March, of alcoholism in Dublin, Brendan Behan, at the age of forty-one; on 22 March, nine months after being ejected from his Chairmanship of City Centre, Jack Cotton; and on 8 August, at the age of fifty-six, the man whose private fantasy projection, after becoming the public fantasy of millions, had, in the opinion of all who knew him, become a Frankenstein's monster, dominating his life with increasing strain and unreality until it killed him—Ian Fleming, the creator and

256

finally the only real-life victim of James Bond. The month before had come the disintegration of the great popular business success story of affluent England, with the crash of John Bloom's washing-machine empire, whose shares, having at the beginning of the year stood at 47/9, fell by the beginning of August to 1d.

Meanwhile, the slide into unreality went on. There were, for instance, some of the curious ways in which England was celebrating the four hundredth anniversary of the birth of Shakespeare.

By and large in 1964, the new English drama was continuing its drift into the violent, sexually obsessed, and freakish fantasy world that had first become apparent in 1962. The year had begun with the staging by the Royal Shakespeare Company of an experimental season in what it described as "The Theatre of Cruelty." The season was directed by Peter Brook, in collaboration with a young American, Charles Marowitz, who had first come to public notice in England in September 1963, his contribution to a conference on the drama at the Edinburgh Festival took the form of having a naked lady wheeled before the gaze of the startled delegates. It was Britain's first introduction to the American avant-garde craze for "happenings." The manifesto of "The Theatre of Cruelty" was a book written in a lunatic asylum in 1938 by the French psychopath Antonin Artaud: their slogan was Artaud's message:

> We need a theatre which wakes us up; nerves and heat . . . in the anguished catastrophic society we live in, we feel an urgent need for a theatre which events do not exceed . . . a transcendent experience of life is what the public is fundamentally seeking through love, crime, drugs, war or insurrection.

Certainly the link between some of Brook's and Marowitz's "playlets" and the "events" of the previous year could not have been more explicit, including as they did not only a short sketch by Artaud himself entitled "The Spurt of Blood" (in which "colour, light and sound are used expressively") but also a "striptease act of 'grotesque symbolism,'" representing Christine Keeler in a scene beside a bath which was also intended to convey the image of Mrs. Jacqueline Kennedy looking down into her husband's open grave.

As the year proceeded, it became clear that this season had set the tone for much of the direction which the new English theatre was to follow. One of the year's more *recherché* successes was the "black comedy" *Entertaining Mr. Sloane,* by a new playwright Joe Orton (Leicester) who, a year before, had spent nine months in prison for obscenely defacing books from a public library. Another was Peter Brook's production of the *Marat/Sade,* with its portrayal of the enacting of Marat's assassination by the inmates of a lunatic asylum, under the direction of the Marquis de Sade; the play (described by Brook as being on the side of "revolutionary change"), until Edward Bond's *Saved* in the autumn of 1965, was the high-water mark of the English theatre's spiraling sensationalism.

Indeed the *Marat/Sade* at last provoked a violent reaction to this trend from the Old Guard, with a series of attacks by representatives of the commercial theatre, such as Peter Cadbury and Emile Littler, on what they described as "filthy plays"; a reaction which of course provoked the progressives themselves to even fiercer excitement, calling forth a telegram from Mr. Michael Foot MP declaring "I CAN SEE THERE IS A RALLY OF THE OLD FORCES TO STOP PEOPLE THINKING BUT IT CAN'T BE DONE STOP IT HAS FAILED EVER SINCE THE SAME RIDICULOUS TRICK WAS TRIED ON SOPHOCLES," and some time later the claim from Miss Penelope Gilliatt that such a play had "the nerve to investigate the sort of violence that Shakespeare himself depicted."*

But the major event in the English theatre in 1964 was the Quarter-centenary of Shakespeare himself. This at least was celebrated by the Royal Shakespeare Company in quite conventional fashion, with the production of seven plays in the historical cycle. There was also, however, a spate of more dubious Shakespearean productions, in-

---

* *Life International,* 13 June 1966. This remark was reminiscent of the defense once offered by Ian Fleming to the charge that his novels were pornographic: "Sex was a perfectly reasonable subject as far as Shakespeare was concerned and I don't really see why it shouldn't be as far as I am concerned."

cluding the heavily cut or reconstructed "pop" version of *Julius Caesar,* staged by Lindsay Anderson at the Royal Court, and of the two parts of *Henry IV,* directed at the Edinburgh Festival by Joan Littlewood, which consisted of little more than an anthology of the bawdier and more sensational titbits from the two plays, played by most of the actors in jeans. "Pop" Shakespeare of a not altogether dissimilar order was Sir Laurence Olivier's almost wholly sensational interpretation of *Othello* at the National Theatre—employing what an awestruck Kenneth Tynan later described as "the minotaur of his talent" to impersonate a rolling-eyed and even ludicrous stage Negro.

The strangest of all the Shakespeare celebrations, however, was the exhibition staged at Stratford by Mr. Richard Buckle. For ten shillings the visitor wandered bewildered through dark passages and caverns surrounded by meaningless shapes in *papier mâché,* aluminum, and wire, huge ill-drawn murals and pop paintings, including contributions by David Hockney, Peter Blake, the "pop" sculptor Joe Tilson, and, from an older generation, Cecil Beaton, all apparently symbolizing aspects of Shakespeare's life. It was reminiscent of nothing so much as one of the sideshows at Battersea Fun Fair in which, for only one shilling, children may be wafted in a small boat past dusty *papier mâché* models of the Taj Mahal and the Eiffel Tower, described as "The Wonders of the World." In the middle of Buckle's Exhibition, entirely out of character with the rest, was a re-created Elizabethan Long Gallery, hung with contemporary portraits of sixteenth-century figures. Nothing was more implicitly a comment on the rest of this absurd freakshow than the fact that, alongside them, was a notice reading "Do Not Touch. These Pictures Are Genuine."

The bubbles continued to surface. In September, it was Fleet Street's turn. First, there was the instance of the *Observer* color supplement, announced to appear on 6 September. For weeks beforehand, a country-wide poster campaign proclaimed the coming of Observer-colour, while in a series of advertisements, David Astor earnestly declared that (presumably in comparison with those of the *Sunday Times* and the *Daily Telegraph,* also launching a supplement at this time) his color magazine would be "more realistic, less escapist, less ephemeral. It's not wise to boast, but I hope and believe it will be more informative, more interesting." In fact when the supplement (edited by Michael Davie, like four out of the first five editors of Sunday color supplements, a member of the New Oxford Group) finally emerged into reality its banality and the shoddiness of its production were hard to credit. The highlights of the first issue were "a long searching look at Paris fashions," a series of reminiscences by Lord Mountbatten ("his pungent opinions and the vigour of his turn of speech stem more from the quarterdeck than the corridors of power") and publicity stills from the forthcoming James Bond film *Goldfinger.* An advertisement for the second issue made even the worst fears seem flattering:

> It is now almost a year since an assassin's bullet abruptly shattered the world of Jackie Kennedy. What has happened in that year? What is she building from the wreckage of Dallas? What does the future hold for her and her children?

Not a women's magazine in the land could have done better.

Still more curious, a week later, was the case of the *Sun.* In March 1961, when his *Daily Mirror* Group had just acquired the Odhams publishing interests, including the ailing *Daily Herald,* Mr. Cecil King announced that the paper's future as "a serious political journal is now assured." In 1963 he moved his empire into a towering new glass-and-steel headquarters on High Holborn and gave it the imposing "dream name" of the International Publishing Corporation. At the end of that year it was announced that the *Daily Herald,* dogged by its "cloth cap image," would after all be closed down— but that in its place there would be launched what Mr. King later described as "a completely new national daily newspaper," "the biggest and boldest newspaper venture likely to take place this century," and a paper "deliberately geared to the mental attitudes and new interests of the mid-1960's."

By September 1964, publicity for the "new newspaper" had outdone in frenzy even that for BBC-2. Almost £400,000 was being spent on advertising alone. From posters, from over 900 television commercials, the "dream symbol" of an incandescent sun glared across the nation—under the clamant slogan "Time for a new newspaper, born of the age we live in." Responsibility for the venture was assumed by Hugh Cudlipp himself, stating that the paper's purpose would be "to stimulate the modernisation of Britain in every sphere." In the *Sunday Times* on 12 September, almost a whole page of *Insight*'s most vivid prose was given over to extolling the vitality and drive of the

> boyish, cigar-burning extrovert of 51 [who] . . . tomorrow night . . . will launch the bid of his lifetime for a place in British social history . . . the Sun by any standard is Cudlipp's baby . . .

He was photographed in action, cigar in mouth; he was quoted as saying "You don't think I'd take all these risks and leave it to somebody else, do you?"; and of all his forthcoming innovations there was none of which he was prouder than the revolution he was working on the paper's middle pages:

> We have utterly destroyed the normal concept of features . . . the centre spread is a great blank sheet of paper. It's a bloody marvellous opportunity.

The following night a champagne party was held at the Café Royal to launch the new paper. Over 3,000,000 copies of the first issue were run off, well over double the circulation of the *Daily Herald*. And then the first issue appeared. It was no more "a completely new" newspaper than the *Observer* magazine was "less escapist" or "meaningful." The *Daily Herald* had merely been given a veneer of modernity, with a few tricks of layout. Within four months the first day's circulation of 3,000,000 had fallen back almost exactly to where it had started. The "biggest and boldest newspaper venture" of the century, "the only newspaper born of the age we live in" had been nothing more than a modish fancy.

With the autumn it was again the turn of television. It had long been apparent that it was by no means in the BBC alone that the once "exciting" dream of the young men who had poured into the television industry seven and eight years before was fading into grey reality—the reality of a conveyor belt feeding on little more than novelty. It was in the summer and autumn of 1964 that the television industry made its most revealing surrender—with a proliferation across both channels of programs that made no greater demand on their producers' ingenuity than arranging for a small group of people to sit chatting in front of the cameras. By the early autumn two such "conversation" programs were established on ITV. Then in November, Donald Baverstock, the head of BBC's Channel One, unveiled his last two desperate bids to prop up the Corporation's disintegrating prestige.

Rarely can there have been a more disastrous beginning to any television show than that of Ned Sherrin's *Not So Much a Programme, More a Way of Life,* a lumbering attempt to revive *That Was The Week,* spread over all three nights of the weekend. Quite apart from the creeping sickness of "television conversation" between celebrities that padded out the program's songs, sketches, and "camp" little dance-routines, it would at any other time have been remarkable that such a grandiose enterprise could have been embarked upon with so little forethought. It was the pattern of the *Sun,* of BBC-2, of the Shakespeare Exhibition, all over again. As indeed was the BBC's second major innovation that autumn, Jonathan Miller's *Monitor.*

When it was announced that the BBC was handing over one of its three major "prestige" programs to a virtual amateur, the *Observer* went almost wild with enthusiasm. Its *Briefing* column on the arts faithfully recorded some of his "exciting" intentions, quoted his enthusiasm for interviews shot in *ciné-vérité* style with "hand-held" cameras, and described him as:

> one of the few "bright young men" to receive the full blast of the publicity machine, who still seems capable of development as an individual and of meaningful work . . . he is, of course, an intellectual, but —English rarity—still in touch with feeling . . .

It was hardly surprising, after the pattern of the previous months, that Miller's first program, a rambling discussion of "camp" and "pop" culture with Miss Susan Sontag from New York, should have been regarded as a baffling catastrophe, and that the remainder of the series should have put an end to the program's six-year run.

A dispassionate observer coming upon the England of that autumn might well have drawn the conclusion that here was a people going out of its mind. For eight years, at least in the theatre, in the press, on television, it had been subjected to a deafening insistence on the supreme virtues of "youth" and "change." And now the stage had been reached where not only were people mouthing these slogans as if in their sleep, but the very invocation of these qualities was becoming almost a guarantee of disappointment if not disaster. The constant search for novelty and sensation had finally consumed everything but itself. Behind the glittering dreamworld facade, "born of the age we live in," behind the pounding sound-track, the "cosmetic canvases," the "happenings," the "hand-held cameras," the frenzy of nervous energy in all directions, lay nothing but dust.

Such also was the nightmare of an observer by no means dispassionate, John Osborne, whose new play opening at the Royal Court on 9 September was as powerful a personal heart-cry as *Look Back in Anger.* The "hero" of *Inadmissible Evidence,* described as "the prisoner of this dream," was a solicitor Bill Maitland, as self-pitiful and demented as Jimmy Porter, but, like Osborne himself, a Porter now older and disillusioned. His youthful dreams, his sexual promiscuity and relentless egotism, had turned to ashes. His hatred for the new "emotionally indifferent" young of 1964, "all cool, dreamy, young, cool . . . forthright, unimpressed, contemptuous" knew no bounds. And in a dream-sequence at the beginning, when he was appearing in court to answer for his life, the only faith he could find on which to affirm was his distracted belief:

> in . . . in . . . the
> technological revolution, the pressing, growing
> pressing, urgent need for more and more
> scientists, and more scientists, for more and
> more
> schools and universities and universities and schools, the theme
> of change, realistic decisions based on a highly
> developed and professional study of society by
> people who really know their subjects, the
> overdue need for us to adapt ourselves to
> different conditions, the theme and challenge
> of such rapid change, change, rapid change . . .

But of all the bubbles in English life based on the fantasy facade of "rapid change, change, rapid change" the greatest was only just coming to its head.

Since the early months of the year and the dying away of the violent echoes of 1963, a lull had come over domestic politics. By July Mr. Wilson's statement (in a television interview with Anthony Wedgwood Benn) that he intended to give the country "a hundred days of dynamic action" fell on virtually deaf ears. More public interest was reserved for the fining of three girls at Bow Street for wearing "topless" dresses than for the renewal of the war between Malaysia and Indonesia that was soon to involve upwards of a tenth of all Britain's servicemen—let alone for the column in the *Guardian* in which Mr. Wedgwood Benn was now weekly indulging his daydreams about "the great awakening" of the forthcoming "big push," when "huge task forces" of "tough young New Frontiersmen" would be moving in to "blast a hole" in Britain's "cotton wool complacency."

By the end of August that enormous Labour lead on the opinion
polls had all but vanished. The National Opinion Poll indeed
showed the Conservatives once more ahead, for the first time in almost three years. When Harold Wilson launched Labour's election
campaign with an almost half-hearted speech to the TUC at Blackpool and again, on 12 September, at an interminable "Giant Rally"
at the Empire Pool, Wembley (featuring a male voice choir and the
Humphrey Lyttleton Jazz band), phrases such as "a dynamic, expanding, confident and, above all, purposive new Britain" sounded
as if they were coming from a different age—tired, half-remembered
echoes of months and even years before.

On 15 September the election date was finally announced, for
exactly a month later. Gradually the country roused itself from its
summer torpor. The election campaign got under way, and slowly
a pattern began to emerge. On the one hand was Sir Alec Douglas-
Home, ineffectual, ill at ease, constantly on the defensive. One of
the most familiar nightly images was that of the Prime Minister
beset by groups of young hecklers, often chanting in unison and reducing him on occasion to silence. This entirely destructive mass-
heckling had not been seen in British politics since before the war;
altogether new was the fact that it was coming largely from the very
young, frequently from teenagers unable to vote.

Harold Wilson, on the other hand, speaking only to huge, carefully staged mass-meetings in the big cities, soon began to recover
much of the public confidence he had shown earlier in the year.
A nervous political excitement was once again welling up in the
press; both the *Insight* and *Daylight* columns again brought their
"blow by blow" journalism breathlessly into play; and a feature of
the campaign was the scale of organized gambling on the result, the
mere £14,000 staked with Ladbroke's on the Tory leadership struggle twelve months before having now mushroomed into a sum of
over £600,000 staked with Ladbroke's alone. As both the polls and
the betting odds swung in Labour's favor, it became apparent that
many journalists were now mesmerized by Wilson's carefully pro-

jected aura as a "tough," "sophisticated," "professional" political "operator," understanding all the "tricks of the game"; not the least of which was the trick of impressing journalists by letting them feel that they were participating in the same relationship, so enticingly glamorized in *The Making of the President,* as had existed between the press and Kennedy in 1960.*

The extent to which Mr. Wilson consciously attempted to project himself in a "Kennedy-style" image over these weeks, with his use of such phrases as "getting Britain on the move," and of course, the "hundred days of dynamic action," marked perhaps the highest point of that process whereby the British had taken refuge in the specific imagery and make-believe of the American dream. In fact during the election campaign, Mr. Wilson was already beginning to see himself in a new role, as he showed by a remark to a Norfolk press-conference:

> I am not a Kennedy, you see. I am a Johnson. I fly by the seat of my pants.

This new attachment was perhaps hardly surprising in view of Johnson's reputation at this time as a "ruthless political operator," which was to bear fruit a month later in the presidential election. What both countries in fact were experiencing was something of that hero-worship and desire for the "rule of one man" often found in the aftermath of crisis: a hunger that would be expressed in Britain, despite the narrowness of Wilson's victory, by the confidence in him found for a short while even in such unlikely circles as those of Conservative industrialists and bankers; and a hunger which, in

* It was not surprising that the journalists most conspicuously hypnotized were members of the 1945–1955 Oxbridge generation from upper-middle-class backgrounds; e.g. Richard West (Cambridge, mid-1950's) and Anthony Howard (Oxford, mid-1950's), authors of *The Making of the Prime Minister,* educated at Marlborough and Westminster respectively; and Henry Fairlie, who in the *Sunday Telegraph* compared Wilson to the "radical Lloyd George" no less than five times in the course of one article.

both Britain and America, would find its ultimate expression over the next twelve months in the language of "consensus" politics.

Wilson's appeal to the nation was couched entirely in "radical" terms. He promised the *"sweeping away"* of *"outmoded* ideas," of the *"old boy network"* of Government by "a *closed* and *privileged circle."* He promised to *"streamline"* the Civil Service and the *"unwieldy"* Cabinet. In roaming back over the follies of *"thirteen years"* of Conservative Government he lashed the property speculators, he spoke of "the *bitter experience* . . . of 7 percent Bank Rate, higher mortgage payments, hire purchase restrictions," he promised an end to "Stop-Go" economic crises. He had already made clear his attitude to the *"nuclear posturings"* on which Sir Alec was basing so much of his own appeal.

Rarely had any political party's campaign so clearly borne the stamp of one man's influence, even down to the style of its Manifesto, with its concluding rallying cry (in fact written, fresh from his triumph on the *Sun,* by Hugh Cudlipp):

> Labour is ready. *Poised* to *swing* its *plans* into *instant action. Impatient* to apply the *New Thinking* that will end the *chaos* and *sterility* . . .

And so, on 15 October, polling day arrived, the wettest day for weeks. Just after six o'clock in the evening came the first confused reports from Moscow of the fall of Khrushchev. Harold Wilson was in his Liverpool constituency, staying only a walk away from the Cavern Club. The past two years had been heady ones for the city: even its football club had won the League Championship, its fanatical and frequently violent fans having made their war cry of "Ee-aye-addio" almost as much part of national folklore as "Fab" and "Gear" and "Yeah, yeah, yeah."

As the election results began to come through, it was soon clear that the swing to Labour on Merseyside had been spectacular, the Conservatives having lost four of their six Liverpool seats. Wilson's own majority had risen from below 6,000 to almost 20,000; in 1955 it had been only 2,558. Elsewhere the swing had been less dramatic; indeed over the country as a whole the Labour vote had actually fallen. The Liberals, as a consolation prize for having seen their support dwindling ever since the month of Orpington, picked up 3,000,000 votes, their highest since 1929—gaining four seats and losing two, and coming close to holding a balance in the new House of Commons.

For the Conservatives, however, consolation was scant; their vote had fallen by 1,700,000. After thirteen years it was the end of Tory Britain; an age which had begun with the return to office of Winston Churchill. It was the end of a ministerial landscape that had come to seem as familiar and firmly fixed as time itself. As the representative of that subterranean tide which had now, after eight years, burst through to the surface, Harold Wilson had achieved what even three years before would still have seemed to many people unimaginable. Like Kennedy, he had received his mandate to "get a tired country moving" only by a hair's breadth—an overall majority of just five seats. Nevertheless, the "hundred days of dynamic action" had begun.

For days the press and television were taken up with new Government appointments. There was the setting up of new Ministries— the Department of Economic Affairs, under George Brown, a Ministry for Land and Natural Resources, a Ministry of Technology; even if the dynamic impact of the last was diminished by the fact that its new Minister was that former champion of the CND Frank Cousins. There was the bevy of academics and "experts" drafted in "Kennedy-style" from outside politics—the Hungarian economists Thomas Balogh and Nicholas Kaldor, from Oxford and Cambridge; Lord Bowden from the Manchester School of Science and Technology, described by the *New Statesman* earlier in the year as "tough," "radical," and "The Computer Man"; Sir Charles Snow, anatomist of the "Two Cultures" and author of romantic novels about "power," to serve as Frank Cousins' deputy; Mr. Alun Gwynne-Jones, Defence

Correspondent of *The Times*, to serve as Minister for Disarmament under the title of Lord Chalfont; and the appointment of the eminent advocate Gerald Gardiner, defender of *Lady Chatterley's Lover* and a founder-member of the CND, as Lord Chancellor, confidently expected to portend a "radical reform" of England's legal system.

All this activity was sufficient to set up at least an impression of "task forces of New Frontiersmen" moving in for "the big push"; and over succeeding weeks the *Observer* and the *Sunday Times*, at least, would find plenty of glamorous copy in "The New Look in Whitehall," as shirt-sleeved Ministers settled down to "sweeping away the cobwebs" with their new informality and zest; and in the impact made, for instance, on the Post Office, by the Postmaster General Anthony Wedgwood Benn's unstuffy habit of lunching, unlike his predecessors, in the Ministry canteen.* But even as the dust was settling, there were sceptics to point out the extent to which the Wilson Government had been forced not just on ability but on the need to settle old political debts and silence potential troublemakers.

The euphoria was still at its height, when on 20 October there came the first signs of trouble—a scatter of stories in the press that all was by no means well with the economy. Six days later the news of impending crisis broke in earnest, with the new Government's first "dynamic action"—15 percent surcharge on imports. At the same time it was announced that the Government was going to cut its spending on "prestige projects" (one of which, it was implied, was the *Concorde* airliner); and on the same evening Harold Wilson made the first of many TV broadcasts to the nation, suggesting that by the end of the year Britain's balance of payments deficit would be between £700 and £800 million. But already the impulsive manner

---

* As he was later to reveal to the *Sunday Times* color supplement (20 February 1966), Wedgwood Benn's private fantasies were no longer, in fact, running entirely on Kennedy's Washington: "I have often thought of the parallel between Castro entering Havana, and a new Government entering power here . . . and had thought that the two events should be *as similar as possible*." It might be recalled that Castro's first act on coming to power had in fact been to shoot 500 members of the old regime.

in which the import surcharge had been imposed, in flagrant breach of international agreements and without any diplomatic warning to Britain's trading partners, was an ominous symptom of the style in which the crisis would be met.

On 3 November, the day that Lyndon Johnson was winning his unprecedented election victory, the Queen's Speech sustained the impression of "dynamism" with a flow of radical proposals for legislation. On November 7 it was announced that Britain had been granted £ 357 million stand-by credit by the International Monetary Fund, and on 11 November the new Chancellor, James Callaghan, introduced his first "emergency" budget. It included a promise of two huge new taxes on capital gains and corporation profits, in the spring—and a further promise of the first increase in income tax since the last Labour Government had been in power. But worse was yet to come; for nine days later the pound began to fall still faster—hardly aided by the Government's own attempts to paint as black a picture as possible of the position it had inherited from "thirteen years of Tory rule." Even in the panic of July 1961, the currency reserves had only lost just over £100 million in a month. Now they were losing £100 million in a day.

On Monday 23 November Callaghan announced a complete return to all the familiar credit-restricting methods of the Tories, so recently and so bitterly condemned. Even so, on 24 November, the pound continued to weaken; not so much as the result of unscrupulous machination by foreign speculators, the so-called "Gnomes of Zurich," now widely invoked by Wilson and others as a scapegoat, but as a reflection of shaken confidence, in the City as well as abroad, in the new Government's administrative competence. The following day the immediate crisis was brought to its end when the Bank of England announced that it had managed to raise a further international credit of £1,071 million. For the moment, at least, devaluation had been staved off. But it was apparent that the pound now occupied an even more important place as the symbol of Britain's international virility than that once occupied by the H-Bomb. It was also apparent that something of the old fever had returned to British politics.*

Not that the economic crisis was the only field in which the Government was taking or promising to take "dynamic action." On 16 November, the press contained strong hints, widely believed to have been leaked by the Aviation Minister Roy Jenkins, that the Anglo-French *Concorde* project was to be scrapped. Mr. Wedgwood Benn too stepped into the act, with a promise that, as soon as the Council of Europe reported on the pirate radio problem, the British Government would take action in its recommendations. On 16 December, amid a fanfare of publicity, Mr. George Brown presided over the signing at Lancaster House of a "Declaration of Intent," by the representatives of both sides of industry, to work toward an effective policy of restraint on rising wages. But by the end of the year wage concessions on the railways and in the docks had made it clear that Mr. Brown would need more than euphoric headlines to achieve his incomes policy. On 17 December the Council of Europe delivered a strongly unfavorable verdict on pirate radios—on the very day that a fifth and the most powerful and "professionally" run station, the partly American-owned Radio London, began transmission from the North Sea. It was soon clear that for Mr. Wedgwood Benn too,

---

* As was shown by the *Daylight* column's reconstruction of events ("How the Pound Was Saved") on 29 November, in prose which even a year before would have seemed a parody of the style: "Nine days ago, a *dark cloud growing* on the financial horizon started to *mushroom* at *frightening speed*. For a *horrible* moment, before *true-blue* bankers from all over the world bailed the Labour Government out, the sterling crisis *over-shadowed* Harold Wilson and *all his works*. . . . Bank of England executives from their *imperial, cavernous listening-post* in Threadneedle Street, had picked up other *worrying* noises. 'The *antennae* reporting in were *sharp*' says an insider . . . on Monday November 16 *white-tied* Wilson delivered reassuring words about keeping the pound *'riding-high,'* speaking in a *hotbed* of City gents and turtle soup . . . At the Treasury *action stations* were maintained all over the weekend . . . *nerve centre* . . . *sleepless* civil servants in sweaters and slacks *manned* the *phones*. *Direct scrambled* lines connected the Treasury knights with the Bank Earl, Cromer . . . 'It was *bloody dangerous*' says one of the Bank *defenders*. 'We were *very near the edge.*' Looking over into the *abyss*, Cromer and his closest aides . . . kept their *nerve superbly*. Parsons is an *extremely tall, immensely powerful banking wizard*, a 54-year old *crisis veteran*. Cromer, only 46 . . . *heavily handsome*, wearing *easily* a responsibility that *suddenly* became *awesome* . . . etc. etc."

"dynamic" words were one thing, "dynamic action" another. By 30 January, after an uncomfortable visit to Paris, Mr. Roy Jenkins was reluctantly conceding that, over the *Concorde* project, Britain had decided after all to "stand by the treaty obligations into which the last Government decided to enter."

If the impression was gaining ground that, behind the "New Thinking" that had been going to "end the chaos and sterility," lay little more than the frenzy of men caught up in an elaborate charade, it was doubly confirmed by, for instance, James Callaghan's quite incoherent attempts to explain his vastly complex taxes; or the leaks and counterleaks which attended Denis Healey's struggle toward a decision to cancel three of Britain's major military aircraft projects in favor of their American counterparts—when less than a year before, he had himself been lashing the Conservatives for the technological implications of their decision to buy the American Phantom and a handful of helicopters.

There is, of course, no phenomenon in politics more familiar than that of a Government saying one thing in order to get into power and then another when faced with the realities of office. A great deal of the Labour Party's initial confusion might be attributed both to their exceptional inexperience of government and to the genuinely considerable economic problems which they inherited. Nevertheless the scale and in particular the quality of their shortcomings was remarkable by any standards. Rarely can any Government have lived and acted to such an extent in the make-believe world of public relations, of press leaks, of meaningless language, of ill-considered actions performed primarily for their immediate effect on people's minds rather than for any lasting effect on events. Yet another, and the greatest victim yet, had fallen prey to the new "English sickness," the slick veneer expressing restless neurosis. In no way was the true character of the Wilson premiership more clearly demonstrated, than by his appeal to a post-election Labour Conference held at Brighton in December:

I believe that the spirit of Dunkirk will once again carry us through to
success.

From three years back came the echo of another Harold Wilson, con-
temptuously facing the Tory front bench on the black morrow of its
crisis in the summer of 1961:

> I myself have always deprecated—perhaps rightly, perhaps wrongly—
> in crisis after crisis, appeals to the Dunkirk spirit as an answer to our
> problems.

As the "Hundred Days" drew toward their close, the country was
in a restive mood. On 14 January a giant demonstration of aircraft
workers marched through London in protest against the rumored
scrapping of the TSR-2 and other aircraft. The weather was wet and
windy, the skies were dark. In Leyton, an East London suburb, the
new Foreign Secretary Patrick Gordon Walker was bidding to
return to the House of Commons in a specially convened by-election;
but the campaign was by no means going smoothly, his meetings
being constantly and violently interrupted by Colin Jordan and various groups of racial extremists. Outside 22 Hyde Park Gate in
Kensington, an army of reporters was keeping vigil, ever since on
15 January the frail figure of Lord Moran had stepped out into the
biting wind to read the first grave bulletin:

> After a cold, Sir Winston has developed a circulatory weakness and
> there has been a cerebral thrombosis. A further bulletin will be issued
> at 10 p.m.

It was only three months since Churchill had ceased to be a member
of the House of Commons.

For day after day, the country waited. The Prime Minister can-
celled a visit to Germany. The National Association of Schoolmasters
called off a strike. Party political broadcasts were postponed. There
was a sense that the world would never wait for news from Britain

with such suspense again. And then, on the night of 21 January, domestic attention was briefly diverted. As Leyton Town Hall was obscured in flurries of snow, television cameras relayed the scenes attending the announcement that Gordon Walker had been defeated —and a "safe" Labour majority of almost 8,000 overthrown by a Conservative candidate who, as chance would have it, was an Old Etonian. The swing away from Labour (on the ninety-seventh of the Hundred Days) was 8.7 percent—while it was over 5 percent in the other by-election of the day at Nuneaton, where Frank Cousins had been elected on a greatly reduced Labour vote. The Labour majority in the Commons was already down to three.

At once there was a renewed frenzy of speculation about the political future. But on the Hundredth Day itself all such diversion was cut short. On a wintry Sunday morning came the news of the death of "The Greatest Englishman of Them All."

The death of Winston Churchill, in his ninety-first year and after a ten-day illness that had been as closely followed as that of a monarch, could in no way have been described as a shock. On the day of his passing, so long awaited, there was even for many people, particularly for the young, a sense of flatness and anti-climax. And then, over the next seven days, the nation found itself gathered up in a great ritual that was as much a remembrance of its own, seemingly so distant past as it was for the career and stature of the man whose passing was its occasion. Here, after all, had been a man whose own intimate links with history ran back to the last cavalry charge at Omdurman, in the year of the death of Gladstone—and whose life span connected the present with the lines of millions who had been contemporary with Palmerston and Peel and the Duke of Wellington, and even with hundreds of thousands, still alive well into his youth, who had lived in the time of Napoleon, Beethoven, and George III. In Britain's last great crisis as an imperial world power, Churchill had stood out like Justinian in the twilight of Rome, as a man who derived his majesty from a sense of the imperial and military splendors of the past. Yet, less than ten years before he had still been Britain's Prime Minister.

As day succeeded day, with newspaper supplements, television programs, pictures of the lying-in-state at Westminster Hall, of the anonymous queues stretching for three miles down the banks of the Thames, the sense of occasion slowly grew—reaching its climax with the State Funeral, the greatest ceremony since the Coronation, watched on television by an estimated 350,000,000 people. Nevertheless, behind the grandeur of the occasion, the steel grey television pictures of that grey January day, the mass of ceremonial prose, many people were aware of an unspoken disquiet. There was a feeling of unreality in the air. It was as if a nation, which for years had been subjecting itself to faked emotions, turning its back on the past to lose itself in the unnatural glare of the present, was now desperately trying to conjure up the real emotion which it knew to be appropriate—and finding that it no longer quite knew how. "The last frail petal of one of the great red roses of all England falls. And the sword sleeps in its scabbard," wrote the columnist Cassandra in the *Daily Mirror.* "You can take tears today and catch them and call them the river that flows through London's heart," ran the *Evening News,* and concluded: "When I get to Heaven, he said, I mean to spend a considerable portion of my first million years in painting. Tomorrow, perhaps, you will look up and there will be a rainbow in the sky. *Winston Spencer Churchill will be at work."*

From the television screens and the pages of color supplements which, for years, had dripped with praise of the ephemeral, the latest sensation, the bright facade of the moment, it was hard to take the pictures of the State Funeral as more than a selection of pretty, impersonal images, to be flipped over and then forgotten. Once again, in a profound sense, the collective fantasy that hung over English life had been put to the test of reality—and found sorely wanting.

Chapter Ten

Echoes of a Nightmare

All sorts of signs may be found, if you look around the
world, of a great storm blowing up.

JOHN VAIZEY
Spectator, 11 June 1965

Search every land, from Cadiz to the dawn-streaked shores
Of Ganges, and you'll find few men who can distinguish
A false from a worthwhile objective, or slash their way
through
The fogs of deception . . . it's universal
This self-destructive urge.

Juvenal, *Satire* XIII

Our teeth are in the real meat, and our muscles exerted
in the real power struggle of politics.

> JO GRIMOND to Liberal Party Conference,
> 25 September 1965

"People rather like all the talk of cliff-hanging: it makes
politics more interesting" . . . Rhodesia he describes as
"My Cuba." "It was eyeball to eyeball for us last week,
but I gave Smith a way out every time."

> HAROLD WILSON in interview,
> *Sunday Telegraph*, 17 October 1965

When I first saw him across a room in 1947, I knew that
Kenneth Peacock Tynan would become the first person on
television to use what the popular papers have dubbed
"that word."

> ALAN BRIEN
> *Spectator*, 19 November 1965

We are in a theatre that is front page news. We are
denounced as subversive, immoral, filthy—it's all terribly
healthy.

> PETER HALL
> *Time*, 13 April 1966

We're more popular than Jesus now.

> JOHN LENNON
> *Evening Standard*, 4 March 1966

Vanity of vanities, saith the Preacher, vanity of vanities;
all is vanity . . .
One generation passeth away and another generation
cometh . . .
All the rivers run into the sea; yet the sea is not full . . .
the eye is not satisfied with seeing, nor the ear filled with
hearing . . .
And there is no new thing under the sun.

> *Ecclesiastes*, I

In the renewed "dream stage" which had come over English life in 1964, the social and political revolution of the past nine years had been finally consummated. Here at last, at the beginning of 1965, was the youthful, vigorous New England which had thrust its way irresistibly up through the decaying, class-ridden atrophy of the Old; an England whose destinies were in the hands of a young, vigorous, Kennedy-style Government; an England bathed in the dazzling release of unprecedented new talent and energy; the England of brilliant young playwrights, of irreverent film directors and television men, of a glittering new classless culture that was the cynosure of the world. Alongside these more prominent standard bearers of the revolution were the host of outriders who had equally helped to transform the flavor of English life—the fashion designers, the hair stylists, the cookery experts, the antique shops, the discothèques, the little restaurants, the casinos, the color supplements, the spy novelists, the interior decorators, the television conversationalists—all interwoven, feeding off each other and providing a unique color and excitement in everyday living.

Here at least was the picture that was taking shape in the minds of many people, particularly certain English and American journalists—and that was to find expression in such articles as that written by John Crosby for the *Weekend Telegraph* on 30 April, unveiling London as "the most exciting city in the world."

It is a characteristic of revolutions, however, that when achieved, they cannot just stand still. Already in Britain the euphoria of the spring and summer of 1964 had passed. In such widely varying manifestations as the disillusionments of Mr. Wilson's Hundred Days and signs of a decline in the sales of pop records, the momentum of this New England was showing symptoms of strain. Where was it all leading to? What was there left to achieve—except to turn the wheels faster and faster in an attempt to stay at the same pitch of nervous excitement? Could the supply of new stimulation, new faces, new sensations, be kept up indefinitely? Were there more Osbornes and Beatles, Quants and Flemings, Finneys and Frosts, more Baverstocks and Bernard Levins, more Harold Wilsons, queueing to take their places in the limelight? Or had the great subterranean impulse which had thrown all these people to the surface, at last spent its force?

In those early months of 1965, as England was becoming self-conscious about the full extent of her social transformation, there was a chill in the air. It was a chill that would by no means affect Britain alone. In 1964, the year in which President Johnson's election victory and the unveiling of his vision of a "Great Society" had marked the renewal of America's own collective dream, Britain was by no means the only country that had enjoyed a new "dream stage." And for America, the nightmare that was to follow the release of nervous energy represented by the Kennedy era and the earlier stages of the civil rights movement was to be worse than anything that could affect Britain itself. For Britain, 1965 would be the year of the Rhodesian crisis. But for America, it would be the year of the Watts riot and the major escalation of the Vietnam war. Reality, in fact, was beginning to call for a reckoning.

In Britain, three weeks after the Churchill funeral, there came an omen. On 25 February, the *Daily Mail* carried an exclusive story from Bernard Levin. Leading the front page, under giant black headlines "BBC MAN OUT," it began:

> A sensational "palace revolution" at the BBC has resulted in the ousting of Donald Baverstock, the most dynamic and talented man the Corporation has thrown up since the war.

The BBC's mounting discontents had come to a head. But the end of the BBC career of Donald Baverstock and his *"Tonight* empire" was more than just the end of a phase in British television. It marked

the downfall of the first man in British public life to whom the fatal
epithet "dynamic" had been regularly and almost automatically
applied.

Barely was the Baverstock storm dying down, when the BBC was
again back on the front pages with a series of incidents surrounding
his last bequest to their screens, *Not So Much a Programme*. The
new show had recovered from its chaotic beginnings and settled
down to some kind of uneasy equilibrium. But lack of judgment
and self-control had led it to invite more and more controversy. By
the beginning of March, the volume of protest had become a flood.
The program was castigated by Lord Longford, Leader of the House
of Lords; two right-wing Conservative MP's put down a Commons
motion calling for Sir Hugh Greene's resignation; while in *The
Times,* that consistent conscience of the Old Guard, Sir William
Haley, himself a former Director General, described the BBC itself
as engaged in "a panic flight from all decent values," "televising
inanities," and in "a surrender to all pressures in favour of so-called
satire and a sick, sniggering attitude to life."

Along with the Clean Up TV campaign, launched in the autumn
of 1963 by a middle-class Midlands housewife Mrs. Mary Whitehouse, which was attracting increasing public attention, this furore
was another example of that pattern which had become so familiar
(as with the attacks on the "filthy plays" the previous autumn)
whereby the aggressions of left and right fed and exacerbated each
other. Only whereas in the fifties it had been most conspicuously the
excesses of the established Old Guard which had enraged the dispossessed young and left-wing intelligentsia—as over Suez, or the chauvinism surrounding Britain's H-Bomb—the balance had now swung
the other way. Now it was the Old Guard who were the dispossessed
enraged minority, and the young and the intelligentsia who, particularly through their control over the vastly more prominent communications industry, represented the prevailing orthodoxy. Yet, such was
the neurosis of this "New Establishment" that it still had to maintain
the illusion that it was battling for freedom against the entrenched

forces of reaction; it still required a supply of right-wing "order" images to feed its aggression. Thus ironically the rise of such figures as Mrs. Whitehouse was even subconsciously welcomed by the avant-garde intelligentsia, as providing them with the exhilarating sense of still having something to rebel against—a process which was to reach its apotheosis a year or so later when their chief Aunt Sally was to become Alf Garnett, a fictitious character actually created by the avant-garde playwright Johnny Speight, as the ludicrously right-wing villain of a television series.

During the last weekend of March 1965, *Not So Much A Programme* caused three separate rows, including one over Bernard Levin's casual reference to Sir Alec Douglas-Home as a "cretin" and an "imbecile." When Sir Hugh Greene was forced at last to make a comprehensive public apology, it was hardly surprising that it should also be announced that the program would be coming off earlier than planned. Television satire, which had once won the BBC such acclaim for its daring, had indeed become a Frankenstein's monster.

Another side to the revolution in English life which in these same months was giving rise to a more general if impotent concern was contained in the statistics compiled by the Home Office, the Ministry of Health, and other official bodies, revealing the price that had been paid for England's social transformation. It was at last being brought home to people that there was something disquieting in the fact that, over the previous nine years, for instance, convictions for drunkenness had risen by three-fifths; the illegitimate birth rate had almost doubled; admissions to mental hospitals had risen by well over a third; the amount spent annually on gambling had increased by four or five times; cases of arson and incendiarism had risen by 250 percent; addiction to such obviously destructive drugs as heroin and cocaine had risen by ten times, and to less obviously harmful drugs by an almost incalculable figure (estimates of the numbers semi-addicted to these drugs ranging between 100,000 and half a million). Graph after graph showed a sharp rise around 1956–1957, and from then on a steady increase, markedly accelerating in the early sixties. In 1964 the crime rate had for the first time topped a million indictable offenses, after the heaviest rise in any of the nine years, and including an increase in those twelve months alone of 17 percent in crimes of violence against the person.

By early 1965, crime in Britain's great cities appeared to be getting out of hand. In London itself, the police faced the new threat of gang warfare. The protection racket, particularly associated with the still proliferating gambling clubs and betting shops, had entered a more dangerous phase; for the main criminal gangs were run largely by men who no longer scrupled to use guns or even torture to achieve their ends. The police seemed more than ever powerless to meet these new challenges. Since 1963, the percentages of cases cleared up had dropped markedly; and even when the authorities did entertain hope of a victory, it was often dashed in the outcome—as when in January the Kray brothers, leaders of the most dangerous of all the London gangs, were remanded on a charge of attempting to extort money with menaces, but in April were acquitted after an Old Bailey jury had been unable to reach a verdict.

At the same time, teenage vandalism was spreading in a rash. On 29 March, young boys derailed a train near Dagenham, killing two people and injuring fifteen. Other trains were derailed. Drivers were hurt by flying stones. In London, Birmingham, and Liverpool, telephones were smashed by the thousand. Over the Easter weekend in April, and again at Whitsun, there were more outbreaks of teenage rioting in seaside towns, similar to those of 1964.

In one view, however, it was still possible to see this wave of crime and disorder as exciting and glamorous. Already, the previous summer, the Kray brothers had begun to attain the status as celebrities which at the end of the year would win their inclusion in David Bailey's *Box of Pin Ups* as among the most "glamorous" figures of swinging London. And in February, the public fascination with the Great Train Robbers reached a new intensity with the serialization in the *Sunday Times Magazine* of a best-selling book which painted the robbery in breathless, blow-by-blow prose as if it had been some heroic wartime exploit. The criminals were each described in that stereotyped capsule language which had been used to glamorize every kind of hero in the collective make-believe, from Presidents to with-it publishers:

> A *wolfishly handsome* man, *long-limbed, deft,* with an *easy manner,* Goody has a *cold face,* a *cruel mouth* in repose. *Active* it becomes the face of a *leader* . . .

It was emphasized that at the trial "one of the prosecution team" had "murmured that in other circumstances Goody could have won the VC," while of others it was said that they were "very attractive to women" or "a stout, popular underworld personality" or "rare among criminals, he is a Left-winger." And from the *Sunday Times* extracts, at least, the subsequent activities of the police might have been seen simply as those of clumsy, interfering grown-ups trying to spoil an exciting game.

It was not only in England that the year 1965 was promising to provide a bleak contrast to the comparatively eventless months of 1964. All over the world there were signs of new storms. On 7 February the Americans for the first time bombed North Vietnam. The number of American troops involved in South Vietnam, which at the beginning of the year had been less than twenty thousand, was now rising by tens of thousands every month—and the full extent of the Vietnamese tragedy was beginning to dawn on Britain and the rest of the world. In London in March and April there were revived stirrings of public demonstration over Vietnam by many of those groups and individuals who had previously made up the now virtually defunct CND. In April, American troops became involved in a second civil war, in the Dominican Republic. At the same time, there was rising tension between India and Pakistan, with armed clashes in the Rann of Kutch. And in May, in Southern Rhodesia, the sweeping election victory of Mr. Ian Smith's Rhodesian Front

Party on a platform of full independence threatened that a climax to Britain's last major colonial problem would not be long in coming.

Meanwhile, back in Britain itself, Harold Wilson's Government was living up to the promise of its first Hundred Days. The headline-catching gestures and statements of brave intention continued to pour out, month after month; a "bridge-building" conference here, a "fact-finding" mission there; at one minute, honors for the Beatles for their "services to export"; at another, a National Plan for Britain's economy for The Next Five Years; one month, a White Paper for the Nationalisation of the Steel Industry, the next, a Commonwealth Peace Mission to stop the war in Vietnam. But in all this parade of bustle and activity the air of unreality surrounding the Government only deepened. As early as 28 April, *The Times* had voiced a generally growing dismay in the words "it is the sheer incompetence of the Government which worries most." As the months passed, the sterling crisis dragged out into the longest for fifteen years. Despite the Government's "stringent" new incomes policy, noisily publicized by George Brown, new wage claims poured in and inflation began to mount. In May, the Government borrowed yet another £500 million from the International Monetary Fund; by July, Mr. Callaghan was forced to bring in his third "emergency" budget in eight months.

Already in the *Spectator* of 11 June, the paper's political correspondent Alan Watkins—one of the few who had retained an objective eye during the foregoing year—had drawn a sharp parallel to the character of Wilson's premiership:

> With every week that passes, Mr. Harold Wilson reminds one more and more of Mr. Harold Macmillan in his last phase. There is the same reluctance to admit that a mistake has been made, the same rather forced unconcern . . .

Despite the Government's bare Parliamentary majority, the left wing of the Labour Party was becoming restless; by the end of June, one Labour MP was calling for the Prime Minister's resignation. After eight months of "dynamic" government, it was hard to point to a single major decision that had been taken. Increasingly it seemed that only one thing maintained the credibility of Mr. Wilson's Government—the continued presence as Leader of the Opposition of Sir Alec Douglas-Home. And then, on 22 July, after weeks of rumor and counter-rumor (and appropriately pushed by a member of the New Oxford Group, William Rees Mogg, in the *Sunday Times*), Sir Alec resigned.

The week-long explosion of "ruthless," "tough-minded," "abrasive" word-spinning amid which Mr. Heath became the first elected Leader of the Conservative Party exceeded anything previously seen. Whereas Wilson in 1964 had at least been his own chief salesman, Heath's new image was merely a projection of the fantasies of others. One of the last remaining bastions of Old England had fallen to the revolution. For the next few days the euphoria of the Conservative Party was complete. At last they too had a leader fit for the "classless," technocratic age; a grammar school product who could "beat Wilson on his own ground." It was not long before both the major opinion polls showed them once again well ahead of the Government, with a lead ranging up to 7.5 percent.

By August, the prospect for Harold Wilson could scarcely have looked bleaker. In Fleet Street and the City, as the financial crisis continued, there were wild rumors of a 9 percent Bank Rate, even of imminent devaluation. In mid-September, when George Brown published the Government's mammoth National Plan, talking airily of an increase of 25 percent in the economy in only five years, the make-believe which marked its every page could not have been more cruelly exposed; after nine months in which the country's production had actually fallen, it was the collapse into reality of that dream of economic growth which had come to dominate English politics in the previous five years. And even when, at the beginning of September, the seemingly endless run on sterling was brought temporarily to a halt, by a further huge international support operation, Mr. Wilson was facing a new threat to his position. For quite apart from the Conservative lead on the opinion polls, the death on 2 September of the Speaker of the House of Commons now threatened to cut the Government's majority to a bare two votes. The Liberals, who earlier in the year had at Roxburgh again won a by-election, now saw the chance which even in the headiest days of their revival they could hardly have seriously envisaged—that they might hold the balance of power in the House of Commons. As Jo Grimond cried to his exultant followers at their Party Assembly in Scarborough: "Our teeth are in the real meat!" But more strains were to come.

For in August and September, something of a storm was breaking all over the world. Overshadowing everything else, the escalation of the war in Vietnam was assuming ever more alarming proportions. In America there was the Watts riot. On 6 September came the news that India and Pakistan, the second and sixth most populous countries in the world, were at open war, with tank battles raging from Kashmir to the sea; a war between two leading members of the Commonwealth with whom Britain, who as late as 1962 had regarded herself as the most natural mediating partner, apparently had no influence whatever. On 30 September, in the fifth most populous nation in the world, the abortive rebellion which rocked President Sukarno's government in Jakarta launched one of the bloodiest purges in history. And on 4 October, there arrived for talks in London the still comparatively obscure Prime Minister of Southern Rhodesia. Before leaving Salisbury, Mr. Smith had defiantly assured his followers: "It is an even bet that, no matter what the British Government does, we shall be independent by Christmas."

The last major crisis of decolonization had begun. And as, in the shires of Britain, the Conservative Old Guard once again stirred to do battle for the cause of the Rhodesians, it is not altogether fanciful to see in their re-emergence, like that of the Liberals, a last gathering before the final curtain of all those groups which had played their part in the politics of the previous ten years. At the Labour Party conference a few days previously, Mr. Wilson had again affirmed his Government's intention to speak only in the "gritty accents of reality." But rarely had reality seemed so far away.

It was by no means in the political domain alone that something of a peak was approaching. Throughout the summer, the nyktomorphic glamor of swinging London had been swelling. The arrival of bewildered American schoolgirls to make their pilgrimage to Liverpool had been familiar for almost a year; now they were followed by tourists as eager to visit Carnaby Street and the *Ad Lib* as they were to see Buckingham Palace; and by the first planeloads of American gamblers flying in to what *Le Figaro* had described in a full-page survey on 1 June as "the European Las Vegas." In May there had been *Newsweek*'s cover story on "the switched-on world of Jean Shrimpton." In June, the Beatles' MBEs had won front page headlines throughout the world. In July, even the violent death of Porfirio Rubirosa had been considered by the *Daily Mail*'s gossip columnist Pearson Phillips (New Oxford Group) a fitting cue to proclaim the passing of

> the time when boring people had money and you didn't have to be particularly clever at anything to be accepted . . . the playboy is dead, and London, ironically, has never been more alive.

During the year, all the different worlds making up London's "swinging scene" had merged into the same iridescent bubble. This was the process which had come to its head in the colored illustration to John Crosby's *Weekend Telegraph* article showing "some of the people who make London swing"—including David Hockney, Mary Quant, David Bailey, John Michael, Peter Blake, Maureen Cleave, John Kasmin, a boutique proprietor named Barbara Hulanicki, a dress designer, two model girls, a hairdresser, and the *Private Eye* cartoonist Gerald Scarfe—all grouped in their pose of frozen solemnity round a piece of cardboard sculpture labeled "Box 1965." By July, the process had gone far enough for *Private Eye* itself to refer disdainfully to the "new aristocracy." Truly appropriate to such a moment in English life, when facade had never been so important, or so unreal, were two of the three vogue films of the summer, Dick Lester's frenetic, fragmented, inconsequential dreams, respectively shot in color and a blinding, under-exposed white, *Help!* (starring the Beatles) and *The Knack*.

But even this frenzy was only a symptom of the gathering strain beneath, as the "swinging city" galvanized itself for a last flight into the stratosphere. Never before had London been a town so fashionably obsessed with kinks, with sexual abnormality and make-believe violence. In June the English Stage Company had been forced to turn the Royal Court into a theatre club, in order to stage John Osborne's latest play *A Patriot for Me*—the set piece of which was a lavish homosexual "drag" ball, starring George Devine as a "baroness," and the protagonist of which, a homosexual spy in decadent Hapsburg Vienna, committed suicide in the final act. In the same week, the centerpiece of the Royal Opera House's summer season at Covent Garden had been Schoenberg's morbid *Moses and Aaron,* staged on unprecedented scale, with its vast apocalyptic orgy scene "realistically" directed by Peter Hall, and including, as a particularly "camp" gesture, the casting of four Soho strip-tease artistes as the Four Virgins. At the Aldwych, Harold Pinter's *The Homecoming* portrayed a man presenting his new American wife to his father and brothers, whereupon they took turns making love to her and laid plans to set her up as a prostitute. The third vogue film of the summer was Roman Polanski's *Repulsion,* an incredibly bloodthirsty portrayal of a young girl's paranoiac nightmares. In the October edition of the *London Magazine,* even the script-writer of *Help!* (who was also the first man to have been commissioned to write a play by the National Theatre) wrote a solemn article entitled "My boyhood life and work in the theatre and how I came to be obsessed with sex and violence" and containing such lines as:

> My plays are about filth, filthily. There is a place for filth in the theatre. I've seen it and lovely camiknick filth it was.

Artistic attention at this time was focused on a series of paintings by an Australian artist, every one a nightmare caricature of the mass-

murderer of the early fifties, John Christie. The most fashionable
new night club was *Danny La Rue's,* the chief attraction of which
was the proprietor's transvestite cabaret act. On the streets and news-
stands, girlie magazines and pornography were displayed with an
openness which even two or three years before would have been un-
thinkable. And yet in no way was the spirit of the times so perfectly
caught as in the song with which the Rolling Stones were heading
the hit parade:

I can't get no satisfaction,
I can't get no satisfaction,
'Cos I try an' I try an' I try
I can't get no,
I can't get no,
I can't get no satisfaction, no satisfaction, no satisfaction, no satisfaction,
I can't get no . . .

Here, as summer turned into autumn, was "the most exciting city in
the world."

At the end of September, it was exactly ten years since this era of
English history had begun. If a visitor from that time could have
been suddenly transported to the London of September 1965, what
would most immediately have struck him? First perhaps, as he sped
along the curving M4 motorway from London Airport below the
unfamiliar howl of jet airliners, would have been the soaring new
glass and concrete blocks breaking the skyline, the tallest of all of
which, the GPO Tower, had only just been opened. They were by
no means a forest, as in New York, and certainly not as tall as the
skyscrapers of Manhattan—but enough to alter the scale of central
London, so that in many parts the older and smaller buildings had
begun to look like toys, or even part of a stage set. Next perhaps he
would have been struck by the change in the appearance of the
young—now in many cases sharply divided from the rest of the
population by their clothes and appearance. He would have noticed

the number of men wearing hair down to their shoulders, and the number of girls with their hair cropped boyishly close. Even more would he have been struck by the girls' clothes—their startling Op Art black and white, their shiny plastics, their little Courrèges boots, above all, their hemlines which, during the summer, had risen two or three inches above the knee. Nothing would have surprised him more than the exhibitionistic violence with which these fashions grabbed at the attention—the contrasts, the jangling colors, the hard glossiness of PVC, the show of thigh. It might even have occurred to him that these hard-looking uniforms were curiously impersonal, like the expressionless stare that so often went with them or the throwaway generic terms—"birds" or "dollies"—that were used to describe their wearers.

As he moved about the town, while his sensibility remained unadjusted, our visitor would have found the same visual violence everywhere: in the ubiquitous neon-lighting, on shop-fronts, on advertisements, in the more garishly decorated restaurants. If he had slipped into an art gallery, he would as like as not have found it again on the spotlit walls, great canvases covered with the simplest, brashest, most highly colored patterns. If he had opened a fashion magazine, he would have been amazed by the black harsh photography and the awkward, even ugly contortions of the models. And if he ventured into one of the discothèques, the sensation of a strange, alienating harshness would have struck him more forcefully than ever—to the weird, space-age garb of the young and the theatrical gloom, he would have found added the blast of deafening, inhuman noise.

At this moment, in September and October, the self-consciousness and frenzy of the English revolution were rising to their peak. In almost every newspaper and magazine, scarcely a day went by without news of the opening of a new boutique, without a feature on Terence Stamp or Michael Caine or Carnaby Street, without a picture of Jean Shrimpton or a mention of Mick Jagger or decorating hints from

David Hicks. It was the time when the twenty-one-year-old Cathy McGowan (South London), a television personality from the "pop" program, *Ready Steady Go* and styled by the press "The Queen of the Mods," set herself up as a "teenage consultant" and was solemnly reported by the *Daily Mirror* as advising the Managing Directors of three large store chains that:

> the kids want clothes to look terrific—and they don't wear them for very long so it doesn't matter if they fall to bits.

In the midst of this feverish city, however, Mr. Wilson suddenly had more serious concerns. For by 4 October, the "great storm blowing up" in so many parts of the world had plunged the Labour Government into the most serious crisis of its eleven months in office. On October 8 the Rhodesia negotiations collapsed. Once again in the London air there was a whiff of the great crisis of 1956. Once again the press was bitterly divided between those calling for violent action and those arguing that Government should bide its time. Only this time the *Daily Express* was on the side of peace and negotiation: while the papers clamoring for the quick solution by force were those champions of "tough-mindedness" and "gritty reality," the *Guardian*, the *New Statesman,* and the *Observer.*

On the night of 12 October, as the Conservatives gathered for their Conference in Brighton, Mr. Wilson addressed the nation on television on "the very grave situation," the "nightmare with which I have to live." He emphasized that the previous night he had discussed the crisis "on the phone" with the Commonwealth's elder statesman, Sir Robert Menzies; and that he had been "in direct touch with nineteen other heads of Commonwealth governments." The following day, when he flew to Balmoral to confer with the Queen, there was little news value left in the deliberations of the Conservative Party, despite the last brief re-emergence as a political force of the Marquess of Salisbury and the enthusiastic ovation given to Sir Alec Douglas-Home. The fact that the opinion polls now showed the

Labour Party, in a sudden surge of popularity, eleven points ahead, only further underlined the metamorphosis which had all but obliterated the "radical" Harold Wilson of a year before. Gone now were the carefully cultivated appurtenances of Gannex raincoat and H.P. Sauce; in their place, the orderly myths of monarchy and Commonwealth, juggled by a silver-haired and gravely visaged "national leader." In a sense, however, it was the last and most revealing comment on the fever which had England in its grip. For at the moment when it seemed that English society was most completely caught up in the frenzy of modernity, the true "two-way" nature of the social revolution was becoming apparent as never before.

At the very moment when Harold Wilson was turning to the monarchy as a symbol of authority and stability—and just ten years after Malcolm Muggeridge's first article on "Royal Soap Opera"— the Royal Family was being subjected to the greatest wave of sycophantic attention from the press in all those ten years. It was not, however, so much as symbols of stability that they were acclaimed by the women's magazines and the popular newspapers as that, almost entirely through the activities of Lord Snowdon and Princess Margaret, they were now gilded with the swinging virtues of the New Aristocracy. The popular press was beside itself with the gay, "irreverent" guests who, it was reported, were more or less regularly received at Kensington Palace—Peter Sellers, David Hockney, Jonathan Miller, Kenneth Tynan. Lord Snowdon's wife was profiled in one magazine as "The Pacesetter Princess"; in the *Sunday Mirror* was a series on "The Little White Room" in the South London dockland where "Tony and Margaret" had spent happy, informal evenings away from pomp in the early days of their marriage; even the *Spectator* published its own glittering account of the new atmosphere prevailing at Kensington Palace, written by the head of the avant-garde Whitechapel art gallery and full of such phrases as "tough resilience" and "direct but spontaneous curiosity."

Not even the Queen herself was immune to such treatment, being accorded by the *Daily Express,* in a long feature about her new relationship with Harold Wilson, the final accolade—"a superb professional."*

On the other hand, Mr. Wilson was by no means the only "new Briton" who was suddenly reaching for at least the outward show of "class," tradition, and stability. Just at the moment when newspaper headlines were announcing, over news of Rolls' most "revolutionary" design for fifty years, "Rolls-Royce Goes Mod," it became smart for the fashion photographers to sell their E-Type Jaguars and switch, like Albert Finney and John Lennon, to old-style Rolls-Royces. Just as the headmaster of Marlborough was observing that, among themselves, his public schoolboys were now affecting what they hoped to be a "classless Radio Caroline accent," it was announced that Mr. Terence Stamp from the East End was acquiring, like Mr. Heath, a flat in the upper-class Albany. Just as one newspaper was depicting the Courrèges-booted and space-age-garbed daughter of a sixth Earl embarking on her first job as a salesgirl in a boutique in Knightsbridge, so another, the *Daily Telegraph,* was reporting Miss Barbara Hulanicki, the proprietor of a boutique in Kensington, as saying (under the headline, on 27 October, "Take a Look at This New Face—It Belongs to 1966"):

> "I love old things. Modern things are so cold. I need things that have lived." Baffling words for such a "with-it" designer . . . with everything around her so fast, so uncertain, she needs to go home to . . . the comfort of dark red wallpaper and Edwardiana. It makes her feel safe.

In the theatre, ten years after *Waiting for Godot* had heralded the "revolution" that was going to "sweep away" what Penelope Gilliatt

* Two other traditional institutions were being similarly gilded at this time. The House of Lords, because of its new found "liberalism," reflected in the passing of bills to legalize abortion and adult homosexuality, and the Church which was the subject of a spate of "swinging" publicity, notably from the *Observer Magazine* in the course of a profile of Coventry on 14 November: "The clergy are making an impact on Coventry itself. The clergymen use the term 'with-it' freely . . . the Bishop, Cuthbert Bardsley, is a cheerful giant who paints . . . he talks about experiments in 'new-look worship.' The Provost . . . a tall, handsome South African . . . talks about the cathedral as a 'gigantic visual aid.' "

has described as "a theatre that had turned into a stuffed flunkey . . . famous old plays decked out with stars," the biggest successes of the autumn of 1965 were being enjoyed by a sudden vogue for "famous old plays," including no less than five revivals of Bernard Shaw, put on by theatres which had discovered the revolutionary effect on the box office of decking out their productions with a canopy full of "conventional" star names. And whereas a few months later the son of the third Earl (Bertrand) Russell was to write in his election address as a Labour candidate that he was "educated at Eton where he acquired a strong dislike of the public school system," only a few months earlier Lord Snow, the Labour Minister from lower-middle-class origins in Leicester, had caused some of his colleagues a good deal of embarrassment by defending his decision to send his son to Eton with the words:

> If one is living in a fairly prosperous home, it is a mistake to educate one's child differently from those he knows socially.

Certainly the English revolution was by no means everything that autumn that it might have seemed. But even now, the frenzy had still to reach its height. For, in the closing days of October, the collective fantasy came to its head in four weeks of almost unbroken hysteria. To ten years of growing make-believe, it was a climactic "Month of Madness."

Friday 22 October: winter arrived with a thick blanket of fog. The M4 motorway was closed for hours by the wreckage of dozens of cars. The papers were now filled with macabre pictures of police activity on Saddleworth Moor near Manchester, where "a number of bodies have been found in shallow graves."

Monday 25 October: Mr. Wilson flew to Salisbury in a dramatic last-minute bid to keep talks going. Wilson obviously becoming increasingly carried away by the crisis, talked excitedly of "my Cuba" and "eyeball to eyeball" confrontation.

294

Tuesday 26 October: Buckingham Palace was besieged for two hours by thousands of screaming teenagers, hoping for a glimpse of the Beatles attending their investiture.

Saturday 30 October: collapse of Salisbury talks. In Australia, Jean Shrimpton appeared at Melbourne race-track in a dress four inches above the knee—and press hysteria over the doings of the New Aristocracy reached its peak.

Wednesday 3 November: on the same day, the cult of sensation reached its climax in both television and the theatre. The BBC was plunged into front-page controversy with its play *Up the Junction*, an ostensibly *ciné-vérité* picture of working-class life in South London (based on a book by a millionaire's daughter and former member of the Chelsea Set). Among the scenes of the play were the detailed seduction of a teenage girl on a bombsite and a horrific back-street abortion, complete with chilling howls. Even critic Peter Black, the most loyal friend of BBC "experiment," was forced to comment:

> I suspect that at least part of the object of *Up the Junction* was a wish, perhaps an unconscious one, of the Wednesday Play boys to see just how far they could go in a television play with sex and cuss words.

On the same evening, at the Royal Court, took place the first performance of *Saved* by Edward Bond (South London), also ostensibly a picture of working-class life in South London—and for the second time the Court had to turn itself into a club to avoid the censorship of the Lord Chamberlain. Among the scenes was one in which a gang of youths rubbed the face of a baby in its own excreta, continued by throwing lighted matches into its pram, and ended by stoning it to death. Even critic Penelope Gilliatt, the most loyal friend of Royal Court "experiment," was forced to comment:

> I spent a lot of the first act shaking with claustrophobia and thinking I was going to be sick. The scene where a baby in a pram is pelted to death is nauseating. The swagger of the sex jokes is almost worse . . .

Thursday 4 November: over the "invasion" of New York by a group of English fashion designers, a stream of headlines: "The Patriotic British Knee," "Now That Shrimp Look Sets New York Staring," "Models Stop Fifth Avenue Traffic."

Friday 5 November: the unilateral declaration of independence by Rhodesia was expected almost any day. The United Nations called upon Britain to use force, if necessary. In Salisbury, a state of emergency was declared. More headlines attended Princess Margaret and Lord Snowdon's triumphal progress from Hollywood to Washington—"The Mod Princess," "Cable Car Serenade for 'Madcap Meg.'" During the night, thick fog again blanketed many parts of Britain; along the M6 motorway, pile after pile of crashed vehicles blazed in the darkness and eleven people died, with over fifty injured.

Sunday 7 November: the death of a second Labour MP cut the Government's majority in the Commons to one. Mr. Wilson made a further last-minute appeal to Mr. Smith that they should fly to meet in Malta.

Monday 8 November: the announcement of a further major escalation in the number of American troops involved in the Vietnam war, now approaching 200,000, was accompanied by the worst case so far of a "friendly" village being obliterated by American bombs and by America's first suicide by fire, on the steps of the Pentagon. From New York a *Sun* correspondent reported on a frantic renewal of civil defense preparations for nuclear war:

> A few months ago, preparations like this would have excited ridicule. Now they are being taken seriously.

Meanwhile at home the BBC had become involved in its second major controversy in a week over its decision not to screen *The War Game*, Peter Watkins' horrifying fantasy, deliberately intended to be as "shocking" as possible, showing the Vietnamese war developing into a worldwide holocaust, and complete with *ciné-vérité* close-ups of men burning in a firestorm, mutilated and scorched bodies, and people having their eyes burned out by the nuclear flash.

Tuesday 9 November: in America it was the day of the "great black-out," the power failure covering New York and eight states; also of a second attempted suicide by fire, outside the UN. In London, the flow of pictures of Jean Shrimpton which had filled the popular press since the incident at Melbourne was interrupted by huge pictures of a film starlet posing at London Airport in a "Shock Dress" six inches above the knee.

Thursday 11 November: the Rhodesian crisis reached its first climactic non-climax in the declaration of UDI. On television, once again in his most statesmanlike mien, Mr. Wilson gravely told the nation, "The world has taken a step backward today, by the action of small and frightened men." Amidst the black headlines of "Crisis" and "Tragedy," there was scant space for the news that, on the same day, at Hyde, Cheshire, two young people, Ian Brady and Myra Hindley, had been remanded on a charge of multiple murder.

Friday 12 November: in New York, Mr. Smith's regime was outlawed by the United Nations, while Mr. Wilson warned wildly of the danger that the Russians might move in under the guise of UN intervention—"the Red Army in blue berets." In the Strand, three hundred demonstrators outside Rhodesia House ended up fighting with the police.

Saturday 13 November: by now the clamor for war against Rhodesia had spread all over Africa; at the UN, African delegates demanded an invasion force; in Dar-es-Salaam, rioting students rampaged through the town, burning Union Jacks and wrecking British offices; mobs besieged British Embassies in Leopoldville and Addis Ababa. But in London, by the late evening, attention had been diverted by a new sensation. In a discussion on stage censorship on BBC-3, a watery relic of Ned Sherrin's "satire" shows, the Chairman, Robert Robinson (New Oxford Group), asked Kenneth Tynan whether he would allow "a play to be put on at the National Theatre in which, for instance, sexual intercourse took place on the stage?" Tynan replied, "Well, I think so certainly," and then continued:

> I doubt if there are any rational people to whom the word "f***" would be particularly diabolical, revolting or totally forbidden. I think that anything that can be printed or said can also be seen.

In a sense it was the high point of Tynan's career. Once again, as in the heyday of *That Was The Week*, the BBC switch-board was jammed with protests. Jonathan Miller and George Melly, it was reported, sent Tynan a telegram of congratulations. Later that night he compounded his inconsequentiality even further by claiming that he had only been "quoting from the evidence in the Lady Chatterley trial."

Monday 15 November: the temperature dropped sharply all over Britain, followed by a huge power failure that was an echo of New York's blackout six days before. Amid noisy scenes as the Rhodesia sanctions bill was hustled through both houses of Parliament, Lord Salisbury gave forth his most distracted imperialist *cri de coeur,* proclaiming that this was "the lowest point our country has ever reached."

Tuesday 16 November: in the House of Commons the last fragment of Harold Wilson's "New Britain" crumbled into reality, when Frank Cousins came to make his first major speech as Minister of Technology. To *The Times* his performance was "clumsy . . . blundering . . . embarrassing to watch." To other papers, "graceless," "maladroit," "a floundering embarrassment," and "a cause of suffering among Government supporters. Mr. Wilson sat chewing his tie in anguish." The only clear statement which emerged was that

the Government had the previous December "sacked" Dr. Beeching
—and even this, Mr. Cousins' Ministry hurriedly had to deny.

The collective fantasy of a time in which even the machinery of
civilization seemed to be collapsing in blackouts, motorway disasters,
and traffic jams, was again moving into a nightmare. Lost in the
murk, tiny human figures seemed to have been reduced to impotent
gestures of self-assertion, boasting of non-existent sackings or proclaiming obscenities into the electronic void. Or, like Harold Wilson
on 17 November, proudly informing the press of his great "Winter
Emergency Committee" which was then never to be heard of again
—an empty charade of "urgent," self-important, meaningless activity.
Even the Rhodesian "tragedy" was now drifting into farce—with Ian
Smith refusing to recognize the Governor and taking away his official motor car, and Britain retorting with the Queen's award of a
very special knighthood to "her" Governor, as if to say "so there!"
Meanwhile, in the unnatural glare of their dreamworld, the blank
faces of the New Aristocracy stared from the pages of the *Daily Express* as it serialized the last great tribute to their hypnotic sway,
David Bailey's *Box of Pin Ups*. And, as it was reported from Vietnam that American losses had suddenly shot up to a quite unprecedented level in "the bloodiest fighting of the war," in Britain, from
the world of pop music, there arose one more phantasm to sweep the
color supplements and the middle-class intellectuals.

It was a long time since a new pop group had risen from the ruck
with anything approaching the excitement that had greeted the
Beatles, the Rolling Stones, or the countless new groups of 1963 and
early 1964. But now, a last meteor flashed across the sky. Dressed in
weird, pop art clothes, often deliberately smashing their electric
guitars and carrying electronic distortion to the bounds of gibberish,
The Who (West London) talked and acted according to a philosophy that in the pop world was entirely new. Their music, as was
quoted by George Melly, now the *Observer*'s "Pop Correspondent,"
on 21 November, had "the auto-destructive bit." And indeed this was

the interesting thing about The Who's new record, now topping the hit parade. Several times the stuttering of *My Generation* expressed the hope that he would die before he got old; and, unlike almost any other pop song, the music did not fade away or stop at the end of a chorus, but tore itself to pieces in prolonged and agonizing cacophony.

For the first time in the ten years since rock 'n roll had arrived, the "death wish stage" was clear and explicit. The final and, in some respects, the most curious phase of the ten-year English revolution had begun.

In the last days of November a remarkable change came over the country's outward mood. The spate of happenings suddenly dwindled. Press interest in the "New Aristocracy" fell away, almost within a week or two, to a comparative trickle.

In comparison with what had gone before, English life seemed to be drifting through a feverish twilight. The December newspapers were dominated by crime, of every variety. From a courtroom in Cheshire came horrific headlines and column after column of bloody detail from the magistrates' hearings of charges against Ian Brady and Myra Hindley.* London experienced its worst wave of robberies in history, and on 15 December the *Sun* declared that "Britain's big cities are being taken over by . . . an engulfing wave of crime . . . indictable crime in recent weeks has risen by leaps and bounds." Preliminary figures released by the Home Office showed that, even before this latest surge, 1965 promised to be by far the worst year on record, car thefts alone having apparently risen by over 40 percent and robberies by 30 percent. At the same time vandalism had risen to a level which even earlier in the year would have seemed unbelievable—the craze for the destruction of public telephones in particular

---

* The so-called "Moors murders," for which they were responsible, were a series of child murders of a particularly gruesome nature, committed between 1963 and 1965. A pronounced feature of the case was the appallingly unreal fantasy life of the two young murderers, centered on books about Nazism and sadistic sexual perversions.

was now spreading so fast that by the end of 1965 more than half the country's 75,000 kiosks had been out of order once or more during the year.

In London, as Ministers openly contradicted each other about the Government's intentions over Rhodesia, the steady flow of new "measures" and "important" pronouncements from the Prime Minister's office—the radio station in Bechuanaland, the Commonwealth "emergency operation" to relieve Rhodesian drought—bore an increasing air of wild futility. And Mr. Wilson's own tired clutching at such clichés as *"seepage* and *leakage,"* "sanctions beginning to bite," "a matter of weeks rather than months," made up a pattern with which any psychiatrist is only too familiar.

During that winter a violent psychosis seemed to have seized almost every part of the world. After its year of raging escalation, the Vietnamese war was beginning to burn in the night like a beacon of approaching catastrophe. In Indonesia, the bloodbath of which the outside world was barely aware resulted in deaths which have been estimated at half a million. In China, November had seen the initial stages of the "cultural revolution" which, in the following eighteen months, was to kill perhaps tens of thousands more. As for the Rhodesian crisis itself, in retrospect we can see that it was only a small part of a fever which was sweeping throughout Africa, toppling many of the regimes which in the previous nine years had won independence from colonial rule.

One by one crashed the dreams of a whole age in African history. Already by the year's end there had been four such *coups d'état,* in each case a takeover of power by the army; and in the first few days of 1966 there were to be two more. New York was paralyzed for twelve days by a giant transport strike; the strike leader Michael Quill was arrested, and within three weeks was dead. In Tashkhent, the leaders of India and Pakistan met to settle their differences— and within hours, Prime Minister Shastri was dead. In Lagos there took place the chaotic travesty of a Commonwealth Prime Ministers' Conference to discuss Rhodesia—and within days of its end, its chief sponsor, the Prime Minister of Nigeria, had been violently put to death, along with other members of his Government and two regional Prime Ministers in yet a seventh African *coup d'état*. Only a month later, the African fever came to its head in the overthrow of the figure who had been central to that continent's mounting hysteria—the archetype of all African revolutionary leaders, Kwame Nkrumah.

If the atmosphere in Britain at this time was by no means as actively nightmarish as in other parts of the world, it was certainly eerie enough. Throughout January and February, a succession of events floated into the headlines of Alice in Wonderland absurdity—such as the caviar and champagne breakfast given by the television "satirist" David Frost at the Connaught Hotel on 7 January.

The episode, known as the "Frost Breakfast," revealed as clearly as any other single event the extent to which, in ten years, television had disoriented the sense of reality in English public life. The list of those who accepted Frost's invitation read almost like a cast list of the New Establishment, headed by Mr. Wilson himself. Among those also present were Lord Longford, Leader of the House of Lords, and two other well-known Labour peers; Mr. Cecil King, Chairman of the International Publishing Corporation, and two other Fleet Street editors, including the editor-proprietor of the *Observer;* the Bishop of Woolwich; the Chairman of E.M.I., a major industrial corporation, including among its interests the Beatles' recording output; the Head of the BBC Television service, and various other leading figures in television; Mr. Len Deighton, the spy novelist; and Professor A. J. Ayer, one of Britain's leading linguistic philosophers and a noted proponent of "permissive" morality. In fact, as was later confirmed by the Prime Minister's Press Office, the only celebrity who had apparently found himself able to refuse Frost's invitation was Paul McCartney of the Beatles.

To appreciate Frost's achievement in gathering together this assemblage of notables, one has only to reflect how, until but a year or two before, the Prime Minister of the day and a similar cross-section of public figures would have dismissed such an invitation from Frost's equivalent—say, a columnist on a popular Sunday newspaper—as an impertinent stunt. What gave Frost the knowledge that his gamble would come off, was his intuitive sense of television's power to re-create the world on its own unreal terms—to reduce everything and everyone, politicians and pop singers, philosophers and journalists, bishops and entertainers, to the same level, as bit players in a universal dream world.

At this time, however, the Frost breakfast was only one symptom of the much wider unreality hanging over English life. It was during this winter that in Chelsea, as in America, the growing ten-year-long drugs craze was entering its prolonged climactic phase, as the pop-Bohemian demimonde was swept by the vogue for what was described as the "fantasy drug," LSD—giving rise to a rash of sensational press reports, with the most horrific nyktomorphic overtones, such as "The Man Who Says Britain Could Be Taken Over by a Brainwash Powder." Even these oddities paled beside the inexplicable announcement in February by the Chief Constable of Durham that he had appealed for the help of the British Army in guarding Durham prison, which held three of the train robbers; "I am satisfied," he said:

> that Goody's friends would be prepared to launch a full-scale military attack, even to the extent of using tanks, bombs, and what the Army calls "limited" atomic weapons.

It was hardly coincidental that, on television and in the cinema, the unrealities of the spy craze had reached their apogee. With such series as *The Spies, The Ratcatchers, The Avengers,* and *The Man from U.N.C.L.E.,* there was a spy or "special agent" thriller on television almost every night, almost invariably concerned with the battle of their heroes, mysteriously representing "our side," against huge, evil, and even more mysterious conspiracies threatening either to destroy or to take over the world. In the cinema, the spy craze was on the whole less nightmarish though equally fantastical, the James Bond films in particular having led to a series of highly colored fantasies so overladen with gadgetry and wish-fulfilment promiscuity that not even their makers could pretend to take them seriously. The latest Bond film, *Thunderball,* a third of which had been shot below the surface of the sea, was the most dream-like of the series; but in this it was only in line with the prevailing mode for that inconsequential and often violent color supplement surrealism which, in such films as *Viva Maria, What's New Pussycat?,* and *Modesty Blaise,* now appeared completely to have taken over the cinema.

After the general euphoria of novelty which had been at fever pitch in English life at least since the beginning of the sixties, and in many senses for five years before that, there was in fact in the early months of 1966 a widespread and acute sense of malaise.

In January, just five months after he had collapsed on stage in a performance of *A Patriot for Me,* George Devine, the undisputed "father figure" of the English theatrical revolution, died at the age of 55. Only a few days later came the failure of Lionel Bart's *Twang!!,* the first real setback in the ten-year career of Devine's female counterpart, Joan Littlewood, who shortly afterwards announced that she was leaving the London stage for Tunisia.

It was also becoming apparent to what extent the nyktomorphic glamor of the "New Aristocracy" had already faded. The "pop dream" that had so dominated the country for two years or more was visibly subsiding. Record sales were down 25 percent, and in some places 50 percent, from a year before. On 28 February, just three months after he had been blazoned across the papers in his "Pin Up" crucifixion pose, P. J. Proby announced that he was being forced to leave the country with £25,000 worth of debts, and was quoted as saying "Britain has fried me." On the same day up in Liverpool, the Cavern Club went into liquidation with debts of over £10,000, and the Liverpool "beat scene" was reported to be "dying on its feet." No less than three out of the four nightclubs which only ten months before John Crosby had been hailing as the center of London's "throbbing nightlife" had now shut their doors, including "the world's most famous discothèque" itself, the *Ad Lib*. One of the two dress designers Crosby had nominated as among the people who most "make London swing" had gone bankrupt—as had the original pirate radio company, Radio Atlanta. And slowly it was becoming clear to what extent even the dukes and princes of the "New Class," the very people who so recently had been considered "the most exciting" in London, had been sadly inflated. In a series of profiles by Maureen Cleave in the *Evening Standard* in March, the Beatles themselves began to emerge, for the first time since the great ballyhoo had started, as rather ordinary young men, bewildered by their success, even infinitely sad. A chapter in England's social history was beginning to draw to its close.

It was in March that the event took place which was to bring home the frightening condition into which English life had been plunged. There had never been such a General Election as that of 1966. Its tenor was set by the BBC's decision to postpone the showing of a children's puppet show, *Pinky and Perky* (two singing pigs), because its content was said to be "political." Once again, as in 1964, a major feature was the continual heckling of leading politicians by groups of teenagers. In East London, George Brown's car was deluged with stink bombs to cries of "Anarchy, anarchy." At Slough, the Prime Minister was hit in the eye by a stink bomb thrown by a fourteen-year-old boy. Mr. Heath's wooden manner and flat, awkward voice, as he recited the facts of Britain's black economic situation—that in the past year wages had risen by 9 percent, prices by 5 percent, and production by only 1 percent—seemed a million miles away.

The contrast between Mr. Wilson's campaign and the one he had fought in 1964 could not have been more striking. On all the broad lines of policy—defense, the economy, foreign affairs—he was defending the position he had formerly so bitterly attacked. The H-

Bomb, the pound, Britain's commitments "East of Suez" were as much the pillars of the "prestige" of Mr. Wilson's "New Britain" as they had been those of the Conservative Britain of yore. Long gone were the days when the Prime Minister imagined himself to be a second Kennedy, or even a second Johnson; indeed in recent months, with his visit to Moscow and his "dramatic" personal settlement of a threatened rail strike, he had been explicitly replaying the role of Harold Macmillan.

Only once, when on television the Prime Minister suddenly reeled off one of his automatic references to "seventeen urgent months" in which the Government had been transformed into a "forcing house of change," was there any whiff of the "great crusade" or the "white heat of the technological revolution." Otherwise, clearly in a state of considerable exhaustion, Mr. Wilson coasted through the campaign, playing the "national leader" above controversy.

Ironically, the newspapers which most forcefully articulated the unreality of the campaign—apart from *The Times* which commented that it "drags its slow length through a morass of mediocrity"—were two of those which, in their different ways, had played more than their part in bringing the atmosphere of British public life to such a pass. The *Daily Mirror,* as so often before, tried to bludgeon its way into reality with towering headlines and violent prose that only helped to drag what it described as "the whole charade" further down into the morass. The *Observer,* trying to "pin down this airless, make-believe election" went on to demonstrate at least one good reason why it was so "make-believe" with a perfect illustration of its own brand of fantasy, full of such capsule descriptions as (of Iain Macleod):

> One of the best TV anchormen in the business, both solid and wily. "He can smile on cue," a professional said admiringly.

On 31 March, after betting on the campaign became more feverish than ever (totaling a figure of over £2,500,000), polling day arrived. On a reduced poll, Harold Wilson won his majority of 97 seats. The triumph begun in 1964 was complete. There were even small but unmistakable signs that, throughout the country, the Labour Party had made inroads into that middle ground which for ten years had provided the main focus of contention in British politics—and which above all had nourished the Liberal revival. To the Liberals indeed, despite their gain of two seats, the election of 1966, in which their vote dropped for the first time in eleven years, was an irrevocable blow.

The real significance of the result, however, lay in the fact that it testified to the desire of the British people to think nothing about politics for another five years. After all the *Sturm und Drang,* after ten years of almost unbroken crisis and excitement, after all the talk about "What's Wrong With Britain" and the clamor for "drastic change" and dynamic government, the great revolution had come and gone. Under a Prime Minister whose appeal to the nation had been couched in almost exclusively Conservative terms, the Labour Government had been returned to power on a Conservative landslide.*

One of the more remarkable things about the fever which had swept through English life since 1955 had been the suddenness with which

---

* Mr. Wilson himself implicitly recognized the extraordinary metamorphosis from the "radical" posture he had adopted in 1964, and even from the excitable talk of "cliff-hanging" only six months before, as he indicated in a conversation reported shortly afterwards by the Prime Minister of Eire, Sean Lemass. Speaking to a public relations dinner in Dublin, Mr. Lemass recalled that the British Prime Minister had told him "a political leader should try to look, particularly on television, like a family doctor—the kind of man who inspires trust by his appearance as well as by his soothing words." Apart from the striking contrast between this and Mr. Wilson's deliberately rousing aggression in 1964, it provides an insight into the extent to which, perhaps more than any other British politician, he was hypnotized by television and the need to create the right "image." It is perhaps no accident that the impact of television on politics and politicians should have become so particularly noticeable both in Britain and in America at about the same time. President Johnson, after all, was said to have installed television sets in various strategic points in the White House so that he could keep a constant check on his own reflected image. And it was noticeable that, in 1967–1968, when the initial glamor of both leaders had worn off, they should both have been the target of exactly the same criticism summarized in the phrase "credibility gap."

it had arisen. The appetite for new excitement had shown itself simultaneously in fields ranging from politics to pop music, from crime to the arts, all in just a few months. Equally remarkable now was the suddenness with which the peak of that fever was dying away.

Already by the beginning of April several bubbles of fantasy had considerably subsided. In the weeks after the election, the process continued: whether in an event as important as the Government's decision on 27 April to resume negotiations with the Rhodesian rebels, or as apparently insignificant as the pricking of the glamor surrounding the train robbers by the surrender in pathetic circumstances of James White. Even the wave of vandalism was falling off; and at Easter (as at Whitsun) there were no teenage disorders for the first time in three years.

One revealing indication of the extent to which the country's mood had changed was provided by the wave of concern which greeted the "Moors Murders" trial at the end of April—in such striking contrast to the sensationalism engendered by the magistrates' hearings back in December. For the child murders by Ian Brady and Myra Hindley had shaken the nation as had no crime since the war. With its mixture of Brady's background as an illegitimate orphan in the slums of Glasgow, and the fantasy world of sadism and Nazism he had been able to seize on through the offices of Manchester's thriving pornographic book shops, for many people the case threw into sharp relief the darker side of the dream into which Britain had been moving.*

In fact, in the still bewildering atmosphere of that late spring and

---

* One of the most interesting expressions of the introspection brought on by the Moors murder trial was a long passage in a book *Bomb Culture* (1968), by Jeff Nuttall, a young writer who had been centrally involved in many of the more influential manifestations of what he called "rebel culture" since 1956, from the CND to the Underground. Obviously the Moors murders brought him to something of a reflective crisis, as there were so many links with the various romanticisms of "rebel culture." "It's possible to get hysterical over the obvious connection between that culture, as it stood in 1965, and the Moors Murders. I did." He was not alone, although I don't think anyone expressed so vividly as he did what some of those connections might be.

early summer, Britain was not only moving toward quieter times, in the purely negative sense that old fevers were exhausted; but for the first time there were signs that a desire for calm and stability was becoming positive and explicit. In some instances, such longings were almost desperate—as was shown, for example, by the issue of the *Spectator* of 13 May, which devoted more than a tenth of its editorial space to a lecture by Lord Radcliffe entitled "The Dissolving Society," and which took for its theme "the shallow and almost perverted idea of progress that constitutes the English sickness of the day." The note of anxiety was sounded even more clearly in a supporting editorial by the *Spectator*'s new young editor, Nigel Lawson:

> The time has come to call a halt to the restless belief that change itself is the only ultimate good, and to seek instead a period of social and intellectual stability during which we can once again put down roots and gather strength. But where are we to find the soil?

Like a switchback ride that decreases in the scale of its rises and falls as it nears its end, there were clear indications in the early summer of 1966 that, in reaction to the nightmare of the winter, the country was emerging into a last miniature "dream stage."

A month after the election, a lull had fallen over the political scene. The Rhodesian crisis had been shelved. The Gallup Poll showed a Labour lead almost as high as in the summer of Profumo. The proportion of the electorate which considered Mr. Wilson to be doing a good job was the highest a Prime Minister had ever recorded. And of all the constitutents of this newfound euphoria, perhaps none was so important as the fact that, at long last, the country's economic troubles appeared to be receding. Exports in the first few months of the year had risen to 9 percent above those for the same period of 1965. The pound was strengthening. The number of people unemployed stood lower than at any time since records were first kept. But it was all, of course, a last illusion. For ten years and more, the country had been caught up in a spiral of ever-rising financial expectation, largely regardless of the consequences. Few ingredients in the history of those years had contributed more to the subtle accretion of unreality. And now the edifice had become vulnerable to the slightest puff of wind.

On 16 May, the national seamen's strike began. One by one, the ports of Britain silted up with abandoned vessels. Exports dropped sharply. The eyes of those bankers across the world, who for the past eighteen months had kept the country financially afloat, were transfixed by the ultimate test of what Harold Wilson himself, in one of his less obviously bromidic phrases, had forecast would be "make or break year for Britain." But the seamen's leaders, like so many other union leaders over the years, were lost in a "dream stage" of their own, brushing away every attempt at negotiation.

It was by no means only the strike, however, that was promoting the languorous atmosphere of this strange interlude. On 2 May, the temperature had risen into the eighties; and over the next weeks, the heat-wave continued. There was an odd spirit at large in Britain —a sense of hedonistic detachment, not just from the strike or the state of the economy, but from anything disturbing at all.

This spirit was most clearly revealed in the phenomenon that had begun with a twelve-page cover story on "London—The Swinging City" in the 13 April edition of *Time*. Over the next two months, the *Time* article was followed in other American magazines by a spate of others in similar vein, ranging from *Esquire*'s intoxicated hymn to "the only truly modern city" to *Life*'s "Spread of the Swinging Revolution: Even the Peers Go Mod." These articles were in most respects much the same as those which had appeared in various journals a year previously, but in two things they were different. The first was that the evanescent landscape they so feverishly described had been dwindling into reality for almost six months. The second lay in the extraordinary welcome they received from the British themselves.

The "Swinging London" phenomenon arrived in those sultry summer days, in fact, like an almost conscious epitaph on that era whose sun was nearly set. For a few weeks, as they reveled, half-mocking, half-flattered, in this strange orange afterglow that was being reflected back from across the Atlantic, the British went on a last, unexpected, narcissistic spree. By nothing else was the mood of the time so aptly caught as by that other exhibitionistic *frisson* that had been brought out in full strength by the summer days, the suddenly ubiquitous mini-skirt—which had turned into the biggest fashion sensation since the New Look.

There were now few matters so weighty that they could not be reduced by the headline writers to the level of a "Mini-Budget" or a "Mini-Pound" or even a "Mini-Deterrent." Off Piccadilly, the latest, most expensively electronic discothèque, *Sibylla's,* sponsored by a partnership which included a Beatle and a 27-year-old Etonian baronet, and named after an upper-class debutante, was nightly packed. In June alone, in a final burst, three more pirate radio stations opened, bringing the total round Britain's shores to eleven. Meanwhile, in the streets of South London, Antonioni, one of the "directors of the sixties," was making a film about a London fashion photographer; down at Elstree, François Truffaut was filming with Julie Christie, just named Hollywood's "Actress of the Year"; Charlie Chaplin had chosen this moment to return, after fifty years, to make another film-set of his own native Old Kent Road; in Park Lane, Mr. Hugh Hefner was opening his first European Playboy Club; while bemused tourists, clicking and whirring their way down Carnaby and the King's Road, could now be numbered in tens of thousands. London had been briefly gilded by its sunset into a legendary Golden City, the focus of the dreams of romantics from every corner of the world.

On 8 June, however, one American who actually lived in London, Mr. Anthony Lewis of the *New York Times,* reported to his paper that the British, "selfish" and obsessed with trivia, were headed down the road to "economic perdition":

> The atmosphere in London can be almost eerie in its quality of relentless frivolity. There can rarely have been a greater contrast between a country's objective situation and the mood of its people.

So soon after the eulogies of his countrymen, Mr. Lewis's remarks, which attracted front-page attention in the English press, came as something of a shock. Even before that, in the *Spectator,* Alan Watkins had descried a curious mood in Parliament—a spirit of "unrest" and "disillusion" spreading through the Labour back benches, directed at the Prime Minister, and ranging over a spectrum of issues, from his handling of the seamen's strike to Vietnam. And then, on 11 June, as the strike neared the end of its fourth week with not a sign of settlement, a Labour MP, Desmond Donnelly, in a speech at Eastbourne, struck the sharpest note of foreboding so far:

> Britain is facing a major crisis of leadership. This once great country is adrift. There is a nasty whiff in the air of national decadence . . . unless we take hold of ourselves, a situation very dangerous to democracy could develop.

In the June heat, the lightning was beginning to flicker. From Hull and Liverpool and the dockland of the East End came the first angry murmurs of rising militancy among the seamen. Two days after Mr. Donnelly's speech, it was announced that, despite all the optimism of less than a month before, Britain had been forced to call on the banks of eleven countries for yet another vast support operation to bolster the pound. A last storm was approaching.

The most striking thing about the events of the following two months was the way in which, as they unfolded, they led not only to the most violent financial crisis experienced by Britain since the war, but also to a kind of grand judgment on the whole of the recent style of English life—and in particular on the political style that had been introduced and established by the Wilson Government since 1964.

The first real sign that the storm was beginning to break was the Prime Minister's taunt that the seamen's strike was only being kept going by a "tightly knit group of politically motivated men." It was a typical Wilson gesture—that combination of the melodramatic phrase and the hint at an alien conspiracy which had so often characterized his reaction to trouble in times past—and it brought tempers exploding into the open. Almost immediately the storm began to break out in other fields—as the nation's attention was diverted by the strange events surrounding the seizure of a pirate radio station in the Thames Estuary and the midnight shooting of its proprietor Reg Calvert (who had bought the station off Screaming Lord Sutch "just for a giggle"), leading to a renewal of the clamor, more fervent than ever, that the pirates should be closed down. Attacks on the country's "decadence" and the "English sickness" had now become the regular small change of leader writers and weekend speechmakers. And then, as the seamen's strike collapsed in a welter of frustrated recrimination, there came the news that, after a comparative lull in the Vietnam war and renewed talk of peace, the Americans had bombed the outskirts of Hanoi and Haiphong—and that for the first time Mr. Wilson had dissociated Britain from an escalation in the war.

Throughout July, the air was filled with drama. As the news was dominated by such headlines as the *Daily Mail*'s "Day Three of the Vietnam Escalation—And World Anxiety Mounts," there took place in Grosvenor Square the most violent CND demonstration since 1963, in which several policemen were injured by a jeering mob four thousand strong. The headlines were full of riots and violence: riots in Amsterdam, race riots in many American cities, a mass-killing of nurses in Chicago, another mass-killing on a university campus in Texas, sectarian violence nearer home in Ulster, and, in the Philippines, the first really hostile mob encountered by the Beatles.

For Britain, despite the continuing emergency of Vietnam, everything was overshadowed by the crisis over the pound—which had been intensified by Frank Cousins' resignation from the Cabinet. On 14 July, the Government resorted yet again to the traditional crisis weapon, the once so awesome 7 percent Bank Rate. At last, however, the price had to be paid for all those eleven years and more of recurrent sterling crises—and for what was rapidly emerging as an international crisis of confidence in the Government. On the following day, the run on sterling continued, even more heavy than before. And for Harold Wilson and his Ministers, the last act of the crisis, two weeks of nightmare, had begun.

Over the last fortnight of July, every possible thing that could have gone wrong for the Government did so—from their loss of a by-election to the first Welsh Nationalists ever to sit in Parliament to the behavior of the Foreign Secretary Mr. George Brown who, whether with abortive threats of resignation or an embarrassingly incoherent speech in the House of Commons, blundered day after day through the headlines. So evident was the strain Ministers were going through that the press referred to them as the "tired-at-the-top Cabinet." But the man who was really caught was the Prime Minister himself.

For Harold Wilson, these two weeks were the first serious foretaste of that collapse of all the dreams which his recent career had embodied. For nearly two years, he had managed to juggle his way between every Scylla and Charybdis in his path, silencing criticism in Parliament by dazzling diplomatic forays abroad, smoothing over criticism in the country by purposive appearances on television and banking up further goodwill through public intimacy with the heroes of popular entertainment. Now faced with his worst crisis at home, he was committed to traipsing off on futile public relations missions to Moscow and Washington. His television manner had become sufficiently familiar to a large part of the populace to seem almost a parody. Even when he fulfilled a longstanding engagement to assist in reopening the Cavern Club in Liverpool, it transpired that he was unwittingly lending the publicity of his presence not just to the innocent teenagers of Liverpool, but to the Club's new sponsors, Radio Caroline, when the Postmaster General, as the result of the Radio City scandals, was at last on the eve of publishing his Bill for the pirates' suppression. When in Washington he was compared by a sympathetic President Johnson to Winston Churchill, the unintended irony of this Texan compliment aroused at home a burst of incredulous derision.

The net result of it all, however, apart from the most crushing credit squeeze since the war, was a freezing of wages and prices for six months, if necessary enforceable by law. After twenty-two months, it was the first major decisive action that the Wilson administration had taken. In doing so, it brought a temporary end to the financial crisis which had been virtually unbroken since the day Labour entered office. It was the beginning of an attack of reality after all those years of inflation which had been the corollary to the greatest boom the British people had ever known. And when the full details of the Government's intentions were published on 29 July, it was hardly surprising that at least one newspaper should have referred back to 20 July, when the "freeze" had officially begun, as "The Day It All Stopped."

The following afternoon, England won the World Cup. But as Londoners danced in the streets (the Prime Minister once again sneaking rather desperately into the limelight, as he posed on the balcony with the winning team), there was also, perhaps, mixed with the excitement, a feeling of something more. For if a poll taken some weeks before by the *Sunday Times* was to be believed, a large majority of the population now held the view that far too much attention was being paid to "mini-dresses, pop music, and bingo," that it was long since time that inflation and financial crises were brought under control, and that a wage freeze was, in fact, positively desirable. Outwardly at least, the spree seemed over.

It was now three years since the summer of 1963, when the collective fantasy had been at its highest pitch of excitement: the time when, as Harold Wilson, the Beatles, and the satirists swept all before them, the Macmillan Government and the forces of order and authority

315

had been in greatest disarray. By August 1966, events could not have conspired more ingeniously to demonstrate what a change had come about. On the one hand, his head still buzzing with bemused suspicions of plots against his leadership, described even by the *Observer* as "The Lost Leader" whose "reputation as a politician magician" had finally "vanished," Harold Wilson once again reshuffled his Cabinet and longed for the respite of the summer recess. The once so "lovable" and "innocent" Beatles were now involved in the second major row in a month, this time in the stream of abuse and hostility which greeted the international publication of the remarks made back in March by John Lennon about Christianity. From New York it was reported that, already half-forgotten, the one-time hero of the satirists, Lenny Bruce, had killed himself with an overdose of drugs, at the age of thirty-nine.

On 12 August came the murder of three policemen in Shepherd's Bush. The public reaction to this tragedy completed the process that had been begun four months earlier by the Moors Murder trial. It was barely two weeks since, on the night of England's World Cup victory, as a result of months of patient planning, the London police had been able to arrest eleven members of the notorious Richardson gang, one of the three gangs (the others being the gang responsible for the Great Train Robbery and the Krays) which during the sixties had come to dominate the London underworld. This constituted perhaps the most significant single victory the police had enjoyed in their war with the criminals in a decade. Now, in the wake of the West London shootings, they received a great wave of public sympathy and support.

It was a revealing episode. As the country sank back, after its two months of nervous delirium, into late summer coma, it proved also to be something of a final curtain. By the end of August, sniffing the new spirit of the time, Mr. Maurice Wiggin could survey the range of recent events to ask almost tremulously in the *Sunday Times* whether it was possible that at long last "The Age of Pop" was "Swinging to a Stop";

Correct me by all means if I'm wrong, but I think I see signs and portents. Unless I am mistaken . . . Britain is entering on a period of
decisive change. The style of living and thinking is about to alter . . .
The period which [I think] is now coming to an end began some time
in the '50's. John Osborne was one of its standard bearers. "You've
never had it so good" was its rallying cry, and "permissive" was a word
dear to both art and politics . . . Now the revolt seems to have spent
its force.

Of course no period of history can ever be said to have ended
overnight: particularly when it is one that turned a society and its
values upside-down, as Britain's had been by her ten-year revolution.
Nevertheless, the last four months of the year were quieter than any
comparable period since the early fifties. Between mid-August and
December, there were only two events which intruded on the sopo-
rific calm over English life. The first was the disaster at Aberfan in
October which, like the police murders, called forth another wave
of communal sympathy. The second, in November, was the nine-day
wonder of Harold Wilson's talks with Ian Smith on board the
cruiser *Tiger*. But even this reminder that, in the background, the
Rhodesian rebellion was still drifting on, by the very manner in
which it flared up into the headlines and was then almost as abruptly
forgotten, served only as further evidence of the coma into which
English life had fallen.

Despite the fact that the unemployment figures were rising rapidly,
the Government's lead on the opinion polls (in such striking contrast, for instance, to the standing of the Conservative Government
in the wake of the financial crisis of 1961) stood higher at the end
of the year than in August. Thanks to the almost complete inertia
of public opinion, the Prime Minister's own position had at least temporarily recovered. Meanwhile, virtually unquestioned, the effects of
the Freeze swept through Britain, clearing away some of the froth
that had accumulated during the years of runaway affluence. The
industries hardest hit by the 1966 measures were not just the nineteenth-century industries such as cotton and shipbuilding which had

317

been the most conspicuous victims of previous recessions, but those which had typified the booming Britain of the previous ten years: the motor car industry, the manufacturers of television sets and household goods (whose sales were to drop by up to 50 percent), and the property companies. Bankruptcies soared, public relations firms closed down, and newspapers and magazines, which for ten years had waxed ever fatter, lost up to a third of their advertising.

As for swinging London, the discothèques which had been so crowded now stood virtually empty. Dozens of casinos shut their doors, also hit by the new gambling tax, and for the first time since the Gaming Act of 1960 had come into force, the number of betting shops in Britain showed no increase. As the first of the pirate radio stations were closed down by Government action and reports appeared in the press that the Beatles might never again sing as a group in public, the sales of pop records reached their lowest level since 1955. And if further proof were needed that the collective fantasy, as it had grown up and engulfed British life since the middle fifties, was subsiding, it came in the news that, in the latter half of the year, the crime rate had registered its first small but distinct fall for over ten years.

The collective fantasy still had a long way to go in any fade toward reality. Nevertheless, in the twelve months since the previous winter, a very considerable transformation had come over the country's mood. And there is no doubt that, whatever was to happen in the future, in the course of the particular collective dream that had sprung up in English life in 1955, the year 1966 had at last marked a turning point.

Chapter Eleven

Fading into Reality

The irregular combinations of fanciful invention may
delight awhile, by that novelty of which the common
satiety sends us all in quest: but the pleasures of sudden
wonder are soon exhausted, and the mind can only repose
on the stability of truth.

DR. JOHNSON, *Preface to Shakespeare*

"Nobody any longer takes Mr. Wilson seriously." This is
what the Tories say, and the public opinion polls and by-
election results more than bear them out. Seldom, if ever,
has a British Government been more unpopular or dis-
credited.

Sunday Telegraph, 14 April 1968

Last week it emerged that the Beatle phenomenon was
ending. There was no formal announcement, no fuss, nor
for that matter any great astonishment . . . Beatlemania is
at an end.

Sunday Times, 13 November 1966

The revolution is over. Behind the ramparts of jackets
more garish than any of those Sir Allen Lane took
exception to there is an air of fatigue and uncertainty,
mixed perhaps with a vague sense of relief. In some places
it's described hopefully as the beginning of "a period of
consolidation."

From an article "After the Revolution,"
on paperback publishing,
Guardian, 12 May 1967

The Freakout is over . . .

JEFF NUTTALL
Bomb Culture (1968)

Our revels now are ended. These our actors,
As I foretold you, were all spirits, and
Are melted into air, into thin air;
And, like the baseless fabric of this vision,
The cloud-capped towers, the gorgeous palaces,
The solemn temples, the great globe itself,
Yea, all which it inherit, shall dissolve,
And like this insubstantial pageant faded,
Leave not a rack behind. We are such stuff
As dreams are made on; and our little life
Is rounded with a sleep.

The Tempest, IV, i

Despite the significance of the events of 1966, it is important not to overestimate the extent to which an era had suddenly "come to an end" in Britain in that year. Such an arbitrary division of history belongs only in school textbooks.

Indeed, in many ways, the changes which had taken place in British society in the early sixties seemed to be continuing after 1966 as fast as ever, not in any cycle, with a rise and fall, but on an ever-rising graph. In the most superficial respect, the continuation of teenage crazes such as those for drugs and the "flower power" vogue of 1967, the heyday of the mini-skirt, the proliferation of erotic books, films, and plays, the legalization of abortion and homosexuality, and the abolition of stage censorship in 1968 (causes for which the progressives had been campaigning for ten years or more), all gave at least the outward impression between 1966 and the end of the decade that Britain's social "revolution" was proceeding as merrily as ever.

Other changes continued in full spate on every side—the tearing down of old buildings in London and elsewhere to make way for new "developments" or motorways, the changing face of the countryside under the impact of new methods of farming (such as the extensive removal of the hedgerows, which for three centuries had given the English countryside its traditional patchwork appearance), the introduction of a whole sequence of reforms affecting the familiar machinery of life, such as the decisions to adopt decimal coinage and the metric system, replacing methods used by the British for upwards of a thousand years. All these changes continued to give a constant sense of restlessness and instability to English life in the years after 1966.

Similarly, despite its temporary lull in 1966-1967, the rise in the crime rate and other signs of social disturbance, such as the wave

321

of violent hooliganism attending football matches, continued in these years almost as actively as before.*

Yet there is no doubt that there was an underlying change of mood in the years after 1966. If the average Englishman had been asked in the late 1960's whether he thought that life in Britain was pleasanter or easier than it had been ten years before, the odds are that he would have agreed without much hesitation. If on the other hand he had been asked whether he was equally satisfied with the broad way in which the country had developed over these years, and with the more general prospects for mankind as a whole, the chances are that his answer would have been hedged about with qualifications.

The answer to the first question would have been a reflection of the material advances which had been made in these years, and also of the sense that English society had become outwardly more relaxed in its convictions and attitudes. Undoubtedly Britain had become a pleasanter place to live in many ways, as was most emphatically remarked upon by foreign visitors, particularly those escaping from the tensions and hazards of life in America.

The hesitation attached to the second answer would have reflected more complicated and possibly more profound considerations—and would, of course, have depended largely on the class, age, and general point of view of the person who was giving it. The lessened stature of politicians, a diminution in the general sense of community and responsibility, a feeling that life had become generally more unreal and fraught with neurosis, a widespread unease at the new power and influence of technology, a sense that too much importance was being attached to the trivial and superficial, a sense of the undoubted moral confusion that was following from the relaxation of

---

* One major victory in the war against crime, however, was the success of the police in at last securing conviction of the Kray brothers on a murder charge in 1969. The full story of how they had become increasingly reckless in the years after 1963, egged on by their growing publicity to the eventual commission of murder almost for "kicks," formed a fascinating and horrifying footnote to the story of London in the sixties.

322

conventional standards—all these things might have been mentioned in connection with such an answer. And so might a more general concern aroused by the terrible events taking place elsewhere in the world, so familiar in their more sensational aspects from the television screen. Many of them seemed, in some obscure way, not only to have grown rather too naturally out of the overall character of the sixties, with its hysterical and violent obsessions, but also to be omens of the way civilization in general might be developing.

The shift in the national mood after 1966 could most easily be measured by recollecting the particular intensity and eagerness with which so many people in the earlier sixties had looked on the emergence of Harold Wilson and the Beatles as in some way heralding the arrival of a new, totally different Britain. Compared with those heady days of 1963–1964, and even those of "Swinging London" in 1965, there was by the late sixties a widespread sense of aftermath, of exhaustion, even of a considerable reaction to the years when all change and novelty of any kind had been hailed without question, save by an embittered and diminishing minority. After the tremendous shock of novelty which had burst on the country after 1955, there was for the first time a sense that the outlines of change were broadly familiar; that nothing that could happen would any longer seem wholly new or shocking; and that even the exhilarations of "permissiveness" were subject to the law of diminishing returns. The generally progressive values established in these earlier years were still the outwardly prevailing orthodoxy of the time; but in every field after 1966, from education to morals, from the faith hitherto placed in the miraculous advance of technology to the progress of the arts, there was a growing undercurrent of questioning. People were at last beginning to raise their heads gingerly to inquire and discuss just what sort of a world it was that had been brought about. And there was a vague but general sense that, beneath the surface, the country was moving through a phase of transition toward new attitudes and new preoccupations.

In no context was this spirit of "hangover" in the late sixties more spectacularly reflected than in the collapse of the public standing of Mr. Wilson and his Government. Between 1967 and 1969, as every major project the Government embarked on turned to dust—the saving of the pound from devaluation, the reform of the House of Lords, the reform of the unions, and the establishment of a secure incomes policy—the Government's reputation both at home and abroad sank as low as that of any administration in memory. Yet despite the Labour Party's unprecedented loss of ten out of the thirteen seats which it defended at by-elections in the first two years of the 1966 Parliament, such was the state of doldrums into which British politics had fallen that there was still no sign of positive enthusiasm behind Mr. Heath's rudderless Conservative Party. The only flurries to ruffle the political calm other than those consequent on the Government's own mistakes, were those surrounding the temporary resurgence of Welsh and Scottish nationalism, and the bid by Enoch Powell in 1968–1969 to make an emotional political issue out of Britain's large, new colored minority. The Liberals, particularly after the departure of Mr. Grimond in January 1967, seemed virtually to have vanished as a political force. And even the devaluation of the pound, the issue which more than any other had dominated the emotional course of the Labour Government since 1964, when it eventually came in November 1967, failed to provoke any political hysteria comparable to the national turbulence which had accompanied the decline of the Conservative administration in 1962–1963.

In those days, the collapse of the Macmillan Government had been one of the focal points of an upheaval convulsing every level of English society. The upper-class father image of Mr. Macmillan had acted as a catalyst for all the aggression that was to unleash the New England of Mr. Wilson and the Beatles. Now, however, in the nervous exhaustion of 1968–1969, there was no great revolution afoot, no New England beckoning as an alternative. Mr. Wilson had become not so much an object of hatred as a shadow, a figure for the time being at least no longer to be taken very seriously. The weary cynicism which greeted his almost every move was no hysterical tide—but merely the sand greeting a wave which had spent its force.

This same sense of a wave having spent its force hung over many aspects of the erstwhile New England of the mid-sixties. Through 1967–1969, the headlines chronicled the continuing fade of the erstwhile pop dream into unhappy reality—the drug scandals of 1967, involving the arrest of many major figures, the slow disintegration of the Beatles, the deaths of Brian Epstein (perhaps the central single figure behind the pop boom of 1963–1964) and Brian Jones of the Rolling Stones, the near-fatal drug overdose of Mick Jagger's girl friend Marianne Faithfull in Australia in 1969. In 1966 and 1967, the strongly drug-influenced "psychedelic" and "underground" movements (as in America) marked a final spiral into even greater unreality for many of those associated with the pop world, but even these were looked on by the rest of the nation with increasing boredom and detachment, until by 1969 they too had entered a phase of exhaustion.

In television, despite the debate which spread from America over its part in creating and heightening the climate of violence in the sixties, the sensational high-water marks of 1965 seemed by 1969 an age away, particularly under the newly conservative regime of Lord Hill at the BBC, whose succession as Chairman in 1967 had heralded the departure of Sir Hugh Greene. The atmosphere of apparently limitless novelty, in which television had in the late fifties and early sixties established itself as a dominant social and political force, had dwindled by the end of the decade into a kind of general resigned acceptance of its predominant triviality. The redoubled disillusionment following the extravagant promises of a new era of "quality" in television made by two new commercial companies, when ITV licenses came up for renewal in 1968, seemed only to underline for the last time the inevitable hollowness of all such promises, made so often and with similar outcome in the past.

As for that most notable of all symbols of the English social revolution, the image of "Swinging London," by 1969 it was already being recalled almost as a historical event, which might have taken place ten or fifteen years before, rather than just three or four. And nothing was a more effective memorial to its passing than the King's Road, Chelsea, where it had all begun when Mary Quant opened her first Bazaar in the autumn of 1965. By 1969, there were more self-styled boutiques in the King's Road than ever before: but the idea of "Swinging Chelsea" had become a Frankenstein's monster. The little shops which had for so long made the King's Road the heart of a real community, one of the most attractive in London, had one by one fallen to a glittering, commercialized invasion, dominated by large fashion chains and other external big business interests. And it was somehow symptomatic that by the summer of 1969 even Bazaar itself had been sold, to become a pharmacy. It was the symbol of a Chelsea that was almost gone.

In a deeper sense, it was hardly surprising that this phase of relative exhaustion should have come about in the late sixties. For the further the events of 1955–1966 faded into the past, the more clearly they could be seen as an inevitably violent transition between one sort of Britain and another, brought about by a coincidence of factors —social, political, and psychological—which could never be repeated.

Britain had had to bear, like every Western country, all the shocks of the coming of affluence, television, and a wave of technological innovation, at the same time as she had been subjected to all the psychological stresses of the last phase of her decline from world power. One has only to draw the contrast between the somewhat unnaturally conservative, elderly, upper-class-dominated Britain of the post-war early fifties, and the Britain that was returning to a relative placidity twelve years later, to see how there was hardly any aspect of her national life in which change had not come to a head in the years between. Even the turnover in generations at the top of English life told its own tale—the age gap between the two unusually old men who had been leaders of the two major political parties in 1955, Churchill and Attlee, and the two unusually young men who had succeeded them by 1965, represented an acceleration of almost forty years, or two complete political generations, in less than a decade.

Obviously such an abnormal concentration of change could not be continued indefinitely—as can be most strikingly seen in the course of Britain's "class revolution" of these years. Nothing had been more symptomatic of Britain's upheaval from 1956 onwards than the extraordinary concentration of new figures and personalities who, year after year, had emerged onto the national stage in successive waves—Osborne, Tynan and the writers of the fifties, David Frost and the satirists, Wilson, Heath, Grimond, and a new generation of politicians, countless television personalities, the Beatles and other heroes of pop culture—all in some way reflecting the scale and depth of the country's renewal, whether as representatives of the lower classes rising to the top, or as upper-class and bourgeois rebels against their own classes.

Just to what extent there had been a real "class revolution" in these years is open to argument. Perhaps, in the long run, it amounted to little more than a continuation of the same revolution which had been taking place for forty years or more, coupled with a general relaxation of social attitudes and barriers and, of course, the new prominence of that glamorous little "classless" minority publicized through television and the mass-media. But certainly in the years after 1966 the flow of new national figures, which had earlier seemed limitless, markedly dried up. And in the last four years of the sixties, it was possible to point to only three new figures whose national impact in any way equaled that of the Frosts, Beatles, and others of pre-1966: the model Twiggy (1966), the student leader Tariq Ali, who achieved temporary prominence through the wave of anti-Vietnam demonstrations in 1968, and the right-wing Conservative politician Enoch Powell who, although well known previously, only passed into national mythology with his speeches on immigration in 1968.

Undoubtedly one aspect of this sense of aftermath in the late sixties was the country's returning conservatism. Despite the somewhat hysterical support attracted by Enoch Powell for his racial views, or even the increasingly scornful use of the terms "trendy" and "leftie" in, for instance, comment on the drug scandals afflicting the pop world in 1967, a remarkable thing about this reaction to the progressive orthodoxy was its generally quiescent rather than aggressive character. It was as if, to a certain extent, the British were once again rediscovering some of the more traditional emotional roots and values of their national life, with a sense of considerable gratitude—as could be seen, for instance, in the nationwide wave of approval won by the police for their civilized handling of the major Vietnam demonstration in London on 27 October 1968, or that which surrounded the monarchy in 1969, at the time of the investiture of Prince Charles as Prince of Wales (when the Royal Family were also subjected to a spate of unprecedentedly informal exposure on television). And certainly in all sorts of ways (for instance, the disavowal of their former positions by various erstwhile pillars of the liberal intellectual establishment, such as Kingsley Amis and John Braine), there were signs for the first time in over twelve years of a fashionable drift back toward the right.*

* It was interesting that the one group increasingly isolated by this changing climate of opinion was the more upper-middle-class segment of the New Oxford Group and the 1945–1955 Oxbridge generation which in the years after 1956 had played such a key role in promoting youthful and lower-class vitality. Whereas their lower-class contemporaries, such as Amis, Osborne, Braine, and Bernard Levin, were in many cases beginning to emerge as somewhat right-wing, the upper-middle-class section of this generation remained by and large frozen in the attitude which up to 1966 had made them so influential, but which was now (particularly as they themselves grew older) inclined to render them increasingly absurd. Not even the earlier period had offered an instance of the cult of youth carried to such lengths as the occasion in the summer of 1967 when Mick Jagger, fresh from trial on a drug charge, was flown by a television company in a helicopter to a "secret rendezvous" with a group which

328

By the closing years of the sixties, however, this changing climate in Britain was only a microcosm of a much wider process taking place in many countries. Particularly by the eventful year of 1968, this phase of exhaustion and loss of momentum, this "fading into reality" of the collective dreams of the fifties and sixties, this rightward swing and the beginnings of transition to a different age, could be seen all over the world. In 1966–1968, as the world continued to be overshadowed by the peculiar horror of the war in Vietnam, by far the most dramatic of all the manifestations of reality which had overtaken the fond anticipations of those earlier years was the condition into which American life had fallen, as a legacy to the bubble of nervous energy which had been generated in the years of the Kennedy renaissance, the heyday of the civil rights movement and of President Johnson's "Great Society." The speed with which, in just a few years, the American Dream, the most powerful image of the twentieth century, had collapsed into nightmare, had left the world quite stunned. Only by the second half of 1968, in the wake of the assassinations of Martin Luther King and Robert Kennedy, in the mood of national introspection over such matters as the influence of television saturated with images of violence, in the comparative lull in rioting in the cities and the beginning of Vietnam peace talks, were there signs at last of a numbed quiescence in the previous apparently helpless drift toward disaster. With Richard Nixon's election victory on a tide of conservatism, recognition of the ending of an era, and of the desire for a fresh, less excitable start in American life became widespread. But it was clear that in the events of 1965–1968, the innocence (if that had ever been the right word) of the American Dream had been lost for ever.

---

included the Bishop of Woolwich and William Rees Mogg, Editor of *The Times.* A similar sense of the growing absurdity of this generation was provoked by, for instance, Paul Johnson's eulogies of the Paris students in the *New Statesman* of May 1968, Kenneth Tynan's performance over the play *The Soldiers,* and the various utterances of Anthony Wedgwood Benn as Minister of Technology, such as the confession that his interest in technology was "spiritual" and his statement in the summer of 1968 that "the public is still stuck with a communications system that has hardly changed since the Stone Age."

A second, by no means unrelated, harvest of the dreams of those earlier years (in that it derived such obvious stimulus from the Civil Rights agitation and the worldwide neurosis surrounding the Vietnam war) was the wave of anarchic unrest which in 1968 came to its head among the students of the world's universities. Apart from its significance as perhaps the most conspicuous of the ways in which extreme left-wing fantasies were in so many countries beginning to arouse a right-wing reaction, one of the remarkable things about this particular psychic epidemic was the number of strands in the history of the sixties for which it marked something of an "explosion into reality"; the trend to permissiveness and the loss of self-confidence by authority; the growth of an increasingly violent tradition of "protest," attached to so many causes that it had eventually come out in its true colors as a condition of indiscriminate rebellion; the way in which governments all over the world had come to regard university education as some kind of national totem, encouraging the mass-production of graduates in many cases quite regardless of the provision of proper conditions for their education, let alone of the purpose for which they should be educated; the growing vogue (which had become particularly marked in the years after 1956) for subjects such as sociology and psychology, which encouraged vague "reformist" thinking without intellectual discipline; and the growing resentment against the impersonality of societies dedicated apparently to serving the Molochs of technology, bureaucracy, and mass-consumption. But above all, it provided a jolt to that adulation of Youth for its own sake that since the middle fifties had become perhaps the predominant characteristic of societies all over the world, from the affluent West to Mao Tse-tung's China; a final tragi-comic disproof of the belief in young people's innate "individuality" and "originality."

By 1968 there were many other examples of disillusionment overtaking the dreams which had been so conspicuous over the previous decade—the chaos afflicting the Roman Catholic Church after the earlier "dream stage" of its *aggiornamento* under Pope John, the continuing collapse into reality of those dreams which had flourished in

330

the vast regions of the earth lately freed from colonial rule. In the Communist world these years saw a phase of disenchantment almost as severe as that prevailing in America, whether it was in the chaos of the "Cultural Revolution" into which China had fallen in the years after 1965, or the "re-Stalinization" which, after the years of liberalization and *détente,* was taking place in Russia, culminating in 1968 in the invasion of Czechoslovakia. This in itself, quite apart from other events in Russia, provided the world with a final disillusionment to that other dream-image which, second only to that of the American Dream, has exerted such a powerful hold over the twentieth century imagination, that of freedom-loving Soviet Communism.

There was also in 1966–1969 a notable series of violent deaths or near-deaths, representing a considerable cross-section of the dreams which had flourished during the previous decade: the deaths of Yuri Gagarin and several other Russian and American spacemen, of Robert Kennedy and Martin Luther King, of Che Guevara, the archetypal rebel hero of the students; the assassinations of Dr. Voerword and Tom Mboya in Africa; a series of show business deaths, including those of Judy Garland by drugs, Jayne Mansfield in a car crash, and Sharon Tate by murder in Hollywood; that in Israel of the radical Bishop Pike; the attempted murder of Andy Warhol, the chief dream hero of American pop culture; and in Britain, the deaths of Brian Epstein and one of the Rolling Stones; those in crashes of Donald Campbell, Britain's last double world speed record holder, and Jim Clark, former world champion racing driver; the suicides of Tony Hancock, television Comedian of the Year in 1959–60, Robin Douglas-Home, and David Jacobs, celebrated show business lawyer and "friend of the Beatles"; and the murder by his best friend of Joe Orton, the "blackest" of Britain's new-wave playwrights. The curious (or perhaps not curious) thing about almost all these deaths was the extent to which, however shocking, they were generally regarded as not particularly surprising.

Of course much of the disillusionment and confusion which hung over the closing years of the sixties ran deeper than the mere dispelling of temporary illusions about the more immediate excitements of the previous few years. One particularly prominent feature of the neurosis of these years, for instance, in many countries was the growing disquiet over the manifestations of modern technology. A noticeable development of the previous decade had been the increasingly impersonal, even in many eyes "inhuman" trend of technology, ranging from the character of the new architecture to the replacement of steam trains by diesels; from the coming of computers to the increasing stranglehold over the environment established by the motor car. The growing unease provoked by these developments (despite the benefits they brought) found particular expression in Britain in the rows which broke out in 1967 over the Stansted Airport Scheme, the Torrey Canyon oil disaster, and sonic boom tests for the *Concorde,* and more generally in doubts over towering-block buildings, in the ever-rising concern about the effects of chemical pollution on the atmosphere, rivers, and wildlife, and even contributed in part to the horror aroused by the Vietnam war. This sense that society was becoming increasingly the prisoner of an all-pervading technological monster, running on out of control, was part of something much larger than just a phase of temporary disillusionment.

Indeed, looking back on the days when the dream of the fifties and sixties had been at its height, it is ironical to recall that one of its most powerful ingredients had been the sense that a new era was dawning. For in the late sixties, when for the first time it was becoming possible to look back on the changes of those years in some kind of perspective, what became more evident was the extent to which they could be seen not so much as the beginning of a new era, but simply as another, very important stage in a process stretching back into the past.

Although its course has sometimes been obscured, the social evolution of the twentieth century has followed a consistent pattern. We

332

have already noted some of the parallels between the climate of our own time and that of the twenties. Now let us look back to an earlier period still, that of the years leading up to the First World War. The years around and after 1900 were an age of exploration in every field from nuclear physics to the reaching of the Poles; they saw the coming of the aeroplane, motor cars, the wireless, the cinema, the first mass-circulation newspapers; in the arts, with Fauvism, Futurism, Cubism, Picasso, Stravinsky, Schoenberg, the revolt against the nineteenth century and the launching of the modernist avant-garde; in the theatre, Strindberg, Jarry's *Ubu Roi* and the beginnings of the tradition of experimentalism and shock; in psychology, Freud and the beginnings of psychoanalysis; in politics, the rise of revolutionary Communism and its milder equivalents, such as the British Labour Party; the emergence of the first movements for colonial independence and the suffragettes; and in America, the first sky-scrapers, the beginnings of jazz and, through ragtime, the first influence of jazz rhythms on popular music.

Here was the birth of the twentieth century dream. It has by no means been always coherent, and from time to time its different aspects have been in direct conflict with each other; but essentially the twentieth century dream has had two chief ingredients, closely related. On the one hand there has been the technological dream, whereby man would achieve a golden age of power, freedom, and silent efficiency, through machines, through ever-rising speeds, through mass-production and instant communications and a complete scientific mastery of his environment. On the other, dominated at every point by the slowly fading image of Victorianism, has been the libertarian dream, whereby man would be freed from the conventions, inhibitions, repressions, superstitions, imperialism, and authoritarianism which had restricted him in the past, and would at last be able to fulfill himself through the sweeping away of social and political barriers and hierarchies, through a complete understanding of his own psychology, and through the pursuit of a new and total freedom in the arts and social relationships.

333

In addition, providing links among these ingredients, has been the hope that, with the elimination of poverty through technologically created wealth, social evils, such as crime and mental illness, would be reduced; and that through mass education and the new forces of mass communication disseminating knowledge in all directions, there would be a steady rise in the level of social culture. This vision, in one way or another, has underlain the advance of twentieth century civilization. In the first fifty years of the century, it transformed the world, with advances in science, with the disintegration of traditional ways of life and social structures, with the rise of mass communications as a major factor in the social and psychic life of the age. And yet today, only twenty years later, even that world of 1950 seems curiously old-fashioned, almost safe and cosy. With its Victorian city centers, its New Look clothes, its steam trains, its map of Africa still painted red, its almost Victorian standards of decorum in public entertainments and the orthodox arts, it seems in some ways more closely linked with the nineteenth century than with our own time.

For what has happened in the fifties and sixties is that, on all sides, the twentieth century dream has taken a step toward fulfilment on a scale dwarfing everything that went before. The coming of the space age, of the H-bomb and the intercontinental missile, the rise of modern technology in its new and more impersonal guise to the point where it has come to invade and overshadow almost every aspect of life, the establishment at the heart of social and political life of the unreal glare of television, the revolt of the young and the overthrow of the last vestiges of Victorian propriety, the reaching of new boundaries of sensationalism in the arts and the widespread merging of popular and avant-garde culture—all this has marked not only a tremendous acceleration of the process which has been under way since 1900, but also a major installment in the toppling of those barriers which kept the dream out of reach and therefore intact. The dream has come true—and the real fruit of the fifties and sixties lies in the fact that, as never before, its hollowness is becoming increasingly exposed.

334

Of course the roots of the "twentieth century dream" lie further back in history than just the twentieth century. One has only to look for a moment behind the caricature of heavy conservative Victorian stability—at the nineteenth century's dizzying belief in progress, at the steady encroachment of industrialization on the nature of society and of science on all man's attitudes to the world, at the seething undercurrent of liberal revolt against traditional structures of thought and belief, the Romanticism rampant in the arts and political thought, the visions of the nationalists, of the Chartists and liberal democrats, of Saint-Simon, of Nietzsche, of Marx—for any clear distinction between our own century and that of the Victorians to dissolve. Insomuch as there was ever a clear break with the past, in fact, it was not around 1900 but a full century before—at the time when the coming of the steam age and industrialism, the French and American revolutions and the birth of the Romantic revolt in the arts, shattered the confines of man's age-old, feudal, pre-industrial society, and launched him on the technological, libertarian road of progress.

The view generally accepted today of these past two centuries is that they have witnessed man stretching up toward his true kingdom on earth, breaking free of the centuries of primitive dependence on nature and religion and divinely ordained hierarchical systems, at last exercising himself to master his environment and to shine the clear light of science into every corner, while artists and thinkers penetrated a whole realm of consciousness of which their ancestors had never dreamed. Of course at the same time it is recognized that this process has brought with it terrible growing pains—the horrors of nineteenth-century industrialism, the two most destructive wars in history, increasing noise, ugliness, frustration, and neurosis, the fragmentation of knowledge, the disintegration of the arts, and so forth. But one of the most prominent characteristics of these years has been the growth of a sort of general schizophrenia, whereby the whole process has seemed so vast and inevitable that we have come to accept its dream and its nightmare aspects simultaneously, with, as it were, different parts of our minds—without ever really fully

335

equating the two. Our attitude to what is happening to mankind has been ultimately based on a dimly sensed and open-ended assumption that some day it would all work out for the best, or that even if it did not, at least that day lay comfortably far off.

If we accept, however, that the dream and the nightmare are inextricably intertwined, then the whole picture becomes more coherent. We can see the particular frustrations, disasters, and disillusionments of the past two hundred years not just as growing pains, but as directly related to and consequential on man's expanding aspirations. With each major catastrophe, he has lurched onward to the next, even greater, fired by a vision that is ultimately unattainable, but which offers the prospect of enough further benefit in each case to inspire him to fresh efforts. This direct link between dream and nightmare applies to the pattern of each specific advance—as we can see in the catastrophic impact on society of that great blessing the motor car, or the two-edged potential of nuclear power, or the terrible unforeseen consequences of the environmental use of chemicals, or in the greatest individual "dream" of all, the advances in medical science and the eradication of disease which bring in their wake the untold dangers of the population explosion. It is only by attempting to see the overall picture that one may perceive the almost mathematical precision with which each new phase of man's advance stretches the potential of both dream and nightmare to a similar extent; and with which each new development, however small, makes its own contribution to the ultimately self-destructive pattern of the whole.

It is thus, for instance, that one may see the true relationship between the technological and libertarian aspects of the dream: that it is the former which, by in some way distorting man's view of his place in nature and reducing his civilization to an ever more unnatural, mechanical conformity, produces the latter, made up of all the individual and group fantasies of a society in disintegration; and the second which expresses the urge to social self-destruction latent in the first.

336

Why should this be so? It is after all rather extraordinary that the very thing man has felt his energies drawn toward, his self-realization as a species, should at the same time be apparently against his lasting interests, dooming him to the most terrible frustrations, if not catastrophe. If man in fact has some sort of "natural" condition and place in nature, against which his awakening has only been some kind of rebellion doomed to eventual failure, what is or was that condition? And above all, if he has such an apparently infinite capacity for deluding himself why did we not recognize such a capacity long ago?

To answer these questions, we must conclude by taking a final and broader look at the nature of fantasy. In doing so, we shall see that, far from being new, this way of looking at the world, under a slightly different set of terms, is almost as old as man himself.

Part Four

Chapter Twelve

The Riddle of the Sphinx

Who sees the variety and not the unity, wanders on from death to death.

KATHA UPANISHAD

Every man has fancies which are contrary to his real
good, when he forms his own idea of what is good. This is
a curious fact which puts man in a class by himself.

PASCAL, *Pensées*

Things and actions are what they are, and the consequences of them will be what they will be; why then
should we wish to be deceived?

BISHOP BERKELEY

It is only too painfully obvious, moreover, that neither
the scientist nor the artist is ever a "creator." The word
"creative," so incessantly misused by our younger critical
schools, is a fiction of that optimism about human
achievement which—it has been said—thrives most
vigorously in lunatic asylums. Nature, as Goethe puts it,
runs its course by such eternal and necessary principles
that even the Gods themselves cannot alter them. The
most that the scientist and the artist accomplish is new
understanding of things that have always been. They
"create" a clearer perception.

H. ZINSSER
Rats, Lice and History

That nature which condemns its origin,
Cannot be bordered certain in itself;
She that herself will sliver and disbranch
From her material sap, perforce must wither
And come to deadly use.

King Lear, IV, ii

During the past thirty years, people from all the civilised
countries on earth have consulted me . . . among all my
patients in the second half of life,—that is to say, over
thirty-five—there has not been one whose problem in the
last resort was not that of finding a religious outlook on
life. It is safe to say that every one of them fell ill because

342

he had lost that which the living religions of every age have given to their followers, and none of them has been really healed who did not regain his religious outlook.

C. G. JUNG
"Psychotherapists or the Clergy?"

This book has been based on the assumption that men's minds work on two quite distinct levels. The first, on which we are accustomed to make a large part of our everyday judgments, is the level of images and the way things outwardly appear to be, or the way in which, however unconsciously, we would like them to be. The second is based on things as they actually are.

In the course of examining the psychic epidemic which swept through English life in the fifties and sixties, we have been looking at a series of events taking place on the first of these levels. At every point, when we have seen individuals or groups acting in certain ways, thinking that they were acting in this manner for such and such reasons, we have seen that in fact they were only the instruments of a much wider pattern, evolving for the most part in quite another direction to the one they supposed. We have seen how that pattern itself followed its own clear laws. We have seen how all sorts of disparate manifestations of the spirit of the time, on the superficial level apparently quite unconnected, were in fact expressions of the same basic, underlying collective fantasy. And we have been able to observe these things because, at least to a certain extent, we have been doing so from outside the fantasy, from the second level of objective reality.

The more one manages to stand outside fantasy, the more obvious it becomes that all its forms are in fact only part of the same phenomenon. Not only does one form of fantasy invariably stimulate another, such as the obvious mutual exacerbation of left-wing and right-wing fantasies; not only is the increase in one form of fantasy in society almost invariably accompanied by increase in others, indicating that they not only lead to each other, but actually spring from a common root; but also each form of fantasy, from the standpoint of reality, is functionally interchangeable with any other. The outward forms they take are only of importance on the level of appearances; on the level of reality, the analogy of one form may be applied to all. For instance, all fantasy works like a drug—whether it takes the form of addiction to power or sex or television or revolutionary politics, it is all progressively addictive, demands increasing gratification, and ends, however subtly, in one form or another of frustration. All fantasy is a form of gamble—a temporary jump out of reality without too nice a calculation of the probable consequences. Drug or gamble—each is part of the other. And ultimately all fantasy is a form of sickness or madness—whether temporary or lasting, a disturbance of our mental equilibrium with the reality of the world around us.

In fact what I have been describing as fantasy or neurosis is what was known to former ages as evil. Nowadays we have more or less lost any exact sense of what we mean by the term evil. We use it either vaguely, simply as a suggestive epithet, or we use it to describe things which are not in fact evil itself but only its consequences—usually crimes on a particularly remote, inhuman scale, such as Hitler's concentration camps or the Moors Murders. But the idea that evil is actually some kind of contagious psychic force in the world, that it is omnipresent both in society at large and in every one of us individually, something that can affect us all the time in even the smallest, most everyday ways, is one that has been all but abandoned as a relic of that superstitious and primitive past from which we have so painfully emerged. The idea that evil might even be perceptible and measurable in objective, scientific terms, is altogether alien to our modern way of thought.

Nevertheless it is perhaps surprising that modern science and psychology should have made so little effort, if not to provide a reinterpretation of the meaning of evil, at least to explain in psychological terms why it was that our ancestors placed so much importance on the idea. We freely pay our respects, for instance, to Shakespeare or Dr. Johnson, Pascal or Plato, as among the profoundest observers of human nature; and yet we somehow manage to overlook that to any of them, the force of evil, whether classified as sin, delusion, or just vanity (that revealingly double-edged word im-

345

plying both self-centeredness and illusion), was something specific and tangible, and that without a recognition of its insidious power it would be impossible to make sense of the human condition.

What our ancestors realized, in fact, was that human beings have a faculty which divides them from all other animals. They have the power of imagination. They have the power to speculate that things might be different from what they are. They do not live unthinkingly by their instincts. For an animal, the way it spends its life, the way it organizes its social system, even the way in which it plays its part in the more general framework of nature by contributing to the life-cycles of other species, are all dictated by innate natural law. The bee accepts its place in a hierarchy, plays its part in building the nest and propagating the species, assists in pollination of the flowers, all in unchanging ritual, generation by generation.

Obviously in the broadest sense man does the same. The history of man shows that he has formed societies, propagated his kind, preserved the chain of life from generation to generation, just like any other species. But a closer inspection shows that, in human societies as in no other, an element of instability has crept in. Looked at in detail, human societies are seen to be at all levels not calm and orderly, but in perpetual flux. Unlike the drones, the workers, and the queens, men do not necessarily accept the position in the social hierarchy to which they were born, but move about from class to class. Unlike the swallow, they do not automatically make any personal sacrifice to protect their young. Men do not obtain their food, build their dwellings, order their relationship with the rest of nature, according to strict unchanging patterns and forms. They have to make choices. Their patterns change. Above all, every part of their society, whether each individual human being or each collective group, family, community, class, generation, nation, shows a tendency to become self-conscious and to measure itself in rivalry with the rest.

The reason for this is not far to seek. For if one looks more closely at this difference between men and animals, one observes a curious thing. Every animal has what one might broadly describe as two sets of instincts: on the one hand, its individual "life" instincts, to survive, to eat, to sleep, to mate; and on the other, acting as a kind of controlling framework, what one might call its collective or "orderly" instincts, which enable it to relate to the world around it, and which lead it to form communities, build nests, tend its young until they too are ready to mate, play its part in the general framework of nature. From the marriage of these two sets of instincts, one may draw the conclusion that the one overriding purpose in any form of life is not so much to survive individually, as to preserve the chain of life in its own species, and indirectly the grand chain of life in nature as a whole. In the animals, in fact, these two sets of instincts, the "life" instincts and the "orderly" instincts, are inseparably intertwined to serve the one supreme purpose. But in man there has arisen a kind of separation, even a potential conflict between the two. His individual "life" instincts remain as intact and unthinking as those of the animals. But the controlling mechanism of his "orderly" instincts, which can alone promote automatic harmony with the rest of the world, has in some way broken adrift. It is in this separation that the unique element of instability in man's nature is to be found.

Of course the breaking adrift is by no means total. Indeed here is the crux of the matter. For on one level, and with what must, on the historical evidence of his survival alone, be regarded as the core of his nature, man attempts to adhere to his basic instinctive pattern, as if no separation had taken place. It is on this level, through marriage and the rearing of children, through subordinating his own interests to those of the community, through accepting the underlying patterns of nature both within and outside himself, that he finds fulfillment. But to preserve this sense of harmony between his two sets of instincts, he must make a continual, conscious effort. For there is another powerful ingredient in his make-up which is continually urging him in the opposite direction, away from his basic core. It is this ingredient which is continually arousing his imagination with possibilities—possibilities which outwardly take the form of projections of his desires for "life" and "order" fragmented into every conceivable permutation and rearrangement, but which must always, by definition, be in some way contrary to the basic instinctive harmony between them, violations of his inner sense or true organic order, projections of self-assertion in one form or another against the containing framework.

Between these two conflicting forces in his character, man thus lives in a state of constant tension. It is his imagination, his ability to choose, which gives him, unlike any other animal, a sense of freedom. But even so, despite this apparent latitude, the laws of nature still retain their absolute control. For it is only when he uses his imagination to return within his basic framework, that man can find satisfaction. The other path, the path of defiance, the path of illusion, leads inevitably to frustration and ultimately, still in a pattern laid down by nature, to self-destruction. This, as our forefathers realized, is the riddle at the heart of man's existence.

So far in this book we have been almost wholly concerned with the power of fantasy to lead men away from reality. But in order finally to see fantasy in perspective, it is necessary to consider some of the ways in which men attempt to re-establish their relationship with reality. The very fact that fantasy is at every point a perversion of man's basic nature means that by tracing back each strand of fantasy to its origin, to the point where it departs from reality, we can build up an overall picture of what that reality is.

What emerges is an idealized portrait of human life and society which, of course, nowhere exists or ever has. It is a society which, like that of the animals, is dedicated to the supreme purpose of carrying on life. It is therefore a society in which no one acquires more of the material things of life than are necessary. It is a society in which no one feels lonely or isolated or bored or insecure or superior or inferior to anyone else, because his chief concern is mutual cooperation and subservience to a common purpose. Inevitably, like many animal societies, it is in some sense divided into classes and hierarchies: but it is not one in which any class, upper or lower, exploits another for its own ends, but in which each has its part to play in the organic whole. Similarly each individual has his own detailed place in the whole. Men and women have their respective roles, again neither being considered "superior" to the other, nor considered "equal," in the sense that their different temperaments and functions are ever confused. The old, because they have seen life and learned its patterns, are wise, and because they have fulfilled their task are not reluctant to die. The young, like any young, are exuberant, but respectful, and learn without reluctance how to take on their responsibilities in turn. In fact as each individual grows up, he gradually builds up an inner picture in his mind, in which his own function, his relationship with others and with the outside world generally, are perfectly and securely balanced. The community is thus at all times united, both within itself and with its wider setting of nature. Its life is governed in harmony with the rhythm of the seasons. Disaster, such as illness, flood, earthquake or death, it learns to accept, without fretting, as the lot of all creation. It is a society whose members can never be disappointed or disillusioned, for they never build up any illusions to lose. Above all, they feel the joy of their overriding sense of being bound together in a common task which goes on forever.

It is this ideal unity from which, by his condition, man has been exiled. And it is this ideal unity which he either attempts to work toward and re-establish, or to dissipate and destroy, with every mental pattern that he makes throughout his waking life. The reason we are capable of dissipating this unity is that we are able to deceive ourselves as to our true interests, by seeing appearances as different from reality. Our minds make partial patterns which do not resolve with the whole. We see the world subjectively—and by definition our subjective view does not tally with the objective.

But the very fact that we think so much in terms of outward appearances, and yet with the most important part of ourselves attempt to adhere to the pattern of underlying reality, means that we help ourselves by giving that pattern its counterparts on the outer level. These counterparts, these shadows of reality, which make up the most familiar of the ways in which we try to re-establish and preserve our unity, we may call in this context "myths"; all that elaborate framework designed to focus men's minds on their inner reality, the framework of tradition, custom, codes of morality, symbols of communal unity such as monarchies and flags, festivals to mark the unfolding of the year and man's relationship with nature, festivals to mark the unfolding of a human life, such as those celebrating birth, adulthood, marriage, and death: all these are the outer shows, vested with a special psychic importance, guarding the central unity of man with himself, with society, and with nature.

Of course, if these myths, these outward shows, lose their link with the reality which underlies them, they become themselves illusions: as when for instance, the power of a throne or the outward trappings of monarchy become not symbols of communal unity, but merely the focus of individual or group fantasies working against that unity; or when a wedding, instead of being the outward sign of a pledge marking a unity for life, becomes transformed into a mere outward show, a sensation of the moment. But so long as they retain their living force, this framework of myths represents that fundamental harmony between man's life and order instincts which shapes his only true and healthy mode of existence.

Within this framework of myth, there are of course other devices by which men come to terms with the destructive force of fantasy. There are, for instance, the safety valves by which he seeks to anesthetize its worst effects, or at least to contain it within certain socially tolerable limits. One such is the system of law and justice, which provides a device for the peaceful "resolution" of social strains arising through fantasy, such as crime and civil discord. Another is the use of games and sport, through which our self-assertive instincts may be safely channeled within a framework of rituals and rules. A third is humor, which provides a social safety valve against the intensity of fantasy, and a harmless way of puncturing one's own or someone else's fantasy or self-importance, without fully exercising a counter self-assertion in the opposite direction (although both games and jokes, like myths, can easily become the vehicle of fantasies themselves, as one can see when a sportsman's successes go to his head or the partisanship of football crowds turns to violence, or when ridicule is pursued, as often in the case of satire, to the point where it becomes as much an act of self-assertion and symptom of sickness as those of its targets).

There are other social safety valves which are more obviously direct concessions to fantasy. One is the use within socially acceptable limits of certain drugs, such as tobacco or alcohol, even though it is recognized that their consequences may be fatal if used to excess.* Another is prostitution, which provides a channel for promiscuity and sexual perversion which might otherwise be turned directly against the fabric of society. A third is that curious phenomenon the scapegoat, who can be made a vessel for the drawing off of society's accumulated aggressions and frustrations; anyone who is familiar with the life of even the smallest and most placid of communities, such as an English village, will recognize the presence of some figure or group, such as an unpopular priest or newcomers or a slovenly family, who become, at least for a time, the butt of that community's gossip and the focus of its group aggression. The same phenomenon is of course familiar on a much larger scale in societies as a whole, and we can even see a variant of it, on an international scale, in the way that certain "crisis points," such as Trieste, Berlin, or Quemoy and Matsu, serve for a time as the focus for international neurosis, and are then more or less forgotten in favor of somewhere else. But even though the scapegoat, or crisis point, serves its continuing purpose at times when neurosis is relatively quiescent, its importance becomes in-

---

* All such drugs (or "intoxicants") of course give their pleasurable sensations by the very fact that they in some way distort our sense of reality, and can do so because they are "toxic"—i.e. mild forms of poison.

finitely greater when the general neurosis becomes excited—as we can see from the history of anti-Semitism and witch-hunting, or, in our own narrative, from the various roles played as scapegoats in the accumulated hysteria of 1963 by Profumo, Ward, and Harold Macmillan.

In fact, for all the power of myth and tradition, and the limited efficacy of these safety valves, in no human society can the reserve of fantasy remain quiescent and under control indefinitely. The condition of man's life is change—whether technical change, or the rise and fall of empires, or just the ebb and flow of generation succeeding generation. The very fact that a society does not live unthinkingly by instinct any more than do the individuals making it up, means that in order to preserve its organic harmony and its sense of a central purpose it must be making a continuous effort to re-establish and perceive afresh its unity with reality; its framework of myths must continually evolve, lest they become stagnant and lose their meaning as "orderly" fantasies, such as those of the Pharisees, who obeyed the outward forms of the law without recognizing the underlying meaning which had originally given it life. With each phase of change it is necessary to re-establish the basic harmony by "resolving" the pattern again; and of course the more change that takes place, the more disorder it unleashes, the harder it is to resolve the pattern, and the more likely it is that society will fragment like a jigsaw puzzle, each group and individual within it becoming neurotic, and being set against the rest.

Indeed from time to time it is inevitable that, as we have seen in our model of what happened to England in the fifties and sixties, the collective fantasy of society should become so excited that all sorts of different streams of infection run together to form a psychic epidemic. The natural mutual attraction of one form of fantasy for another will reach the point where a whole range of group fantasies can find common cause, merging into one general collective sickness —which eventually comes to a head in some grand self-destructive catastrophe, such as a war or revolution. A classic example of this is the history of Europe in the fifty years leading up to the Great War, when developments in politics, social movements, revolutionary fever, the spate of assassinations, the pace of scientific advance, and violent changes in the arts, all heralded the mounting collective psychosis that was to culminate in the events of 1914–1918.

Human history in fact presents so continuous a record of such psychic epidemics, some large, some small, and the dying down of one merges so closely with the first symptoms of the next, that it seems sometimes as if there were never any real periods of quiescence in between. The process of change is never smooth and regular, but seems only to consist of periods of stagnation when the established order becomes conservative and out of touch with reality, interspersed with periods of chaos when the pent-up forces of change explode out of control. Even in the most stable states, the same pattern can be seen in the life of almost every individual government, the hopes and energy which attend its inauguration souring almost inevitably to the disillusionment and exhaustion which attend its downfall.

What a dismal picture it presents, this endless round of discord, change, and decay, of dreams raised up only to be shattered and replaced by nothing more substantial than new dreams! And even this is only describing human affairs on a grand collective level. It says nothing of all the shattered hopes and aspirations, the private insecurities, miseries and frustrations attendant on the life of almost every individual human being. But then what we are looking at is nothing less than the bitter fruit of man's eternal failure to overcome the unique flaw in his nature, to solve the riddle which every mere insect, bird, and beast of the field solves all its life long without thinking.

So shifting and illusory is the level on which myth vainly attempts to hold together man's sense of unity, that he naturally tries to find ways of achieving a deeper and more stable relationship with reality. One such is through the patterns of art. It is a natural corollary of the failure of our own times to draw a clear distinction between good and evil, that we have come to see the function of all forms of artistic expression as more or less the same. Classic and Romantic, Shakespeare and Shelley, *War and Peace* and *Finnegans Wake,* even Bach and the Beatles, are all regarded ultimately as only different forms of "self-expression." Such a confusion is hardly surprising, for it is after all one of the most insidious properties of fantasy that, by diverting attention solely to outward appearances and away from the meaning that underlies them, it strives continually to blur or erase the distinction between itself and reality.

Similarly we have come to regard such qualities as "talent," "imagination," "intelligence," "sensitivity," as absolutes, demanding respect and requiring no further qualification. In fact the artist is in a sense suffering from a kind of sickness. What we call his talent is part of an extra flaw in his mental make-up which makes it more necessary for him than for most people to make patterns in his mind to establish equilibrium with his surroundings (it is no coincidence that so many artists should also have been sick in more obvious ways, dying young, going deaf, going mad, and so forth). But as with every other form of mental activity, he can either achieve that equilibrium, by resolving with reality, at a deeper level than is open to most people; or his art becomes just another expression of neurosis, albeit expressed perhaps with a high degree of "talent." By the very virtue of his extra degree of sickness, if he succeeds in overcoming it, the rewards in terms of insight into reality are greater than most people's; but by the same token, if he fails, so are the penalties in terms of spiritual frustration and mental sickness. In the same way, what we call "intelligence" may be just the expression of a particular kind of insecurity, a mind stretched and quickened by having to make a special effort to comprehend the world; and again the result may be successful, in which case the man of intellect may truly have a wiser and deeper knowledge of the world than most men; but as we have seen from the role of intellectuals in our narrative, the result may be just the opposite, and, despite his undoubted "intelligence," the intellectual may be simply more prone than most men to neurosis and delusion.

Once we manage to stand outside the confusions of fantasy, in fact, we can see the distinction between two very different kinds of art. On the one hand, we have the "suggestive" art of all ages, including the avant-garde and "experimental" art of our own time, made up of innumerable unresolved patterns, and of all the suggestive "life" and "order" images which are the fragments of our sense of unity in disorder. These are the patterns produced by what D. H. Lawrence crudely but accurately described as "the masturbating consciousness," the mind racing out of touch with reality, as an engine races when it is put out of gear; patterns based, as in the cinema or pornographic literature, not on the underlying patterns of reality but on an attempt to stimulate, through sensations, the illusion of actual "experience."

On the other hand, we have that whole realm of art which is drawn from the other side of man's nature, designed to focus his mind on the natural unity from which he feels exiled, designed not to escape into some imagined and subjective "heightened reality," but calmly and harmoniously to accept and portray the real world, behind superficial appearances, as it actually is.

We have, for instance, the plays of Shakespeare. We have already touched on the extent to which Shakespeare's tragedies provide perfect depictions of the unfolding of the fantasy cycle, viewed externally from the standpoint of reality. From observation on a cosmic scale of one of the fundamental patterns in nature, right down to the precise observation of his individual, everyday images, the essence of his greatness lies in his unwearying perception of the world exactly as it is, unclouded by any subjective notion of what it might be. "Life with Shakespeare" as Mr. Christopher Hollis has put it, "is not a debate on principles. The principles are settled. Life is the pageant of men living up to them, or failing to live up to them." And to Shakespeare, those principles were the outward expression of a whole framework of order, which equally encompassed personal morality,

355

the social order, and the natural order of the universe, all making up a harmonious whole which can only be flouted at ultimately fatal risk.*

Then we have the novels of Tolstoy. In his two major novels, *Anna Karenina* and *War and Peace,* Tolstoy not only provides us, on Shakespearean scale, with the classically tragic picture of some great offense against the natural order, swelling through all its stages toward catastrophe; on the one hand, the adulterous liaison of Anna and Vronsky, on the other, cast on a much grander stage but still in essence the same pattern, that of Napoleonic ambition rising to its nemesis in the unconquerable expanse of Russia. But also, in both these histories, Tolstoy gives us something which Shakespeare never really attempted; the other side of the tragic picture, the detailed account of individuals painfully finding their personal path back to their own inner health and sense of purpose, culminating both for Levin and for Pierre in the fulfillment of family life, and a refound faith in the order and purpose of the universe.

In the finest examples of the arts of painting and sculpture we find a more distilled and concentrated sense of man's inmost sense of harmony, and in their choice of subject matter, a representation of the symbols which most deeply affect the core of his being. The very language we use to describe great pictures, on the one hand that of

* In all literature, there can be no more concise and magnificent description of the working of fantasy in society than Ulysses's famous speech from Act I, scene iii, of *Troilus and Cressida,* beginning with the parallel between the natural order and the ideal of human order:

The heavens themselves, the planets and this centre
Observe degree, priority and place,
Insisture, course, proportion, reason, form,
Office and custom, in all line of order . . .

continuing with the picture of what happens when "degree is shaked, which is the ladder to all high designs" and concluding with the lines:

Then everything includes itself in power,
Power into will, will into appetite,
And appetite, an universal wolf,
So doubly seconded with will and power,
Must make perforce an universal prey,
And last eat up himself.

proportion and form, representing order, on the other that of invention and color, representing life, reveals that our highest ideals of beauty can only exist where there is a perfect marriage between the two, at a point where life and order, imagination and discipline, are so totally intertwined that it is no longer possible to distinguish one from the other. Similarly, when we criticize a work of art it is because it fails to achieve this exact balance between life and order—we say on the one hand that it lacks life, is mechanical, dull, uninspired, on the other that it lacks order, is undisciplined, showy, chaotic. For of course ultimately, as all great art implies, without perfect order there cannot be true life, and without the pulse of life there cannot be true organic order—this being the supreme guiding principle of nature, and the balance between the two being upset only in human fantasies.

In architecture, the most functional of the arts, we can see this expression of unity or discord in the contrast between the cathedral-centered skyline of a medieval town, expressing the harmony of a social organism grouped round its central symbol of communal unity, and the chaotic skyline of a city of today, dominated by towers each one of which is designed deliberately for commercial or other reasons to draw attention to itself, and to assert itself against the unity of the whole. Whether they be built as office-blocks to promote the "prestige" of a particular company, or as flats to give their inhabitants a better view than anyone else, one has the impression of a society in which each individual part is striving to vie against and outdo every other.

Finally, as the most abstract of the arts, through which the perfect marriage of life and order can be conveyed in all its purity, simply in terms of sounds, there is music. In music, as in no other art, do we see how this harmony alone can open the door to that full range of the profoundest human emotions—true joy, sublimity, nobility, exultation, majesty, pathos, grief—as compared with the tiny emotional range of any art based on fantasy, alternating as it only can, between different expressions of excitement and frustration, its pale reflections

357

of real emotions (as in jazz) being on the one hand a sort of strained gaiety, and on the other the howling plaint of grief that is only disguised self-pity.

Not for a mere conceit was it that our ancestors should have employed the analogy of music to convey their sense of the most profound unity, and the rich chord which is struck in man's inmost being between contemplation of "the starry heavens above" and his sense of "the moral law within." For, as Sir Thomas Browne wrote in the seventeenth century:

> there is a music wherever there is a harmony, order or proportion; and thus far may we maintain the music of the sphears; for those well-ordered motions and regular paces, though they give no sound unto the ear, yet to the understanding they strike a note most full of harmony. Whosoever is harmonically composed, delights in harmony.

Similarly, two thousand years before that, Plato had declared that, since music was of the utmost importance in reflecting and shaping the moral character, mind and temper of the Greek citizens, and therefore ultimately the harmony of their society:

> the introduction of a new kind of music should be shunned as imperiling the whole state, since styles of music are never disturbed without affecting the most important political institutions.

Although we may think that Plato is here slightly confusing the chicken and the egg, in that, as we saw from the coming of rock 'n roll to Britain in 1955–1956, the appearance of a new style of music is likely to be as much a symptom of a new wave of excitement as its cause, his implication that there is no clearer window on the psychic health of a society than the condition of its arts is indisputable.

But this very fact that the arts are in themselves a reflection of the health or sickness of a society, and that in unhealthy times even the finest works of previous ages can have no fundamental significance to people who no longer sense the underlying reality which gave them birth, means that ultimately the arts too are only a form of myth,

358

however potent. To an age like our own, of what real significance, for instance, is Bach's B Minor Mass or a Duccio Madonna or Salisbury Cathedral? They are magnificent images, no doubt, amazing marriages of imagination and form—but not fundamental statements of man's proper relationship with himself, with society, and with the universe. We live in a period when, for nearly two hundred years, the arts have concentrated more and more on the level of appearances, have become more and more ends in themselves, acknowledging no higher end—and have more and more lost their links with the underlying harmony and unity of all things. There are critics today who could tell Beethoven more about the construction of his music, in terms of his favorite tonal intervals, recurring rhythmic figures, and so forth, than he was aware of himself. The next moment they may be happily applying the same approach in praise of a piece by Boulez, or even the Beatles. But how far would they have patience with, or even start to comprehend, the spirit of Beethoven's own belief (a spirit which is still, of course, expressed in his music for those with ears to hear) that:

> like all the arts, music is founded upon the exalted symbols of the moral sense; all true invention is a moral progress. To submit to its inscrutable laws, and by means of those laws to tame and guide one's own mind, so that the manifestations of art may pour out: this is the isolating principle of art . . . thus every genuine product of art is independent, more powerful than the artist himself . . . connected with men only inasmuch as it bears witness to the Divine of which men are the medium. Music relates the spirit to Harmony.

One cannot ultimately balk the fact that, down through the ages, the central and most important means whereby man has sought to establish unity with the reality underlying his existence, the means comprehending the vast preponderance of art, myth, and all the rest, has been religion. It is precisely in order both to explain the "flaw" in man's condition, and to provide the means whereby he may come to terms with it, that all the great religious systems have been instituted. Unfamiliar or inimical though it may seem to the generally prevailing twentieth-century Western view, this survey would not be complete without a sympathetic look at the world view which all the traditional religions have, with only minor variations, put forward.

One of the most vivid expressions of the fact that man has somehow become "separated" from his true nature, and that he can therefore make a continuous, endlessly frustrated effort to re-establish his unity, or take refuge in an infinitely more futile attempt to escape from it, is contained in the Judaeo-Christian story of the Fall of Man, giving birth to the two paths of Good and Evil. It is again indicative of the temper of our age that, in all the derision which has been heaped on the book of Genesis for providing such an "unscientific" account of man's beginnings, the one thing which has been lost sight of is its central reminder that no explanation of man's condition can be of the slightest worth unless it begins with the fact of his basic flaw. Whether the apple eaten by Adam and Eve be called Knowledge, or Self-Consciousness, or just Imagination, it still points to the truth, underlying all others, that man has been given two distinctive paths to follow—and that one leads back to fulfillment, the other to frustration and destruction.

An even more significant factor in the decay of religious belief in recent times than the decline in belief in God, has been the dismissal from rational consideration of belief in the Devil, evil and Hell. For without the realization of the power and nature of evil, it is impossible either to see man's plight in perspective, or to appreciate fully the necessity and means of finding one's way back to the other side. There are plenty of victims of the most advanced stages of fantasy who are prepared to admit to some kind of belief in God: whether the God allowing total freedom glimpsed by the hippies in LSD visions, or their right-wing counterparts who believe that God is identified with Protestant White America, the sacred principles of free enterprise and a booming Gross National Product. Even Himmler, the architect of the concentration camps, came to a belief in God in the closing stages of the war, through his surmise that only a benign Providence could have worked the miracle of saving Hitler from the July bomb plot of 1944. But it is unlikely that any of these believers would admit to a rational and unhysterical belief in the power of evil.

All the great religions contain some version of the Fall, or man's separation from his "true" existence, usually pointed up with a picture of some paradise or golden age before he became thus separated —as in the Greek myth of Pandora's Box which, when opened, released evil into the world. Similarly, in their different versions of Hell and its punishments, all religions contain their own projections of the nature of fantasy and its consequences, whether the fate of Sisyphus and Tantalus, doomed for their offenses to the eternal alternation of anticipation and frustration, or simply the straightforward nightmare-cum-death-wish culmination of hellfire and eternal damnation. Again, all religions contain their mythical projections of the consequences of fantasy in a straightforward worldly sense, such as the story of what happened to Sodom and Gomorrah, or the fate of the builders of the Tower of Babel, or the nemesis that overcame the world when it had become wicked in Noah's time. Other peoples (for obvious reasons) had their own version of the flood myth, such as the Greek story of Deucalion and Pyrrha. But in each case the common factor was that mankind had become so evil that it had brought upon itself an unparalleled disaster, from which a tiny handful survived to carry on the chain.

For of course the essence of the death wish that lies at the heart of all fantasy is that it is not just personal, but that it also comprehends the death of the species as a whole, of all life. In one context we can see this desire taking explicit shape in the closing stages of some gigantic group fantasy, such as Nazism, with the longing for a *Götterdämmerung* in which the whole world may be engulfed. In another, we can see it in the way in which the pursuit of the vitality image of sex for its own sake eventually turns more and more toward the sterility of perversions and confusion between the sexes. Was it wholly coincidental that in the winter of 1965–1966 when, as we have seen, the psychic epidemic running through English life had reached its second death-wish stage, the peaks of sensation employed in several of that winter's plays and films should have encompassed not so much the deaths of their central figures, but those of children, of the next generation? The abortion scenes which marked the sensational climaxes of *Up the Junction* and *Alfie,* the stoning to death of the baby in *Saved,* coincided with a phase of obsessional interest in abortion shown by the press and politicians.

In fact, ultimately, all life on the level of reality is one. Each individual man, or animal, or plant, is merely the temporary vessel of a tiny part of that one substance, and their deepest instincts are to preserve it in not just their own species, but in the grand chain of all creation. An offense against one part is an offense against all, and nothing has been more illustrative of man's mounting self-assertion against his natural setting over the past few hundred years, than his steady destruction of all forms of wild life, from the growing pollution of earth, air, and water, and the destruction of forests, flowers, birds, beasts, and butterflies, to the actual extinction of whole species.

At his deepest level, man feels his unity with this whole sum of life, the precious, intangible thing that is in him, and of which he forms such a minute fraction. The desire for eternal life, so often seen on the fantasy level as simply a self-centered desire for personal immortality or reincarnation, is in fact a desire, having handed on the gift of life to the next generation, for the peace of merging back once again into that whole—a whole which, beyond the material world where it is alone divided into life spans and measures of time, has no beginning and no end, and is therefore truly eternity. As Prince Andrey says in *War and Peace,* "to die means that I, a part of that love, shall return to the great whole, the eternal source of things."

This sense of a total harmony is the ultimate reality of man's existence, the point where life, order, and purpose meet in the unity which he calls Love. His consciousness of this unity he calls Faith.

And the unity itself, comprehending all things, he calls God. True belief in God is not simply assent to an intellectual or emotional proposition—which is why no one can be talked into belief by intellect alone, or swayed into it by mere uncontrolled emotion. It involves a complete attitude to life, combining intellect, emotion, and will. Nor is it merely a subjective psychological condition, an anthropomorphic projection rooted in individual insecurities, which happens to have been shared by many thousands of millions of people at all times and in all societies. It is indeed a psychological condition —but one according with man's desire for true mental health or wholeness, at the deepest level of his being.

The word religion comes from the Latin *religare,* meaning "to bind." Its function is to provide the means whereby man can bind himself, his life and order instincts together, in the harmony of his true purpose. It is to enable him to focus all his faculties and being on the one center of his life where all images and patterns finally resolve. It is to enable him to counter the dis-ease which is his lot, and to find a sense of wholeness or "holiness," a sense of being at one or "at-oncment" with the inner moving of all creation.

The one psychologically essential step toward attaining this sense of harmony (marking the central difference between all true and pseudo-religions) is the acknowledgment, not just that there is vaguely something greater outside himself, but that in the most exact sense he is only a tiny part of an infinite organic whole—and that the only barrier between him and the whole is that part of his mind which I have called the fantasy-self. No man can be at unity within himself unless he is in harmony with the entire unity outside himself. The hardest thing for any man is to bow the knee, for in so doing he must first break his pride and overcome his self-consciousness, by recognizing the fantasy-self within him as his one true enemy.

This act is often interpreted from outside as in some way an act of surrender, particularly of intellectual surrender—which is why true faith is more easily attained by simple people who have no innate conviction of their own uniqueness. But in fact it is only by taking this step that a man can begin to see the world as it really is. In a sense, compared with those who are still living on the level of outward appearances, and therefore being continually baffled and disillusioned, he will be seeing the world upside down—or rather the right way up. For only thus will he begin to see the way in which all things work together, according to the unchanging laws of reality—just as we were able in our narrative to see on the level of reality one aspect of what happened in England in the fifties and sixties; and he will come to see how everything which happens in his own life and that of the world is part of the same overall pattern. Many people half recognize that there are remarkable subterranean patterns in their lives, catching tantalizing glimpses of another level of existence with its own rules and purposes—which, if they stop to think about it at all, they variously attribute to Fate or coincidence or chance or telepathy or even "the stars." But once they reach the level of reality, they see how all those glimpses fall into place and resolve, how everything that happens to them is part of a pattern working for good or ill. As Francis Bacon put it:

> a little depth in philosophy inclineth man's mind to atheism; but depth in philosophy bringeth man's mind about to religion; for while the mind of man looketh upon second causes scattered, it may sometimes rest in them and go on further; but when it beholdeth the chain of them, confederate and linked together, it must needs fly to Providence and Deity.

Both by learning to observe these patterns in his life, the way they work for good or as continual reminders to set him back on the right path, and by learning to compose himself to unity, shutting out as far as possible the operations of his fantasy-self, in the state which we call prayer, a man may come to have a continual intimate relationship with the real self within him and the reality outside him that is God. However clearly he recognizes his fantasy-self, or the

364

Devil, and tries to curb it, it will always be present, introducing into his mind a stream of suggestive images and temptations to self-assertion; but he will learn that the more he concentrates on the building-up of his inner unity, the greater the resistance he can put up. He will be fighting an endless battle—but once he has appreciated the need for that battle, he will never really lose sight of it, and the continuing reward which its waging provides.

He will learn too how everything that he does, every pattern which he makes in his life, can contribute to that unity; and not just through his prayer, his rituals, the festivals and ceremonies which he uses explicitly to focus his life, even though these in themselves transform the plain of everyday existence into a landscape of hills and valleys, affording a framework in which all the familiar landmarks of life take on new depths and meaning. Nor is it only the artists who can transform their actual means of livelihood into an expression of their relationship with reality; although it is not incidental that the greatest artists, such as Rembrandt or Beethoven or Michelangelo or Dante, should have regarded their art as an expression of relationship with God, in the way that Bach stated that "music has only one purpose—to honor God and recreate the mind." Anyone whose work is not based on fantasy itself or his own self-advancement, anyone who can take pride in his workmanship and contributing to the lives of others, can see a greater satisfaction in a job well done, a pattern resolved, than simply in the fact that it is over and that they can get on to the next thing. The way we speak, the way we dress, the way we conduct ourselves toward others, are all outward signs of our inner sickness or health; the way we spend our spare time, what we read, our regular habits of life, all these things can be based on a continual attempt to resolve our lives in a general unity, and on avoidance of all those distractions and diversions which however harmless they outwardly seem, bring only a nagging disquietude of mind. There is nothing so trivial or menial which, if it is not in itself evil, cannot be transformed into a joyful expression of the greater glory of the Divine Whole. As George

Herbert wrote, "who sweeps a room as for Thy laws, makes that and the action fine."

So far in this chapter, I have concentrated as much as possible on those things which have been common to human nature since the beginning of recorded time. Yet the fact remains that we are obviously today in a situation mankind has never been in before. Whether in terms of religion, art, or just the myths which hold our societies and minds together, we can hardly be said to be displaying a growing sense of fundamental unity. And if such a sense of unity is the measure of spiritual, political, moral, or even mental health, then there are signs that we are indeed in an unusually unhealthy condition.

Of course, even by these standards, we must not be too hasty about judging our state. The number of societies in which the majority of people has a true religious sense, governing all their actions, cannot have been large: it would be hard to find a more contemporary-sounding view of the religious outlook than the attitude expressed in these words:

> Can't you see how naive and comic a figure you cut these days, with your adamant belief in all this religious guff? That was how primitive man lived, long ago . . .

even though they were written in Juvenal, describing Rome in the first century A.D.

Yet over the past few hundred years, led by the civilization centered on Europe, mankind has embarked on a unique collective endeavor: namely, the unprecedented extension of what he calls scientific knowledge, and its application to the everyday life of society in terms of technology. This enterprise has had the most profound and unforeseen repercussions on his psychology, on the nature and constitution of his society and on his basic attitudes to the world. The first signs of this process began to appear as long ago as the Renaissance, which marked the first real breaking-open of that secure world-picture which had, at least in theory, prevailed in the Middle Ages, whereby God, the universe, the continent of Europe, Christendom, and the feudal order of society had all been bound together in an organic whole. With this fragmentation, men began to assert themselves against every part of that organic frame which had given them, at the deepest level of their minds, such security: in science, with their new gunpowder, and the perhaps even more subtly unsettling discovery that the earth was no longer the center of the universal frame; in exploration, with the discovery of the New World, blowing another hole in the frame; in religion, with the Reformation, and Luther declaring "here I stand—I can say no other" against a fifteen-centuries-old tradition of authority; in philosophy, with Descartes proclaiming no longer "God thinks—therefore I am" but "*I* think, therefore I am."

The second great turning point came, as we have seen, two hundred years ago, with the French and Industrial Revolutions; when nothing more vividly betrayed the new phase into which the European subconscious was moving than the sudden eruption, in all societies and all fields, of the wave of Romanticism which, in all its later growths and developments, has been with us to the present time. To the Royal Academy in 1778, Sir Joshua Reynolds spoke for more than just a tendency beginning to appear in the arts, when he warned in vain of the approaching dissolution:

> We cannot on this occasion, nor indeed on any other, recommend an indeterminate manner or vague ideas of any kind, in a complete and finished picture. This notion, therefore, of leaving anything to the imagination, opposes a very fixed and indispensable rule in our art— that everything shall be carefully and distinctly expressed, as if the painter knew with precision the exact form and character of whatever is introduced into the picture. This is what with us is called Science and Learning; which must not be sacrificed and given up for an uncertain and doubtful beauty . . .

Since this time, the process has galloped away. Technology has reshaped society, breaking up the organic unity in all directions. It

367

has cut man off from nature, distorted the scale and pace of his life, deprived him of the chance to make meaningful patterns out of his work. The onetime servant, the Machine, has become the master, on whom he may become dependent for his whole life, from cradle to grave, for food, for physical health, even for the illusion of purpose. Having cut him off from his roots, deprived him of all that truly nourishes his being, and reduced him to a state of neurosis, it even supplies, through television, films, and advertising, through all the tricks and toys of his technologically shaped wilderness, the almost ubiquitous stream of unresolved imagery to keep his mind drugged in a state of acquiescence. It is hardly surprising that the arts should have broken up, or that the greater part of public religion should have been watered down into almost total meaninglessness—for the whole pre-condition of their healthy existence has been removed. And in place of the old certainties, rooted in the supreme reality of existence, we have transferred our faith to science, the explanation for everything which explains nothing, the ever-more-fragmented picture of reality which becomes ever more unreal.

Step by step, from those first discoveries of Kepler and Copernicus, through the theory of evolution which knocked away the last prop of stability from underneath man's stable world-picture by giving him the illusion that he was on an escalator moving ever more rapidly upwards into the future, to the total disintegration of today, with physical sciences, biological sciences, psychology, sociology, anthropology, bifurcating and trifurcating in all directions, each one examining an ever tinier fragment of reality and therefore seeing the world in terms of ever more superficial outward appearance, science has led mankind into the darkness of a universe made up only of shadowy nyktomorphs. And behind it all, with every stage, the underlying pattern becomes ever more apparent—of mankind's blind self-assertion, mounting toward what?

The hardest discipline of all in overcoming one's fantasy-self is learning to face reality and at the same time to accept it, whatever it may bring: to keep faith and to keep courage, and above all not to take refuge in the fretting of pointless speculation as to how things might have been different, or might still be. The miracle of existence is that, however black and confused the world may become, even if it seems totally to have lost its head, the eternal, unchanging reality is still within us, if we can but learn to give it our ear. Behind the world of appearances, no matter what goes on or is decided there, it is still open to any one of us to have the same faith and inner stability as have ever been experienced by man. The words once written by Ronald Knox:

> We have to accustom men's minds to the notion that it does not matter what the politicians do, does not matter even if our bishops seem to betray us, we belong to a spiritual kingdom complete in itself, owing nothing to worldly alliances . . .

really can apply for any of us, and not just to the doings of politicians and bishops, but to the findings of science, the prospects of mankind, and to every kind of misery or horror, imagined or unimagined, that takes place only on the material, outward level.

Once a man has learned to see below that level, to the inward reality of things, he can truly learn to accept, not just with stoicism or resignation but with joy, whatever the unfolding of his conscious life may bring. No one ever had so much cause to fret and rage against his material fate as Beethoven, or had such a violent, ungovernable ego with which to rage. And yet, in the music of his last years, we see the total serenity in which his inner struggle was resolved. Over the last movement of his last complete work, the Quartet Op. 135, appears the famous motto, "Muss Es Sein? Es Muss Sein." Then we hear his interpretation of these words. "Must it be, must it be?" asks the music, in all the discordant anguish of every man who has ever fretted against his condition since time began. And then comes the reply, full of joy, "It must be, it must be!", dancing and singing on its way to the final shout of nothing less than complete triumph. "It must be, it must be, it must be SO!"

What is fantasy? Is there no final explanation of this fate of man, this cosmic joke, that should have placed him in the terrible dilemma of his condition? I do not mean that we can answer in scientific terms just why or when it was that man took this fateful step, and became separated from the rest of creation. But there is in fact one time in his life when the essence of fantasy, rebellion, the violation of order, is essential to man—when, as we grow to maturity, we must learn to reject that inward subservience to the framework of authority represented by our parents and the grown-up world, in order to reassume authority and responsibility ourselves, so that the pattern may be carried on.

Here we are obviously touching on a complex of the most profound myths of the human race—the myth of the King who must die in order that a new King may reign; the myth of the Golden Bough; that the old year must die in order to give way to the new: the basic rhythm of the eternal renewal, not just of life but also of order, the framework in which alone life can be maintained.

Our fantasies are thus, in a sense, our way of learning. We rebel against the framework of order so that we may learn through our mistakes where the confines of order lie. Even the endlessly repeated pattern of fantasy art, the Romantic tragedy with its implied death wish, can eventually be seen from outside as an unconscious moral lesson—but only so long as we do eventually learn from it, and no longer identify with it. In order to become mature, in short, we must not only reject the authority of our parents—but at the same time, in order to replace them, we must also learn to kill off our own fantasy-selves. Only by killing this fantasy-self can a man become fully mature. Unless he does so, he is still in a perpetual state of rebellion, a perpetual state of immaturity.

Of all the instances of fantasy we have seen in this book, every one has been in fact an example of immaturity. The state of someone who has failed to overcome his fantasy-self, and find his central unity, is that of someone who still cannot, at the deepest level of his being, take anything seriously except the projections of his own ego. Of course it is true that many people in a state of fantasy act as though they are taking something seriously, often too seriously; but what they are taking seriously is only fantasy itself, which they attempt to invest with all the outward trappings of reality. The claim that it is pursuing "reality" is one made by every sort of fantasy, whether it be Mr. Wilson talking of his "gritty reality," or the innumerable schools of self-conscious "realism" in the arts, which are always the disguise for some kind of subjective or distorted view, often of an unusually sensational and unreal nature (the pop art of our own time, for instance, has been described by critics as "the new Super Realism"). Similarly, it is a familiar trait of fantasy to deck itself out with the trappings and language of religion, as when we see Peter Brook talking of "Holy Theatre" or Anthony Wedgwood Benn describing his interest in technology as "spiritual." And again, immaturity, the more immature it becomes, increasingly takes cover in a pretense of maturity—as when the cinemas of Soho advertise a film as "truly adult," or the avant-garde theologians talk of mankind's "coming of age."

The most puzzling and powerful of all Shakespeare's plays is *Hamlet*. Like all his tragedies, it describes the unfolding of a fantasy cycle, perhaps more profoundly and explicitly than any. And yet what is the offense against nature for which Hamlet must die? It is not some obvious crime like Macbeth's, or delusion like Othello's. On the face of the story, in fact, it is that he *cannot* commit an offense: he cannot revenge his father by killing his uncle. But if we accept that in some way Claudius and his father are the same, and that it is his subconscious urge to "kill" his father and "marry" his mother that he cannot fulfill, then we see why the play exercises such an extraordinary and subtle hold over our own subconscious minds. *Hamlet* is, in fact, the most abstract and profound study in literature of man's central problem, the problem of immaturity, of the inability to grow into a full man. Hamlet cannot basically take anything seriously: "to be or not . . ."; he cannot commit himself to the central unity of his being. He is so clever that like many brilliant and immature men, he can see the truth of everything except the truth itself. He cannot grow up. And therefore, by the laws of fantasy, he must die.

From Hamlet we may move logically to Oedipus: most famous of all legends about a man who actually did kill his father and marry his mother. But Oedipus was also the man who solved the Riddle of the Sphinx. The Sphinx was the ultimate symbol of fantasy, the unresolved image of beast and woman. She sat at the top of a cliff, asking all men who passed by the riddle, "What is it that has four legs in the morning, two in the afternoon, and three in the evening?" The answer, of course, was "man"—but behind the outward question lurked the real riddle, "What is man?" Unless the passerby could solve the riddle, he was thrown over the cliff. Oedipus solved the riddle, and it was the Sphinx who threw herself over the cliff. Every man, in order to play his part in maintaining the survival of life, must solve the Riddle of the Sphinx for himself.*

As we have had confirmed by over half a century of research, and by the writings of such experts as Professor Eliade, there is scarcely a primitive society in the world which does not in some way formalize this act of coming to maturity by means of "initiation" rites into the full status of adulthood. Frequently such rites act out with terrifying power the process of "dying" in one's immature self, in order to be "born again" as a fully responsible member of society. Such ceremonies are an outward recognition of that truth, relevant to all societies, that ultimately to overcome his fantasy-self is the one supreme contribution that any man can make to his fellow creatures.

---

* It was not of course coincidental that these same myths, interpreted in a somewhat different sense by Freud and his followers, should have played such a large part in building up the mystique of modern psychology, which has in turn played such a considerable role in the twentieth century neurosis. The essence of Freudianism, the supreme expression of that profound revolt against the "father figures" of Victorianism, tradition, and religion which sprang up in the late nineteenth century, lay in its uncovering of all the temptations to violation of order which make up the dream-fantasy level of the mind. But instead of recognizing them as imperatives of the way the mind must *not* work, Freud interpreted them as symptoms of "inhibition" and "repression," which must be cleared away in order that the individual may fulfill himself. It would be hard to find a clearer example than this basic confusion of the self-destructive urge at work in the twentieth-century subconscious.

Of course we cannot overcome our fantasies altogether. They are the waste products of the mind, as constantly present in our waking life as dreams in our sleep. But we can learn to recognize them, to distinguish them from reality, and to prevent them from influencing our thoughts, opinions, and behavior. In some way, all the fantasies that are around us in society, that infect the collective human organism, are in the end just one fantasy, made up of all the separate unresolved images and acts of self-assertion that are fed into it from each individual fantasy-self of all the thousands of millions of human beings on earth. Every man who asserts his own ego against the general framework in any way, however small, or adds to the sum of unresolved imagery, however idly, is playing his part in increasing the sum of the world's discords and miseries.

In recent years, there has been a tacit reflection of this fact in, for instance, the discussion of the relationship between the portrayal of violence on television and the growth of actual violence in society at large. The relationship is obviously not so direct that it may be statistically measurable, and that is why such apprehensions are so hard to "prove" scientifically. But it undoubtedly exists, just as any contribution to the general neurosis serves ultimately only to arouse people's fantasy-selves, cut them off from one another, and heighten the level of disorder in society. This is true on the grand scale of the whole complex of different neuroses and self-assertions aroused in all parts of the world by such an "outbreak of demonic power" as the Vietnam war; it is true on a tiny scale as well, for instance, in the succession of antagonisms (with all their possibly infinite repercussions) aroused by a man who drives his car aggressively and recklessly to work in the morning, jarring the nerves in turn of everyone whom he meets, passes, or vies with on the way.

However upset one may be by wars or the government or fellow drivers or one's children, it is *never* a fruitful answer to assert one's own ego in opposition. Any such act of self-assertion at worst only provokes feelings of counter-assertion, and at best is as fruitless as railing at the weather. However much one may wish to change the outside world, the only thing one can ultimately be sure of changing or having any control over is oneself. This is why the most practical measure any man can take to change the world for the better is the least dramatic act of all—to withdraw his own contribution from the general sum of evil. As Carl Jung put it:

> Such a man knows that whatever is wrong in the world is in himself, and if he only learns to deal with his own shadow, then he has done something real for the world. He has succeeded in removing an infinitesimal part at least of the unsolved, gigantic social problems of our day.

Or, as he was exactly echoed by an old Vietnamese quoted in the *Guardian* at the time when the Vietnamese war was at its height, tearing his country to pieces around him:

> Humanity is *one*. Each of us is responsible for his personal actions, and his actions towards the rest of humanity. All we can do is hold back our own brand from the fire. Pull it back—do not add to the flame.

When I began writing this book, as a typical child of our time, I regarded the practical relevance to our modern plight of collective human experience in the past to be very small. I could see little direct relation between our modern world and even much of the great literature of the past, let alone the teachings of the great religions. Nevertheless, when I began to look into these things, as an heir to the Christian tradition, it was inevitably to the literature and teachings of Christianity that I at first turned.

The story of Jesus of Nazareth must, if only by its intimate connection with the efflorescence of Western civilization, be regarded as the most powerful myth in the history of the human race. Naturally it is almost impossible for those who have not crossed over the gulf of "disbelief" to understand what Christians mean when they say that "God sent his Son into the world." Automatically it conjures up for them the picture of someone being sent as a sort of celestial ambassador from "out there." But gradually I came to see that all it means is simply that, at one particular moment in history, the unfolding of the collective human organism, by that same pattern which from time to time throws up both men who represent abnormal concentrations of evil, such as Hitler, and "antibodies" to evil, such as those great artists whose work can comfort and illumine the lives of men for generations after they are gone, resolved itself in the creation of one human being so closely in harmony with the underlying reality of man's nature that he could be called wholly an expression of God.

Jesus came into the world symbolizing the eternal renewal of life in one sense in the image of the mother and her child which has inspired so much great art in all societies. In the wilderness, since he was a man, he was tempted, and to become a full man, had to wrestle with and overcome his fantasy-self. From then on he taught the living truth which is at the heart of human life—that on the material level of this world, because of their fantasies, men will find perpetual tribulation. But that, by finding the level of reality, the drug of appearances may be overcome.

All this in itself, however, was no more than the teaching of the truth which has been perceived and passed on by all the great masters, of all religions. What transformed Christianity into a myth of such unique power was the fact that this perfect man, so perfect that he was God, took on himself as a model the pattern and consequences of evil. In the events of Passion Week we see the portrayal of the fantasy cycle, moving from the Dream Stage of the entry into Jerusalem with the crowds cheering, through the Frustration Stage of Gethsemane ("Oh Father, if it be possible, let this cup pass from me") to the Nightmare Stage of the betrayal, the taunting, and the trial, with the same crowd which had cheered five days before, howling for his blood. And so to the Death Wish Stage of the Crucifixion. Yet, on Easter morning comes the Resurrection, completing the full cycle of the perfect man; who had acted out the pattern of the world's sins, and yet was reborn.

The rebirth of Christ coincides, of course, with spring—the rebirth of the year. But it is also a rebirth which can coincide with the inmost experience of every man who goes through the same pattern: of dying in his fantasy-self, in order to live in his real self—the real self which, because it is part of God, goes on for ever and ever.

Index

Cardus, Neville, 96
Carleton-Greene, Hugh, *see* Greene, Sir
    Hugh Carleton
Carnaby Street, 6, 32, 81, 155, 246,
    287, 311
Carnegie Hall, 244
Carstairs, George, 197
Carve Her Name with Pride (film), 142
Casinos, 6, 278, 318
Cassandra (Columnist), 275
Castle, Barbara, 148
Castro, Fidel, 269n
Cavern Club, 176, 267, 304, 314
Censorship, stage, 258, 295, 297, 321
Central School of Art, 154
Chalfont, Lord, *see* Gwynne-Jones, Alun
Challenor affair, 216
Chamberlain, Neville, 89
Chaplin, Charlie, 57, 96, 311
Charge of the Light Brigade, Brook
    Street restaurant, 7
Charles, Prince, 328
Charter-house, 154
Chartists, 335
Chataway, Christopher, 91–92, 126
Chatterton, Thomas, 51
Cheadle, 148n
Chelsea, 40, 153, 154, 176, 177, 326;
    "Set," 31, 140, 200, 208; and
    LSD, 303
Cheltenham Ladies College, 253
Chequers, 207
Chicago, 313
China: Cultural Revolution of (1965),
    58, 301, 331; and Russia, 176, 217;
    and India, 190
Chips with Everything (Wesker), 187
Christianity, 374–376
Christie, John, 289
Christie, Julie, 311
Church of England, 107, 203; attacks
    on, 128; "radical" theologians of,
    144; "swinging" publicity, 293n

Churchill, Winston S., 89, 93, 105, 108,
    113, 131, 145, 268; and Eden, 113;
    member for Woodford, 256; death of,
    273, 274–275; State Funeral of, 275,
    279; Johnson compares Wilson to,
    315; and Attlee, 327
C.I.D., 92
Ciné-verité, 191, 225–226; and night-
    mare stage of 1963, 229; during
    Month of Madness (1965), 295
City, The (financial establishment),
    270, 285
City Centre, 184–185, 214, 334
Civil discord, 350
Civil Rights Movement, U.S., 111, 162,
    173, 279, 329, 330; and violence of
    summer 1963, 213, 219; and Watts
    riots, 279, 286
Civil Service, 167–168, 222
Clacton, 249
Clark, Jim, 331
Clark, William, 122
Class, social, 90–91, 95–108, 327–328;
    in the arts, 93–94; lower-class ur-
    ban young, 96–98; authors' defini-
    tion, 96n; upper-class young, 98–
    102, 153, 160, 164; upper and
    middle, 103–108; and the theatre,
    114–119; and avant-garde, 127–128;
    youth cross lines of, 140; and pop
    singers, 245–246; merger of teen-
    agers and avant-garde middle class,
    252; in animal societies, 349
Classicism, 354
Classlessness, image of, 14; and New
    Aristocracy, 9–10; and election of
    Mr. Heath (1965), 18–19; and the
    teenager, 185; and pop culture, 245–
    246; in 1965, 278
Clean Up TV campaign, 280
Cleave, Maureen, 197, 201, 287, 305
Cliveden, Astor's home, 168, 202, 210,
    212

Dream figures, 55; Kennedy as, 160; in 1960 Britain, 164–165; and Beatles, 244–250 *passim;* fashion photographers as, 250–251; hairdressers as, 251; designers as, 251–252. *See also* Hero

Dream image, *see* Image

Dream stage, *see* Fantasy cycle

Dress, 6; designers, 6, 8, 287; of twenties, 48; and classless youth, 140; titillation in, 252; topless, 264; of youth of 1965, 289–291. *See also* Fashion

Drugs, 29, 33, 321; hallucinogenic, 66; addiction to, and death wish, 77; increase in addiction to, 281–282; and LSD, 303; scandals of 1967, 325, 328; as fantasy safety valve, 351

Drunkenness, 77, 281

Duccio di Buoninsegna, 359

Dufferin and Ava, Marquess of, 253

Duffy, Brian, 41, 250

Duncan, Ronald, 106

Dunkirk (film), 142

Durham prison, 303

Dynamism, image of, 160, 163, 179, 182; and election of J. F. Kennedy, 160–161; in art, journalism, 163–164; and BBC television, 165; and Macmillan Government reforms, 183; and Election of 1964, 264–268; in economic crisis of 1964, 269–271; and Queen's Speech (November 3, 1964), 270

Ealing comedies, 94

East End, 10, 14, 96, 117, 140, 305, 312; photographers, 41; lower-class immigrant communities of, 97; and youth club for "Rockers," 144; pop stars of, 246. *See also* London

East Germany, 174

East Pakistan, 212

Eastbourne, 312

Echoes of the Jazz Age (Fitzgerald), 49

Eclipse, The (film), 228, 231

Ecology, *see* Pollution, environmental

Economic crisis, 88–89, 103, 151; of 1961, 166, 169, 179; in Wilson's 1964 platform, 267; after 1964 Election, 269–271

Economic planning, 182; National Plan (1965), 284, 285

Economist, the, 88–89, 181–182, 222; "Farewell to the Fifties," 136, 147; on CND protests, 149; and Britain's application to Common Market, 153; on English social revolution, 154

Economy: postwar recovery in, 25; of early fifties, 92–93; of mid-fifties, 107; boom as a cause of disquiet (1960), 151–153; in 1961, 166, 169, 179; in 1962, 184; in 1964, 256, 267–271; issue in Election of 1966, 305; strengthening of (1966), 309

Eden, Sir Anthony, 93, 108, 112–113, 131; and Suez crisis, 120–124

Edgecombe, Johnny, 192n, 201

Edinburgh, 242, 257

Edinburgh, Duke of, *see* Philip, Duke of Edinburgh

Education, 323, 334. *See also* Public school; Universities

EEC, *see* Common Market

Egypt, 91, 113, 121, 122, 123

Eichmann, Adolf, 162

Eisenhower, Dwight D., 150

El Alamein, battle of, 79

Election, *see* By-elections; General Election

Elephant and Castle, 214

Eliade, Professor, 372

Eliot, T. S., 44

Elizabeth, Queen Mother, 108

Elizabeth II, Queen, 9, 10, 90; quoted, 86; Coronation, 89, 91; and Royal Tour of Australia and New Zealand,

Genesis, 360

Geneva Conferences (1954, 1955), 91

Genius, and self-destruction, 77–78

Gentry, 93. *See also* Aristocracy

Germany, 58, 79, 93. *See also* East Germany; West Germany

Gilliatt, Penelope, 116n, 258, 293, 295

Gilmour, Ian, 126

Gladstone, William E., 169n

Glasgow, 96, 97

Glubb, Sir John (Glubb Pasha), 113, 119

Goa, 174

God: belief in, 360–361; nature of, 363–367. *See also* Religion

Godard, Jean-Luc, 253

Gogh, Vincent van, 78, 118

Golden Bough, The (Frazer), 231

Goldfinger (film), 260

Goldsmith, Oliver, 22

Goldwater, Barry, 156, 230

Goody, Douglas, 218–219, 283, 303

Goon Show, 86, 105

Gordon, Lucky, 215, 220

Gordon Walker, Patrick, 273, 274

Gore, David Ormsby (Lord Harlech), 167

Gorky, Maxim, 45

Government Publications Office, 220

Goya, Francisco, 51

GPO Tower, 289

Grade brothers, 98

Graham, Philip, 219

Grand Prix, 77

Gratification, of fantasy, 64–71, 345

Great Britain, *see* Britain

Great Depression, 79, 100, 200

Great Gatsby, The (Fitzgerald), 70, 76

"Great Society," American, 279, 329

Great Train Robbery, 5, 218, 247, 303, 308, 316; and image of "New" England, 243; public fascination with, 282–283

Greece, 216

Greene, Graham, 88

Greene, Sir Hugh Carleton, 165, 193, 229–230, 280–281; leaves BBC, 325

Grigg, John, *see* Altrincham, Lord

Grimond, Jo, 100, 131, 147–148, 221, 286, 324; quoted, 277; in "class revolution," 327

Grimsby, 159

Grosvenor Square, 190, 313

Grosz, George, 187

Guardian, see *Manchester Guardian*

Guerilla warfare, 221

Guevara, Che, 59, 331

Gun, 60

Gwynne-Jones, Alun (Lord Chalfont), 268–269

H-bomb, 92, 125, 127, 145, 157, 270, 280, 334; New Left opposition to, 130; national debate over threat of (1958), 132; national protest movement against (Easter 1958), 132–133; issue in Election of 1966, 305–306

Hailsham, Lord, 210, 225

Haiphong, 313

Hairdressers, 8, 251, 287

Hairstyles, 6, 27, 246, 278, 290

Haley, Bill, and his Comets, 31, 118

Haley, Sir William, 87, 90n, 121, 210, 280

Hall, Peter, 106, 188, 227, 253, 277; and Royal Shakespeare Company, 144; and staging of *Moses and Aaron,* 288

Hall, Willis, 155

Hamilton, Dennis, 149

Hamilton, Richard, 37

Hamlet, 371–372

Hammarskjöld, Dag, 176

Hancock, Tony, 331

Hanoi, 313

Happenings, 257, 263

Hard Day's Night, A (film), 250

I Vitelloni, 30
I Want to Hold Your Hand (Beatles), 231
Ice Cold in Alex (film), 142
Illegitimacy, 34, 129, 281
I'm All Right Jack (film), 151
Image, 344; of New Aristocracy, 8–16; of Edward Heath, 17–21, 285; in view of early fifties, 29–31; and language, 32–33, 39–40, 49–50; of sex, 34–35; use of term, 36–37; in late fifties, 37–39; of modernity, 38–39; and photography, 41–43; in fantasy, 53–56, 60–64, 66–71; term used in Election of 1959, 146; and satire movement, 178; and pop culture, 252–253
Imagination, 346, 348, 354
Immigrants, colored, 139, 324; communities, 96–98; and Notting Hill race riot (1958), 143; and Conservative Party, 180
Immigration Bill, 180
Immorality, 47
Imports, surcharge on, 269–270
Inadmissible Evidence (Osborne), 236, 263–264
Incendiarism, 281
Income control, 183, 284
Income tax, 270
Incomes policy, 284, 324
Independence, colonial, 333. *See also* Decolonization
Independent Group, ICA, 28, 29, 37
Independent Television News, 126
India, 5, 87, 88, 174; immigrants from, 180; and China, 190; floods of 1963; 221; and Pakistan, 283, 286, 301
Indonesia, 221, 264, 286, 301
Industrial Revolution, 367
Industrialization, 59, 335
Industry, 103, 129; and wage restraint (1964), 271; and nationalization,

284; and wage and price freeze (1966), 317–318
Infanticide in the House of Fred Ginger (Watson), 188
Inflation, 103, 104, 107, 151, 315; Macmillan on, 137–138; worsening of (1960), 162; of 1965, 284
Insight column, 205, 211, 225, 265
Instability, 346
Instinct, 346–347; and myth, 350
Institute of Contemporary Arts (ICA), 28; and Independent Group, 28, 29, 37
Intellectuals, 125; liberal, 33–34; and cause of moral freedom, 35–36; dream heroes of, 59; and British Labour Party, 64; Shil's essay on (1955), 93; and upper-class young, 98–102, 154; and theatre of mid-fifties, 114–119; and political ferment of 1957, 130; avant-garde, and teenage interests, 252–253; and The Who, 299
Intelligence, 354–355
Intercontinental missiles, 334
Interior decorators, 6, 8, 278
International Monetary Fund, 270, 284
International Publishing Corporation, 260, 302
International Test Ban Treaty, 217
Ionesco, Eugène, 252
Iraq, 168, 213
Ireland, 214
Irish: of East London, 96; "emancipation" of, 97, 98
Iron Curtain, 215
Islington, 40
Israel, 122
Italians, 97, 98
Italy, 142
ITV, 193–194, 261, 325
Ivanov, Eugene, 168, 191, 210, 211
Ivy League (pop group), 245

influence on Wilson's Cabinet, 268–269

New Left, 130

New Look, 25, 27, 32, 95, 334

"New Mood in Politics, The" (Schlesinger), 150

New Morality, 35, 80, 210; Bishop of Woolwich on, 203–204

New Oxford Group, 100–102, 116; and Colin Wilson's *The Outsider*, 118; and Suez crisis, 123n; and New England revolution, 126, 127, 129; and Angry Young Men, 127–128; and Labour Party, 130; and European dream, 152n; and *What's Wrong With . . .* series, 163, 168; compared to satirists, 178; and editors of color supplements, 260; growing absurdity of (late sixties), 328n

New Statesman, 34, 86, 107, 163, 186, 192, 204, 236, 329n; and H-bomb protest, 132; "The Menace of Beatlism," 247; on "mod" art, 254; and Rhodesian crisis (1965), 291

New Wave, 80

New York, 242–243; and pop culture, 253; and power blackout, 297; transport strike in (1966), 301

New York Times, 311

New Zealand, 200

Newley, Anthony, 243

News of the World, 149, 192, 210, 220

Newspapers, 59, 103, 229, 318, 333. *See also* Press

Newsweek, 10, 219, 222, 287

Nha, Ngo Dinh, 227

Nietzsche, Friedrich, 335

Nigeria, 301

Nightclubs, 304–305

Nightmare, link with dream, 336. *See also* Fantasy cycle

Nijinsky, Waslaw, 118

Nixon, Richard, 329

Nkrumah, Kwame, 199, 301

Nonconformity, 31, 57

Norman, Frank, 142

North, the (of England), 96, 97, 139, 202

North London, 96. *See also* London

North Vietnam, 283. *See also* Vietnam war

North West London, 97

Nostalgia, 93–95

Not So Much a Programme (BBC program), 262, 280–281

Notte, La (film), 187

Notting Hill, 33, 143

Nottingham, 96, 143

Nouvelle vague, 154

Nova magazine, 11

Novelists, 126, 163, 245, 278. *See also* Literature

Novels, 229

Nuclear deterrent, 194–195

Nuclear power, 92, 336

Nuclear testing, 174, 176, 217

Nuclear weapons, 124, 127, 152, 174, 194, 207

Nude Reclining (painting), 208

Nureyev, Rudolf, 244

Nuttall, Jeff, 308n, 320

Nutting, Anthony, 113, 121, 122

Nyasaland, 146

Nyktomorphs, 54–56, 66, 67, 70, 368; and Romantic poetry, 55; and literature of mid-fifties, 118; and New England, 125; and satire movement, 187; and scandal, 210; and image of "Swinging London," 251, 287; and LSD, 303

Obscene Publications Act, 35

Observer, 12, 17, 36, 110, 177, 186, 215, 261, 302; on Heath's election, 18–19; on drama, 94; and Wilson's *The*

413